AF575458

Re:

GARRETT BRADLEY

Devotion

The MIT Press
Cambridge, Massachusetts
London, England

LISSON GALLERY

Contents

Introduction

The work of Garrett Bradley is an affirmation and an entreaty for us to slow down and focus, to look around and wonder, to question history and to live in the moment. Despite its externalized and fictional nature, filmmaking itself seems transformed in her nurturing hands, as an internal and intimate medium, a craft to be furthered and molded, or as a vessel for stories to be retold anew and pried open, with an indelible yet ethereal atmosphere left in its wake. The adrenaline-fueled pace, manufactured spectacle and relentless exposition of most mainstream releases are also refuted by Bradley's measured approach to the production of moving images—hers is one of holding back, unfolding, abstracting the observable and allowing for subtlety and intuition at every step. This is her Devotion.

Bradley's work is devotional too in its quiet dialogue and considered collaboration between camera and subject matter, but her wider practice—encompassing film, photography and installation—remains a moveable feast, with rigid meanings shifting out of shot before they can be fully grasped. Rather than try to define or delineate Bradley's practice—perhaps by gathering reviews or commissioning essays on her career to date—this book aims for devotion and joy, for homage, inspiration and introspection, through a mixture of new conversations with peers and fresh reflections on past influences.

Before the reading begins, there is a film to watch. Or rather Bradley has created a durational experience of stills from her entire back catalogue, which reads or "screens" like a sequential, stop-motion kaleidoscope of freeze-frames. This reconfigured, achronological survey of her work in page after page of specially selected shots hopefully stands in for an abstracted filmography, perhaps acting as a temporal IMDB of her archive, as well as a counternarrative to traditional surveys of artistic development, instead providing pulsating glimpses into an ongoing creative process. These pages take a whistlestop tour beginning (in high school) in 2001 for a work called *Autumn*, through to Bradley's first feature, *Below Dreams* (2014), following the threads of three lives intertwining across her hometown New Orleans, all the way up to her Academy Award-nominated documentary *Time* (2020) and beyond.

This section might also embody a stream-of-consciousness image bank touching upon social inequalities, deprivation, incarceration, loss, relationships, dreams and memories.

Among the remarkable text contributions that follow this cinematic prelude are favorite essays of Bradley's or sources of inspiration for her films, one example being the 1926 play by Zora Neale Hurston, *Color Struck*, in which protagonist Emma is rejected—on the basis of her skin tone—both by mainstream, white society and her own, darker-skinned community. Reproduced here in its original form, as published in the Harlem Renaissance magazine *Fire!!*, started by Langston Hughes and others, *Color Struck* is followed by another excerpt, taken from Hurston's biography, *Wrapped in Rainbows*, in which she faces some of the same struggles as her character. The author, Valerie Boyd, deftly blends research and prose in the retelling of a racially fueled power dynamic that went on to influence Bradley's own film addressing the topic of colorism, entitled *AKA* (2019).

Just as Joan Didion admits, in interview with Hilton Als, that she would always watch *The Third Man* before sitting down to write a movie, Bradley too returns—not just to the writing of Hurston, Didion and Als—but to touchstone films by William Greaves (*Symbiopsychotaxiplasm* of 1968) and Charles Burnett (*Killer of Sheep* from 1977). Curators and critics directly address Bradley's own seminal works here, or else explore their origins, as Ashley Clark reveals how the raw material for *America* (2019) was discovered in the surviving rushes of an ill-fated 1913 production known as *Lime Kiln Club Field Day* (Hollywood's first all-Black cast), while Bradley dissects her own practice in conversation with fellow artists Alexandra Bell, Arthur Jafa, Tyler Mitchell and others. Not insignificantly, Bradley talks to her mother, the painter Suzanne McClelland, about abstraction and duration in art, through the lens of Pieter Bruegel and Robert Altman. Elsewhere, Claudia Rankine's excoriating takedown of any number of Serena Williams detractors bears some relation to Bradley's Netflix documentary series on Naomi Osaka, which featured another tennis player trialed by her own truths, while having an attitude and identity imposed on her by others.

The Black experience and depictions of the Black body in society are elevated and problematized in Bradley's output and this volume, with a refrain from one contributor ringing at every page turn: "What if we could wait for Blackness?" This phrase, from an exchange with author Kevin Quashie during the book's editing process, is instructional as an antidote to the lack of patience associated with the current need for instantaneous or "urgent" Black presence (a filmic and photographic form of repression or control). Quashie's preexisting notions of Black quietude and expressiveness can also be discerned in Bradley's films, especially in a newer, lesser-known three-screen meditation on interior life and abstracted selfhood, titled *Safe*, which was first shown at Lisson Gallery in 2022.

Lisson Gallery is indeed proud to be partnering on this new series of books, each focusing on a different artist or theme under the *Re:* title. This prefix not only suggests an email chain or a reply, but *re*fers back to someplace else, suggests a body of *re*search or a text that *re*gards, *re*views, *re*draws, *re*engages or *re*addresses the context and associated influences of this group of some seventy contemporary artists—themselves similarly corralled loosely and adventurously under one umbrella, since Lisson Gallery's inception in 1967.

With each more-or-less annual volume and each artist differing greatly from the last, it is no coincidence that *Re:* is to launch with the wide-reaching and emotionally sensitive world of Garrett Bradley, following her path of *re*verberation, *re*search, *re*collection and *re*imagining. There is more than one way to reach an in-depth appreciation of an individual artist and their cultural contribution, but a few good starting points must include time, osmosis and, of course, devotion.

A final note of thanks goes to MIT and commissioning editor Thomas Weaver, to colleagues at Lisson Gallery including Kojo Abudu and Elissa Goldstone (for invaluable direction), Zoë Anspach (for overall vision and design of the series), Lotte Parmley (for picture research) and to Garrett, her studio and every individual contributor to this book.

—Ossian Ward, series editor, Director of Content, Lisson Gallery

Sardines, 2008

Practice, 2004

Autumn, 2001

Dante 9-5, 2013

Below Dreams, 2014

Like, 2016

Alone, 2018

The Earth Is Humming, 2018

America, 2019

AKA, 2019

Time, 2020

Naomi Osaka, 2021

a Negro, a Lim-o, 2022

Safe, 2022

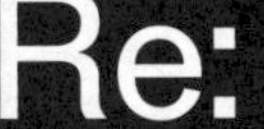
Re:

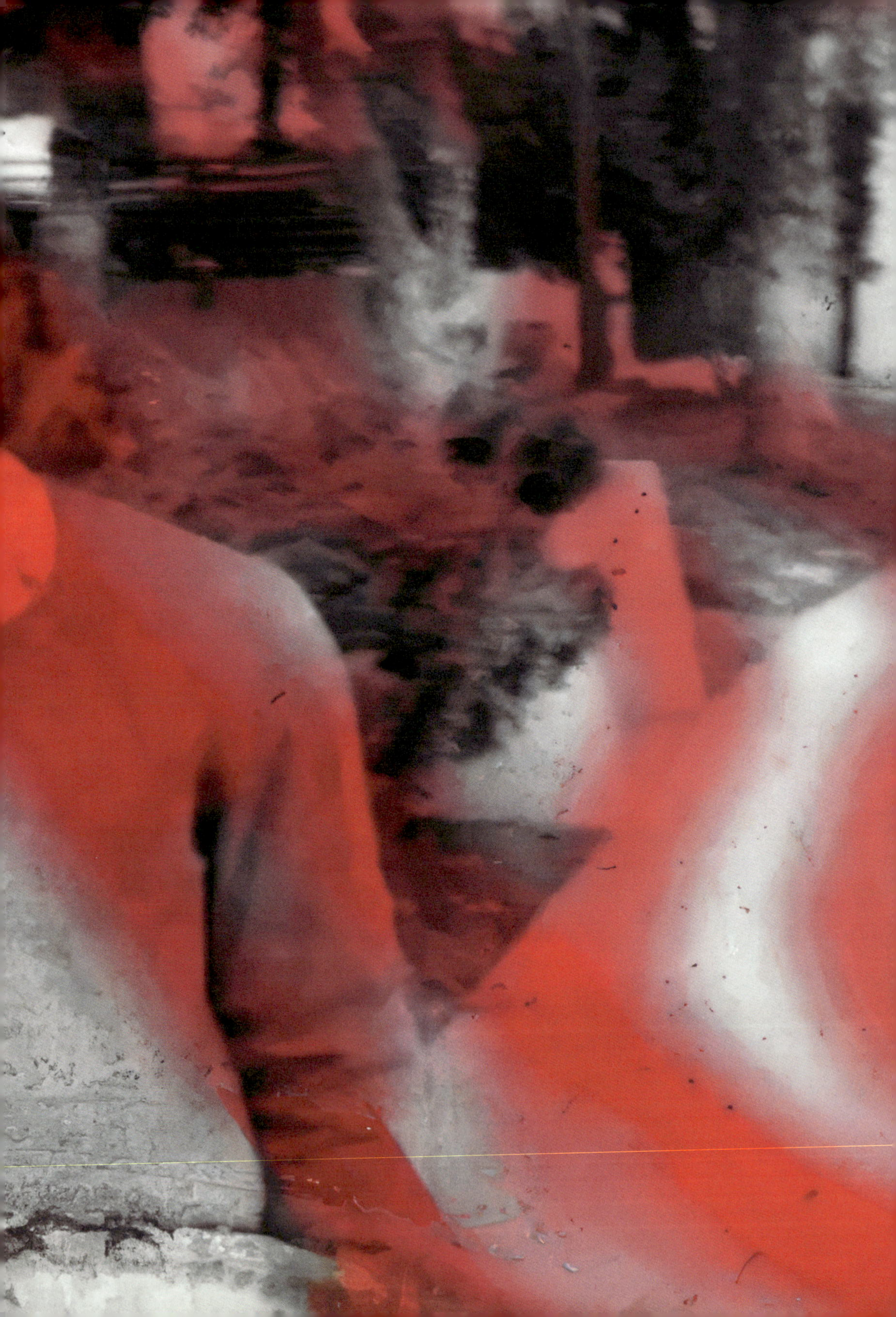

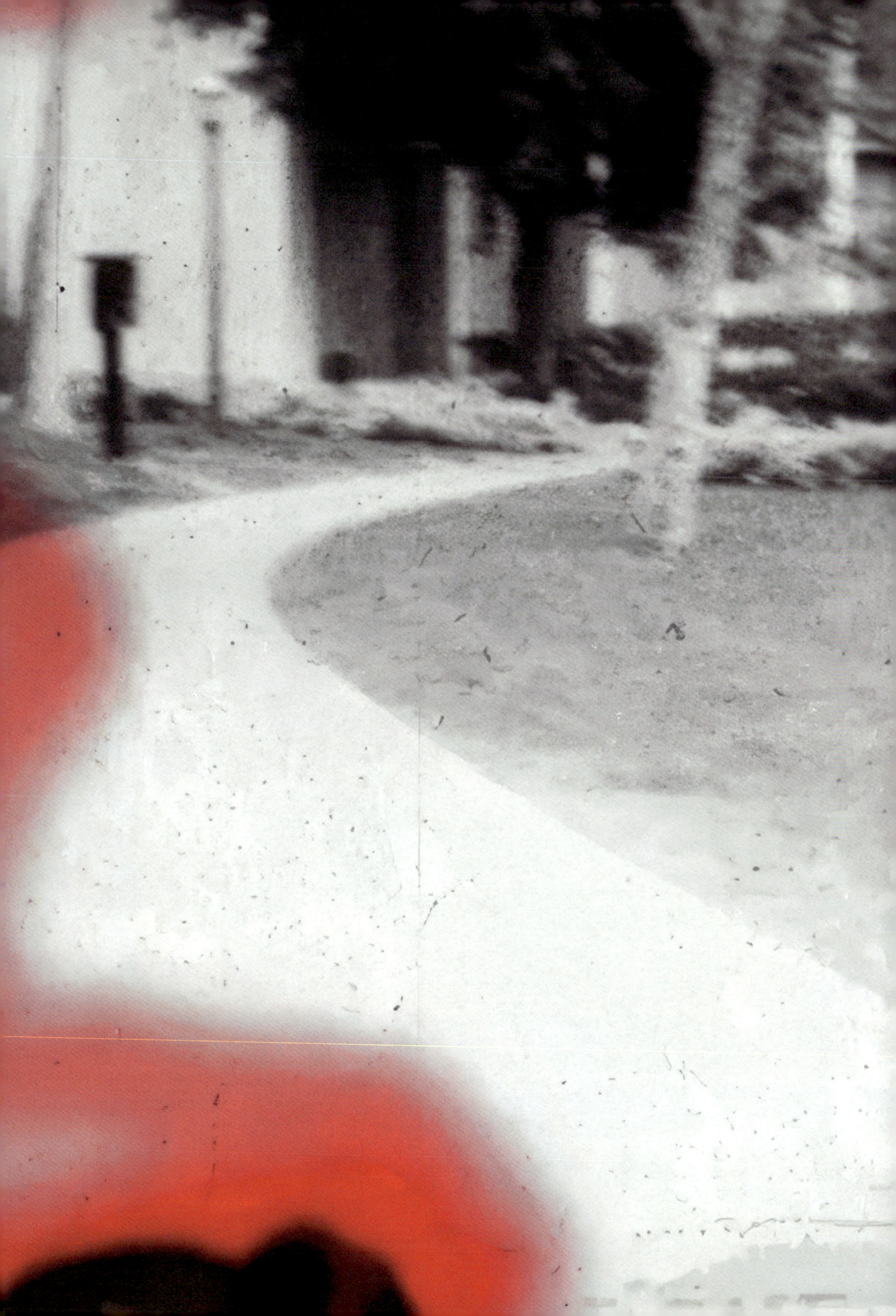

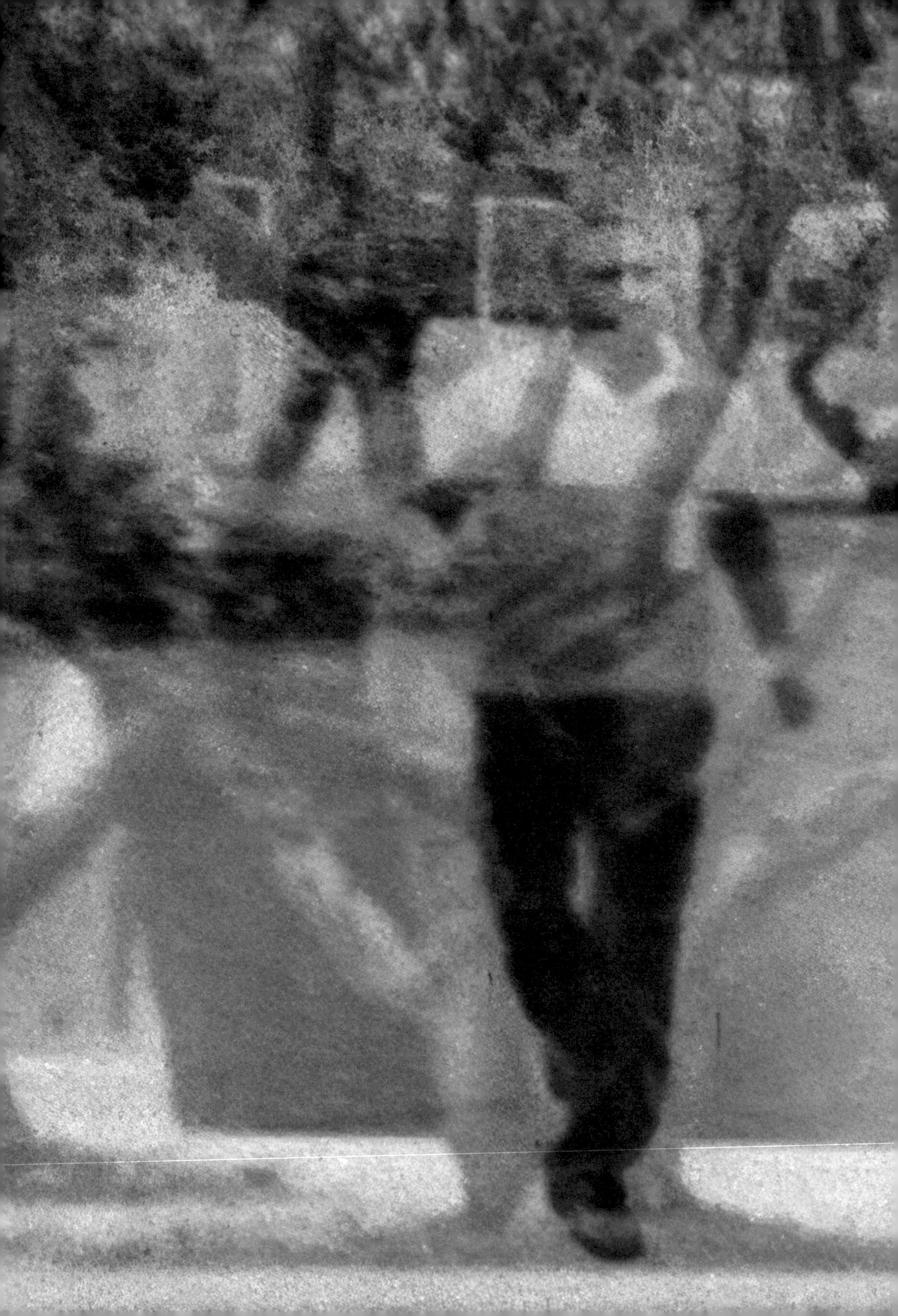

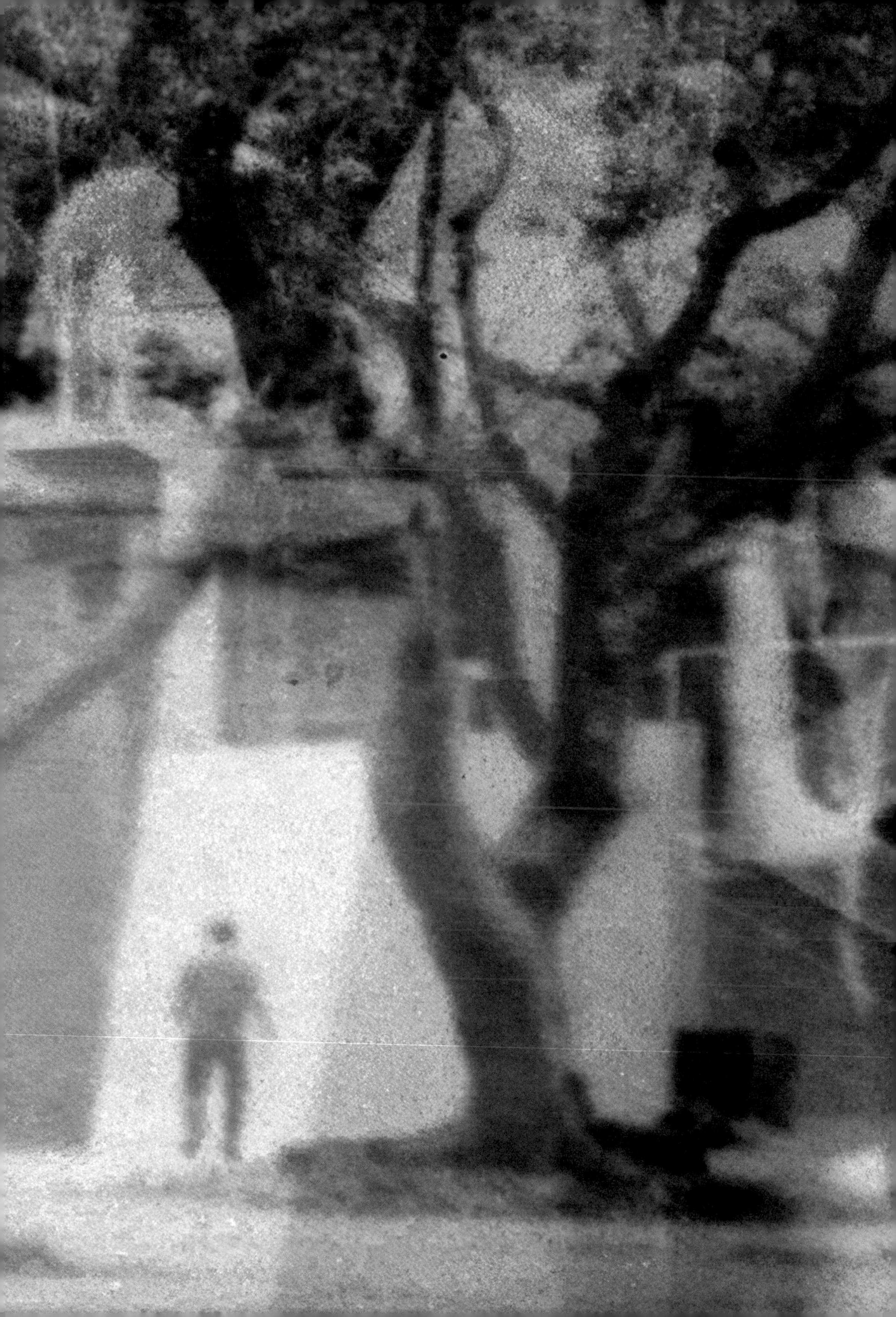

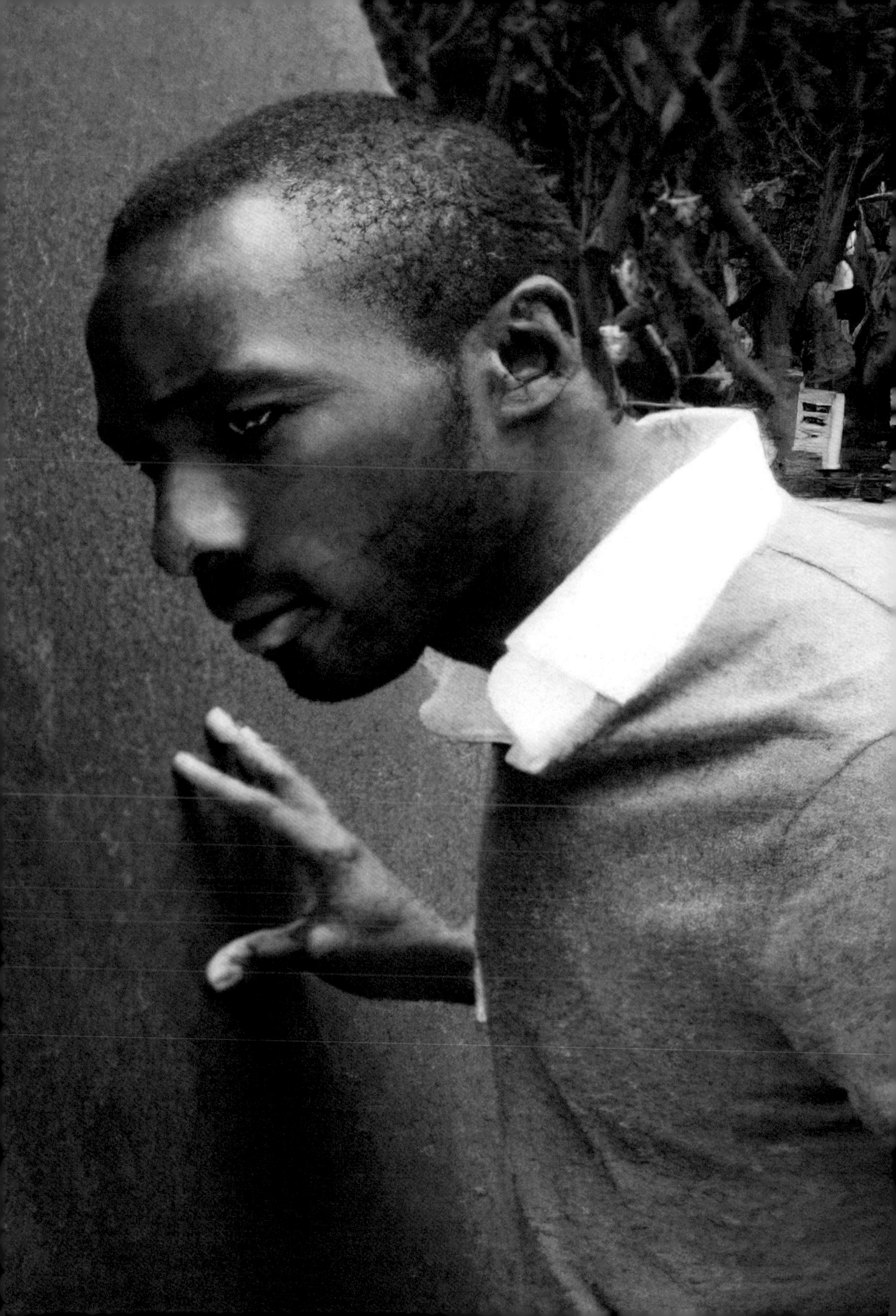

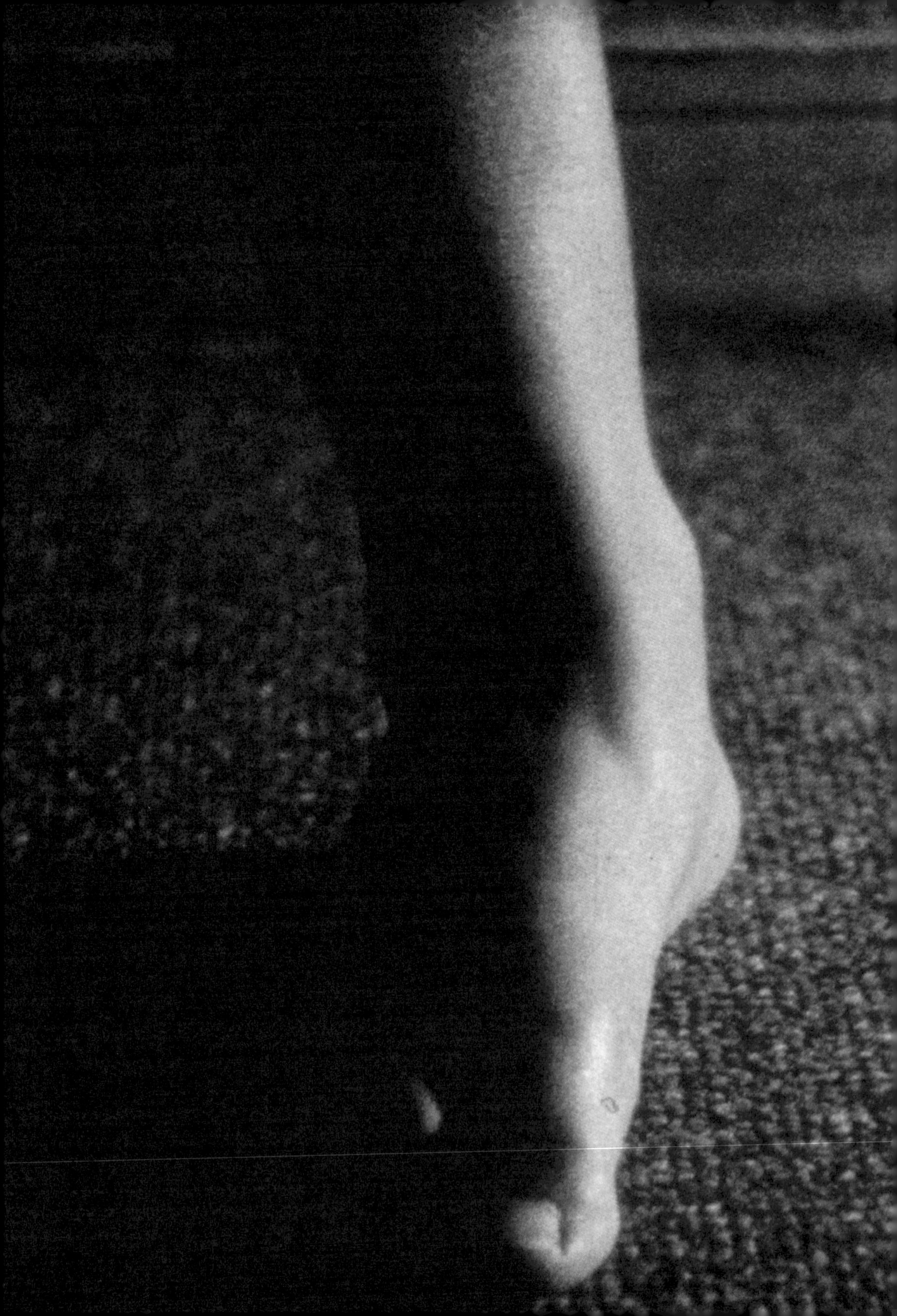

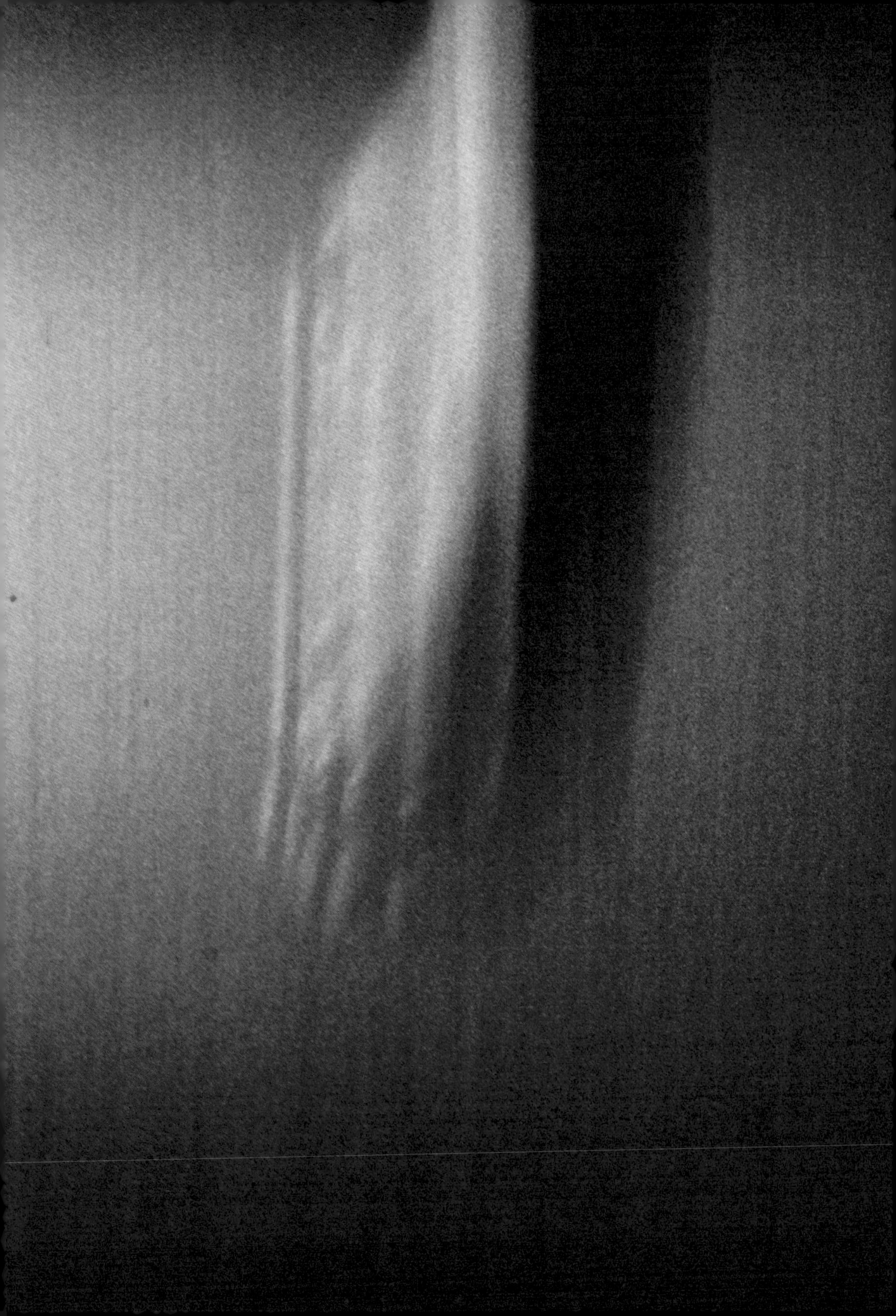

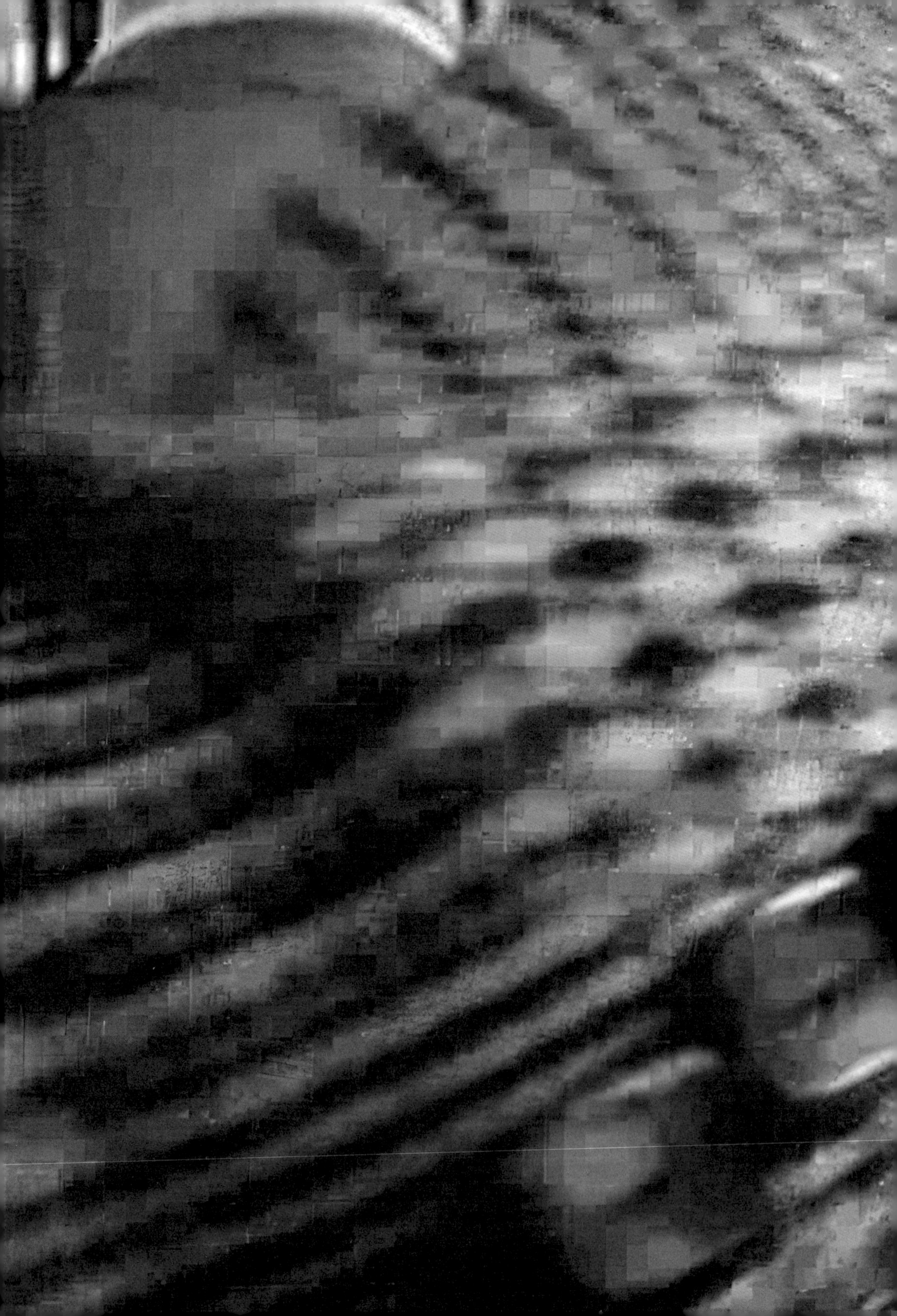

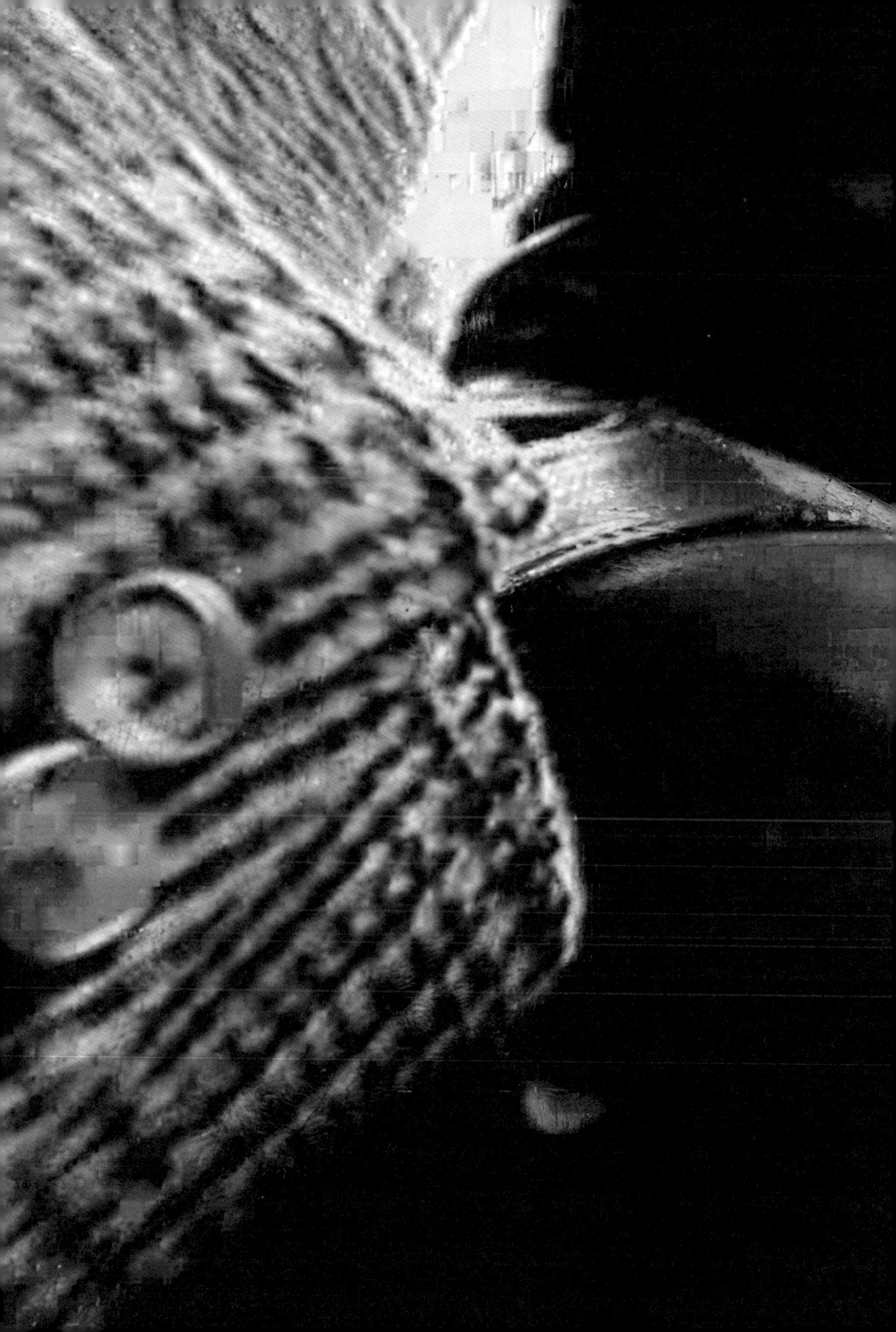

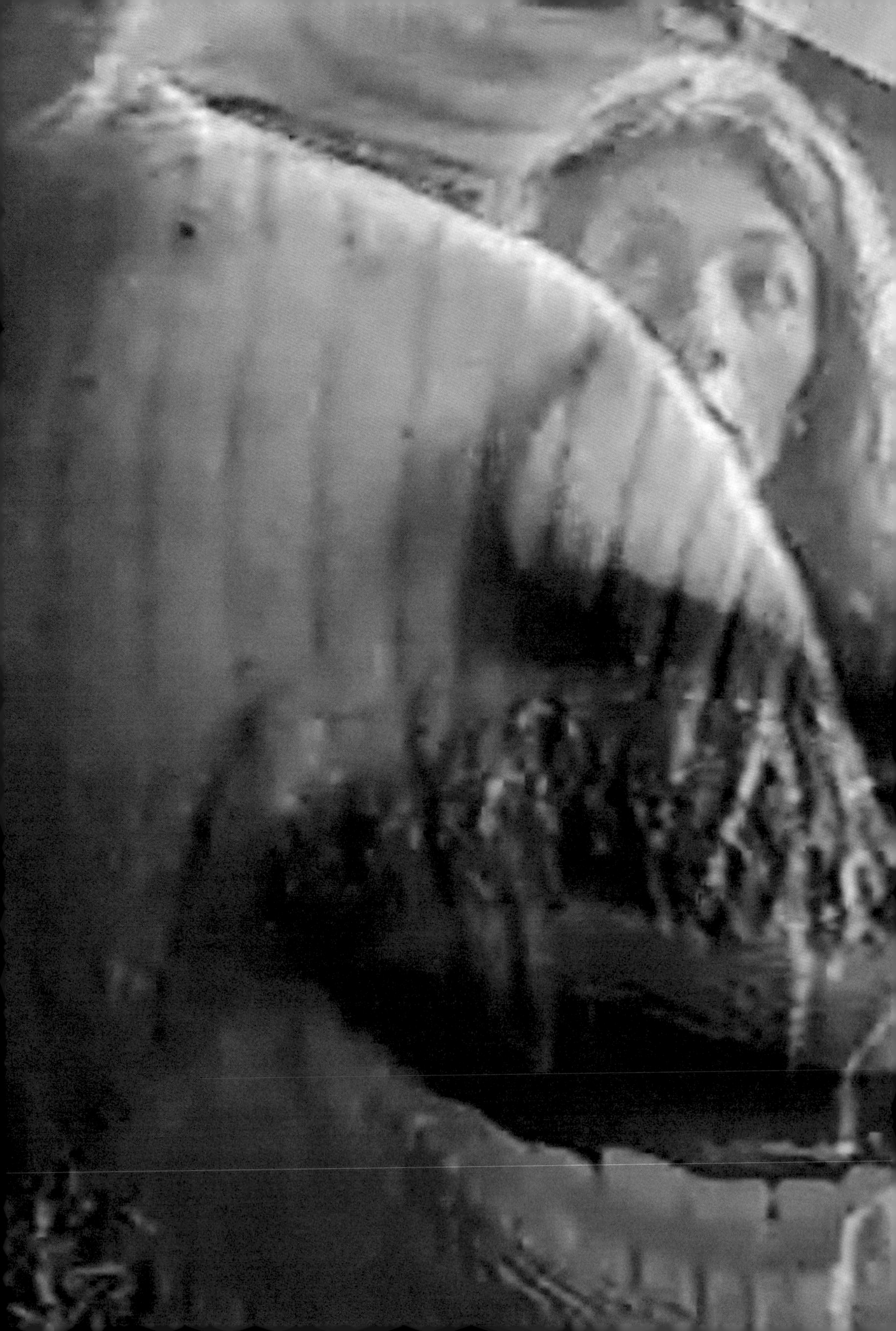

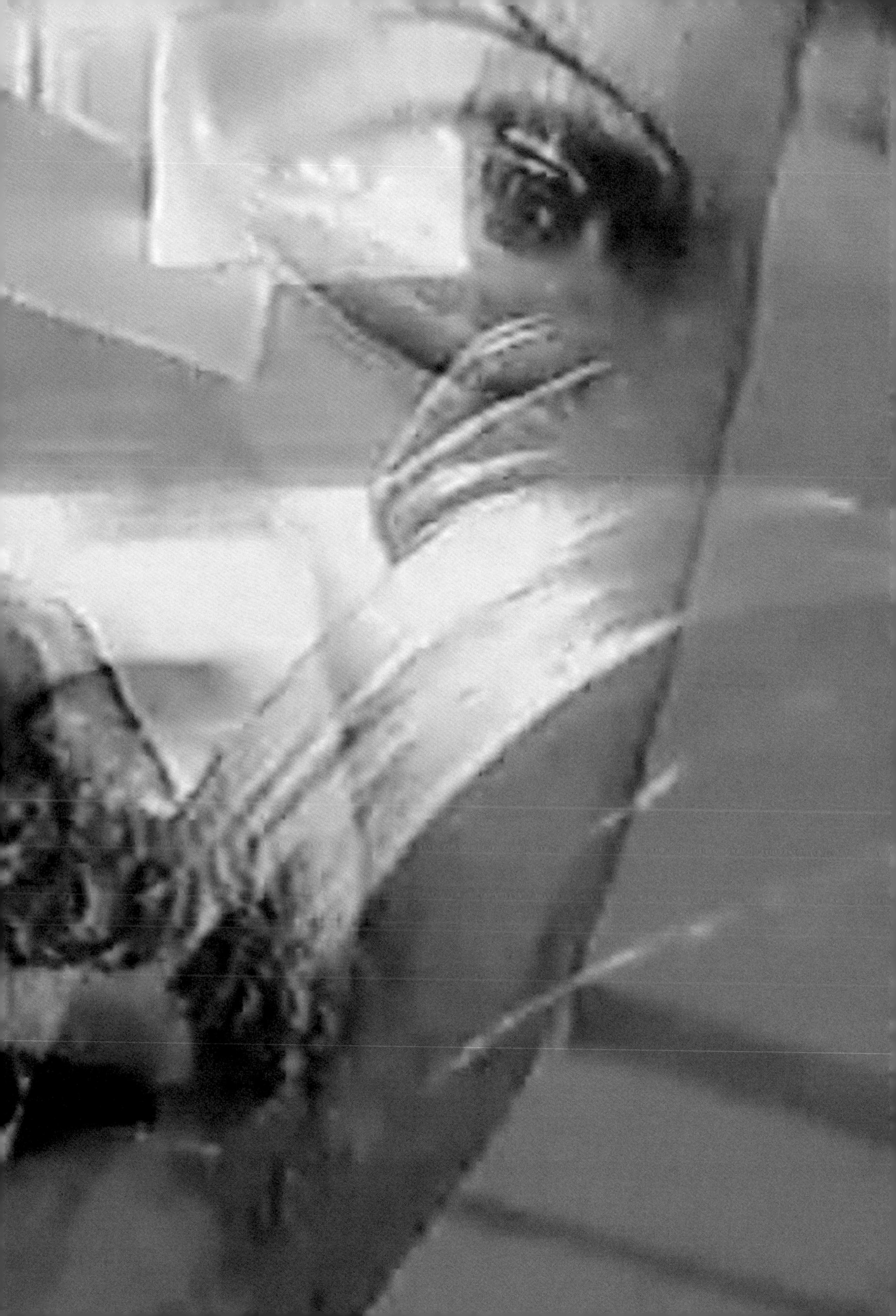

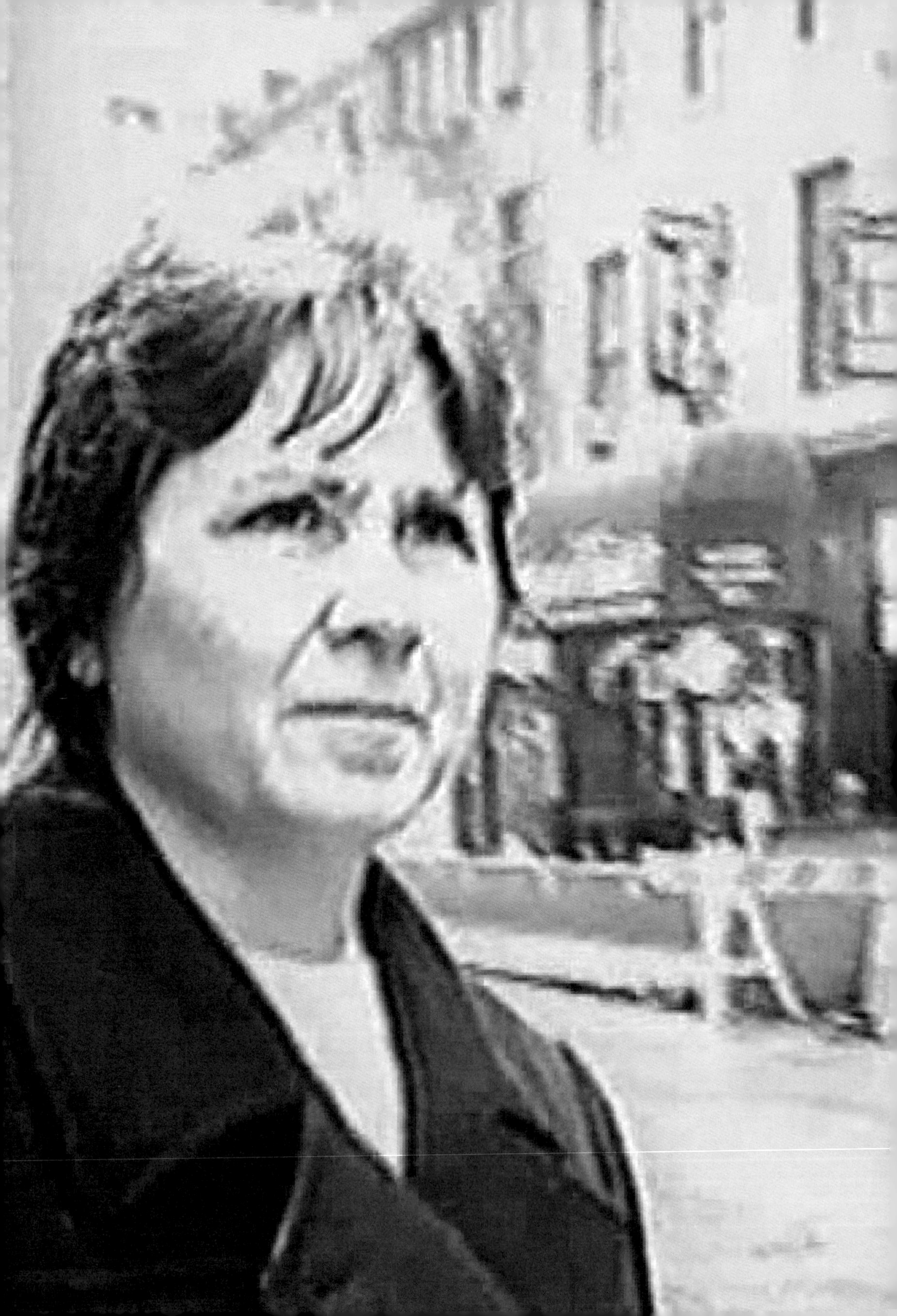

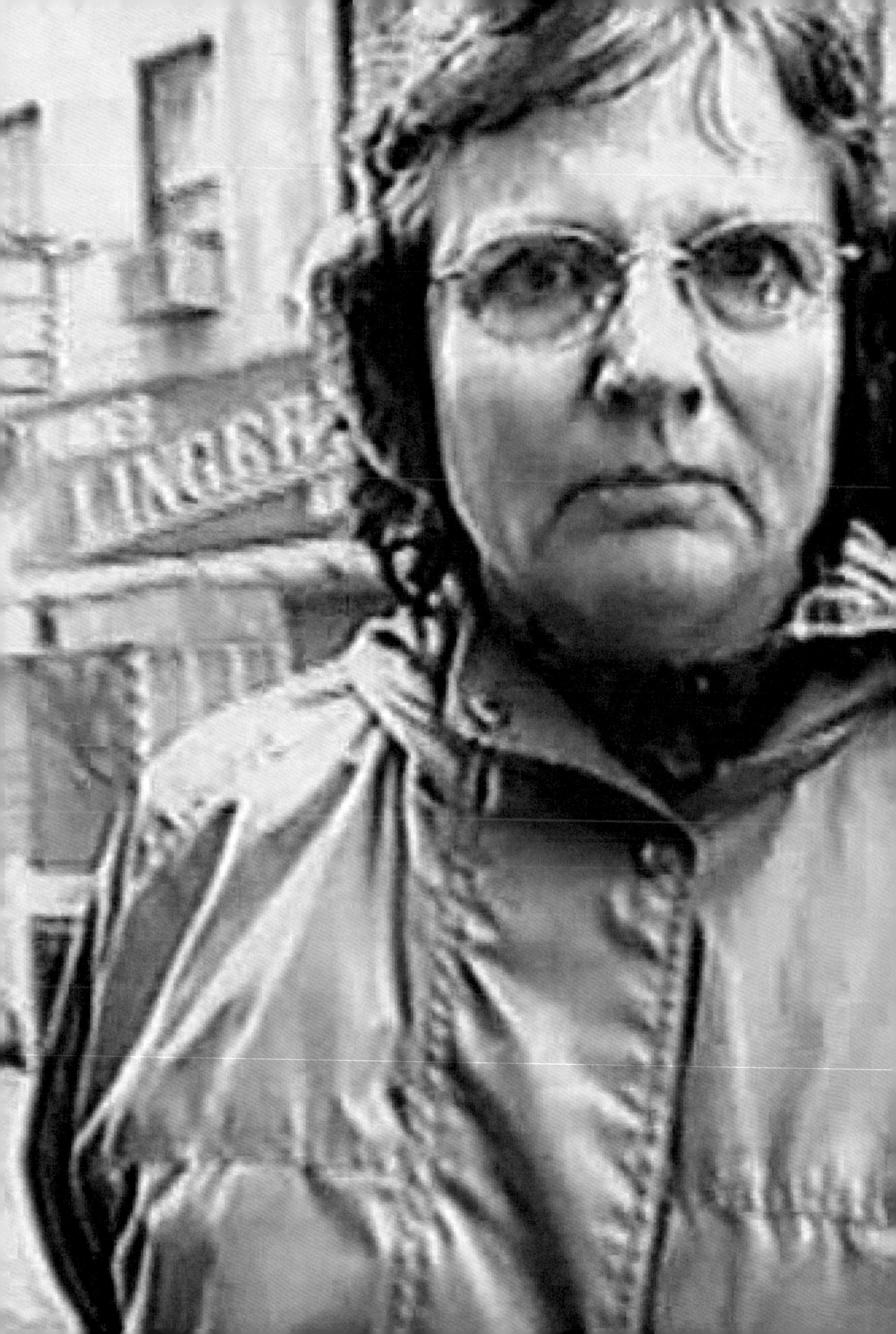

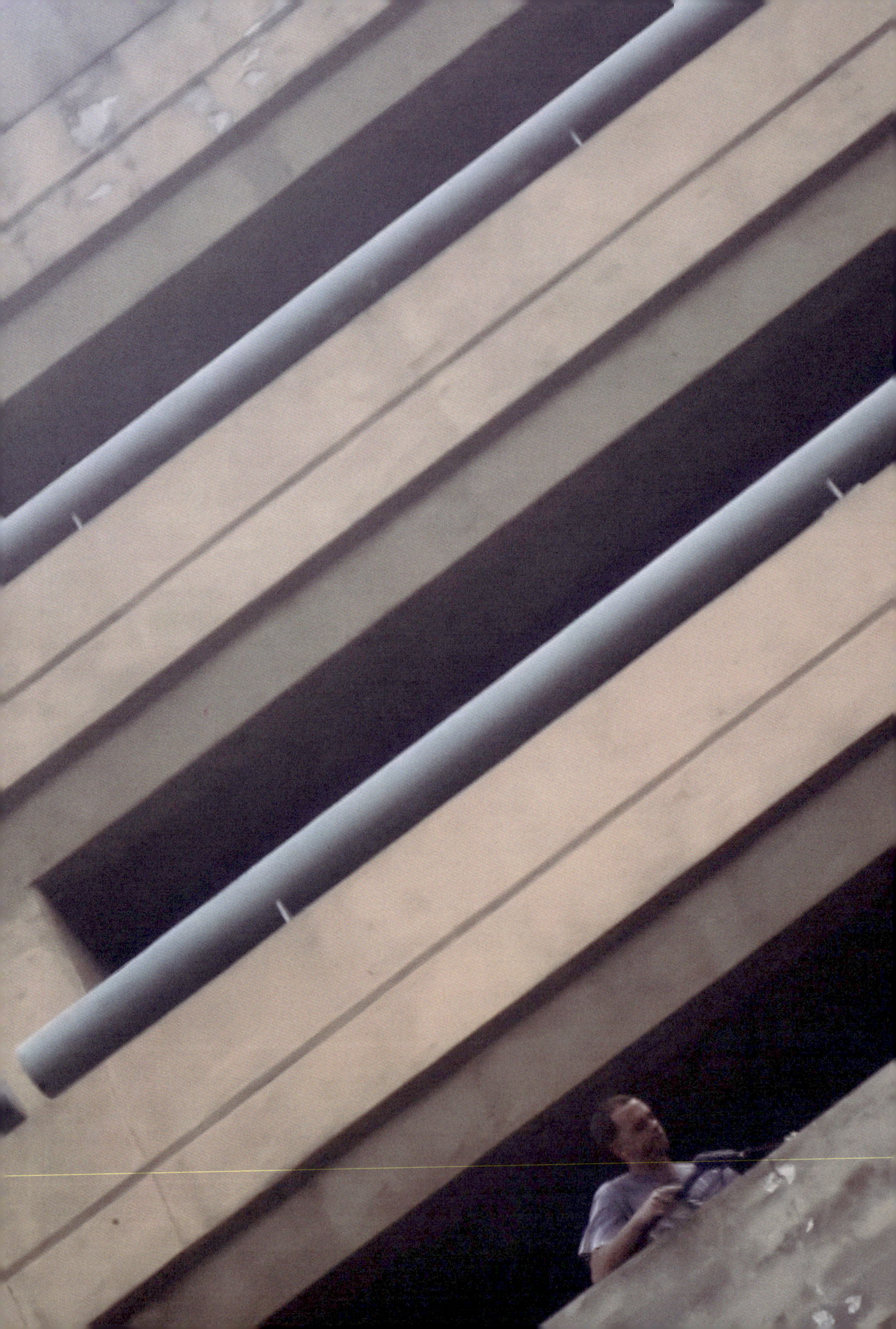

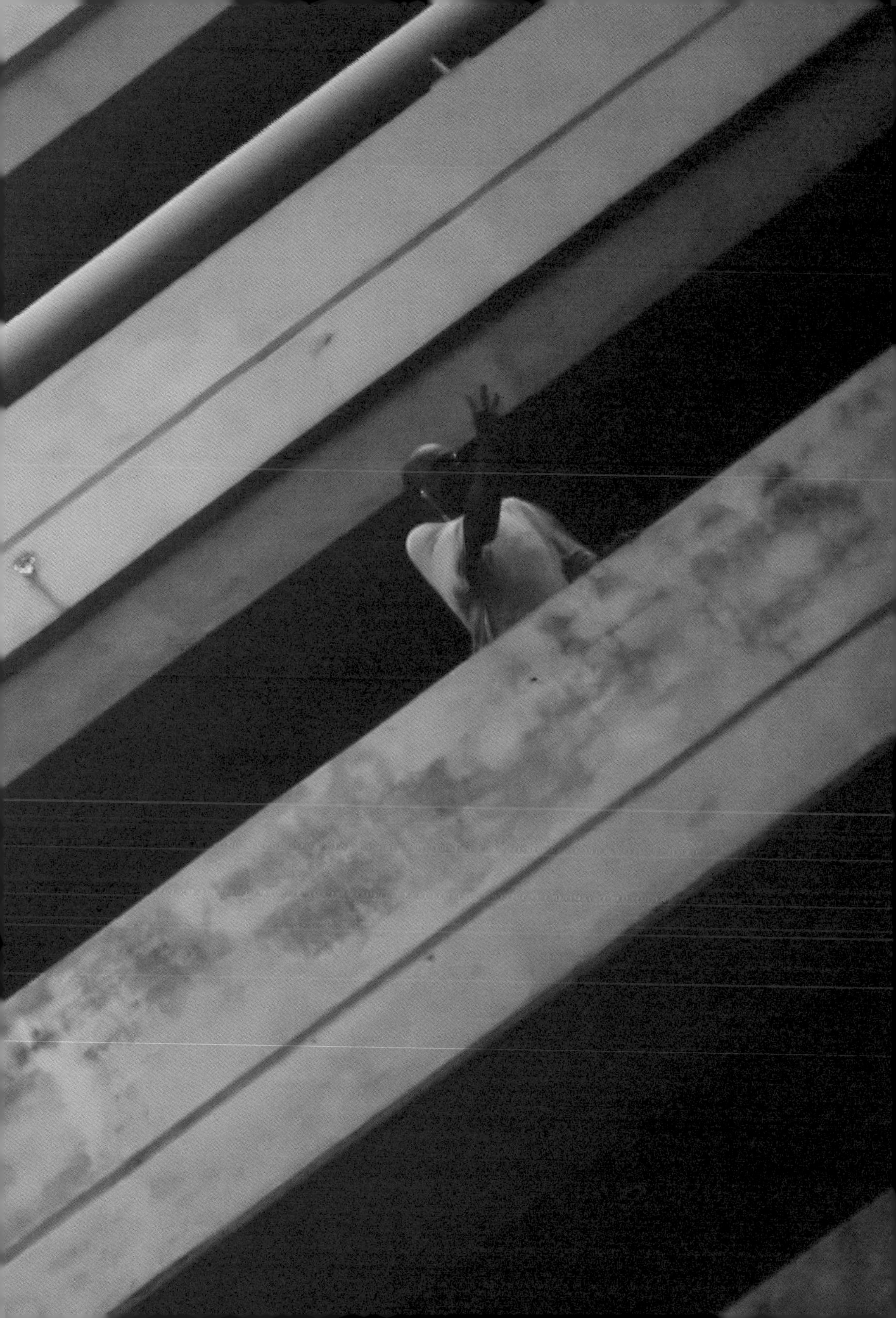

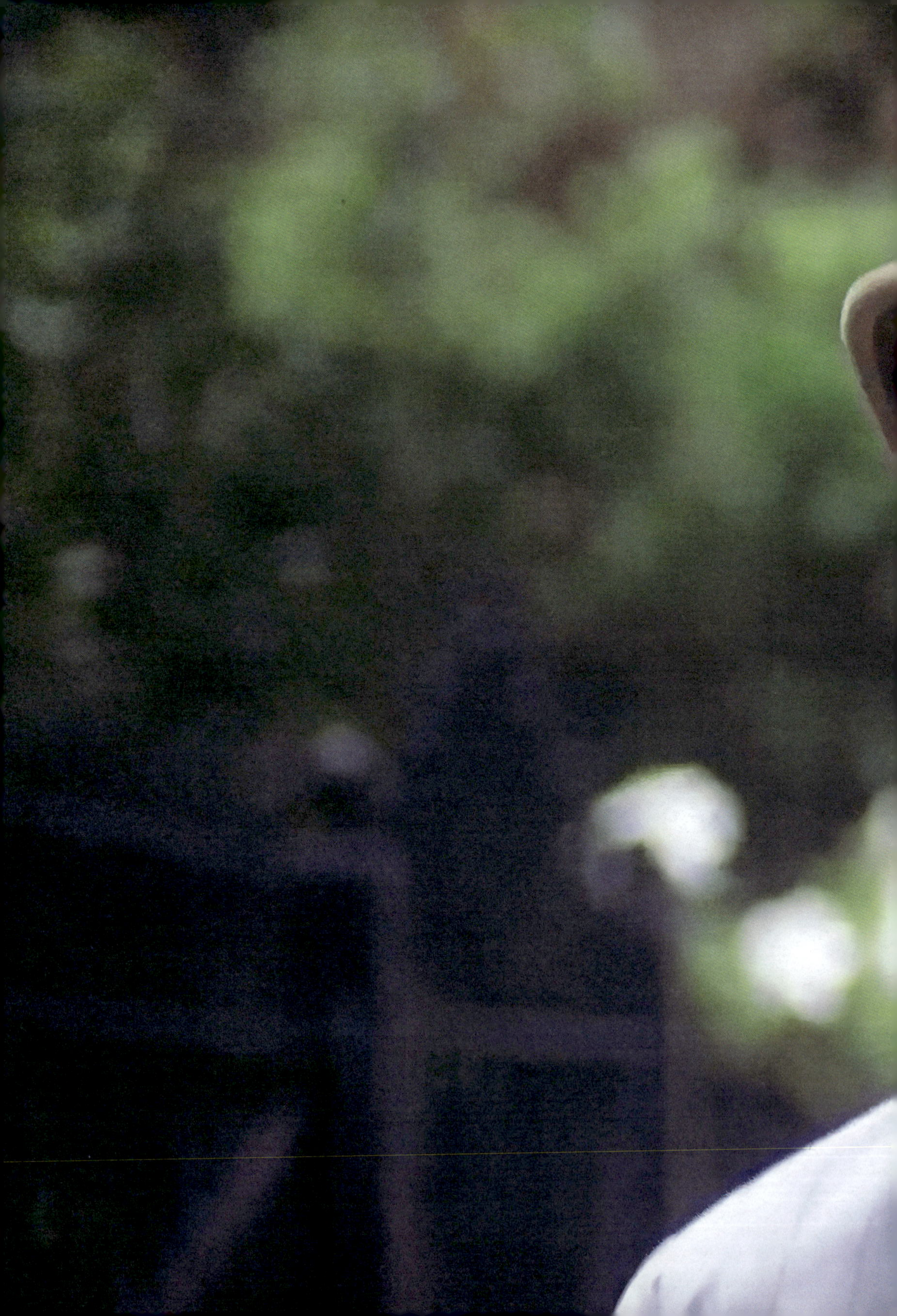

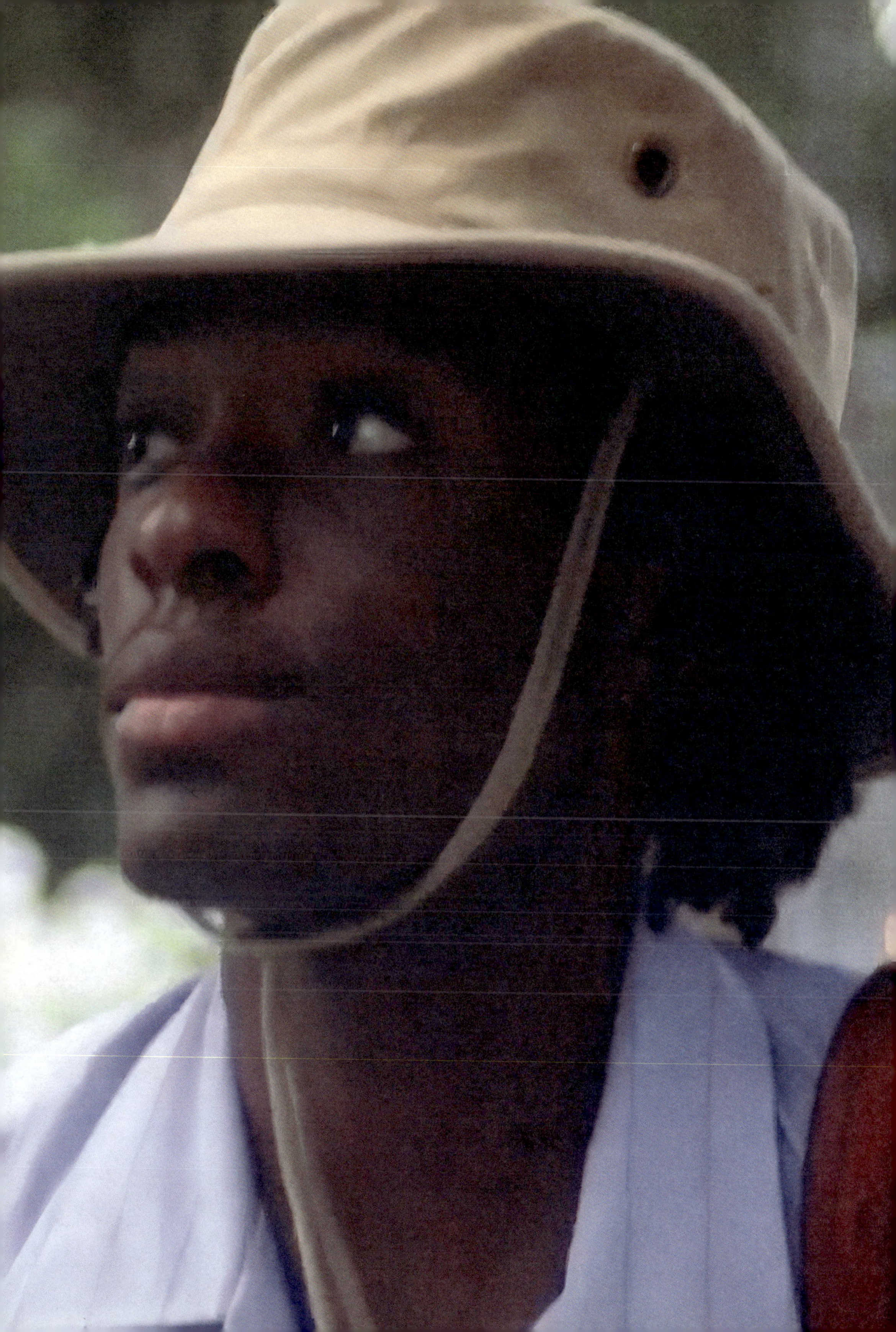

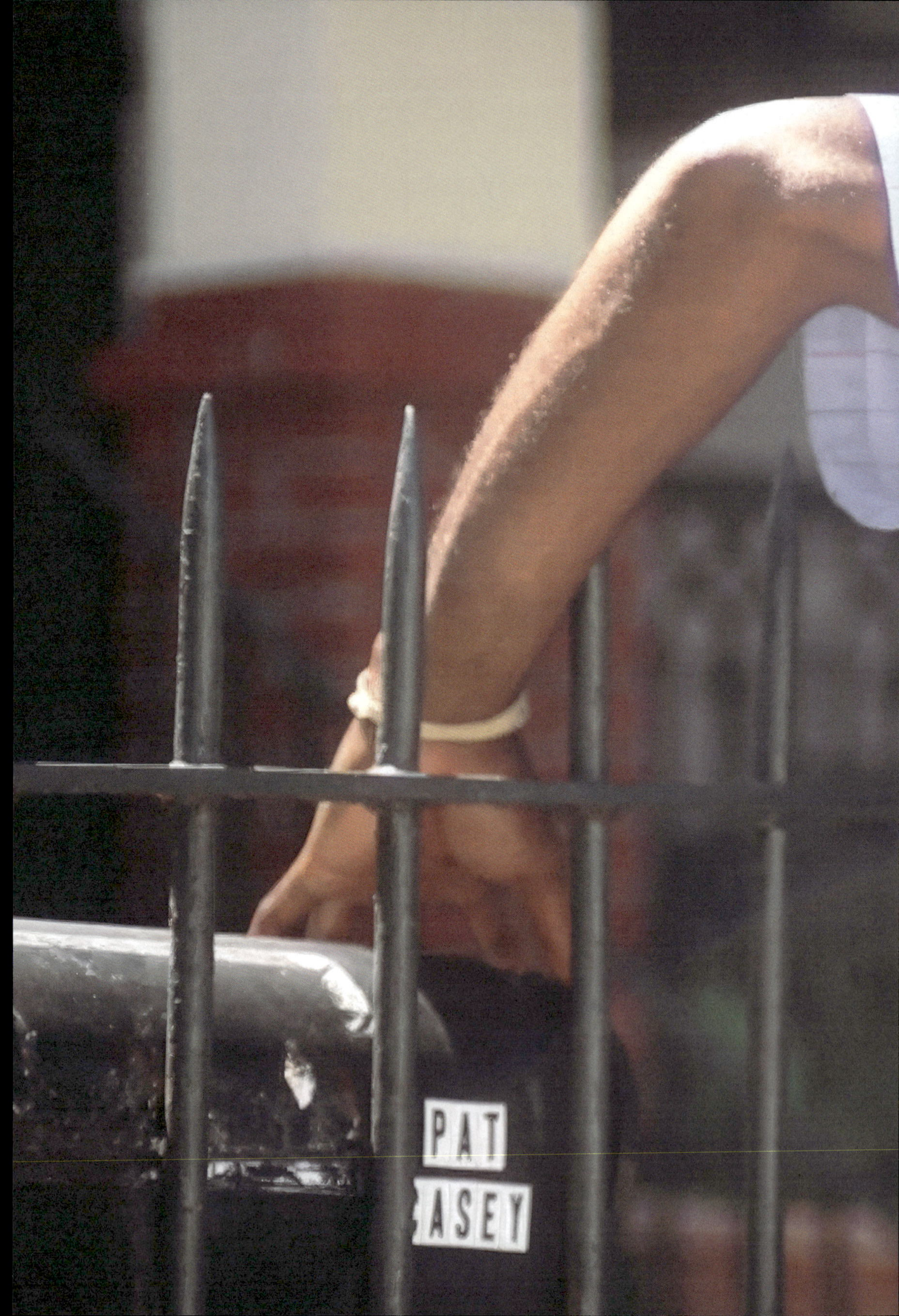
PAT
ASEY

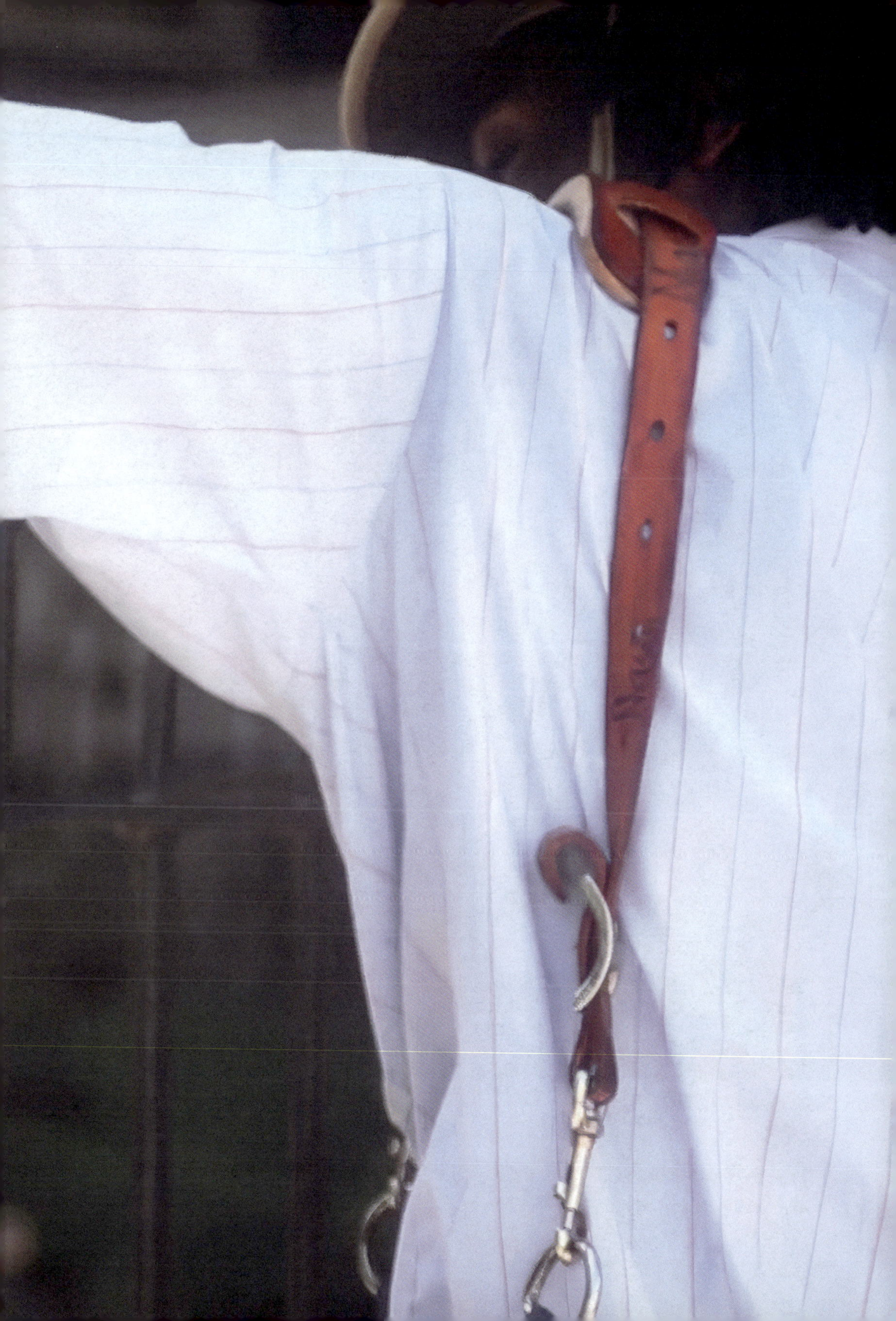

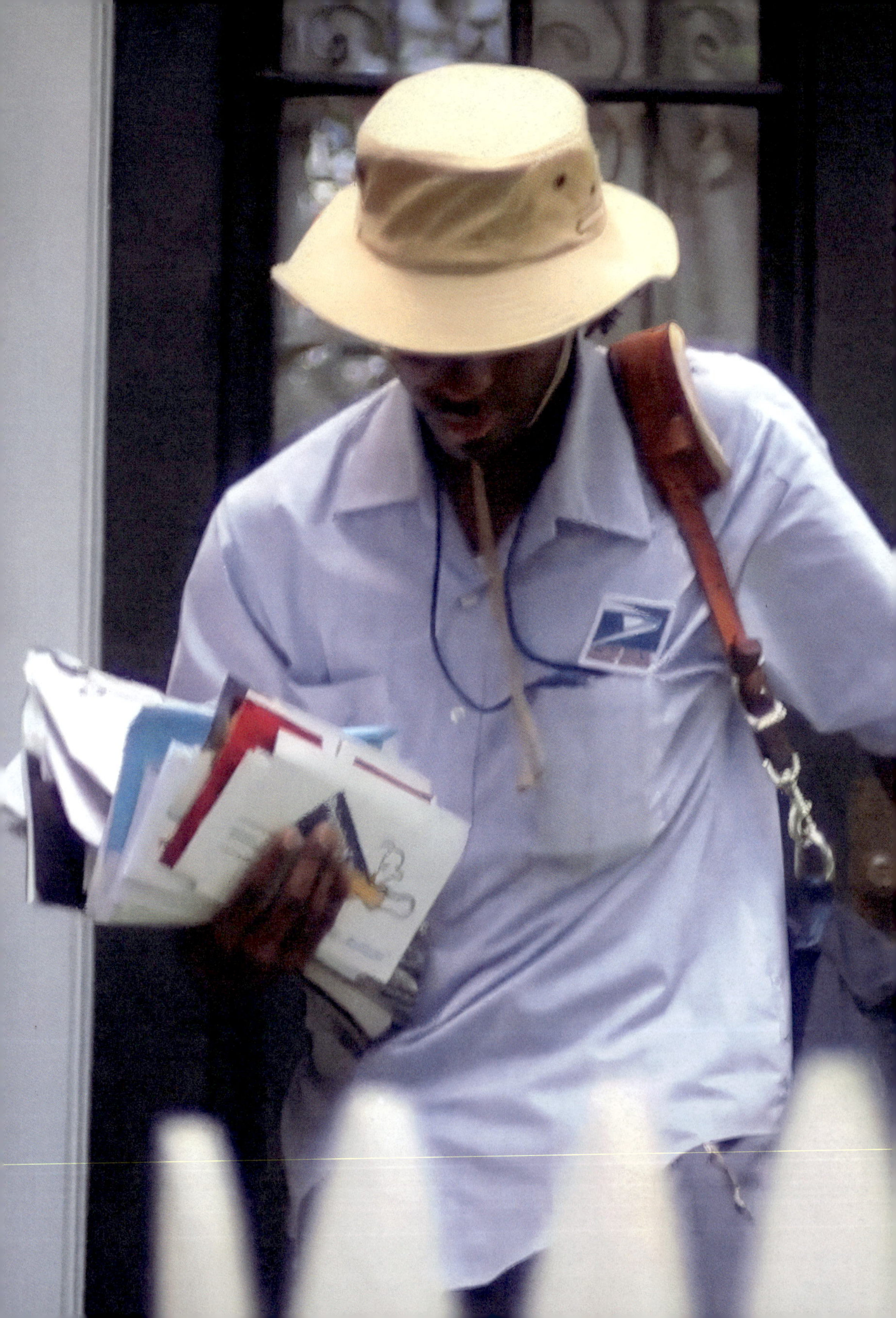

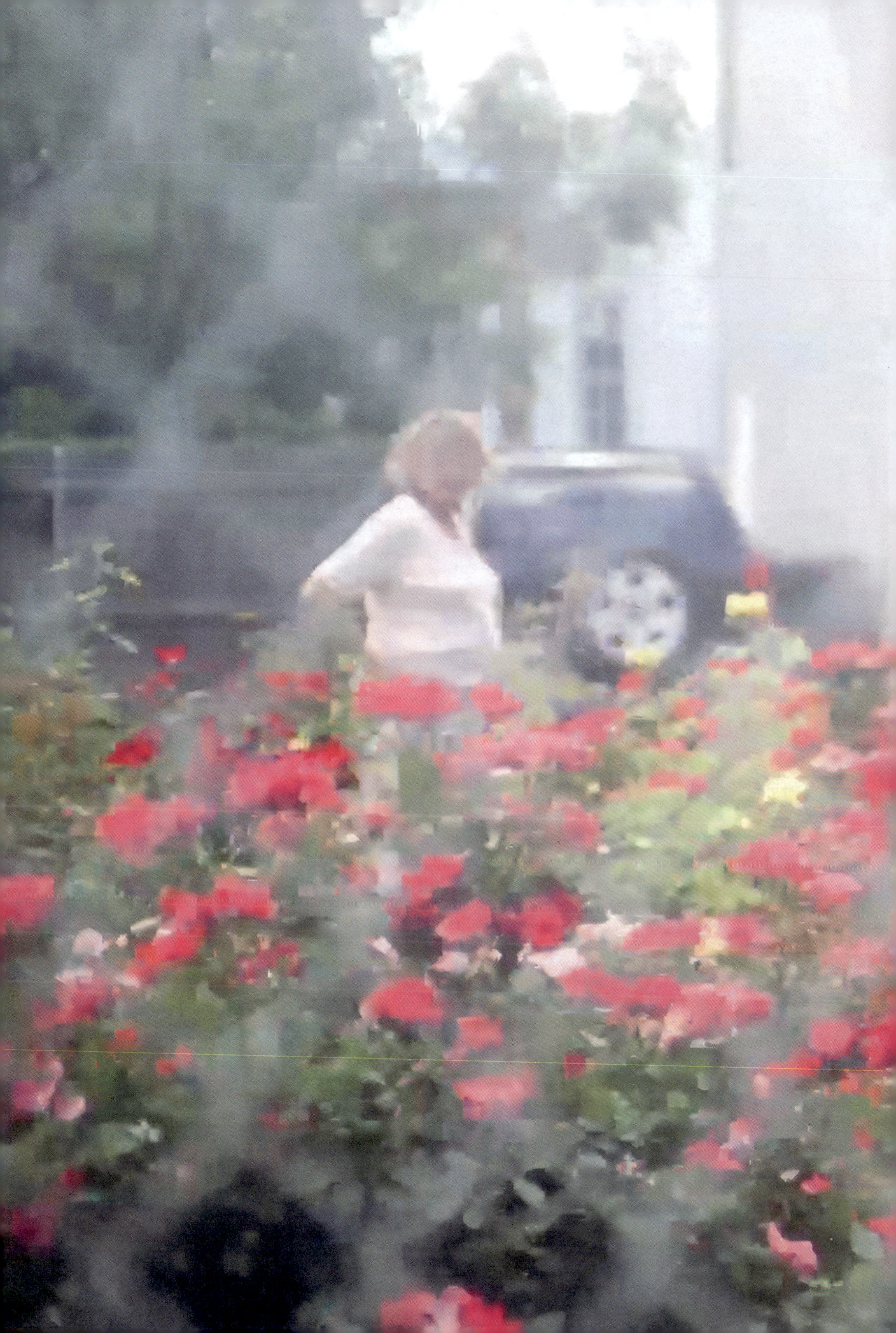

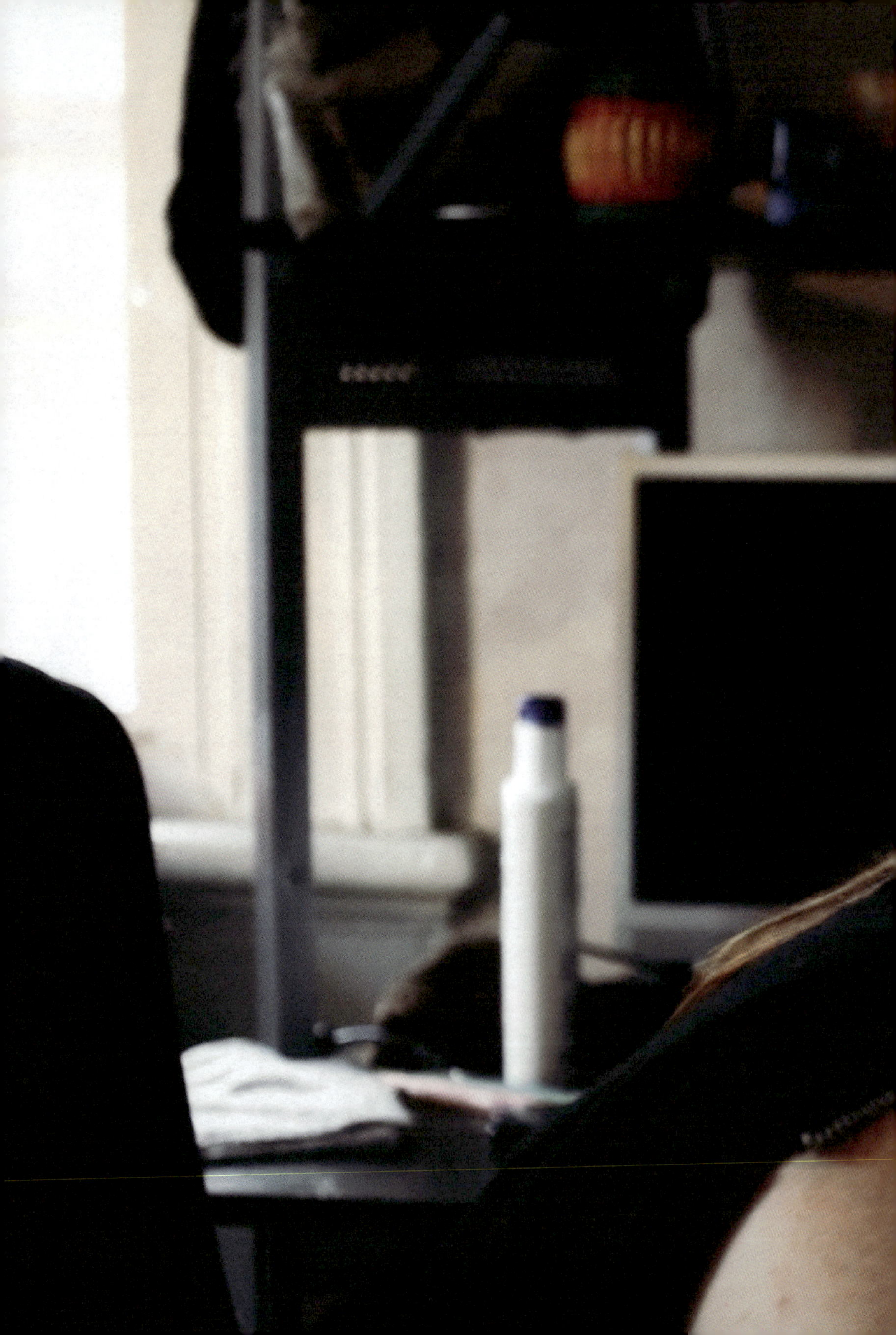

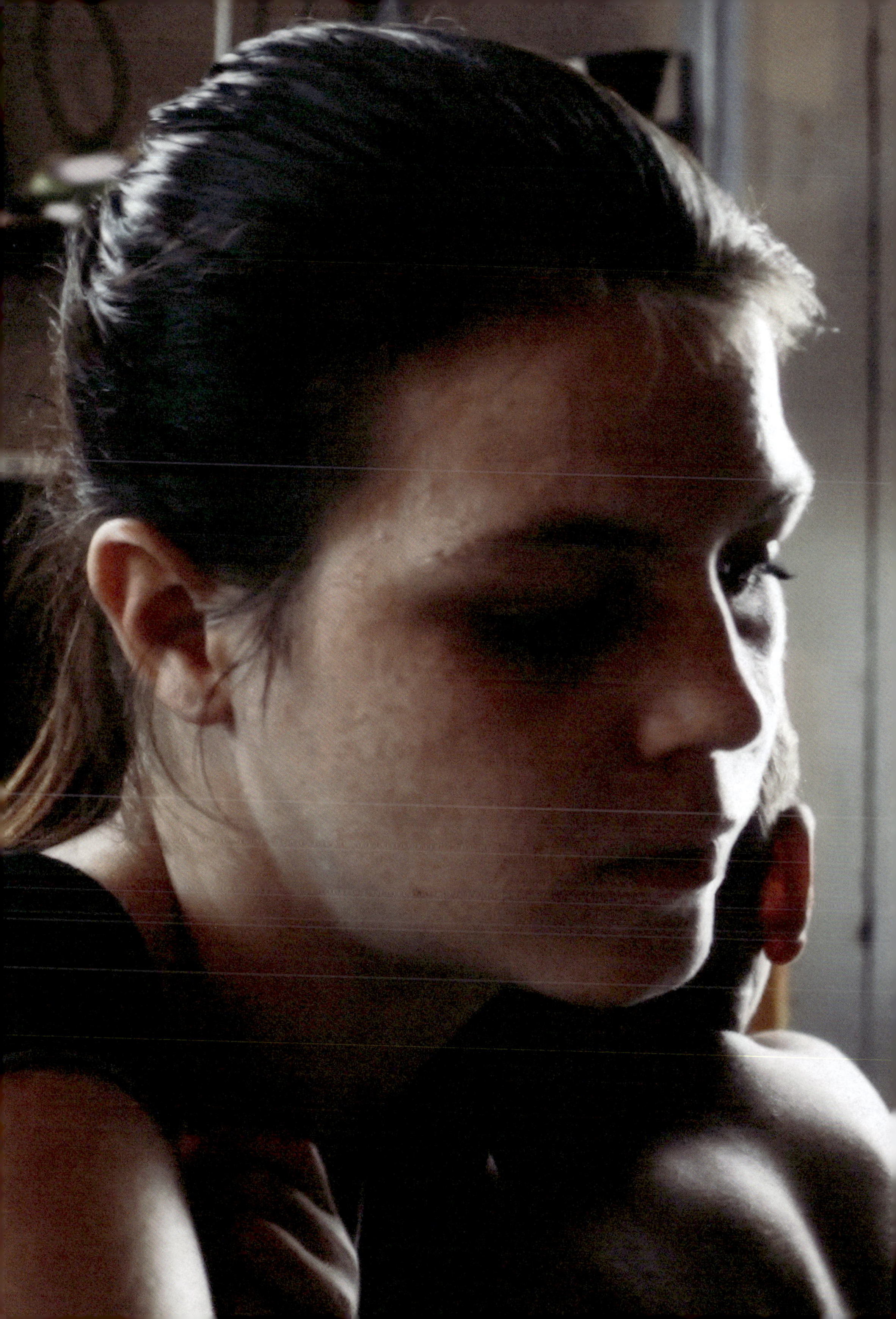

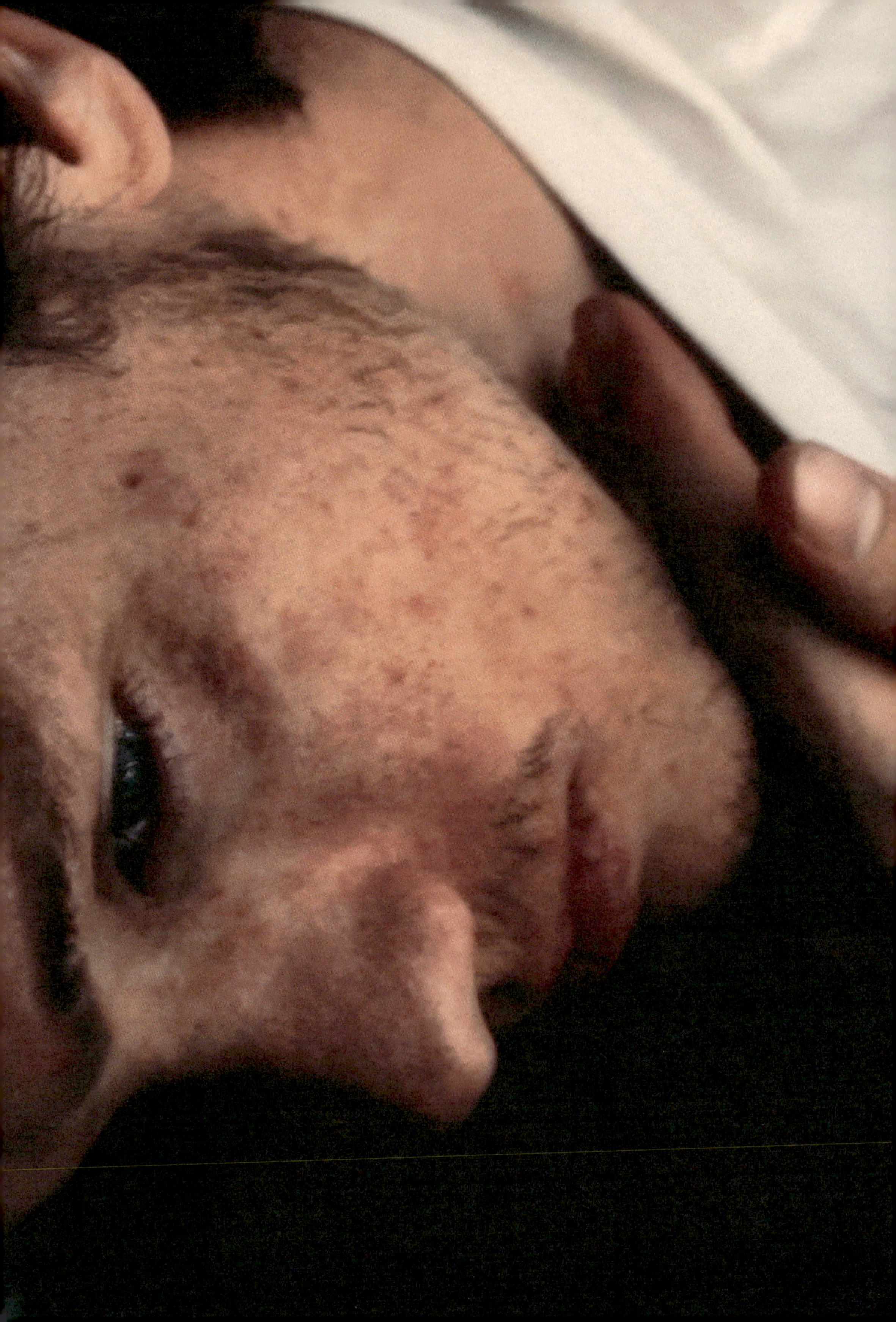

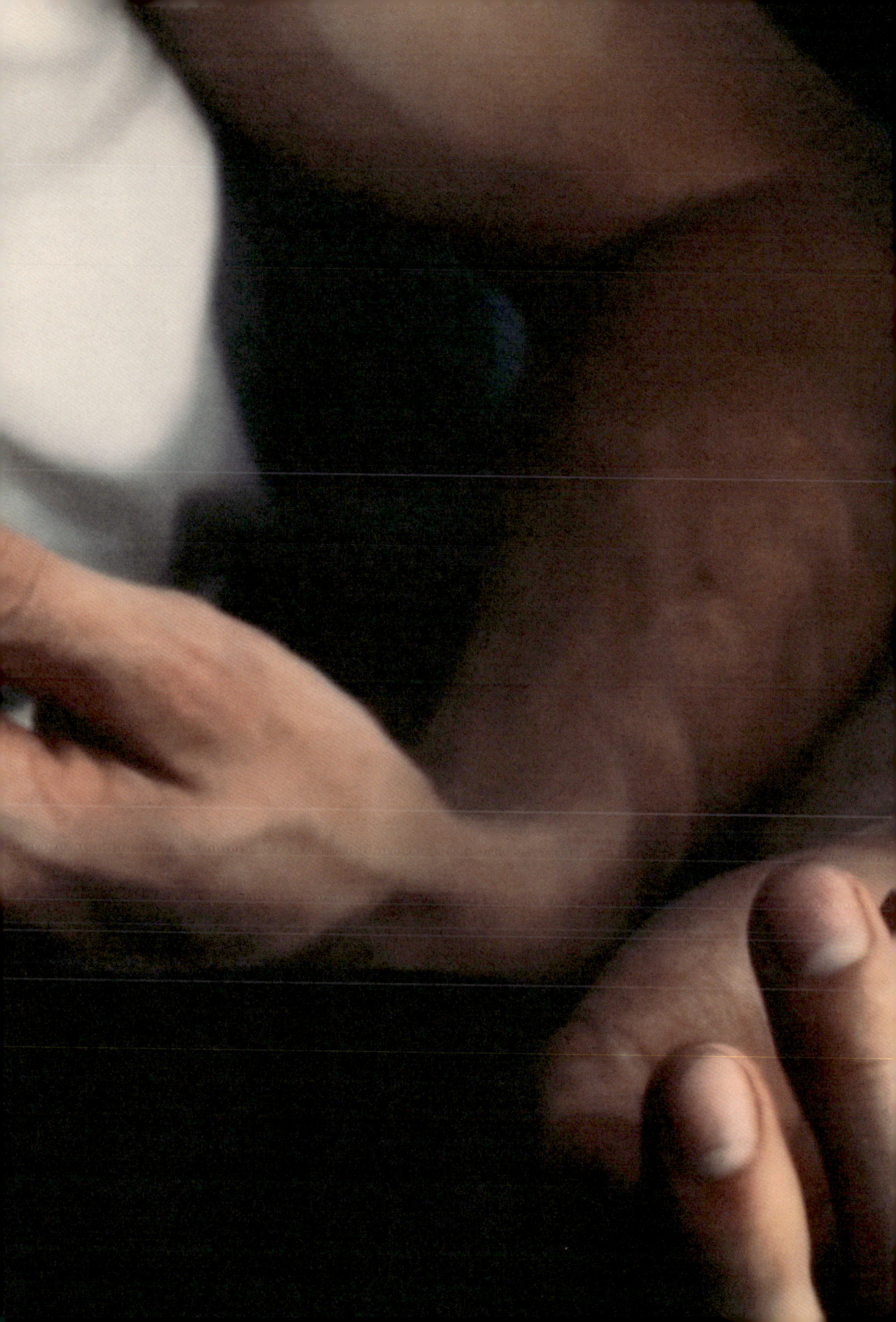

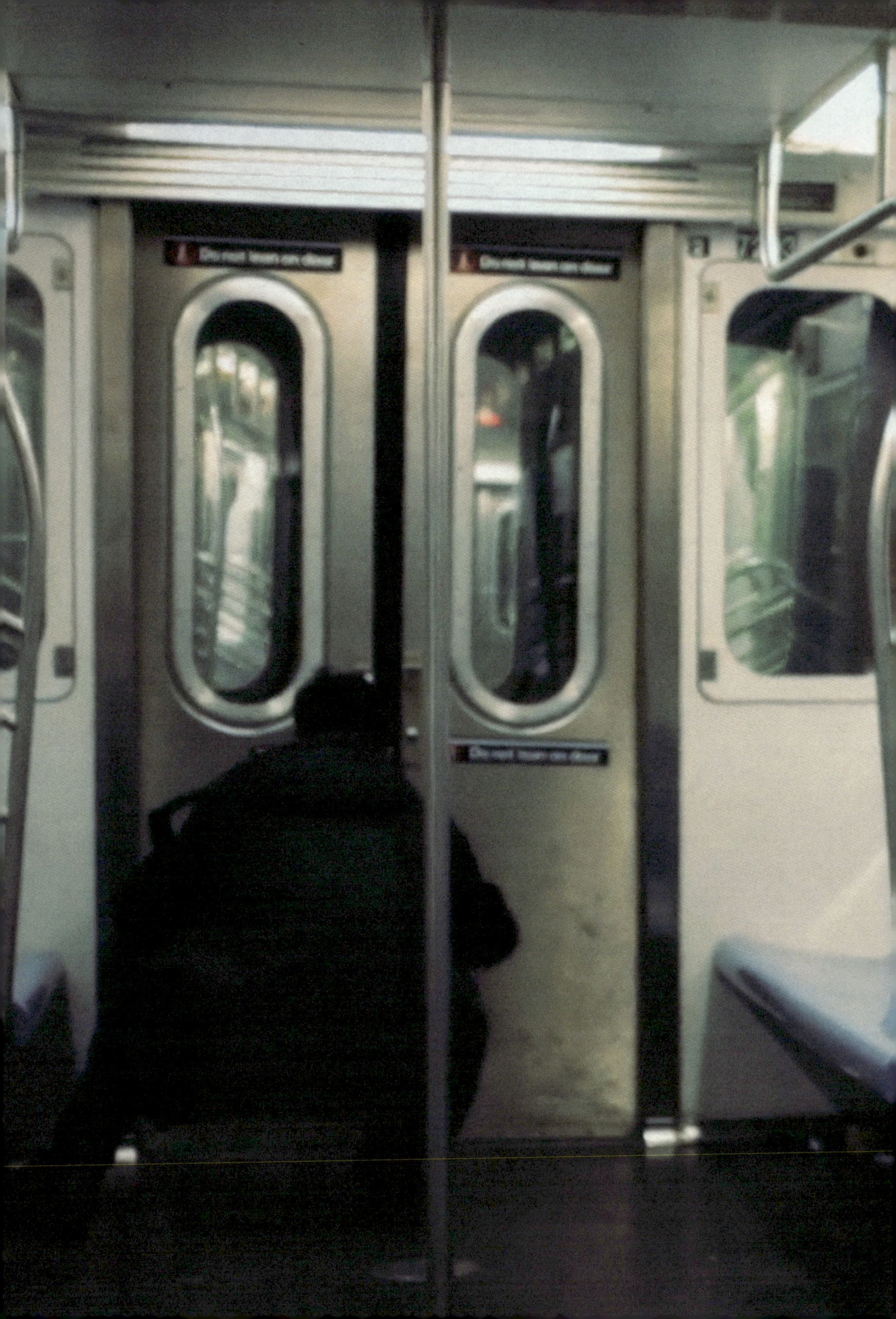

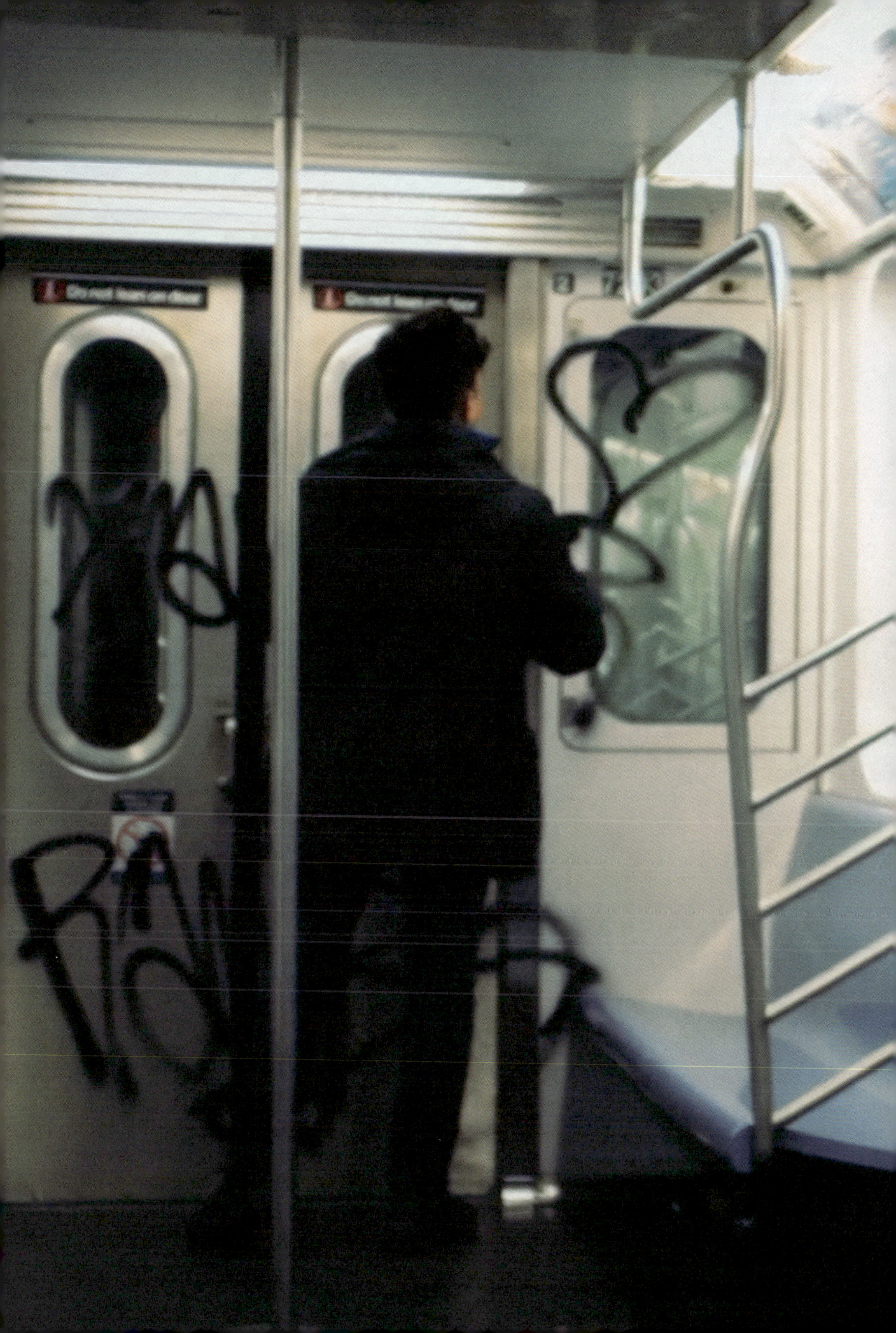

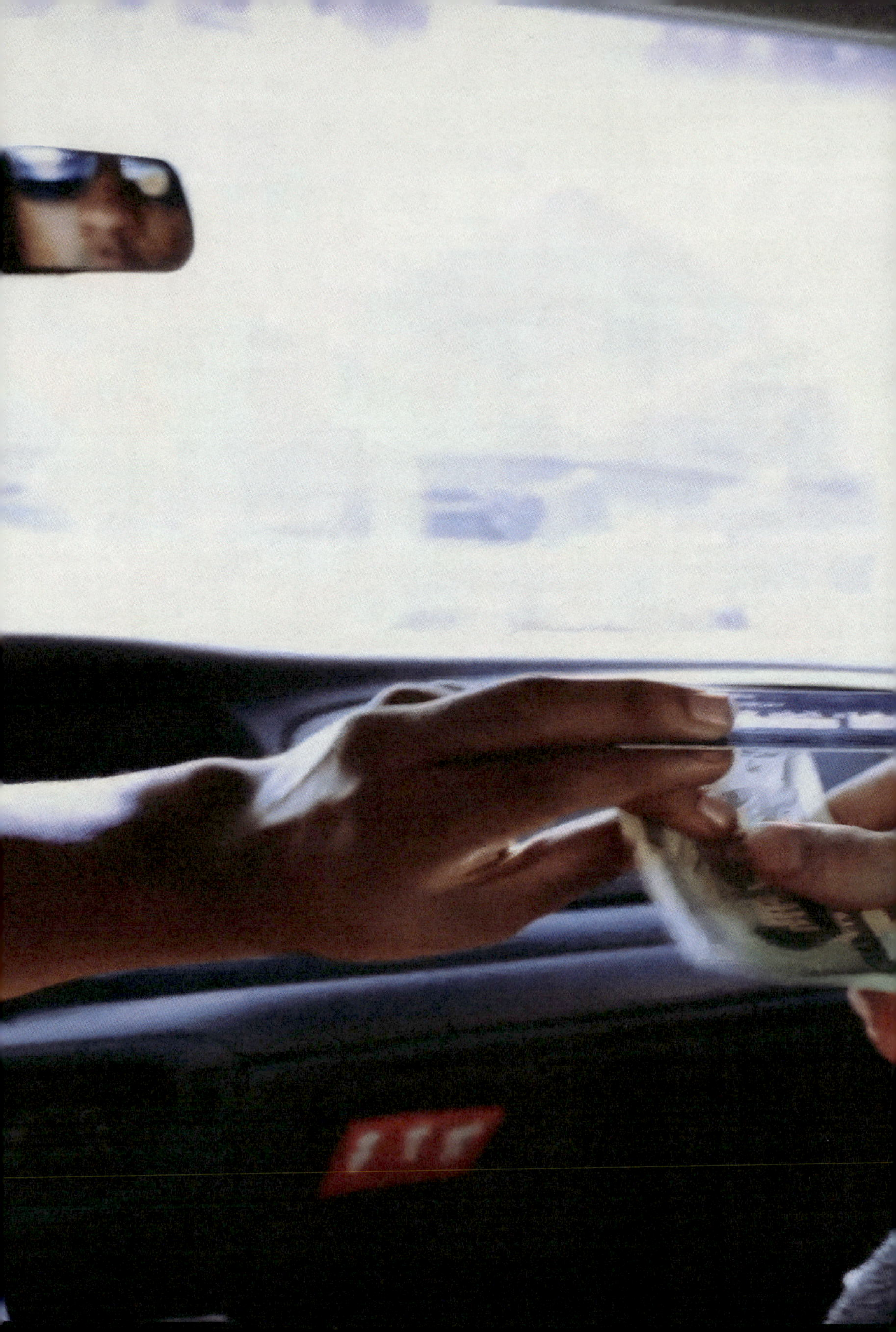

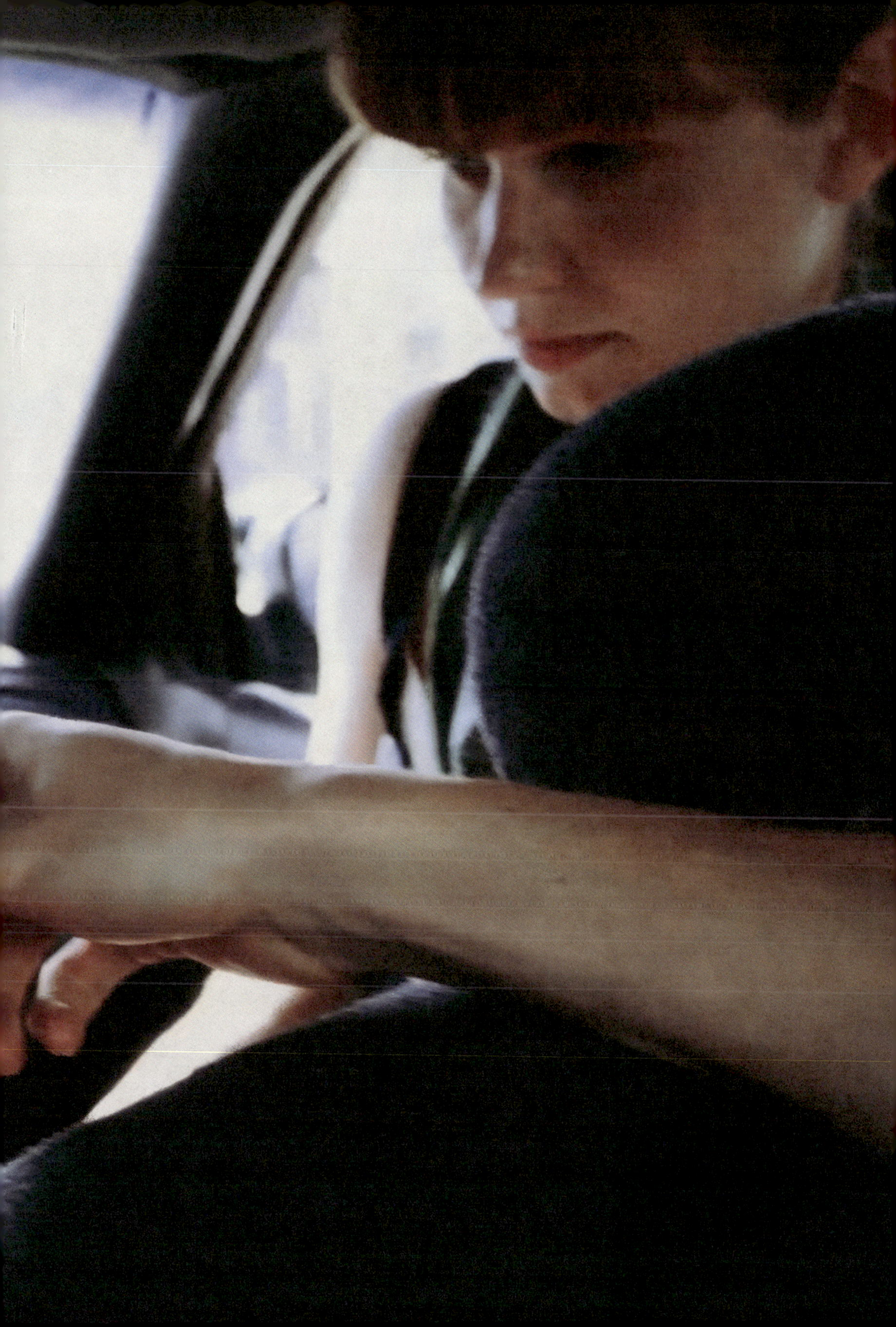

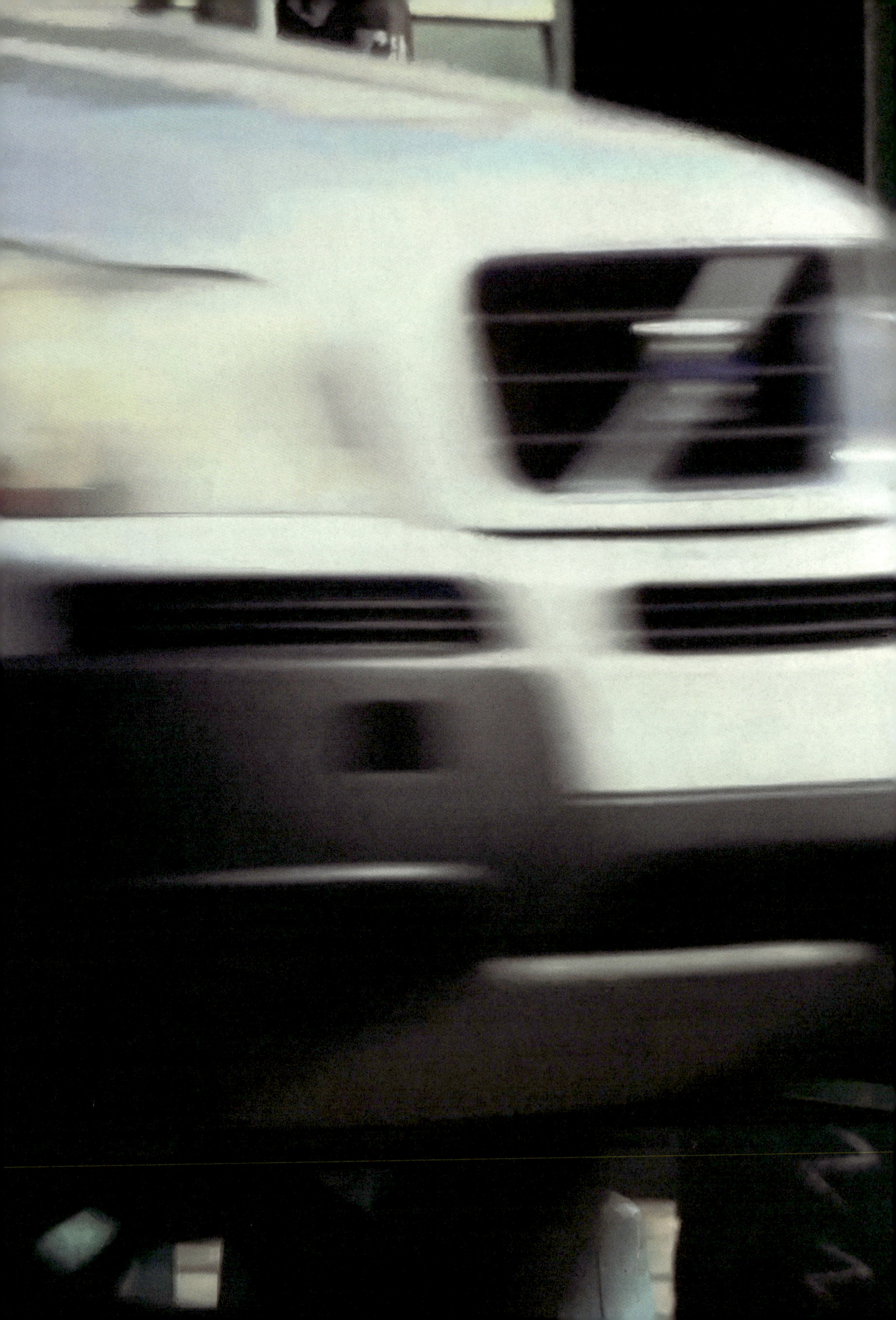

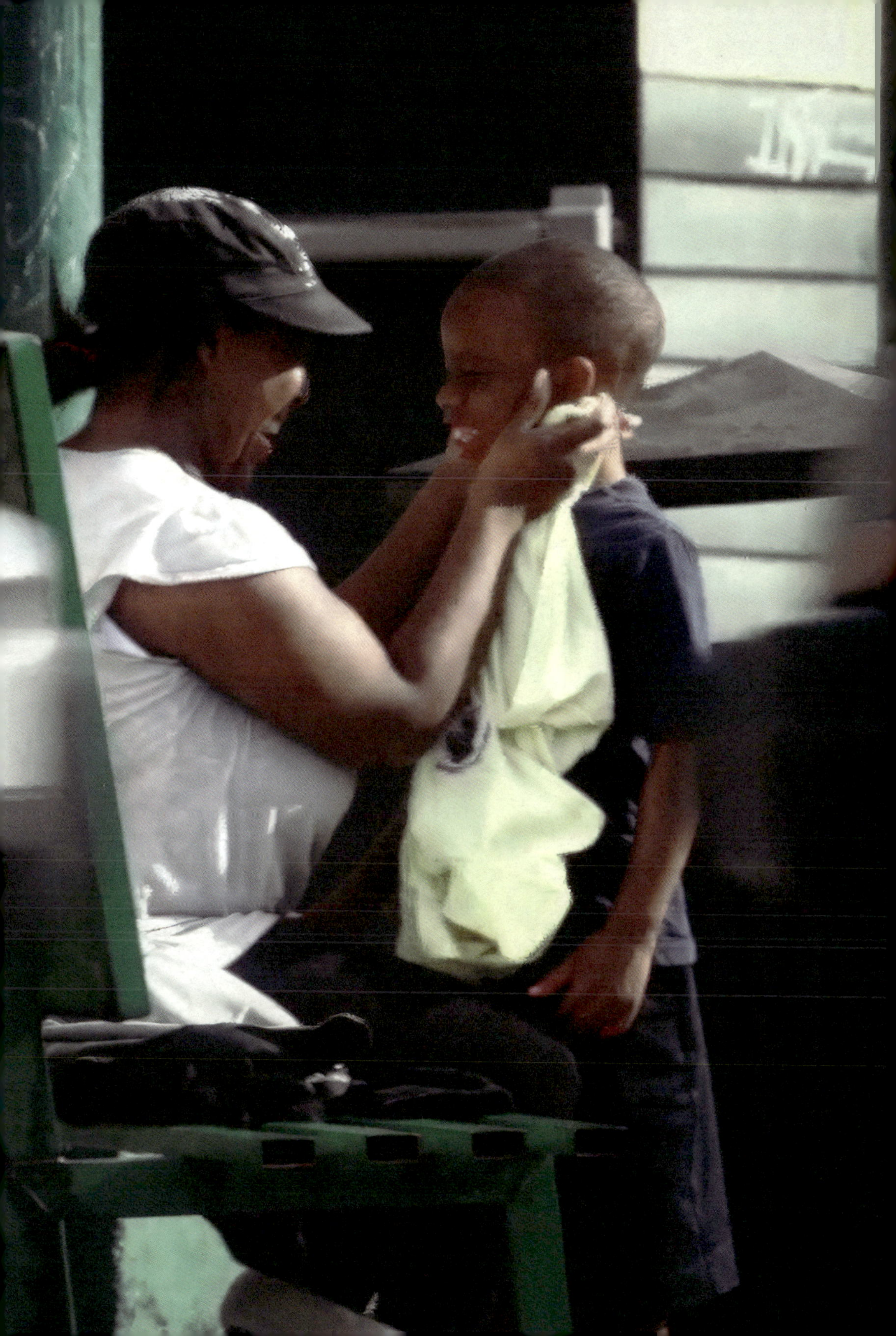

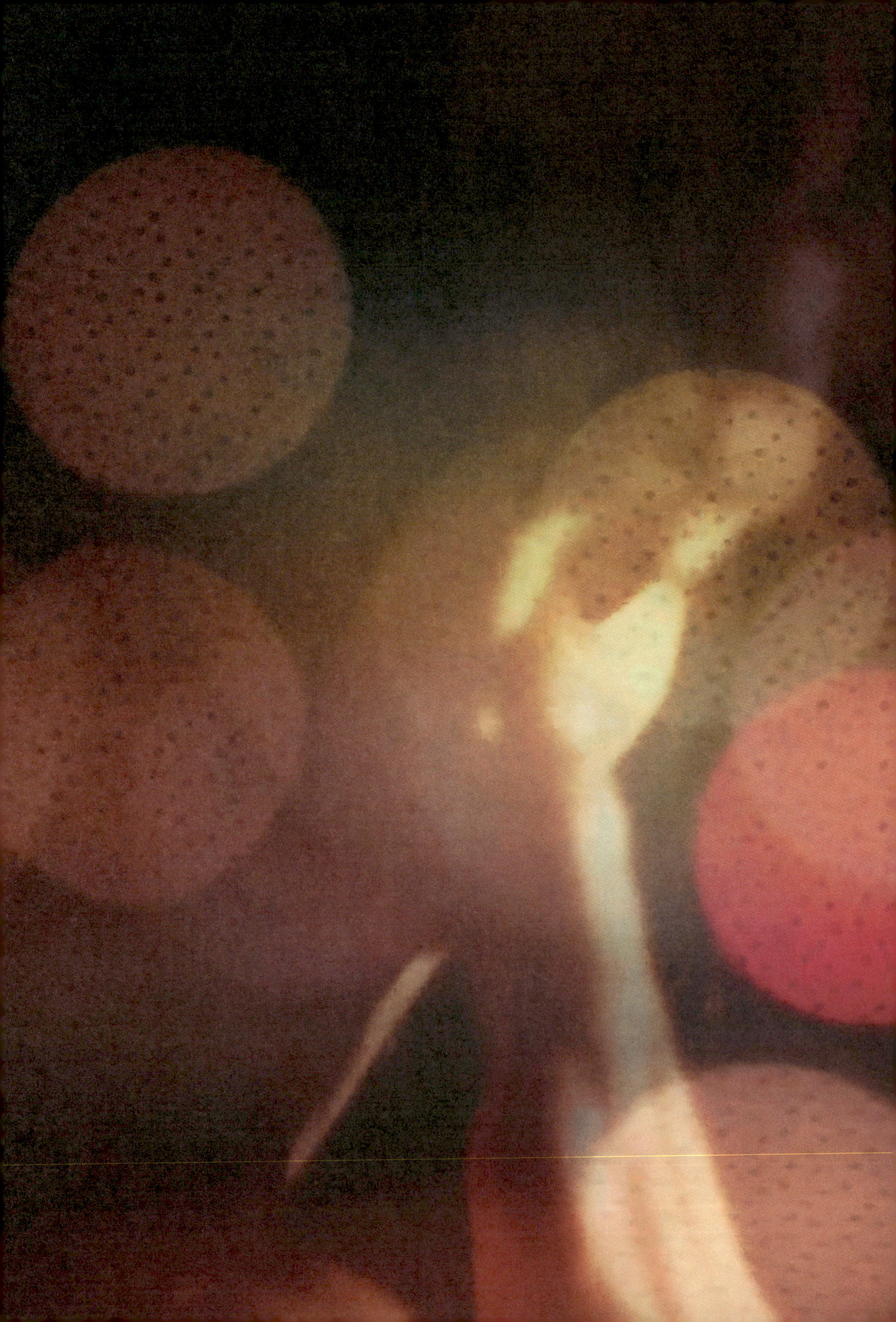

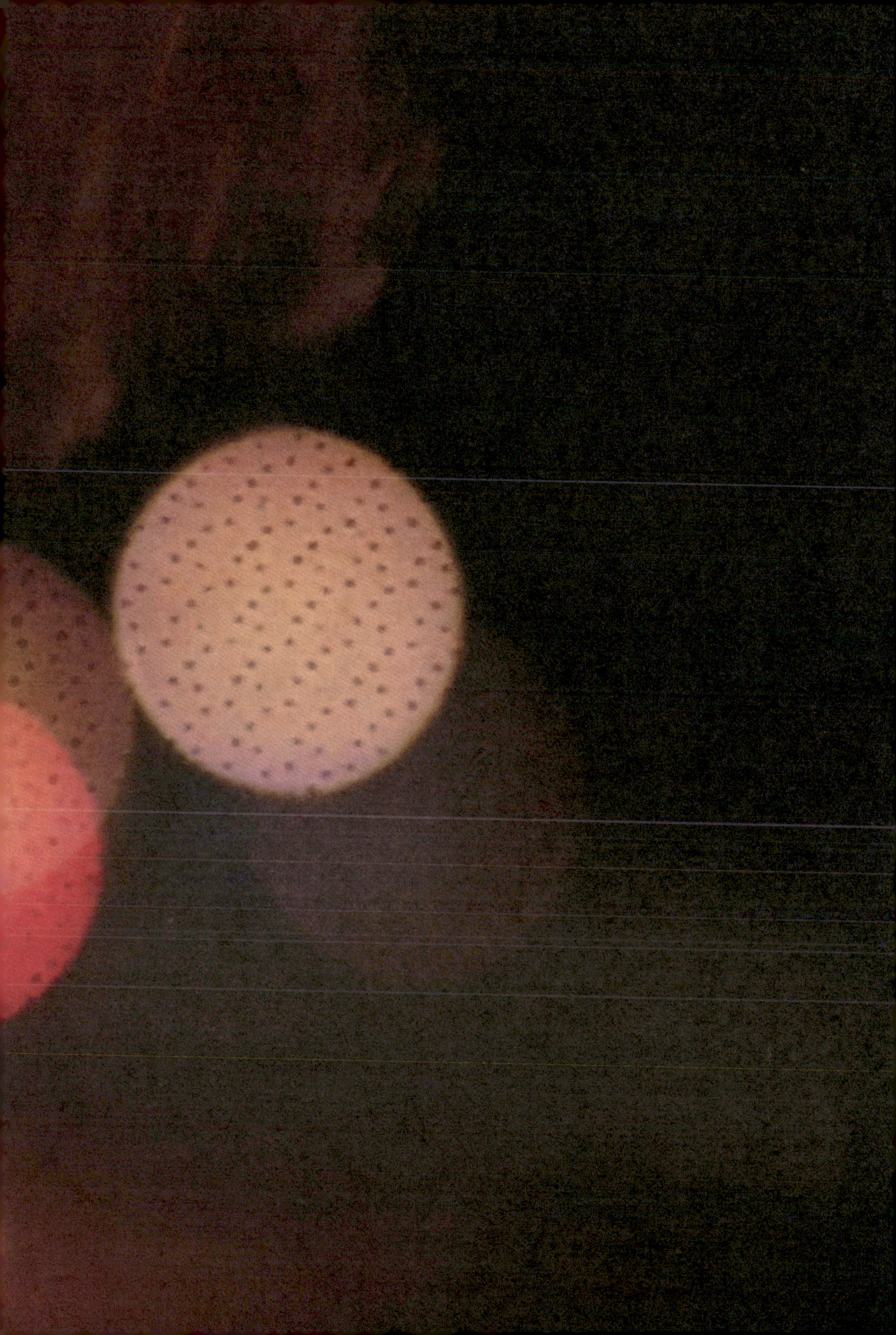

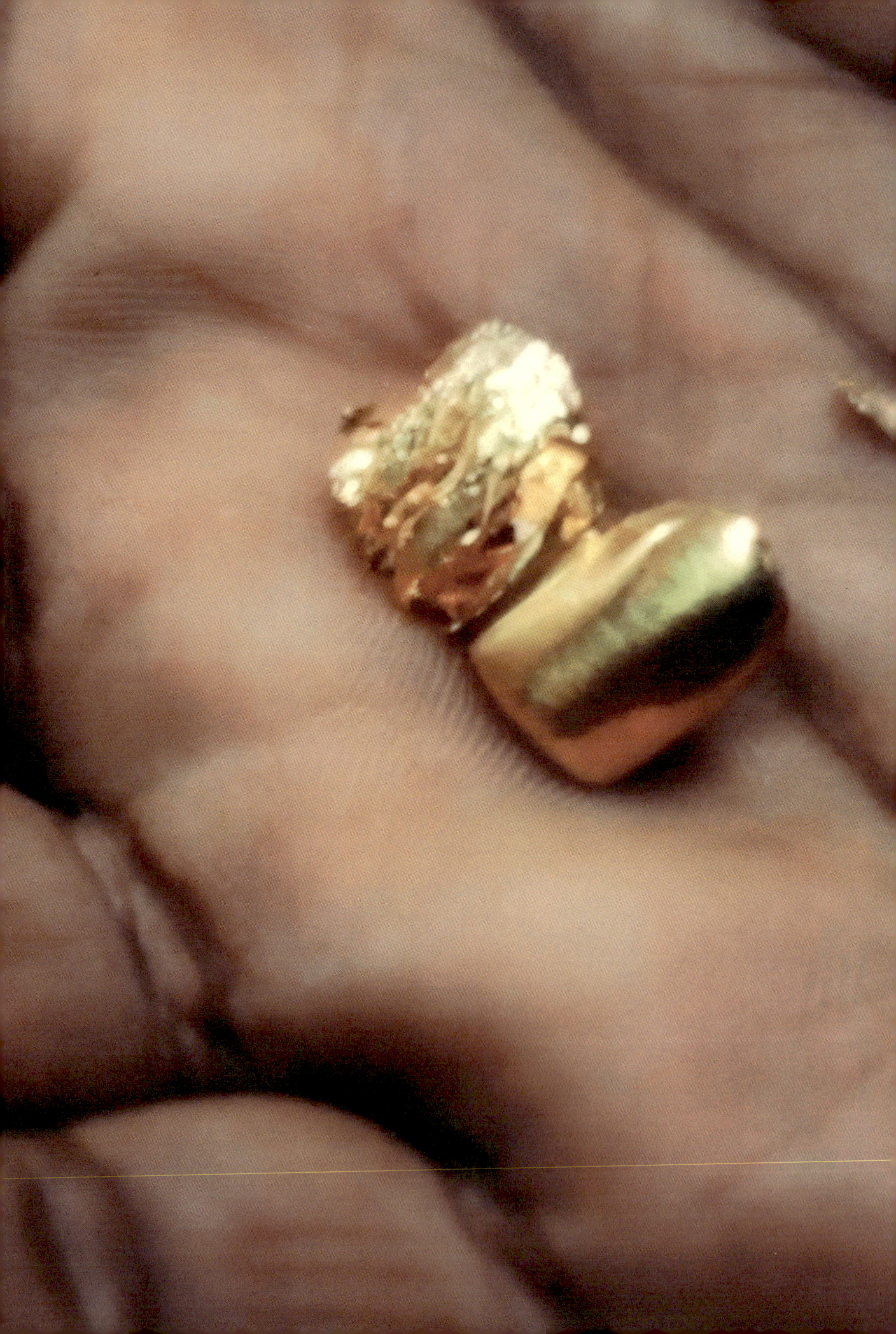

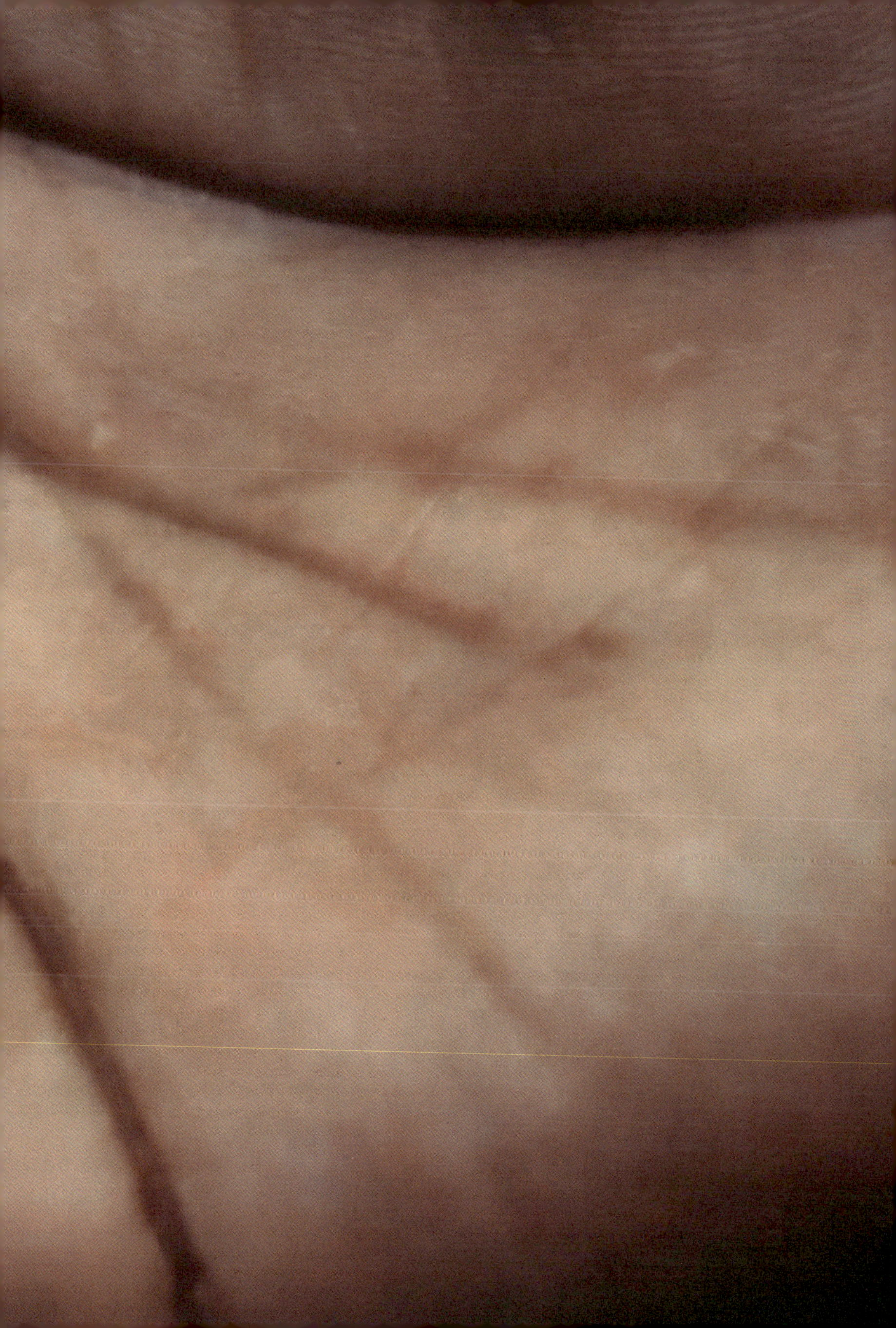

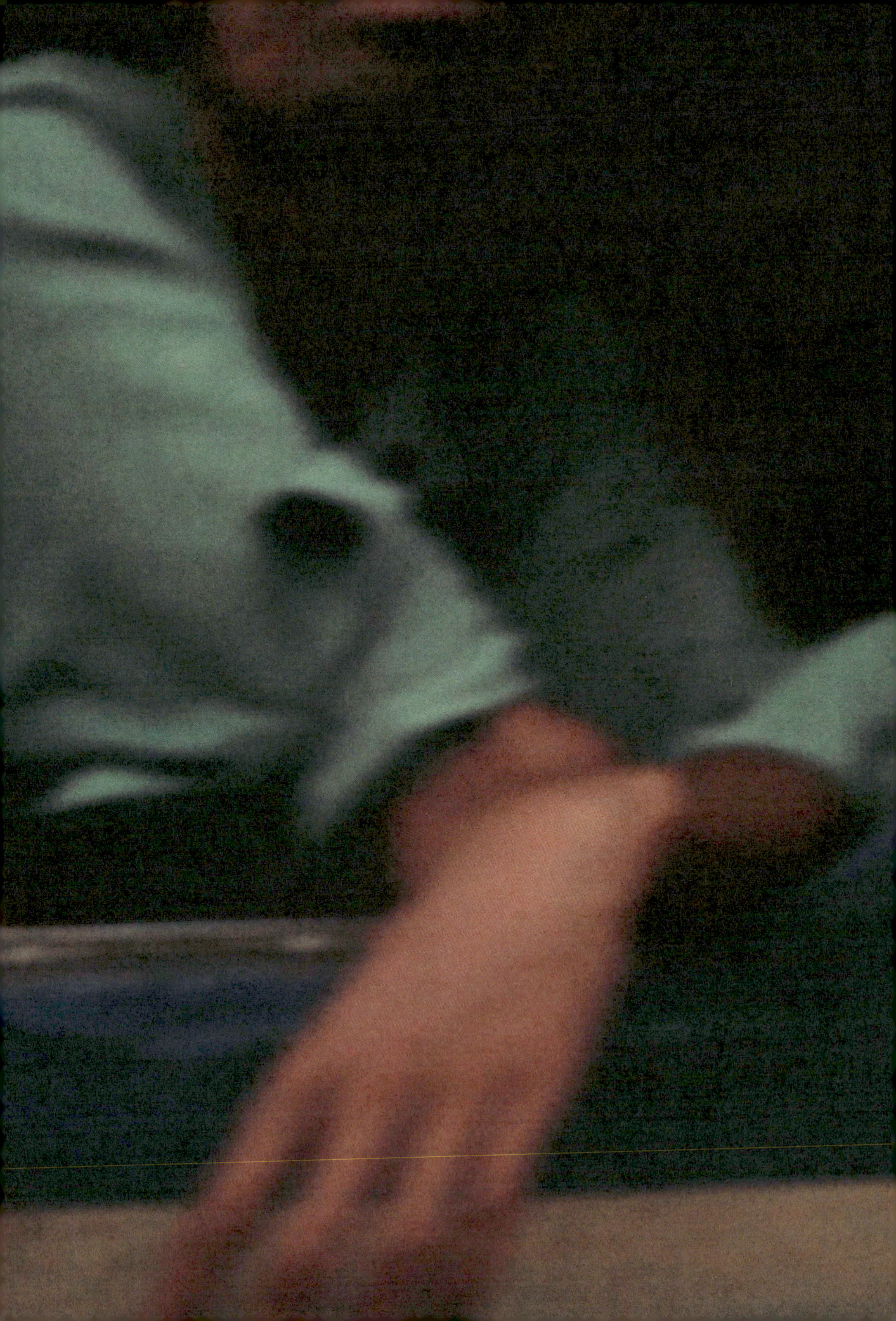

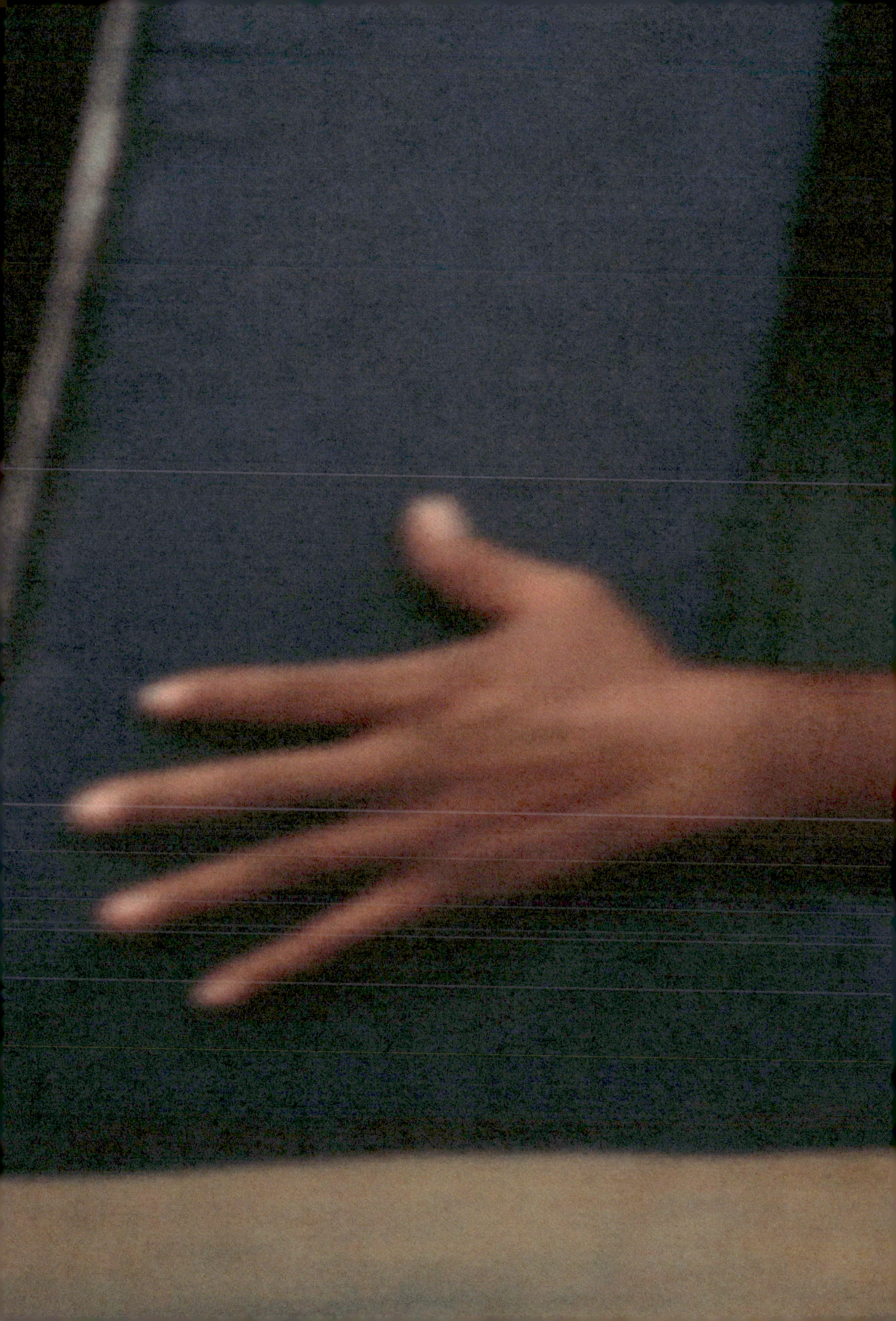

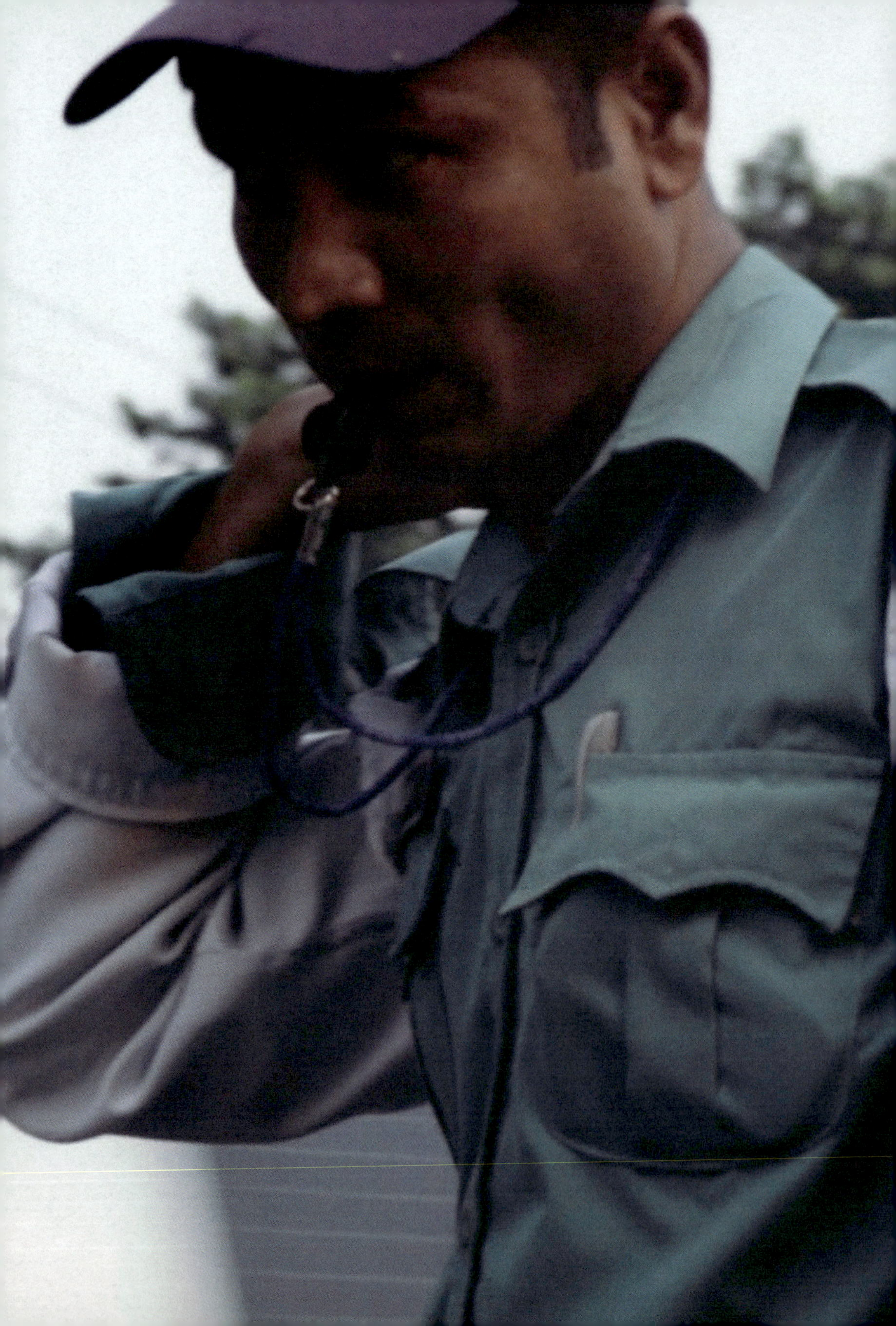

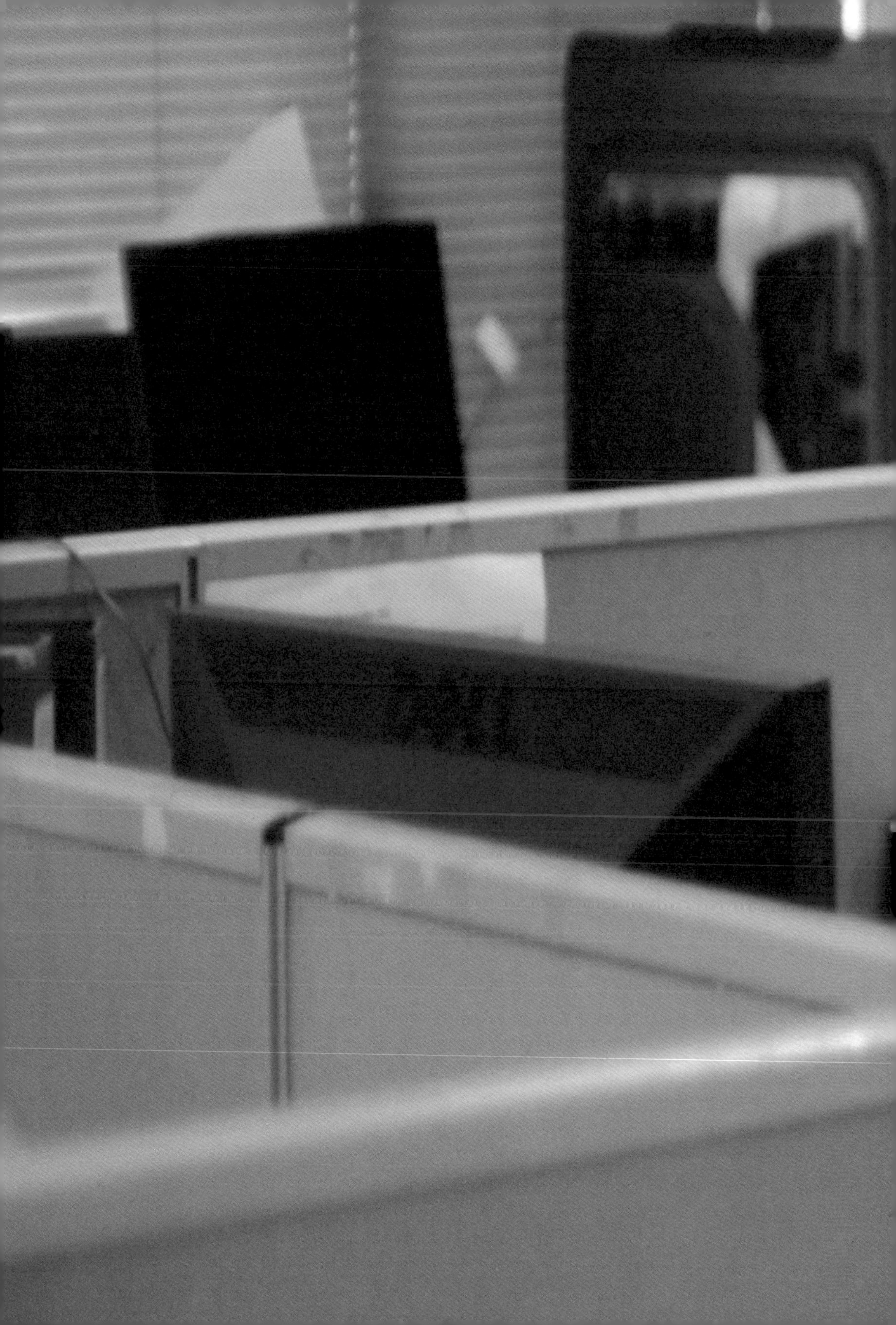

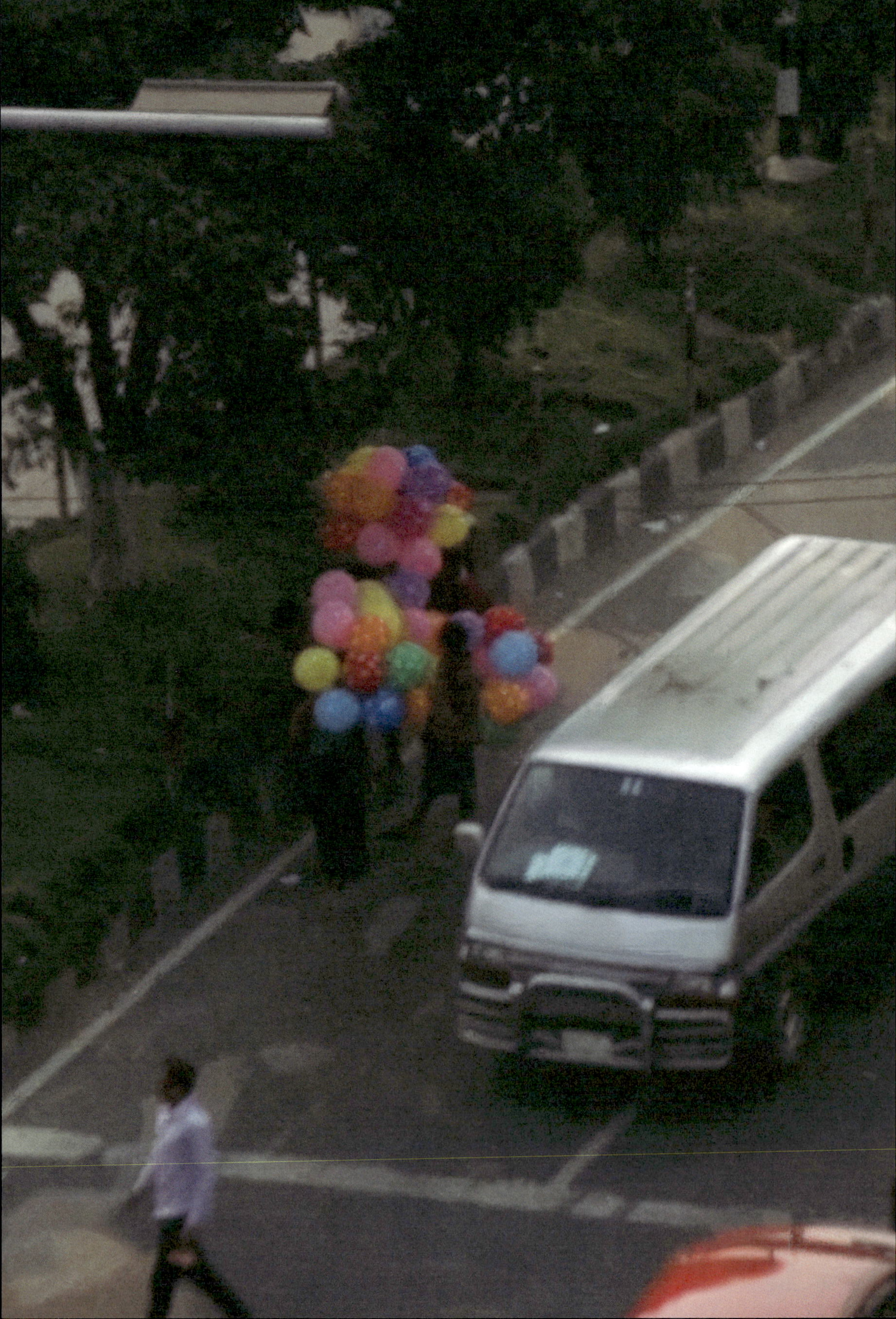

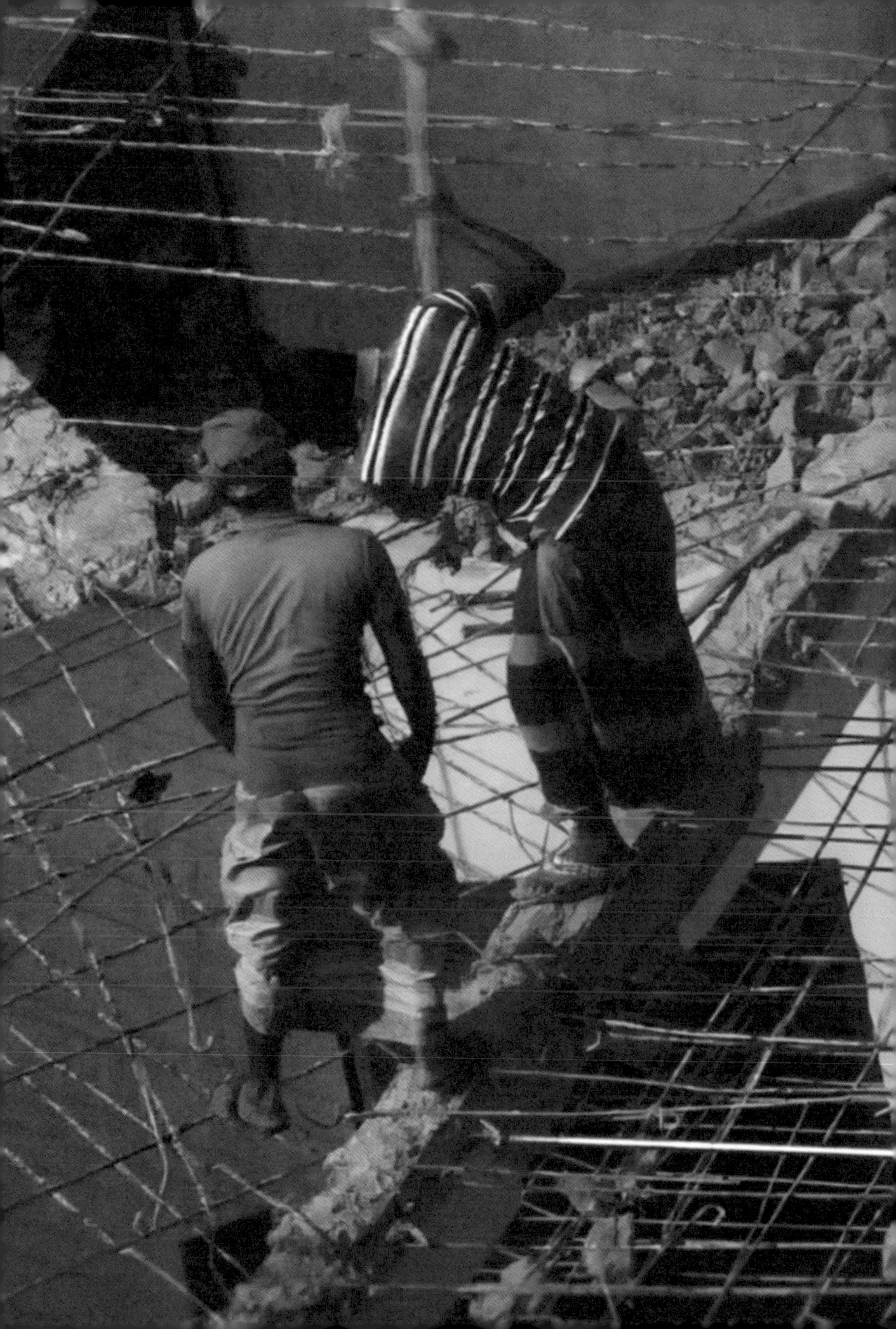

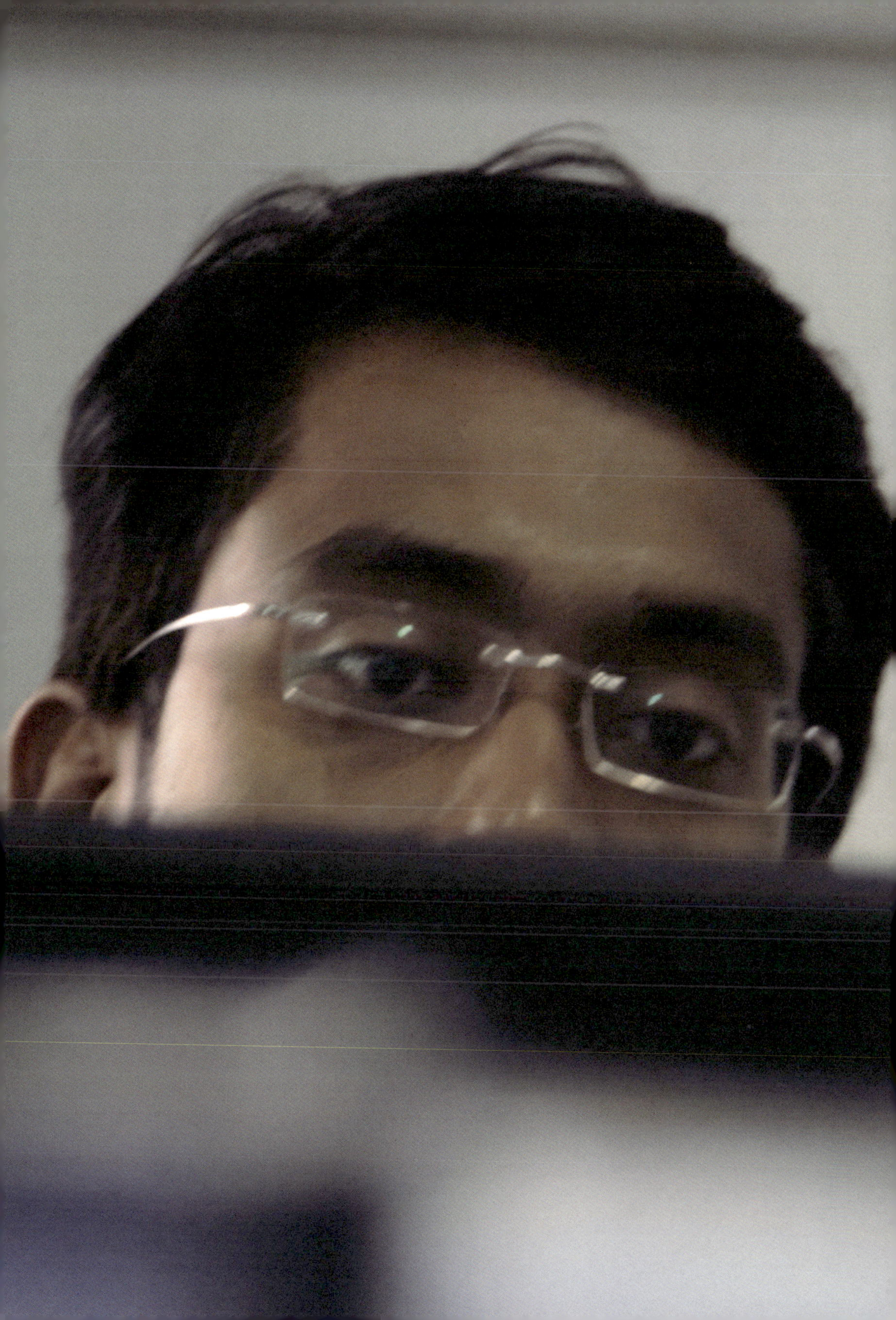

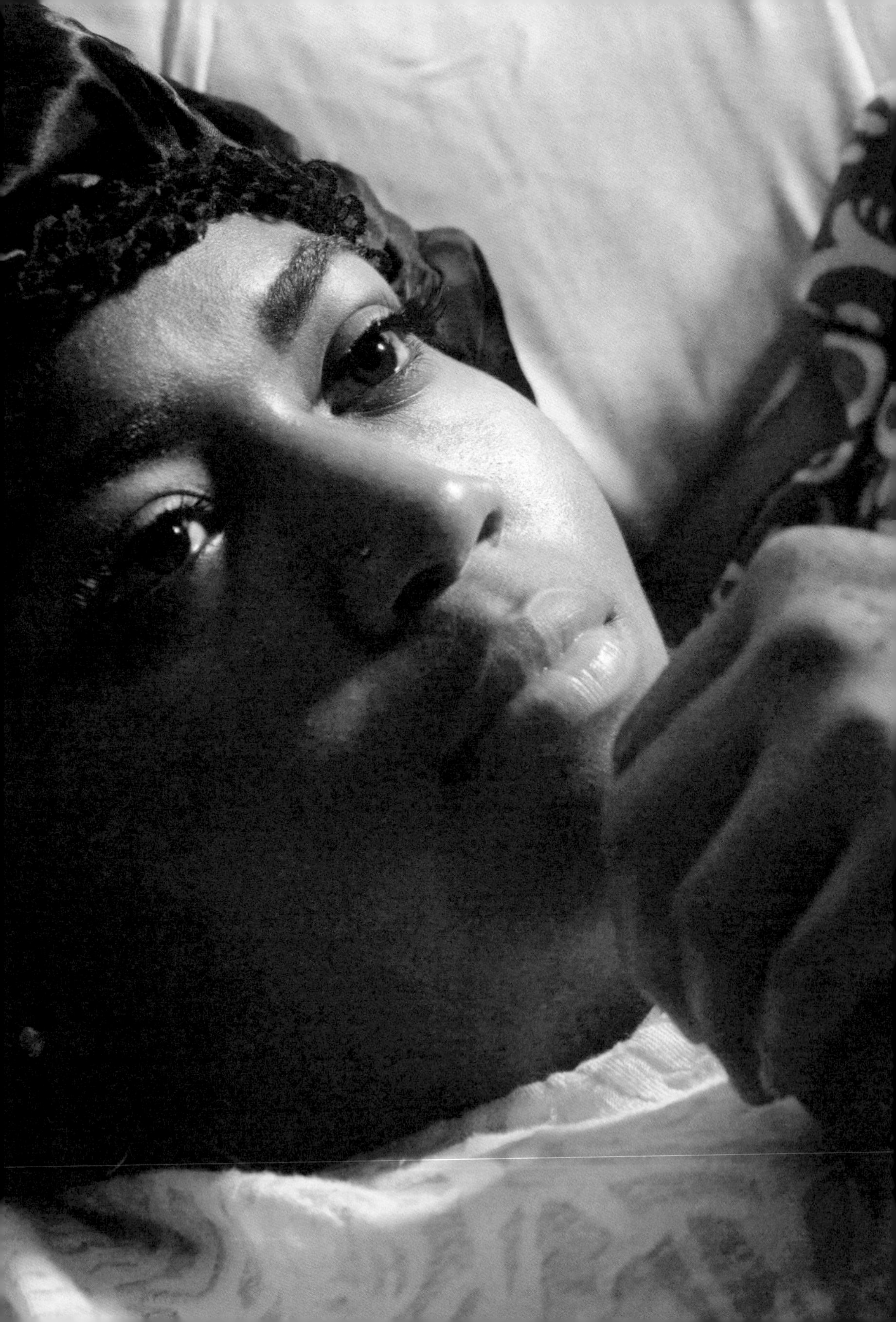

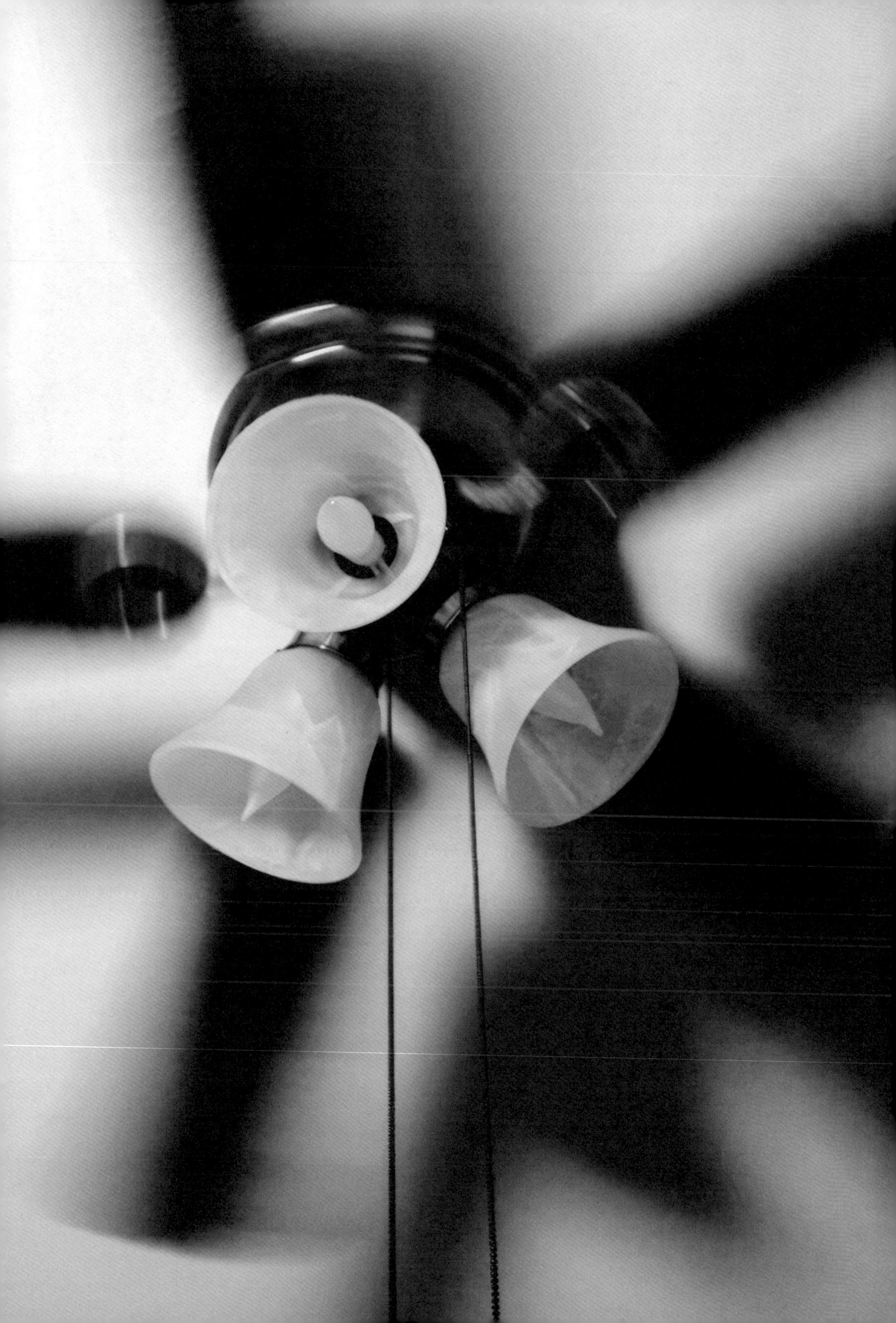

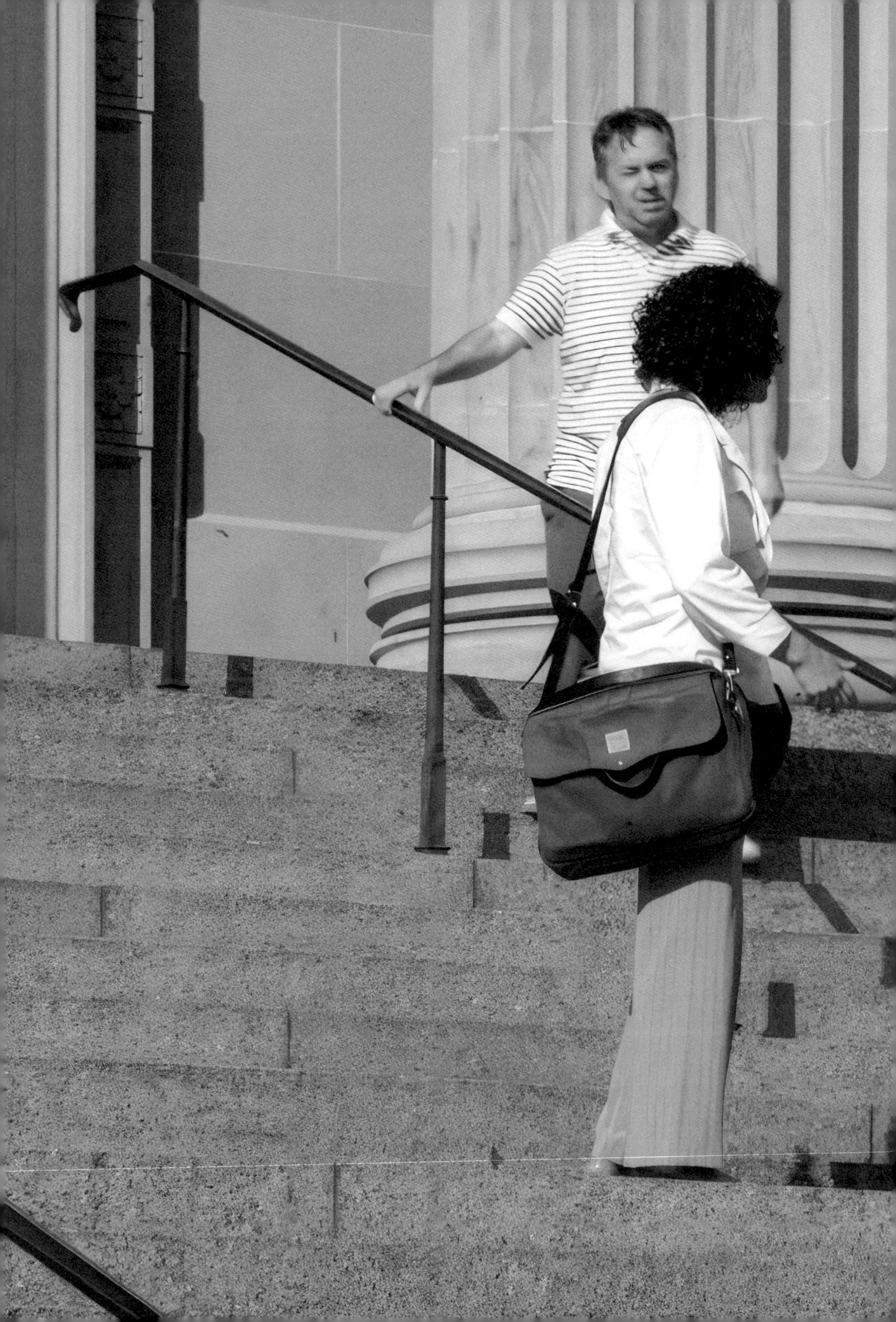

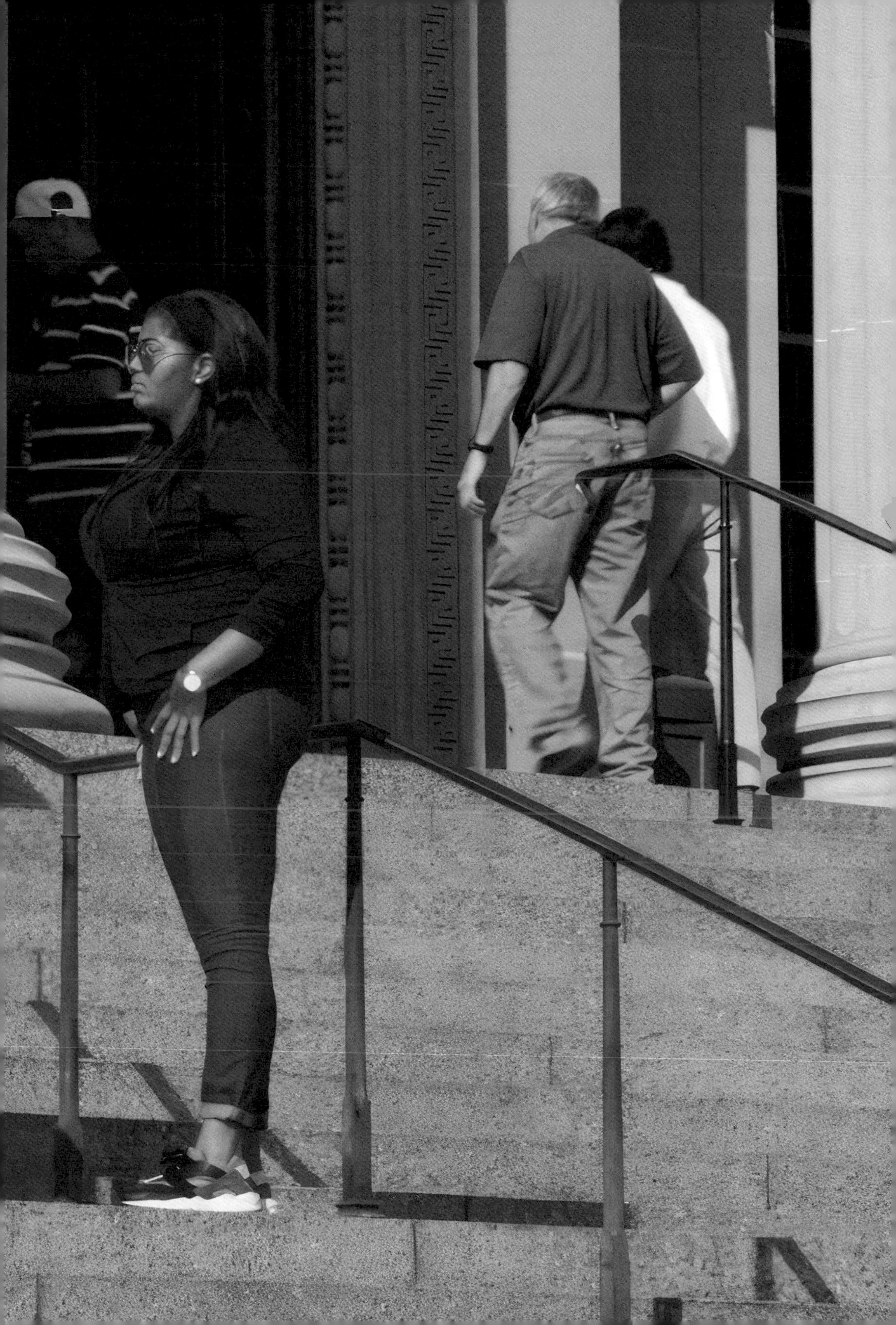

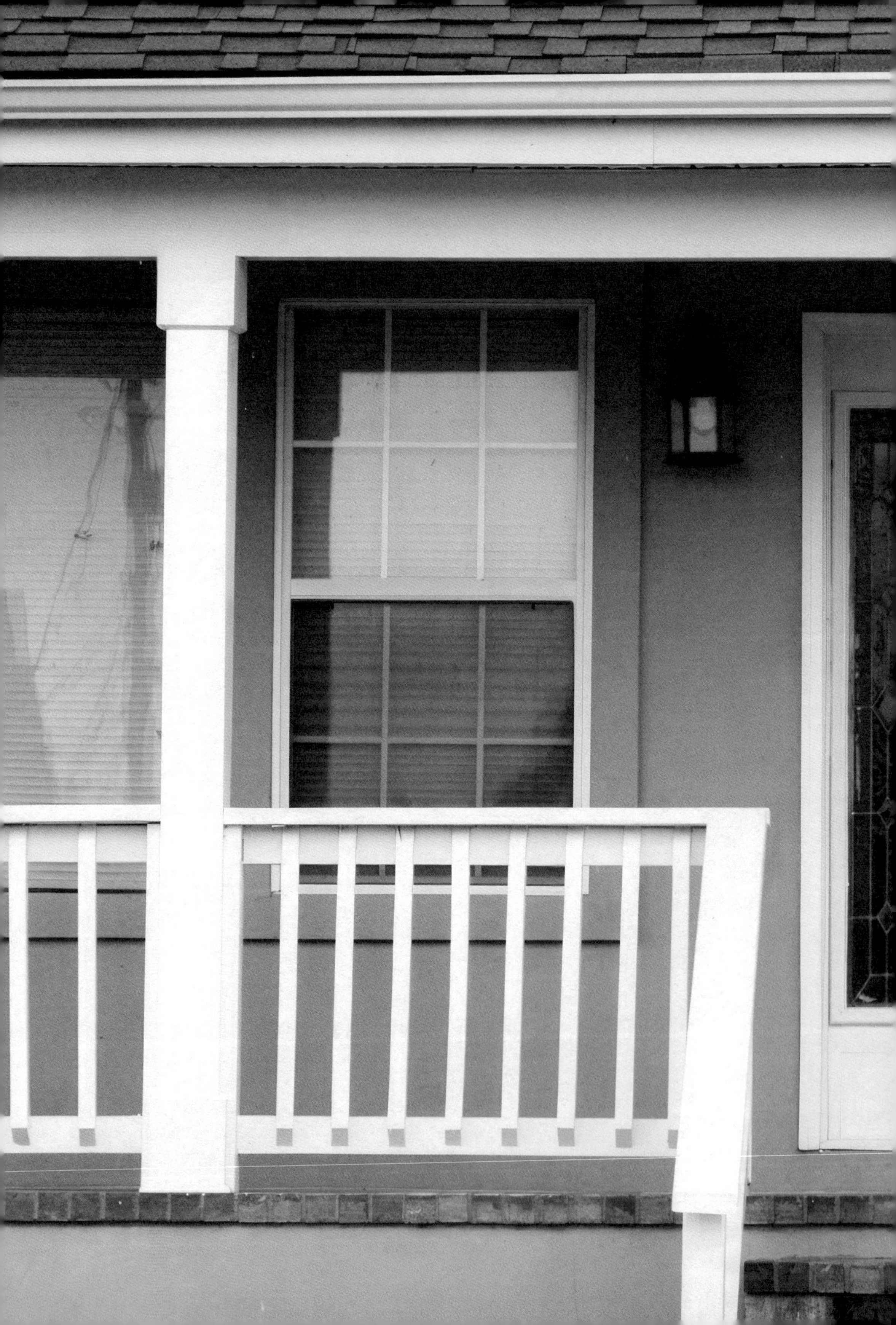

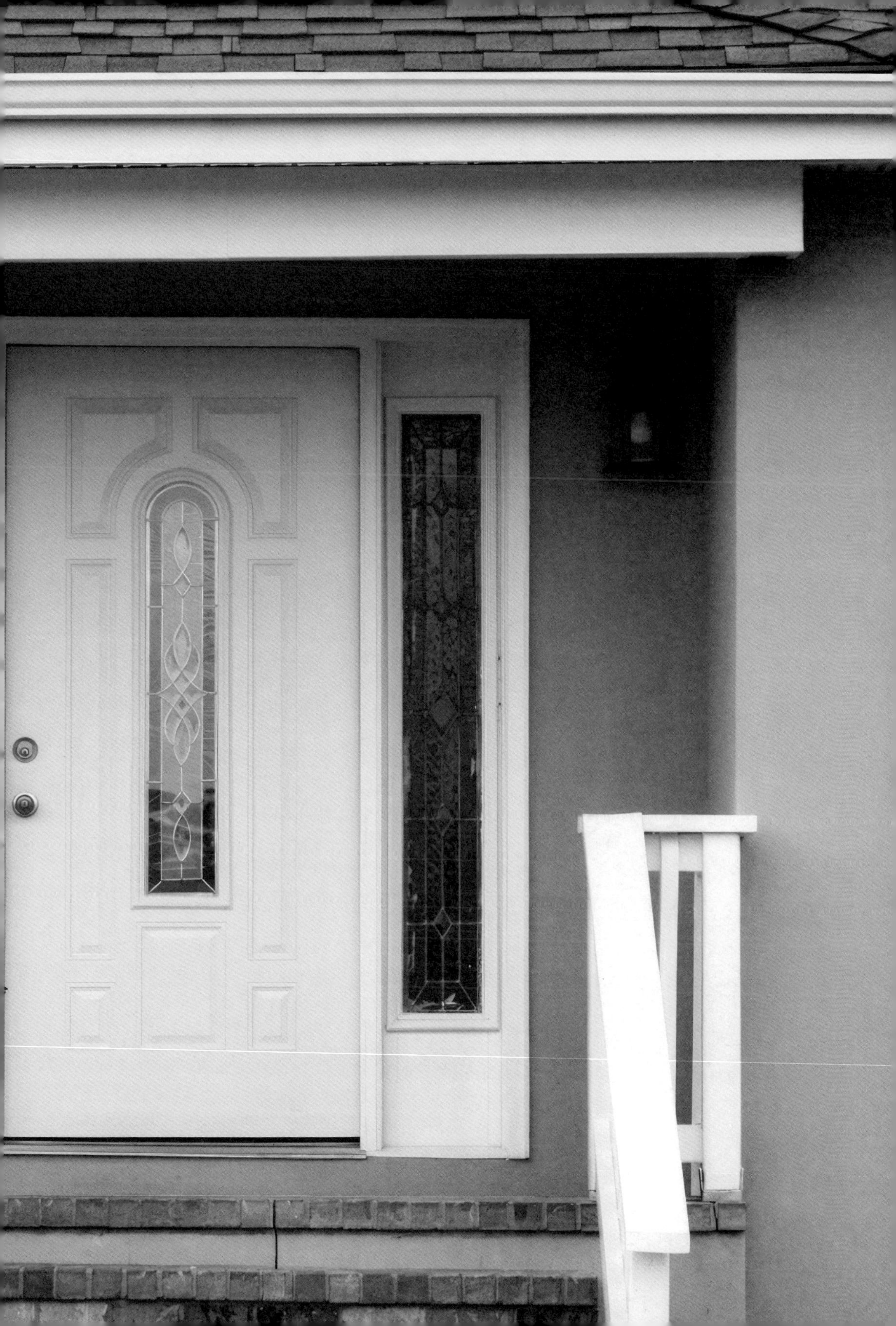

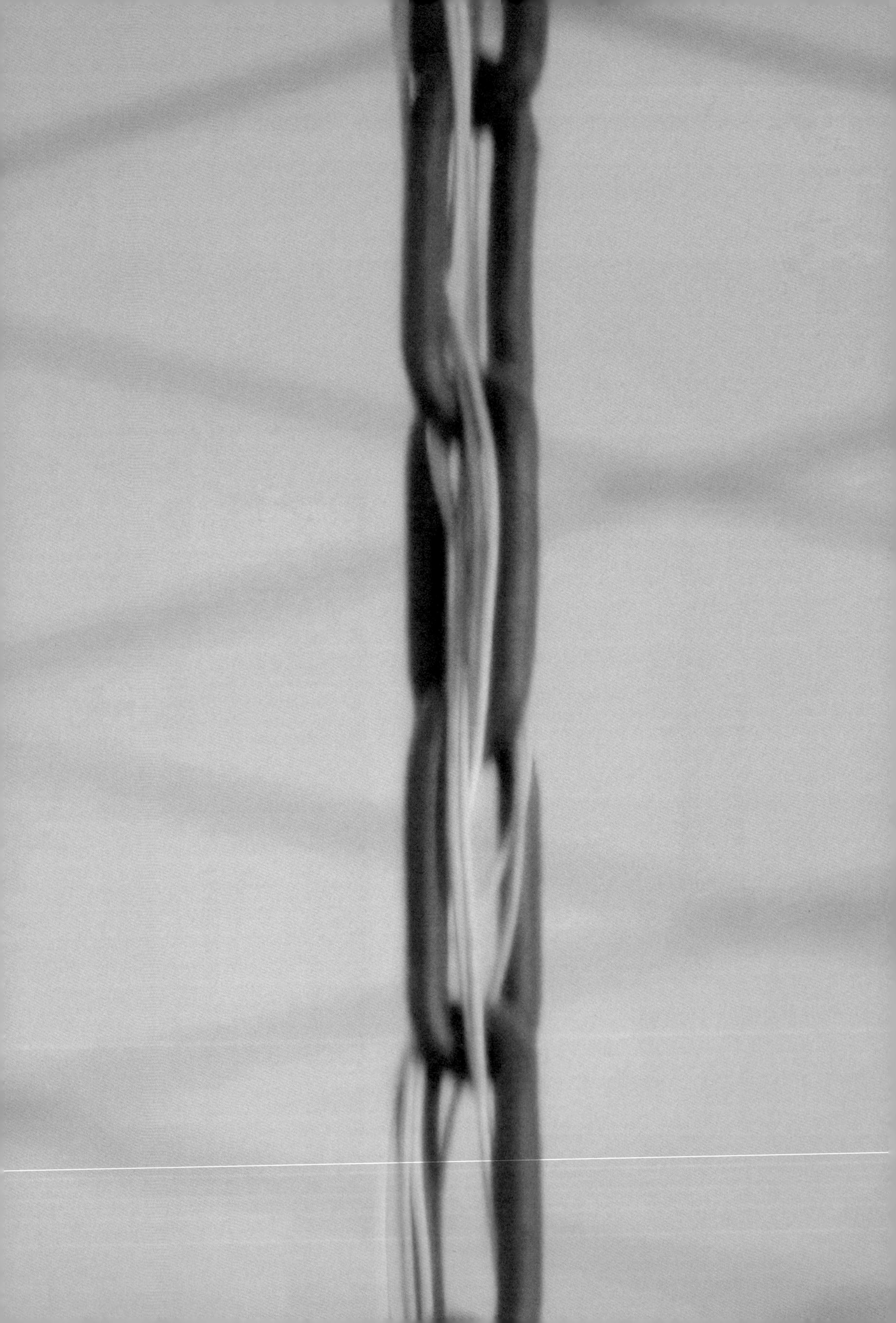

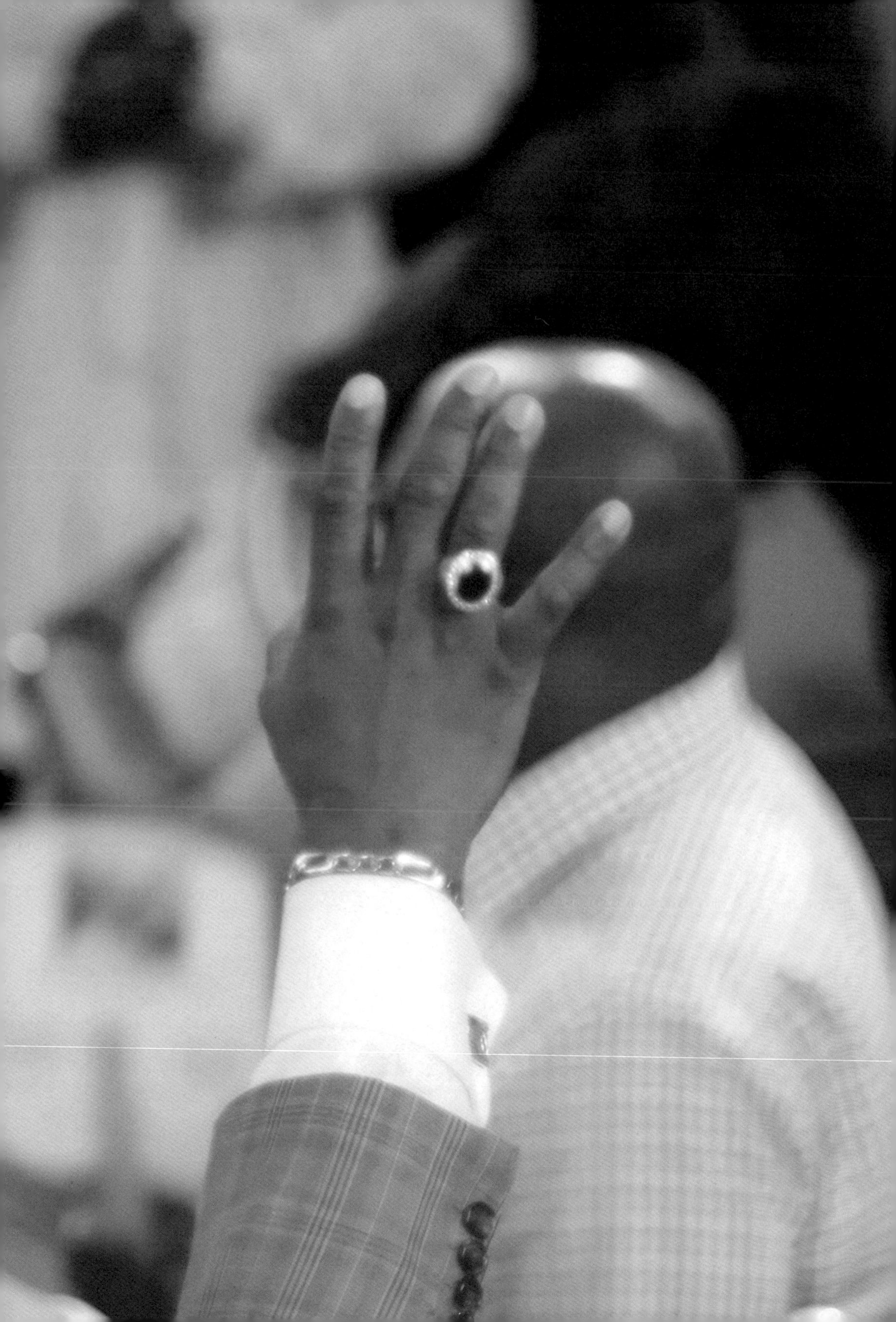

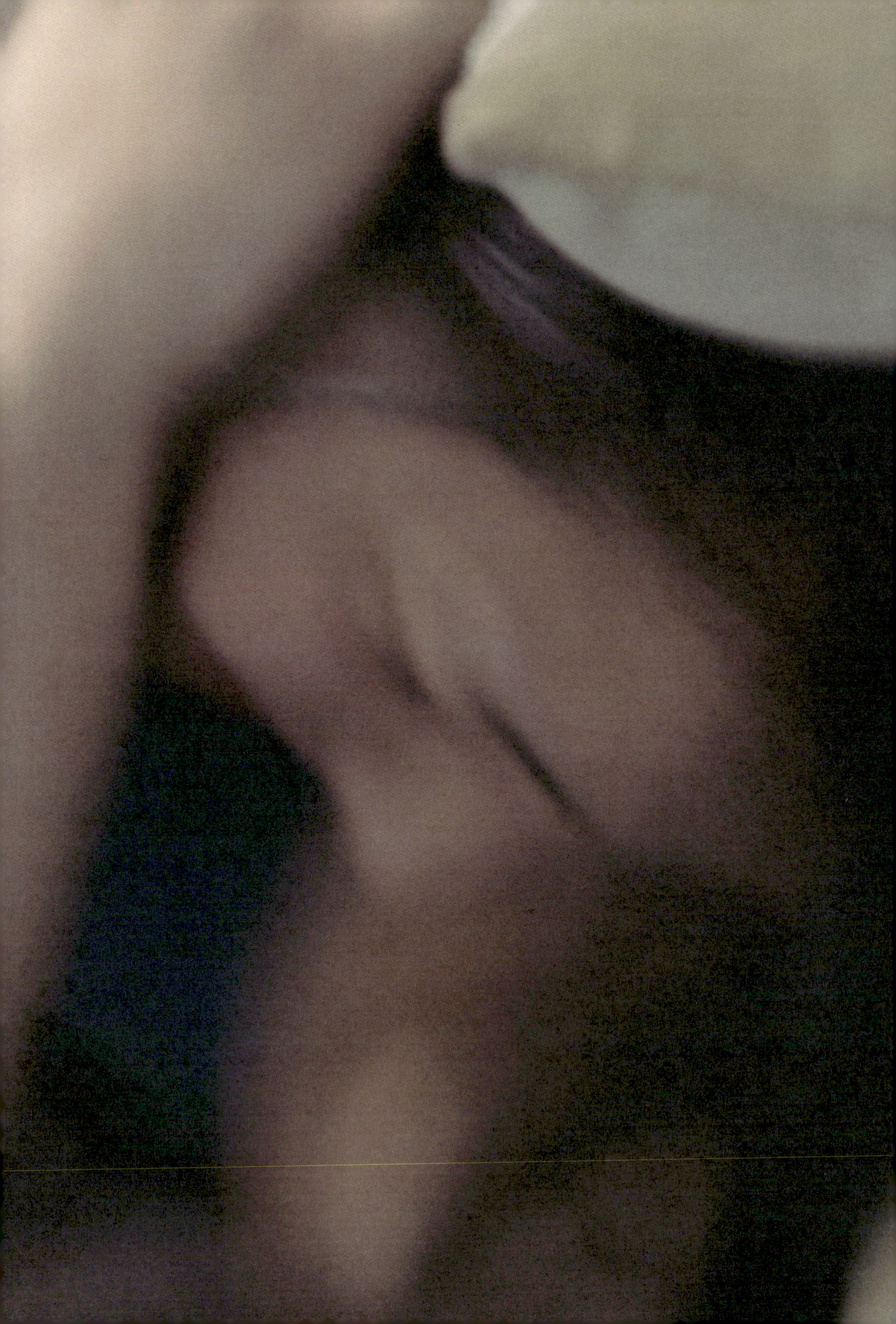

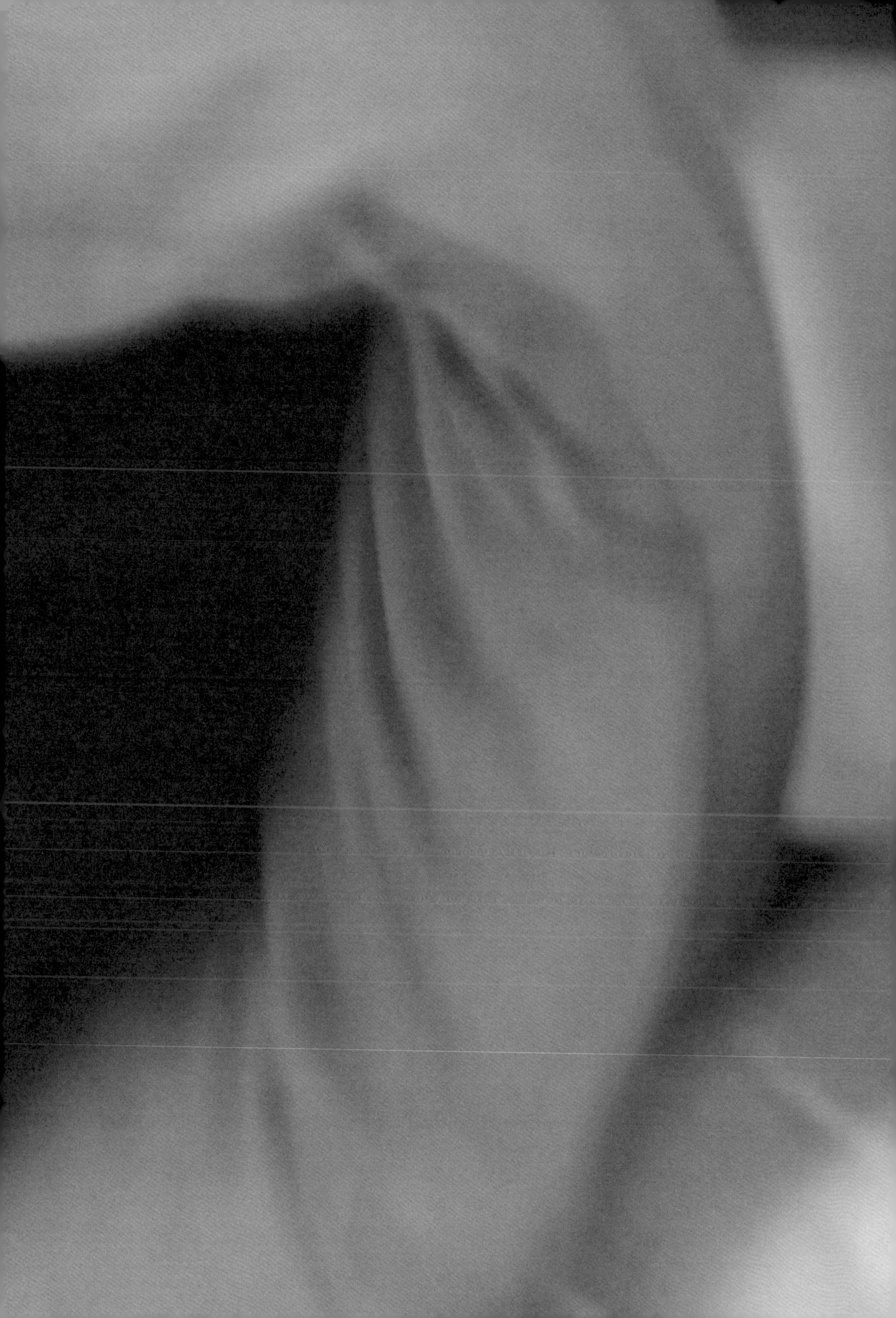

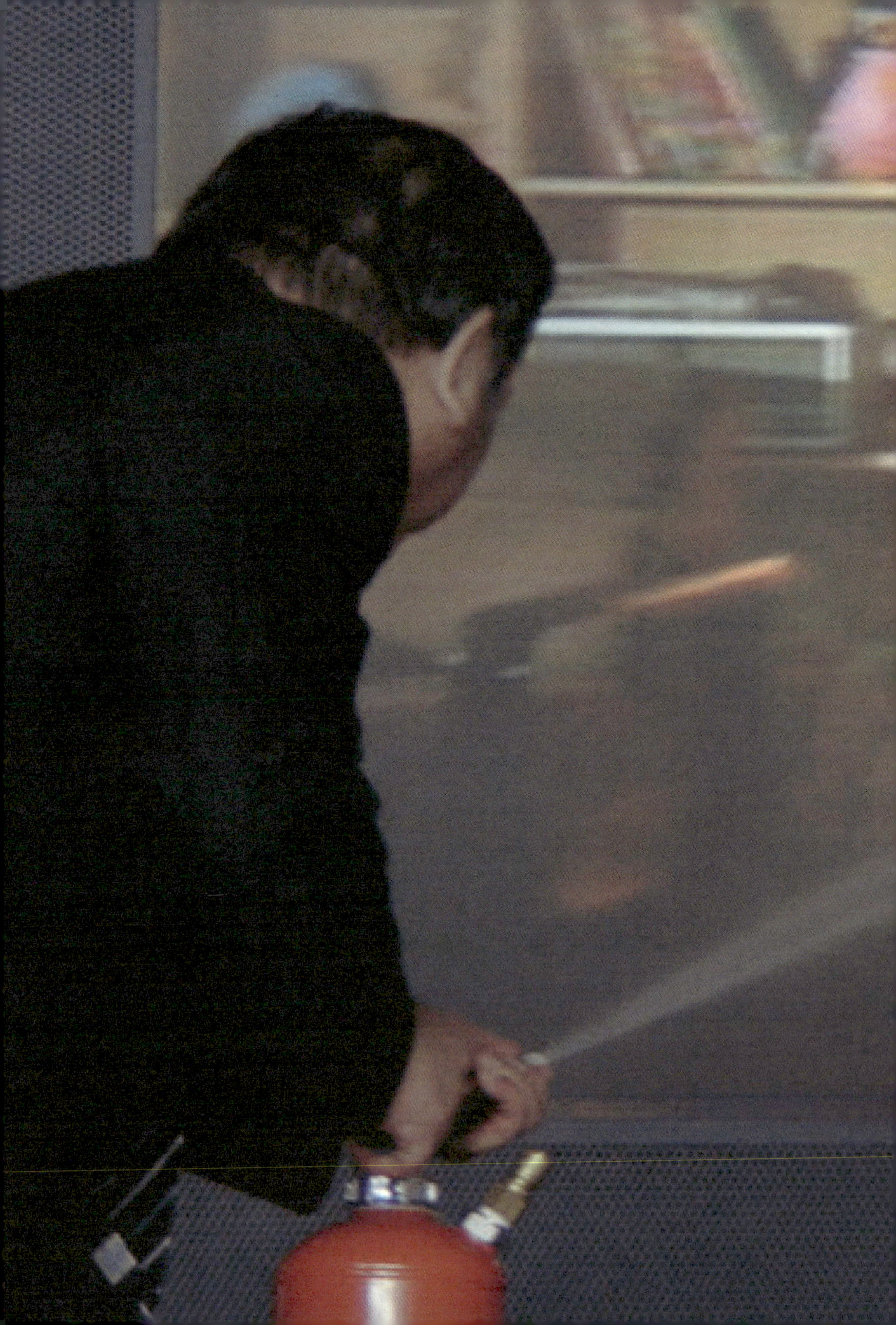

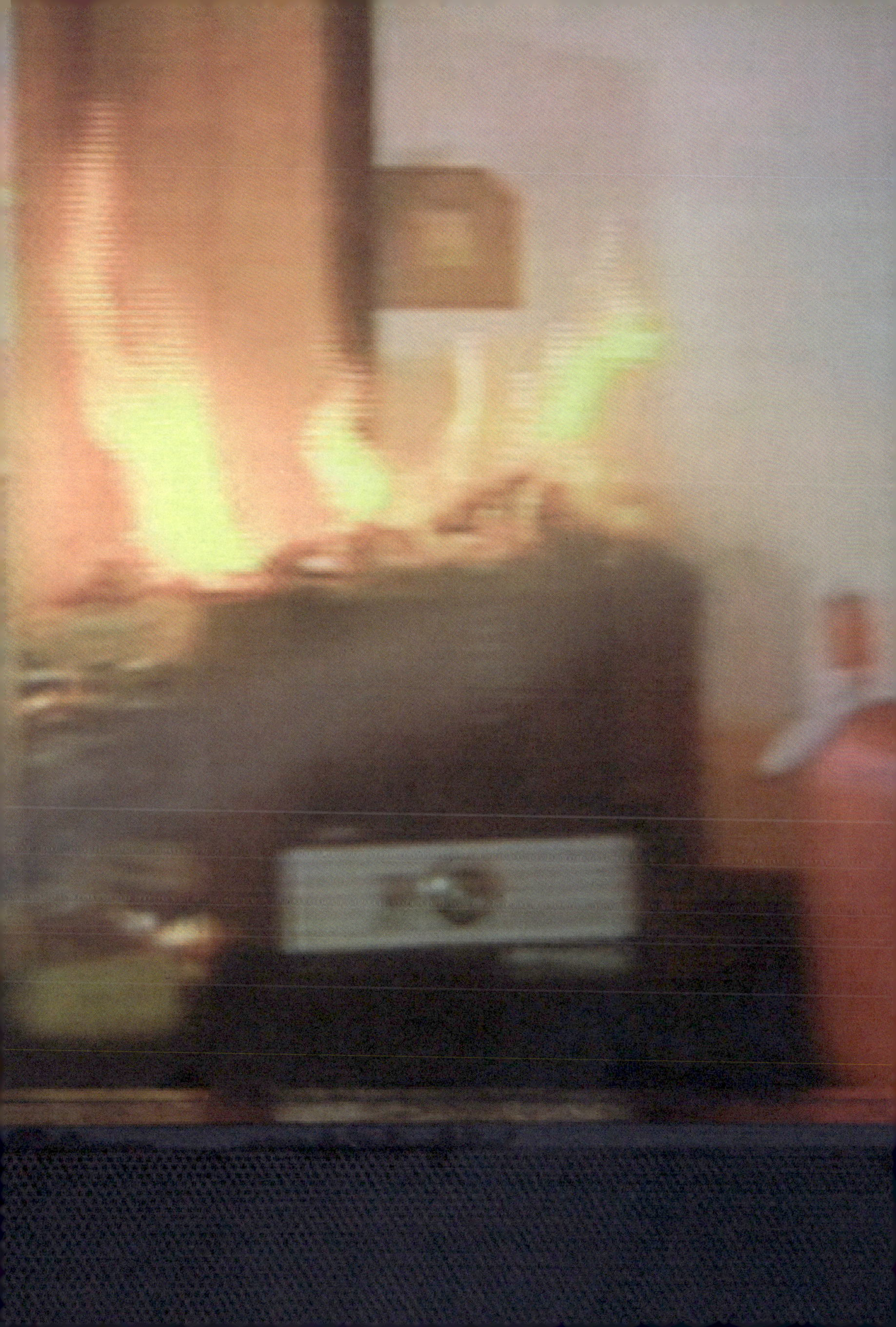

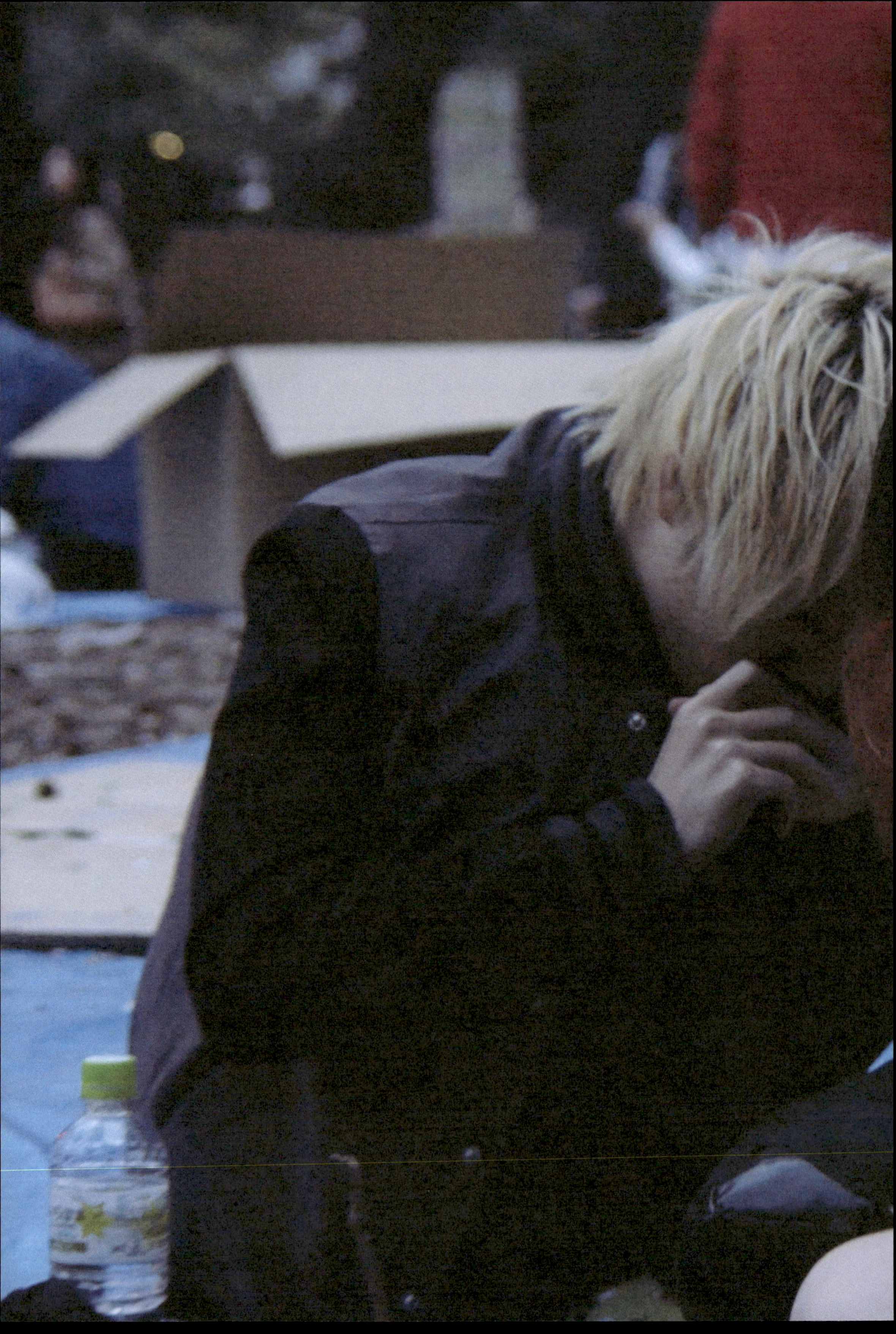

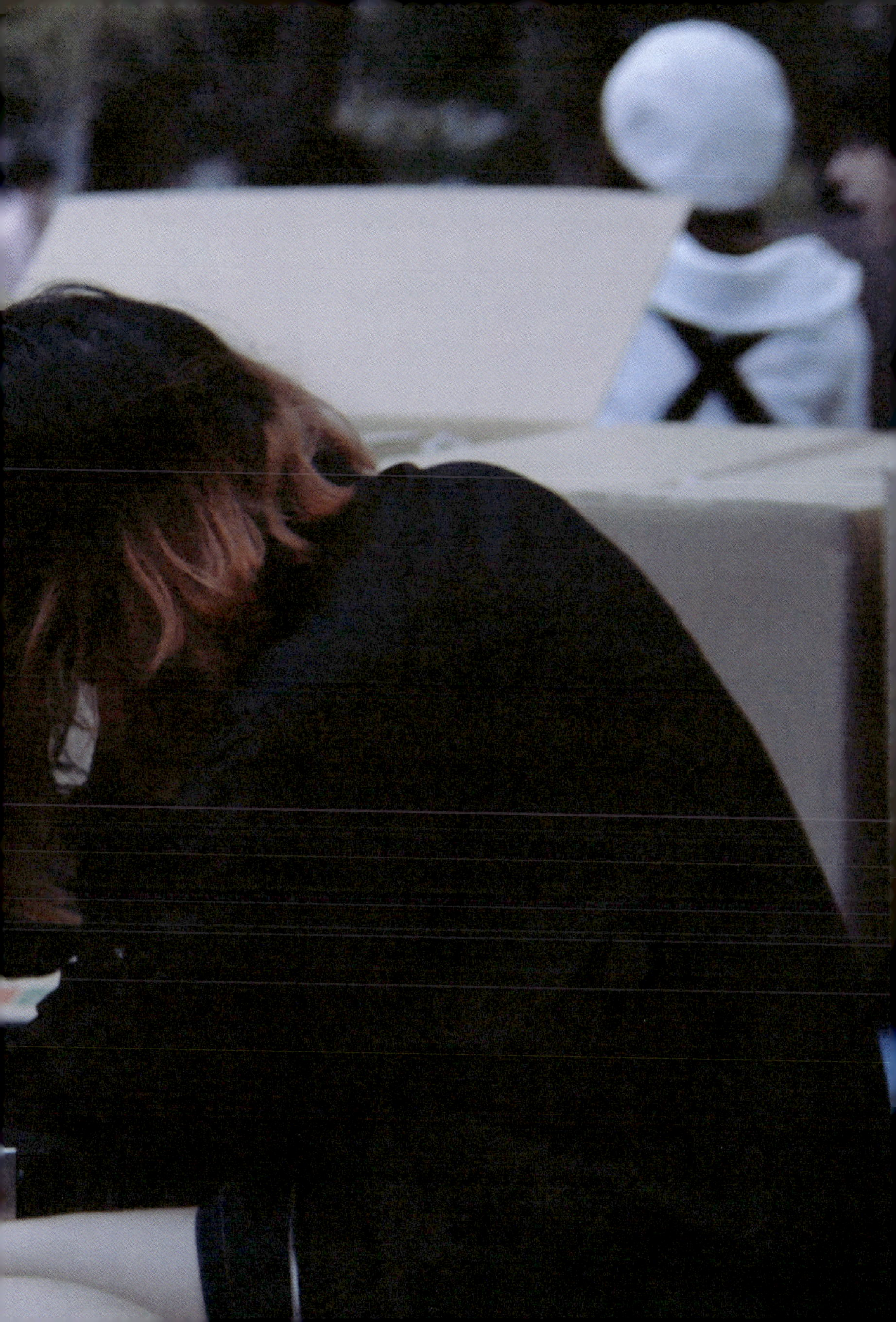

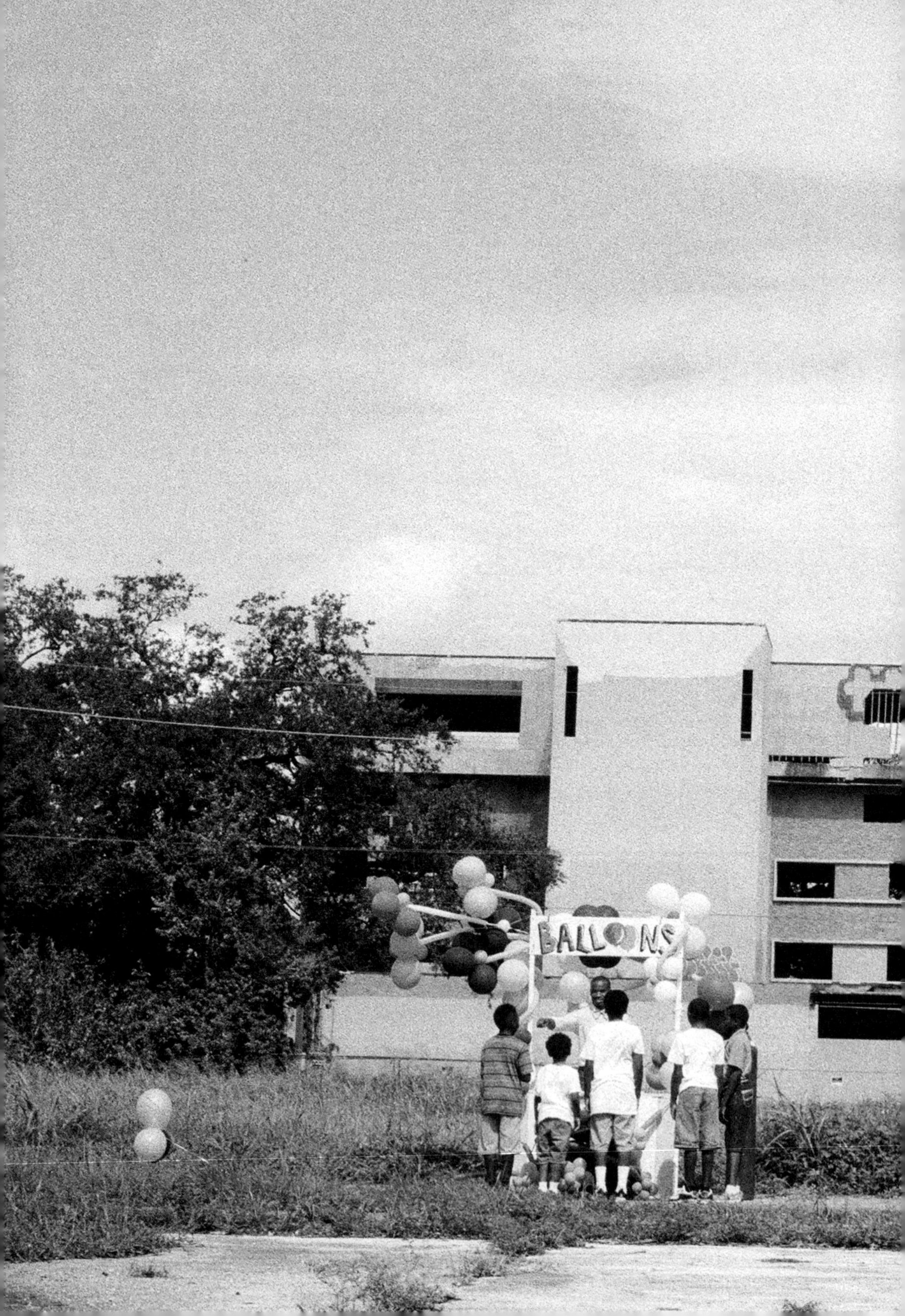
BALLOONS

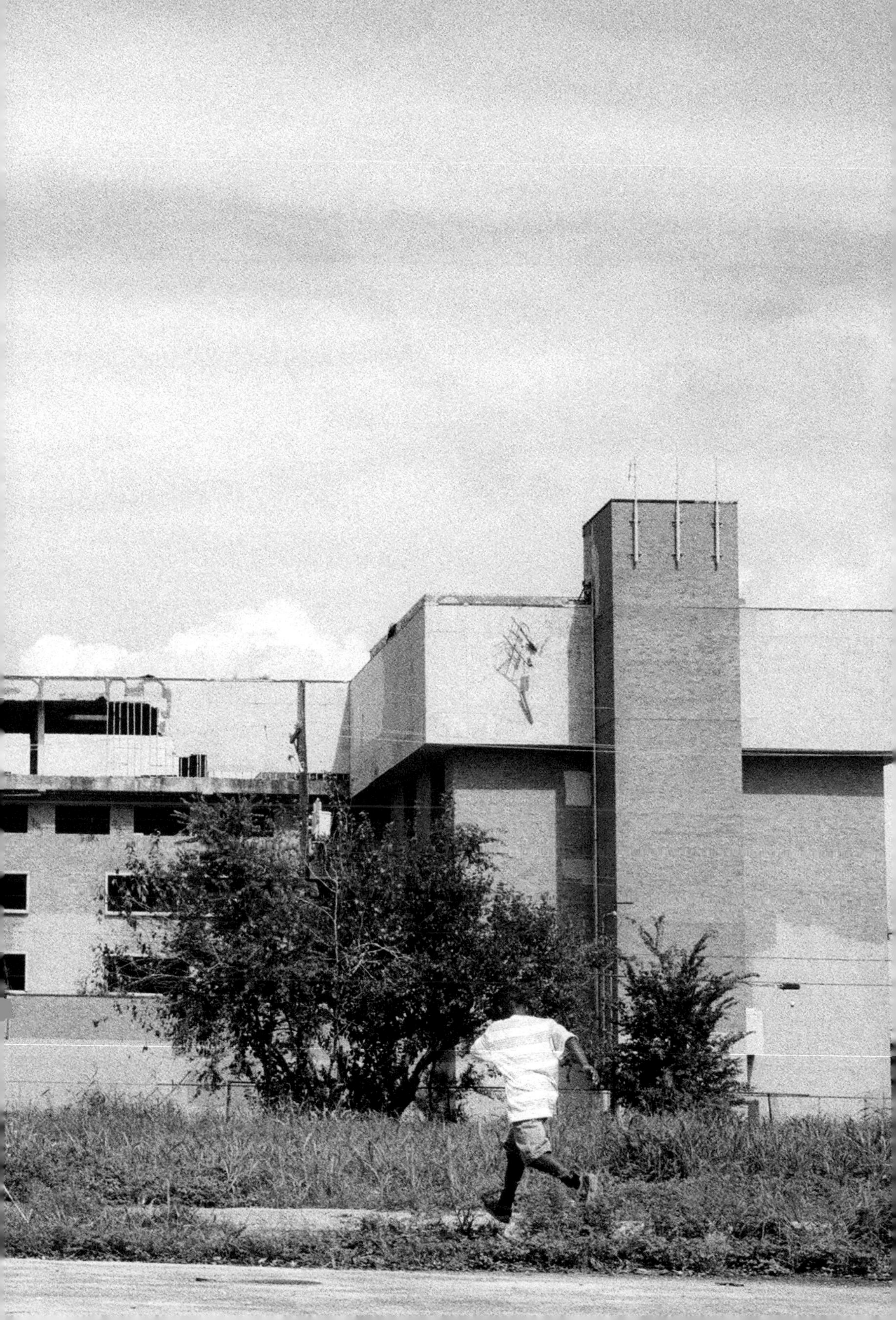

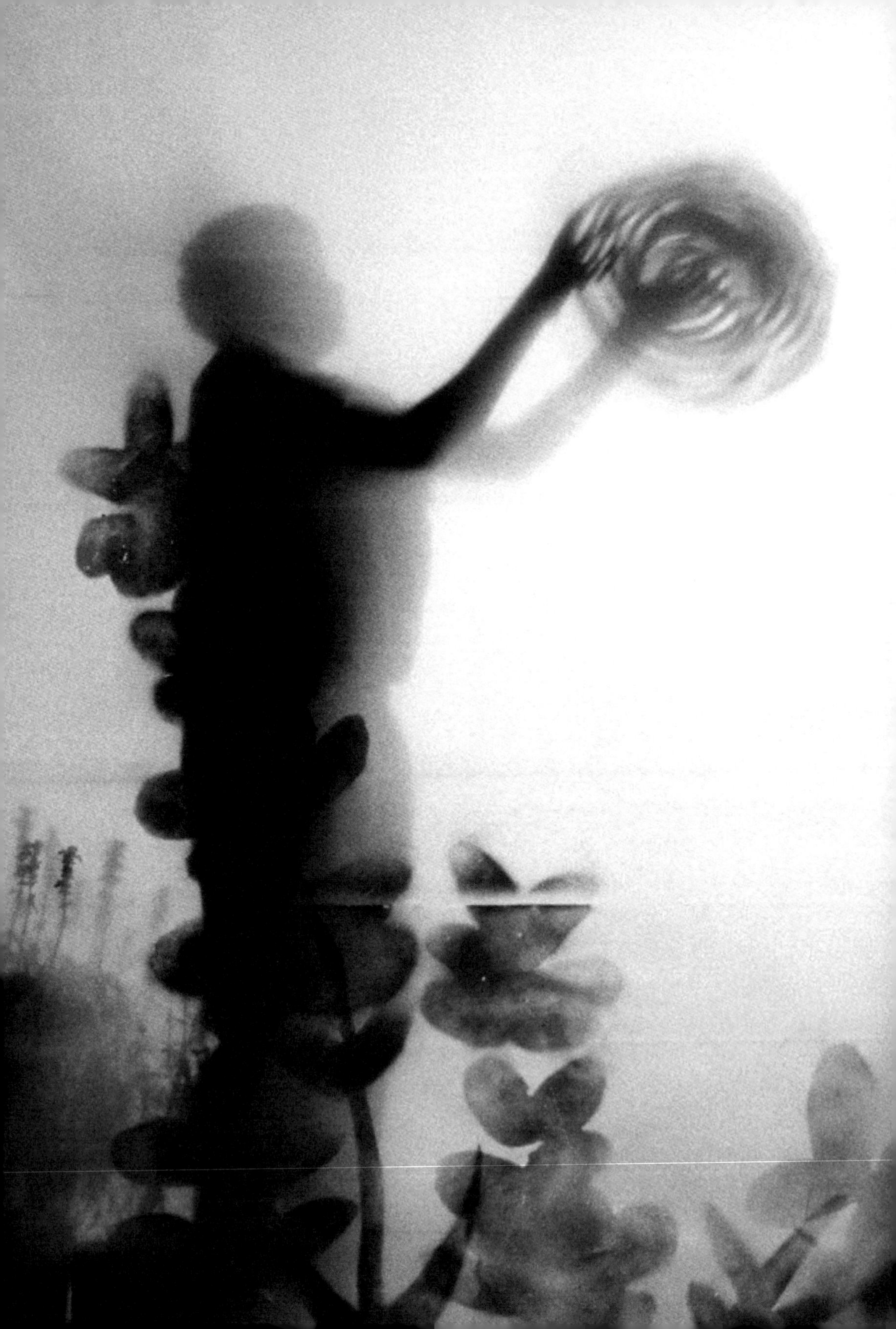

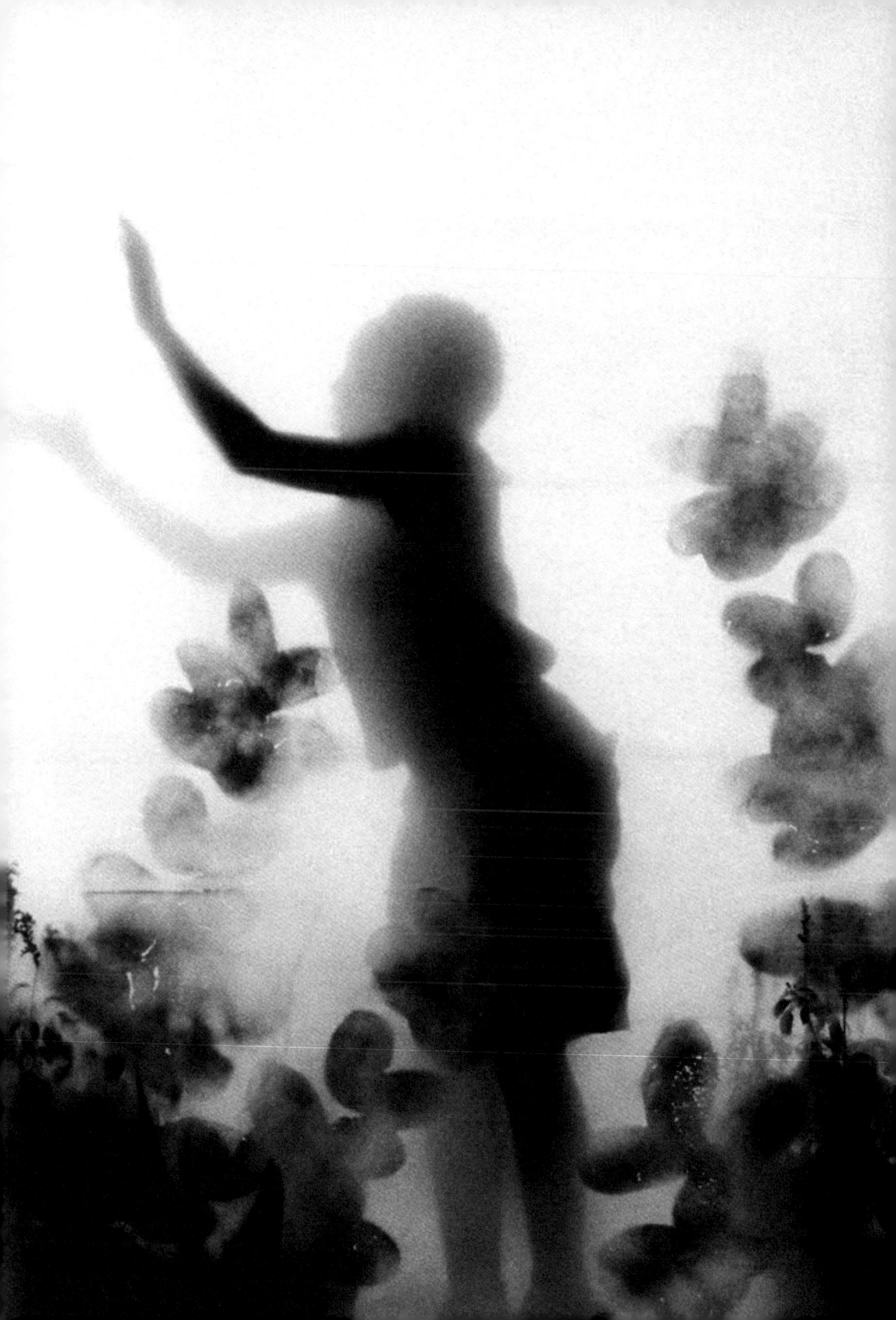

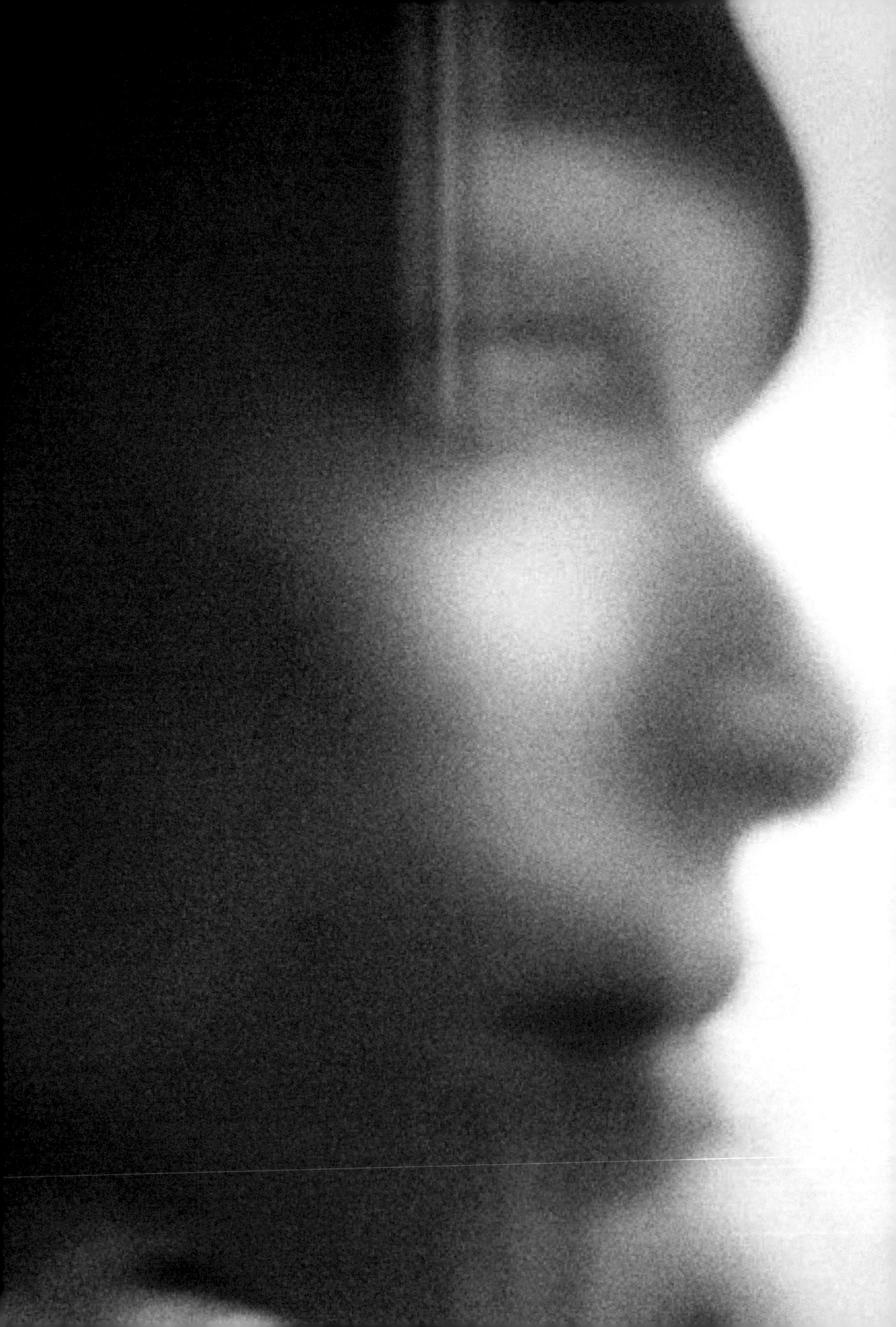

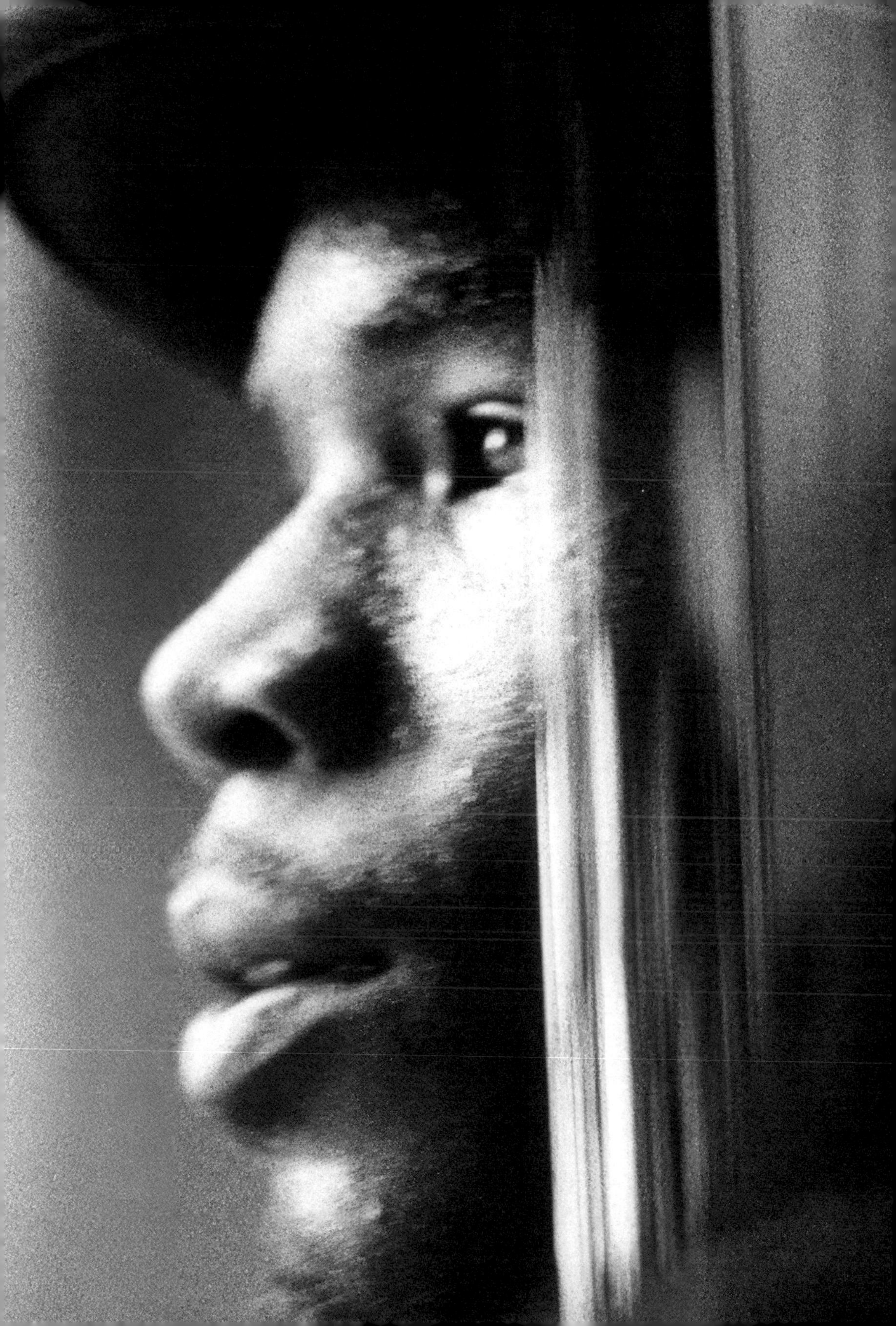

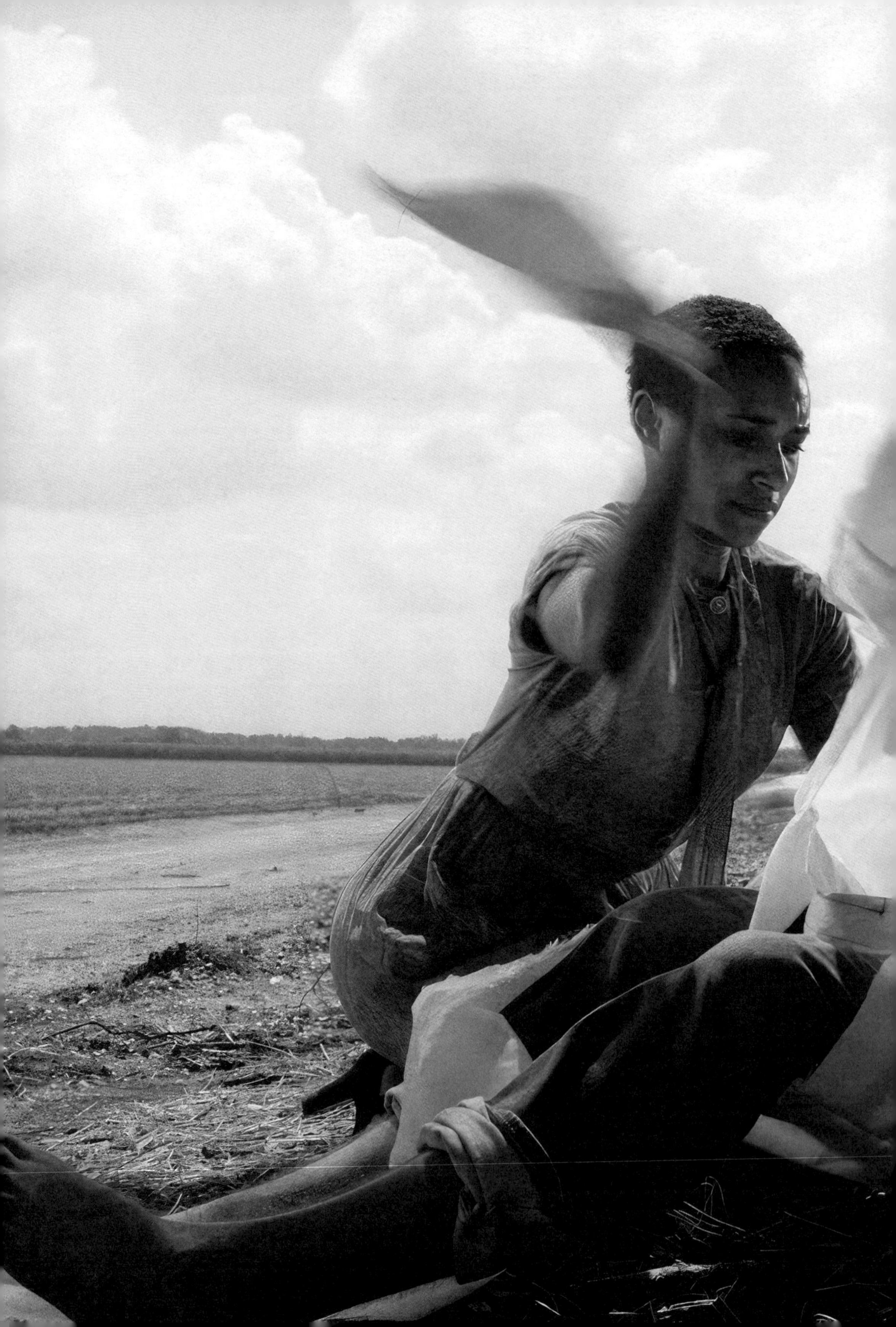

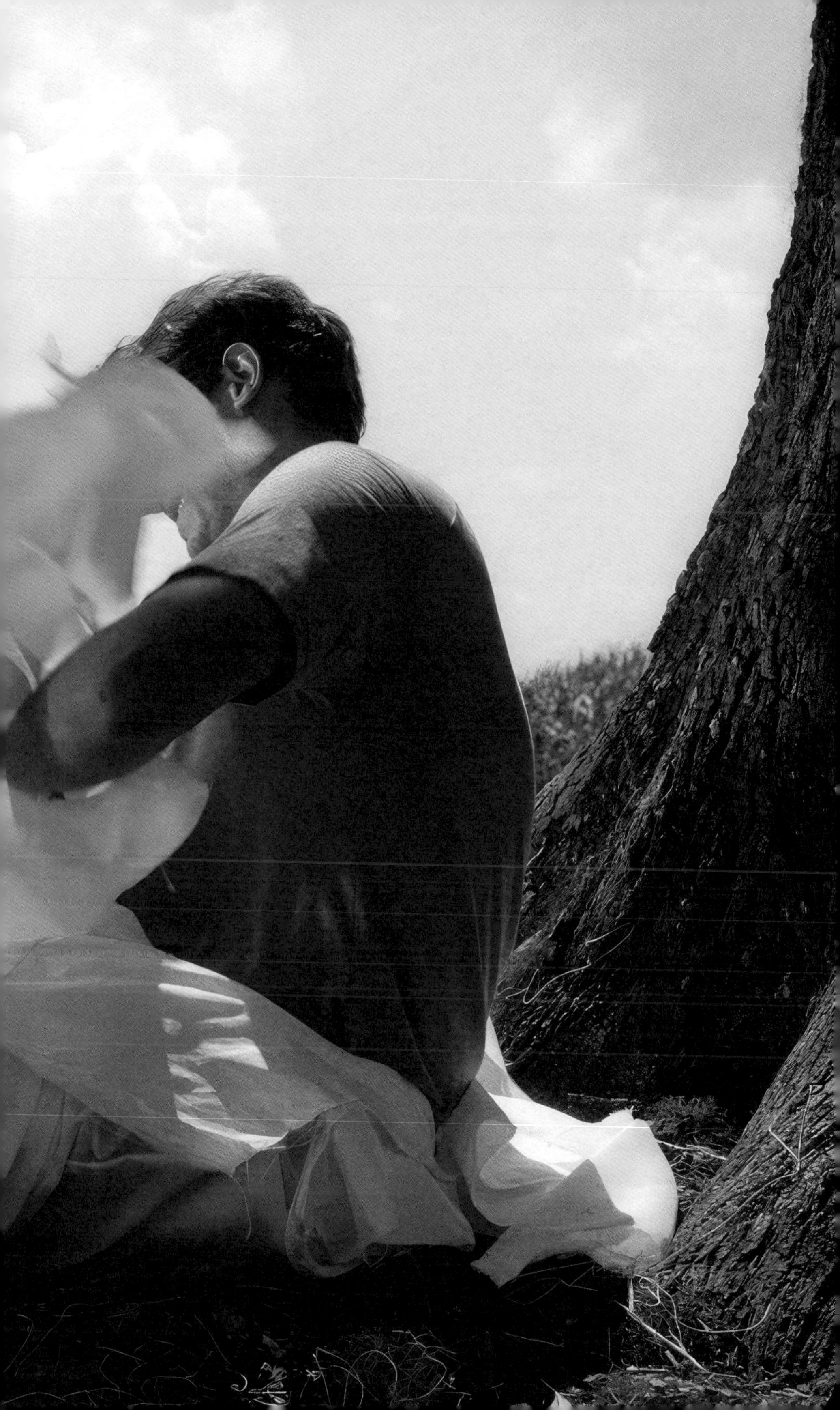

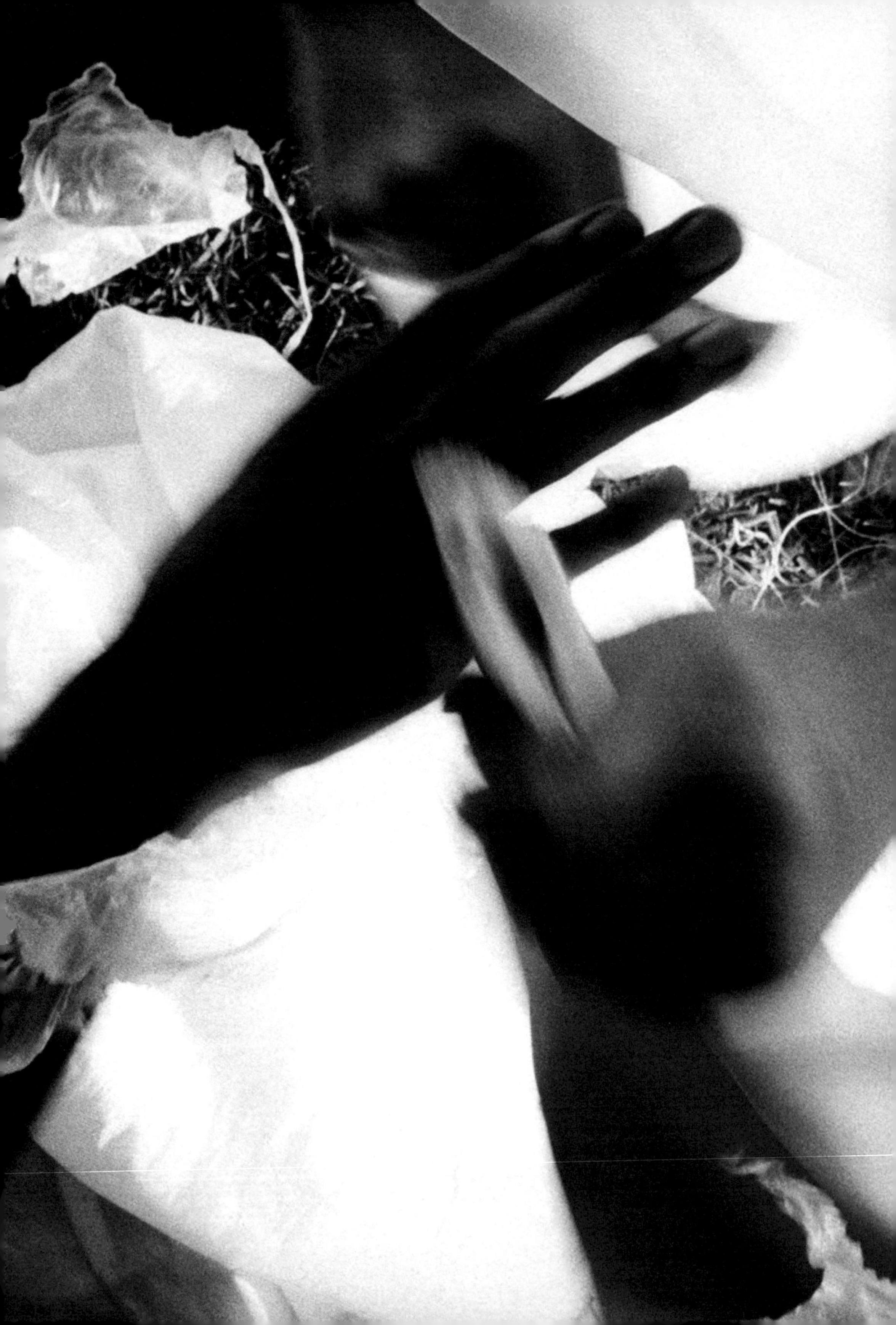

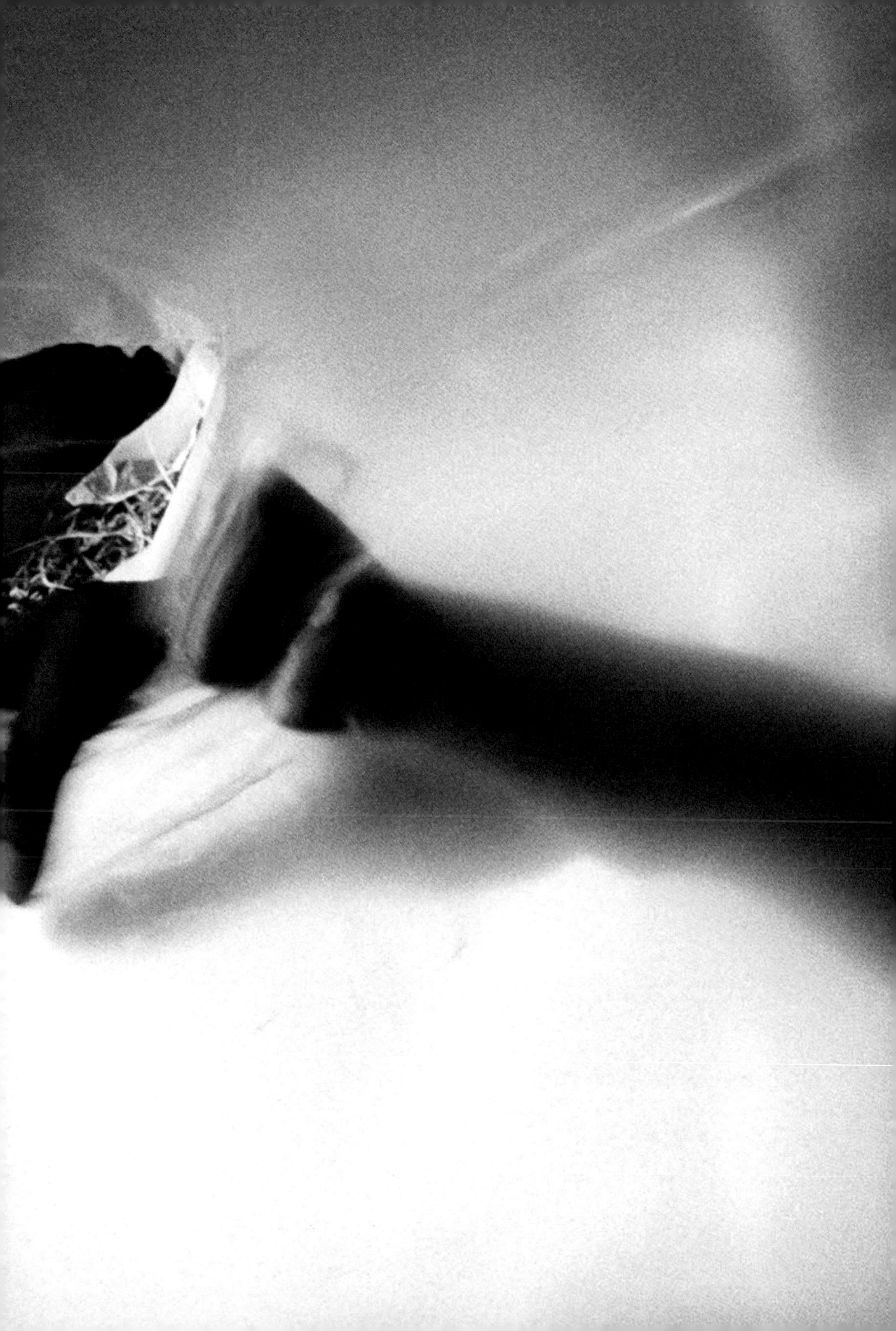

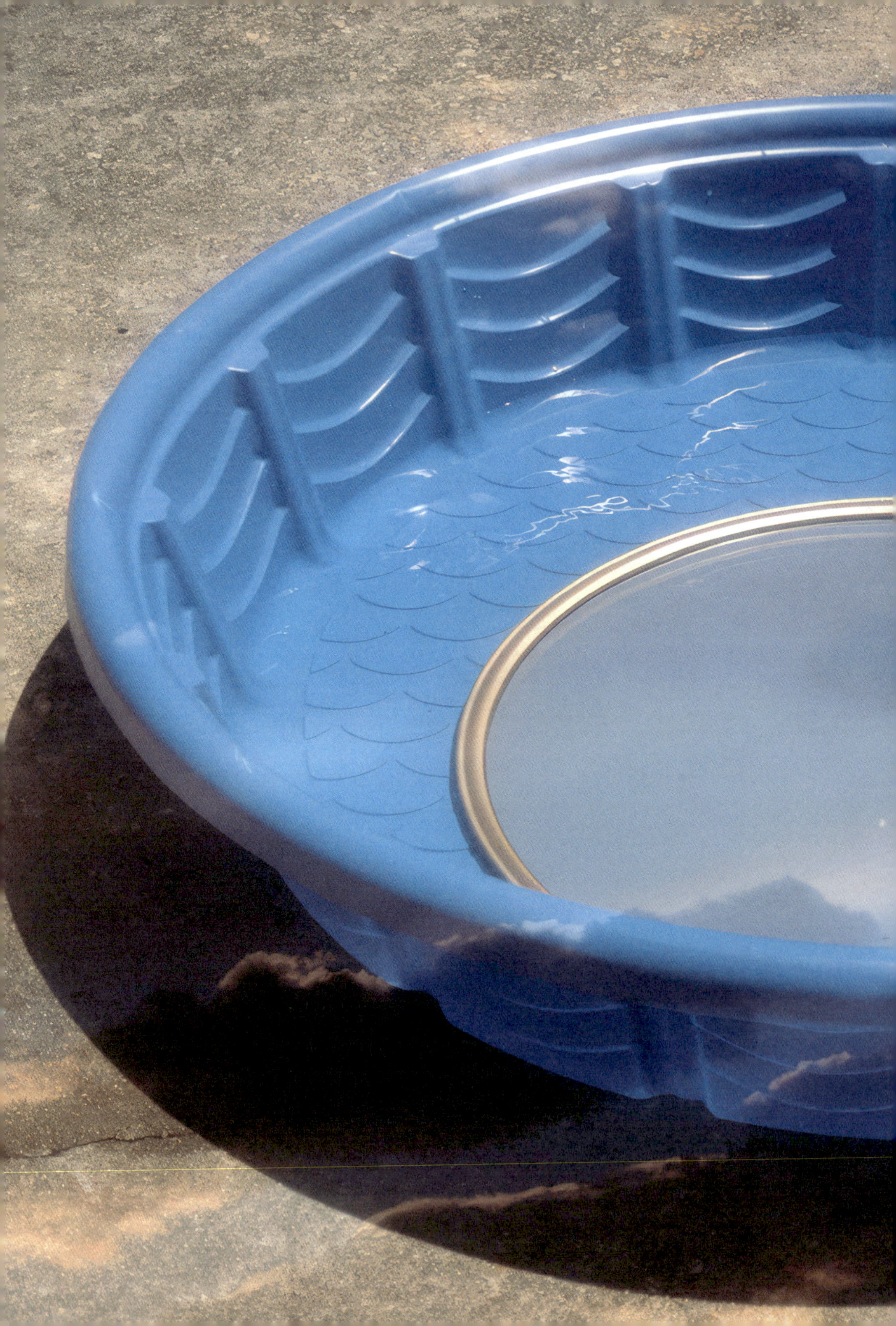

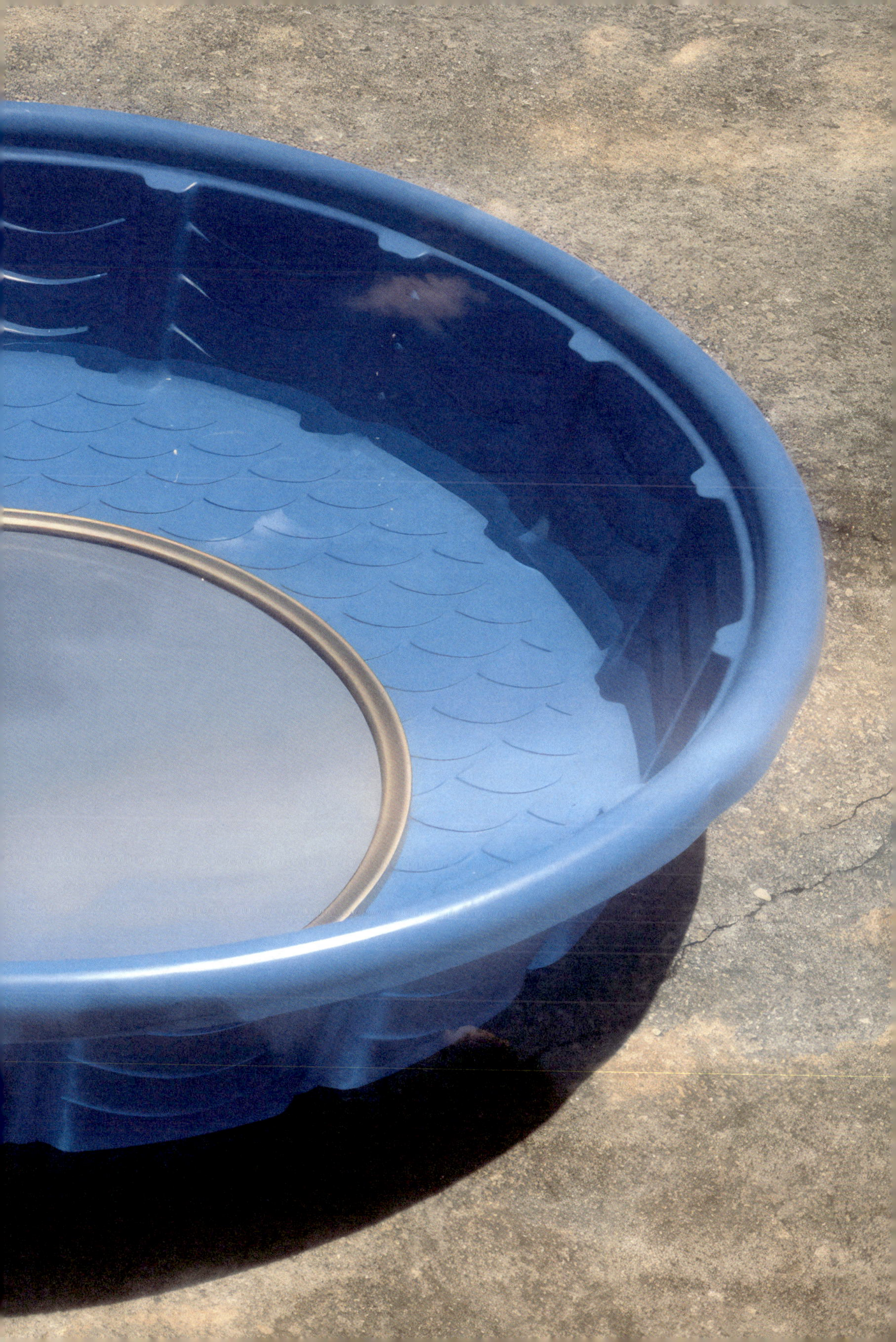

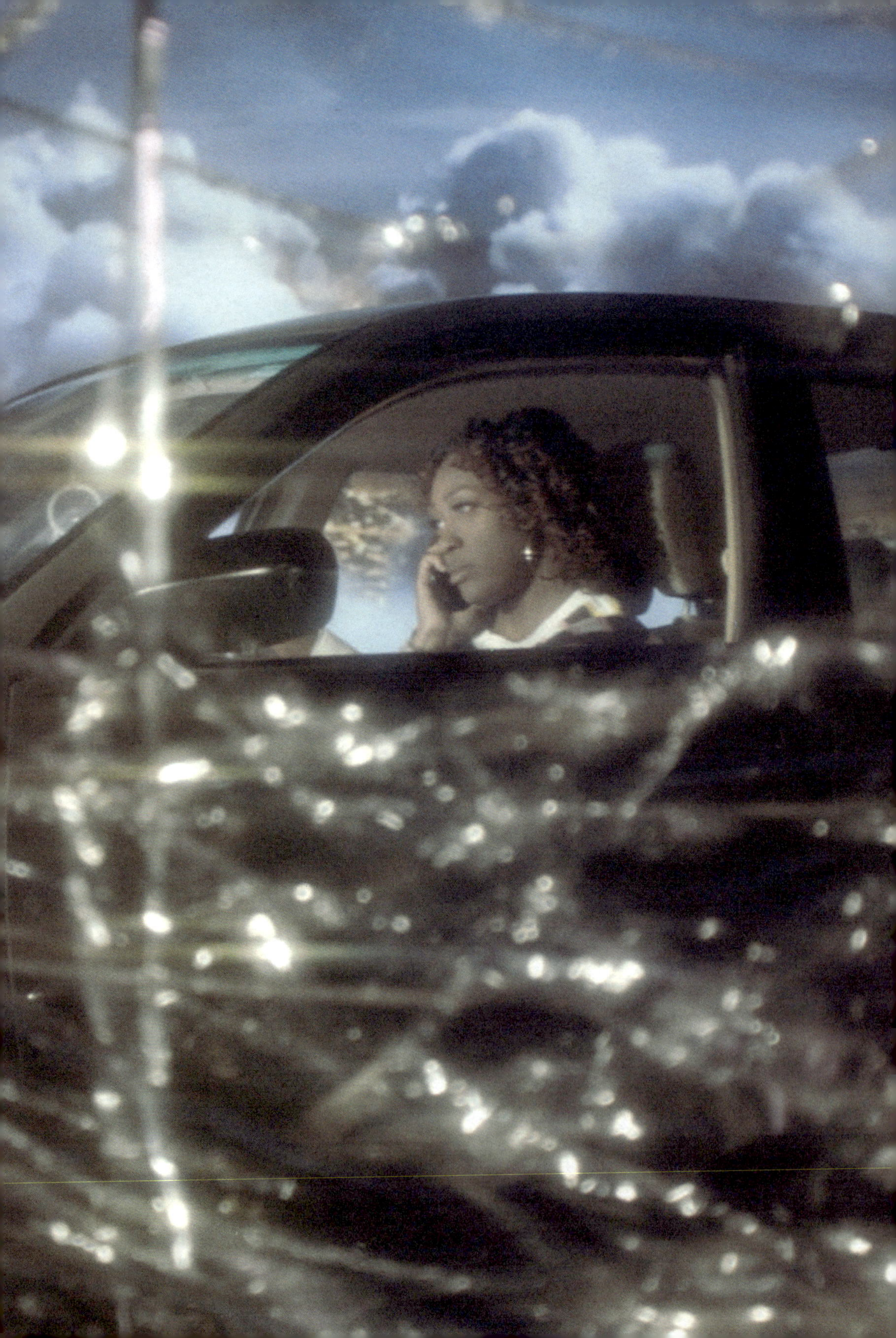

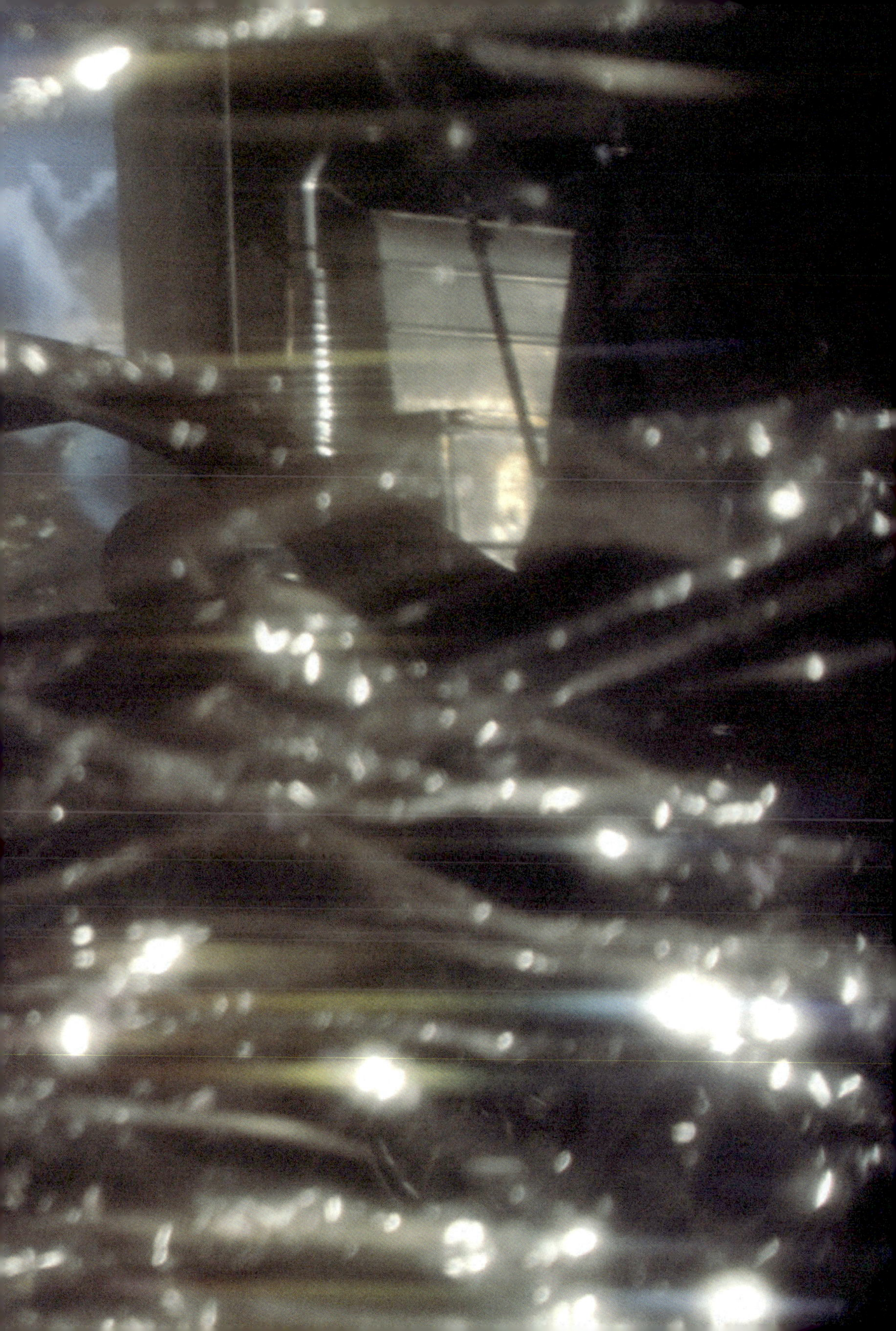

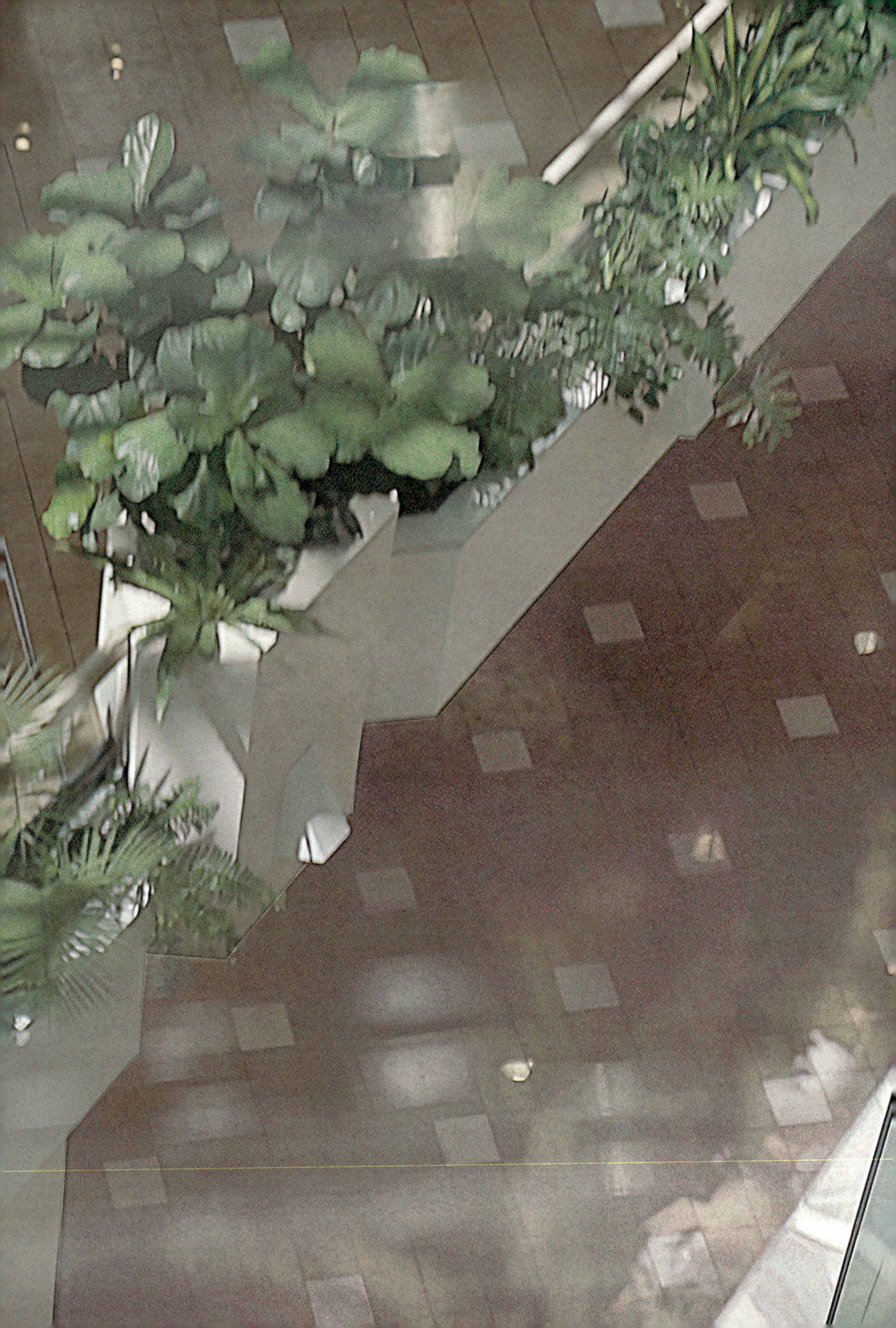

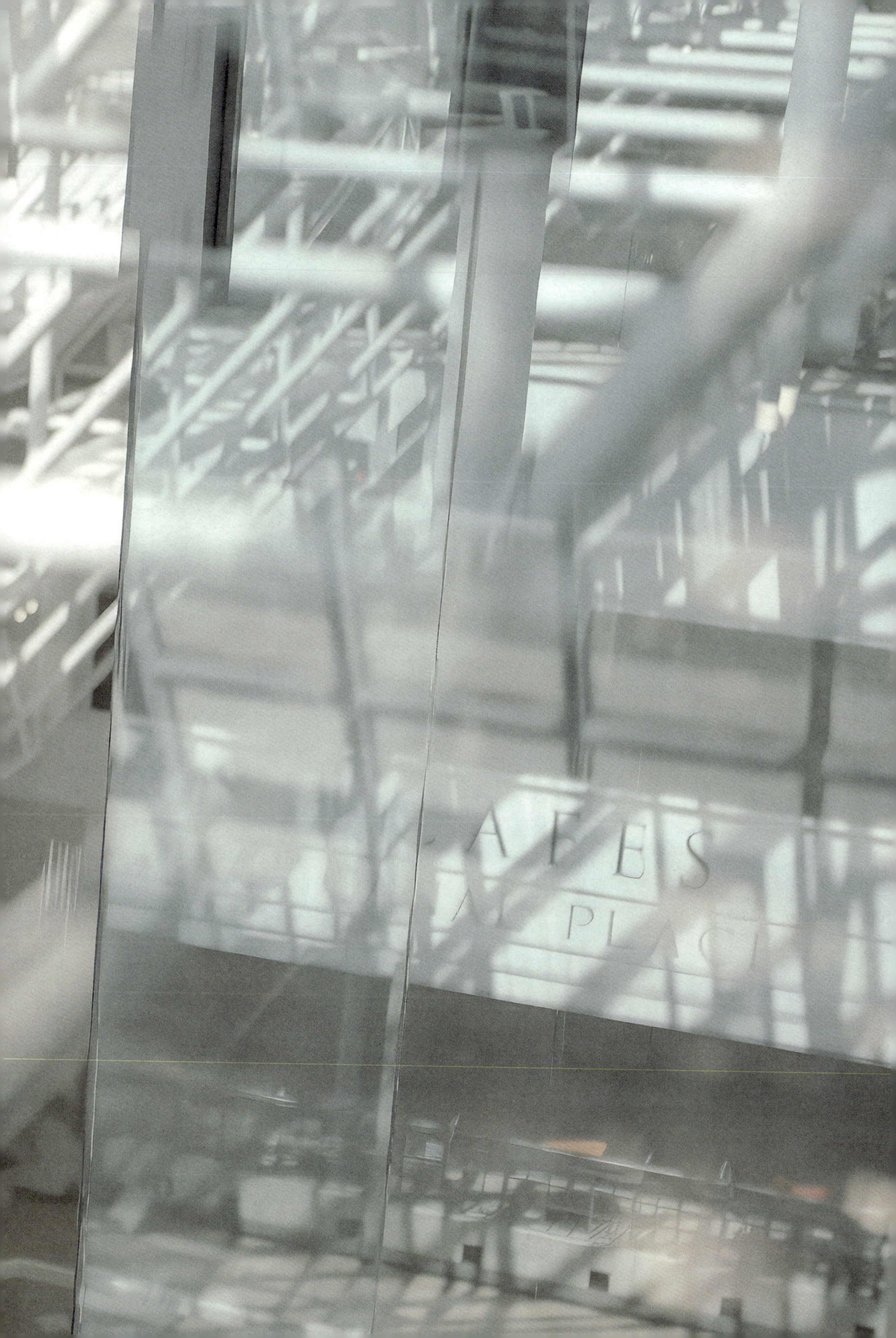

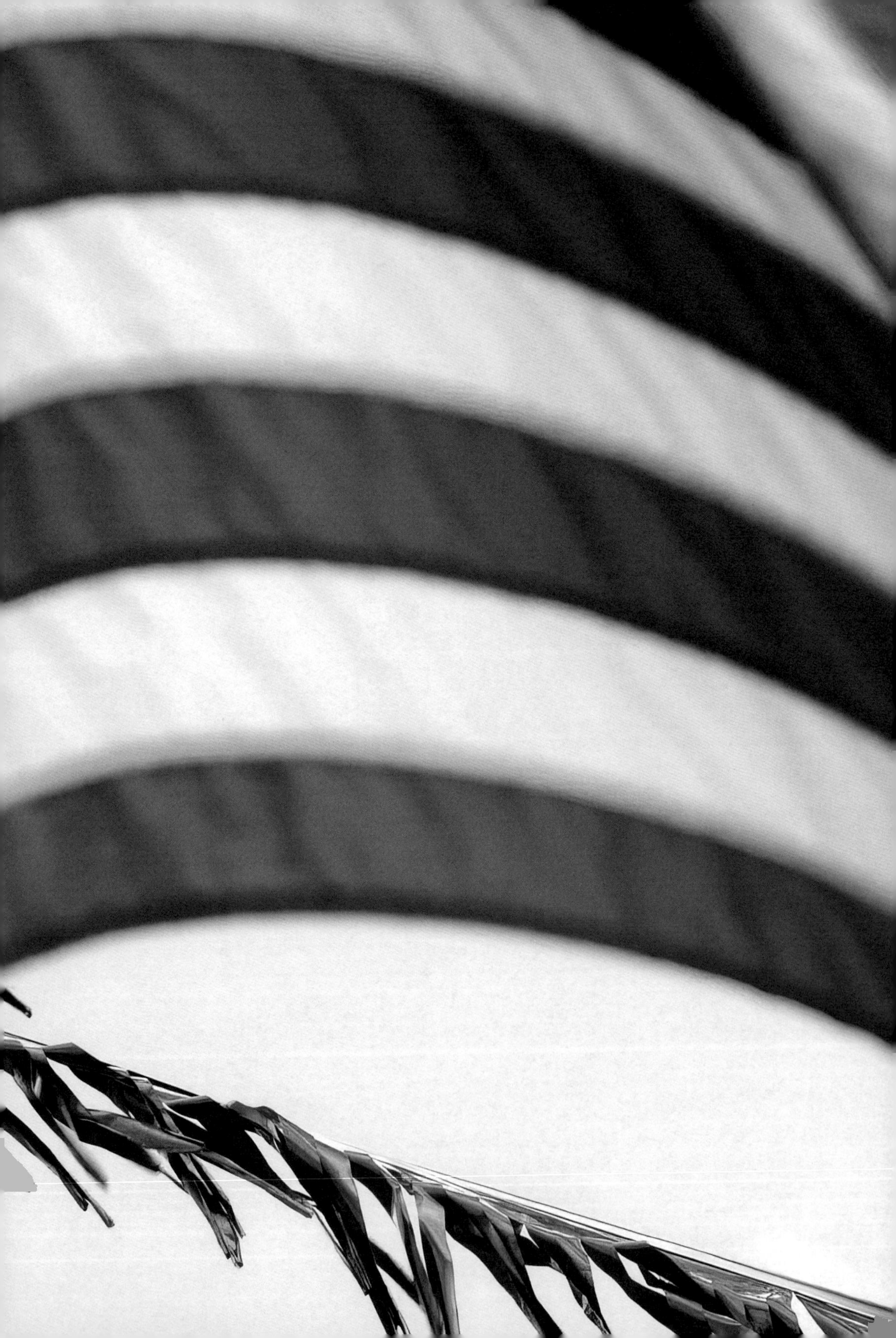

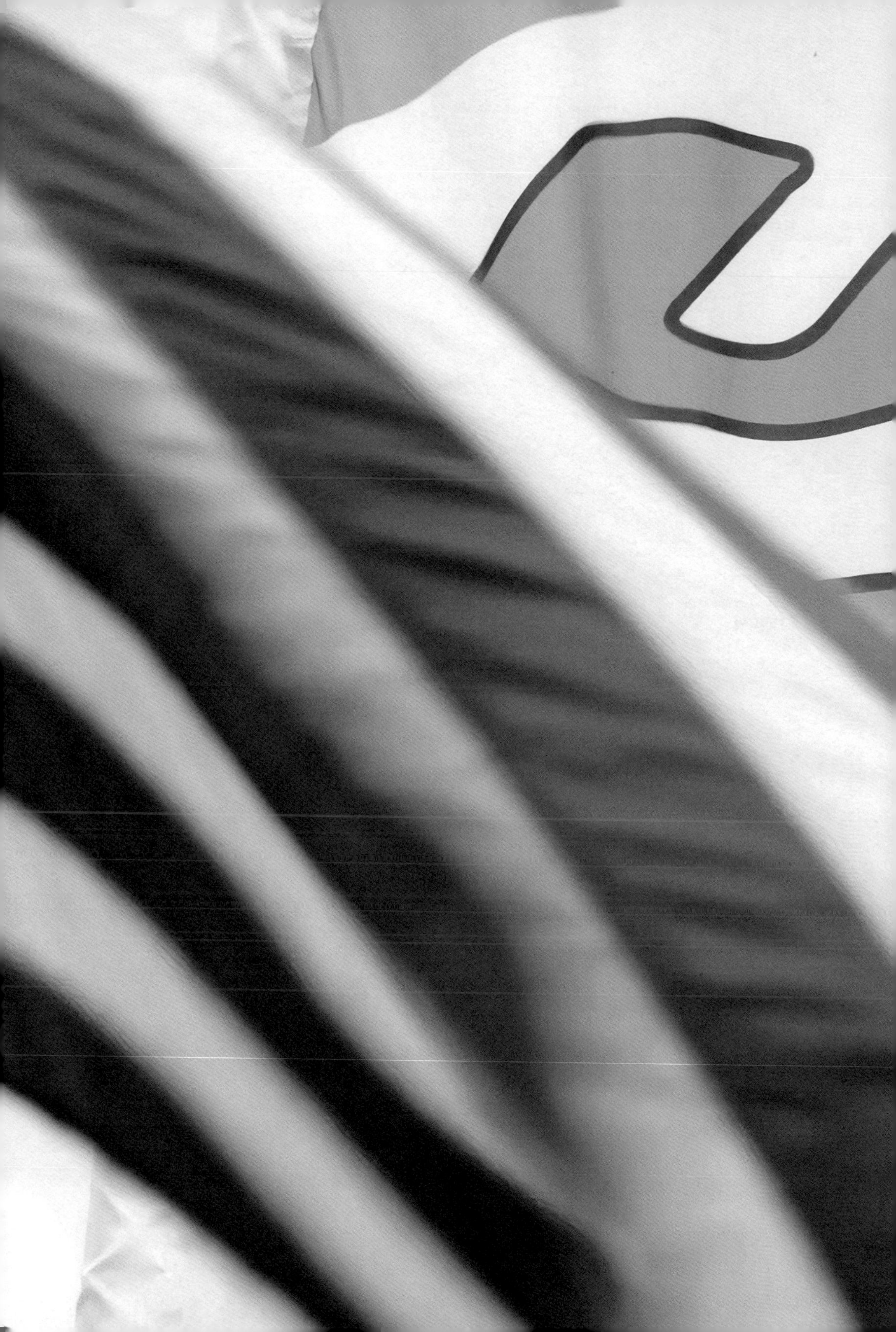

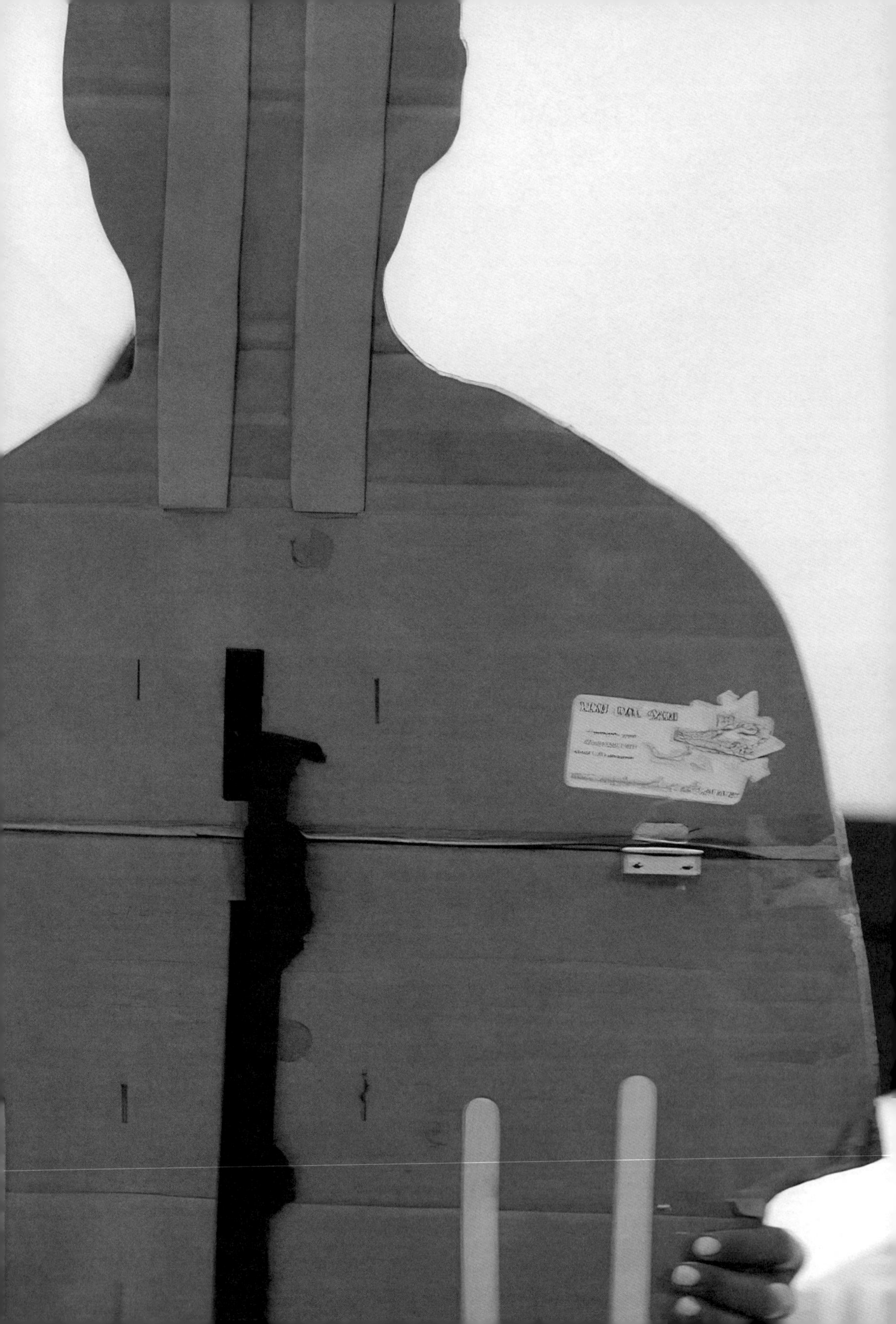

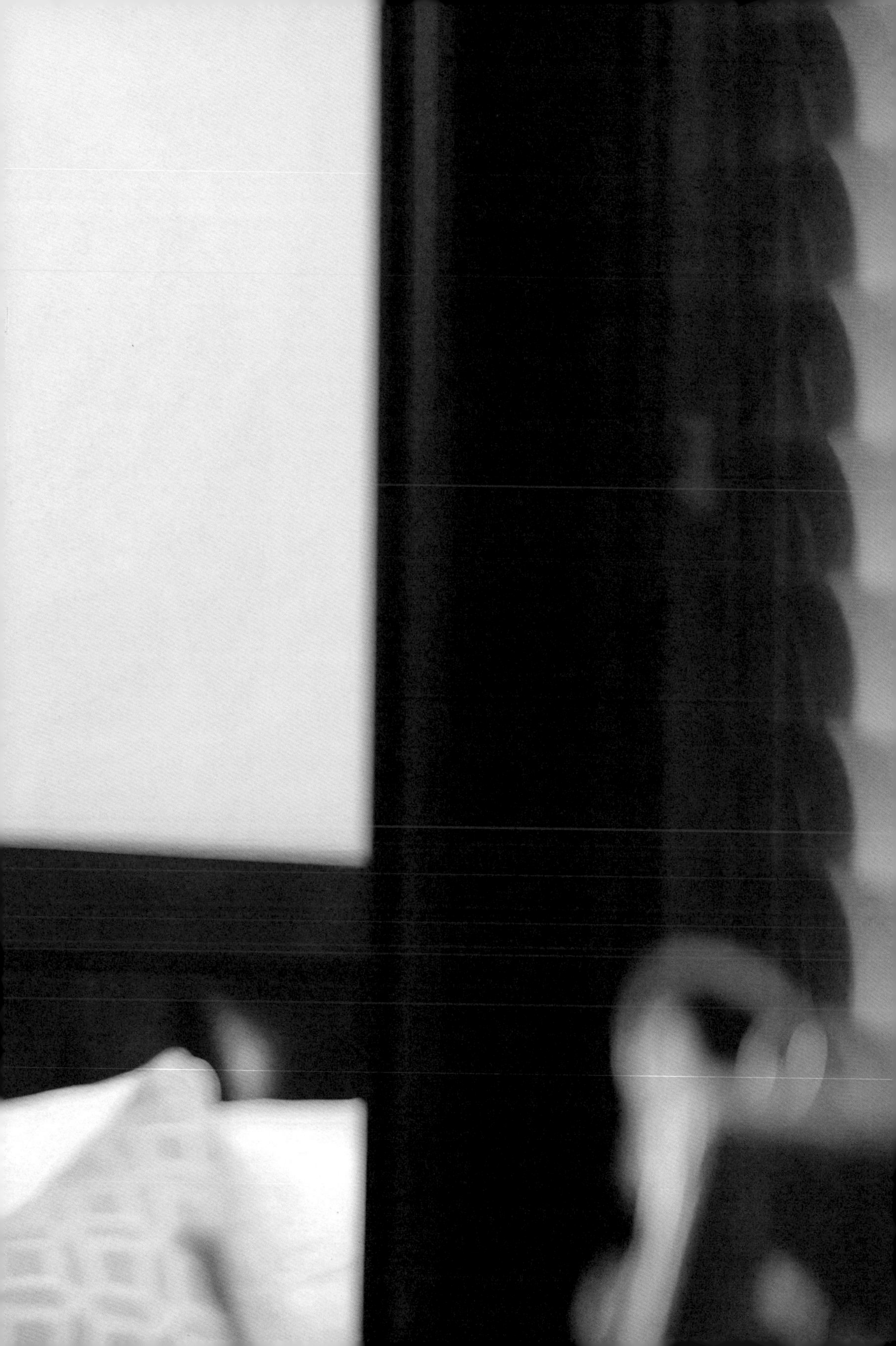

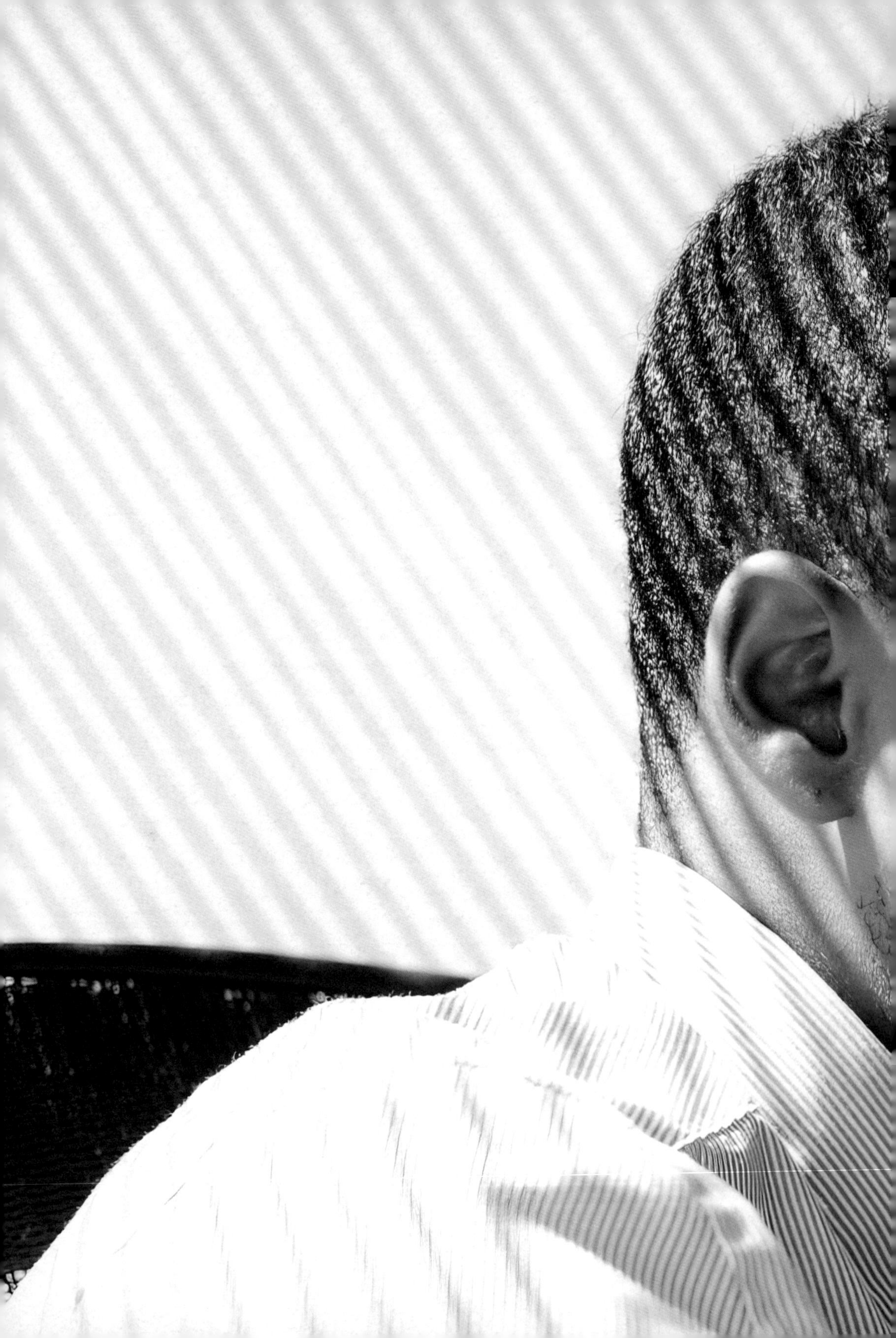

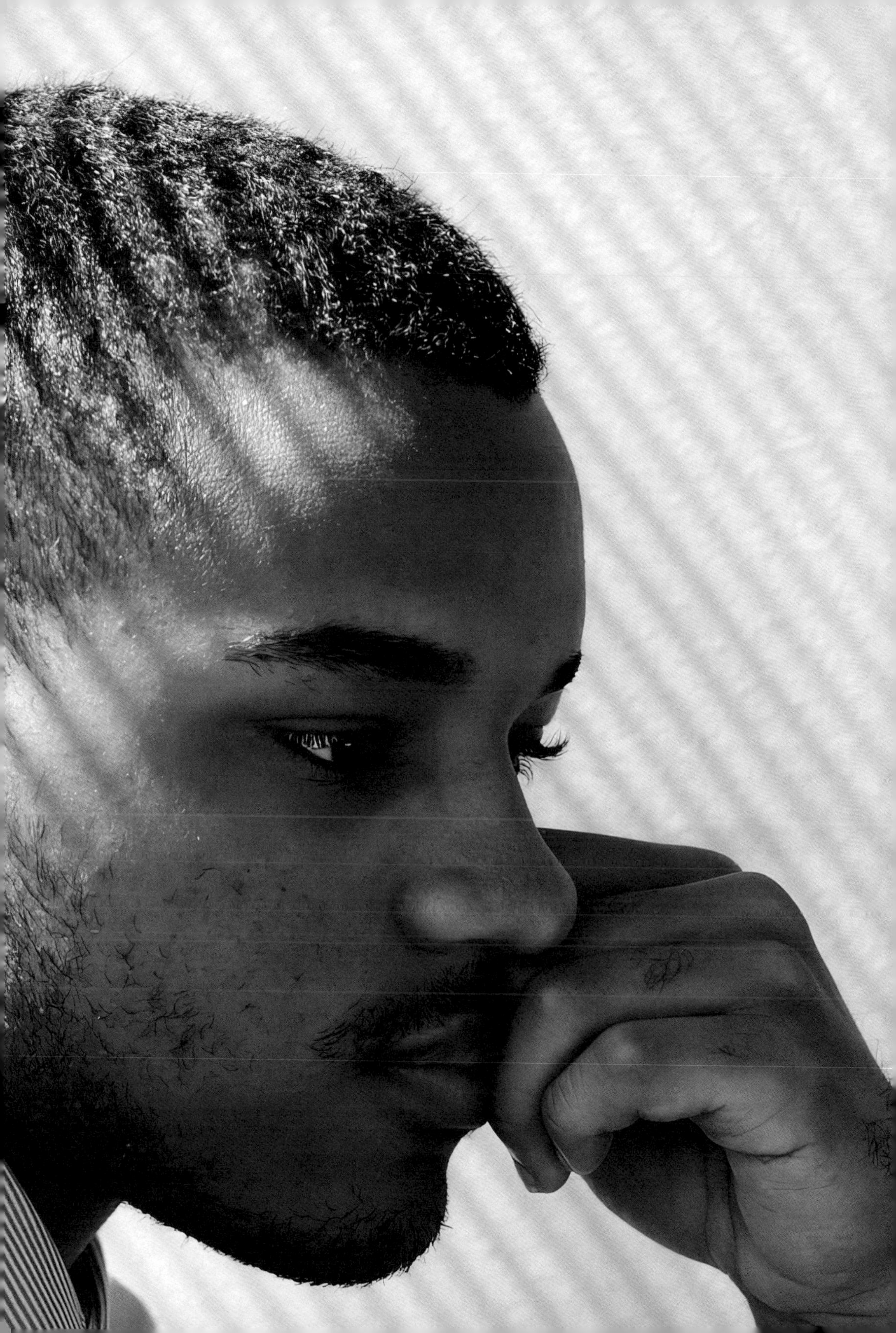

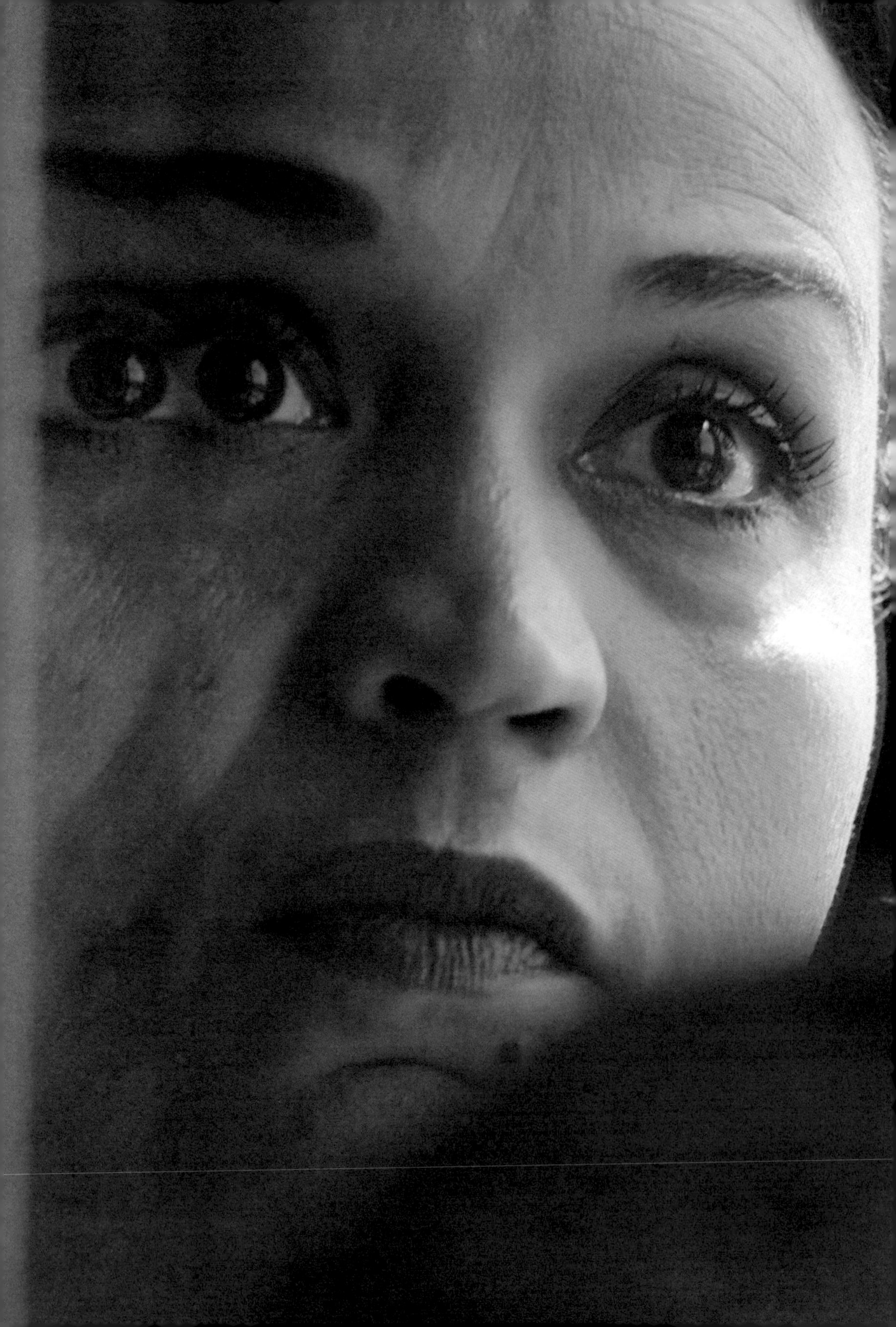

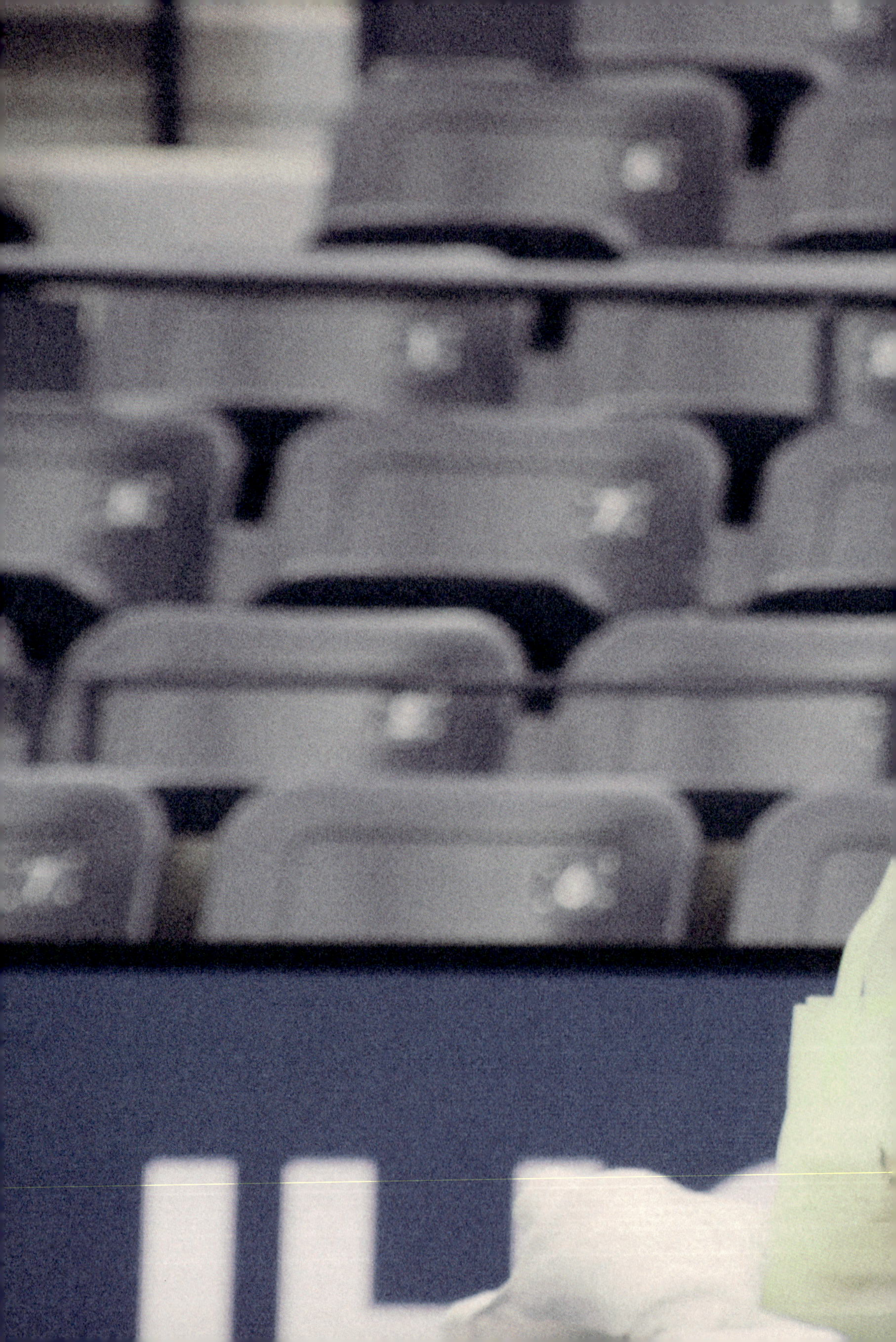

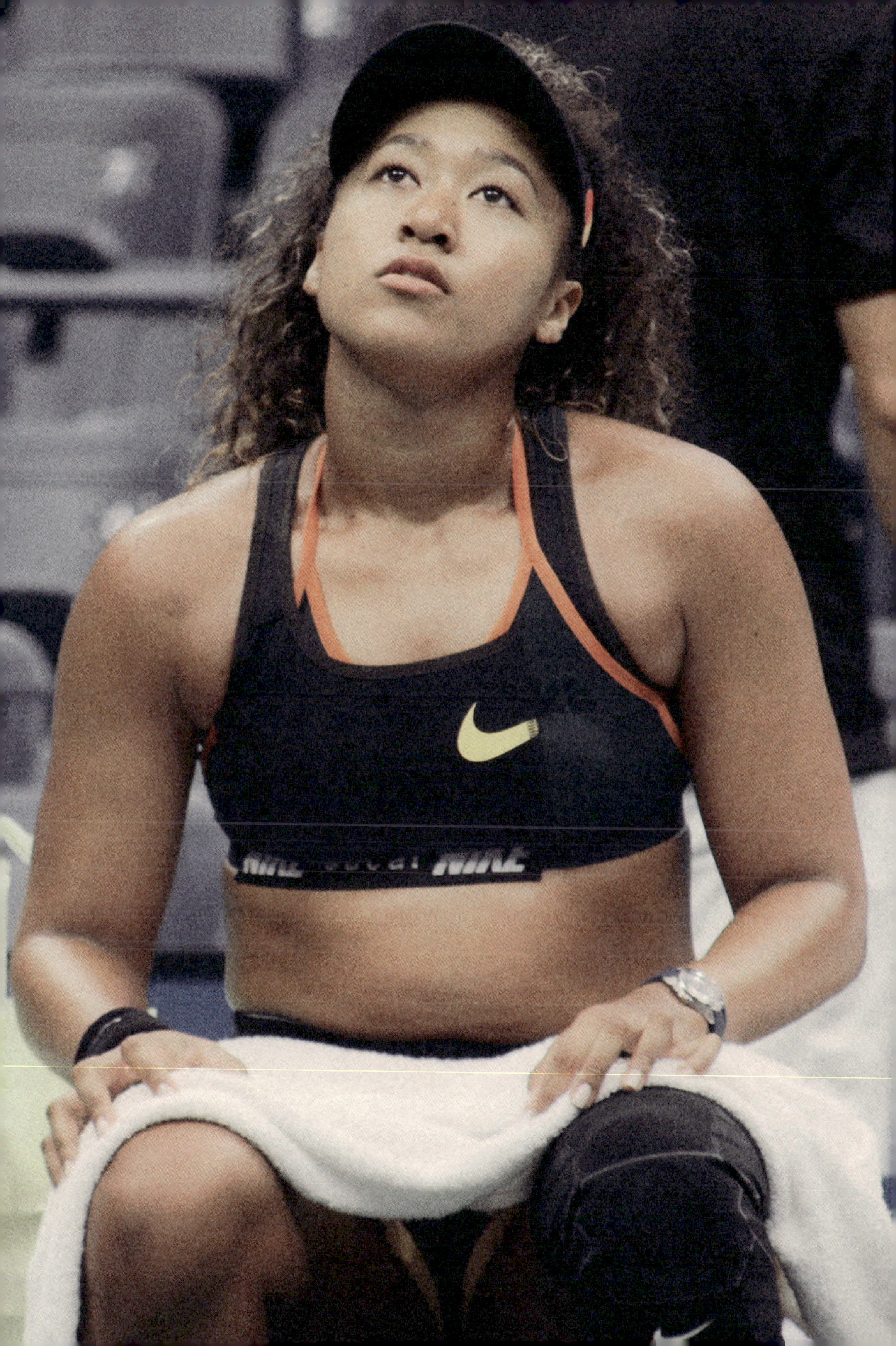
NIKE

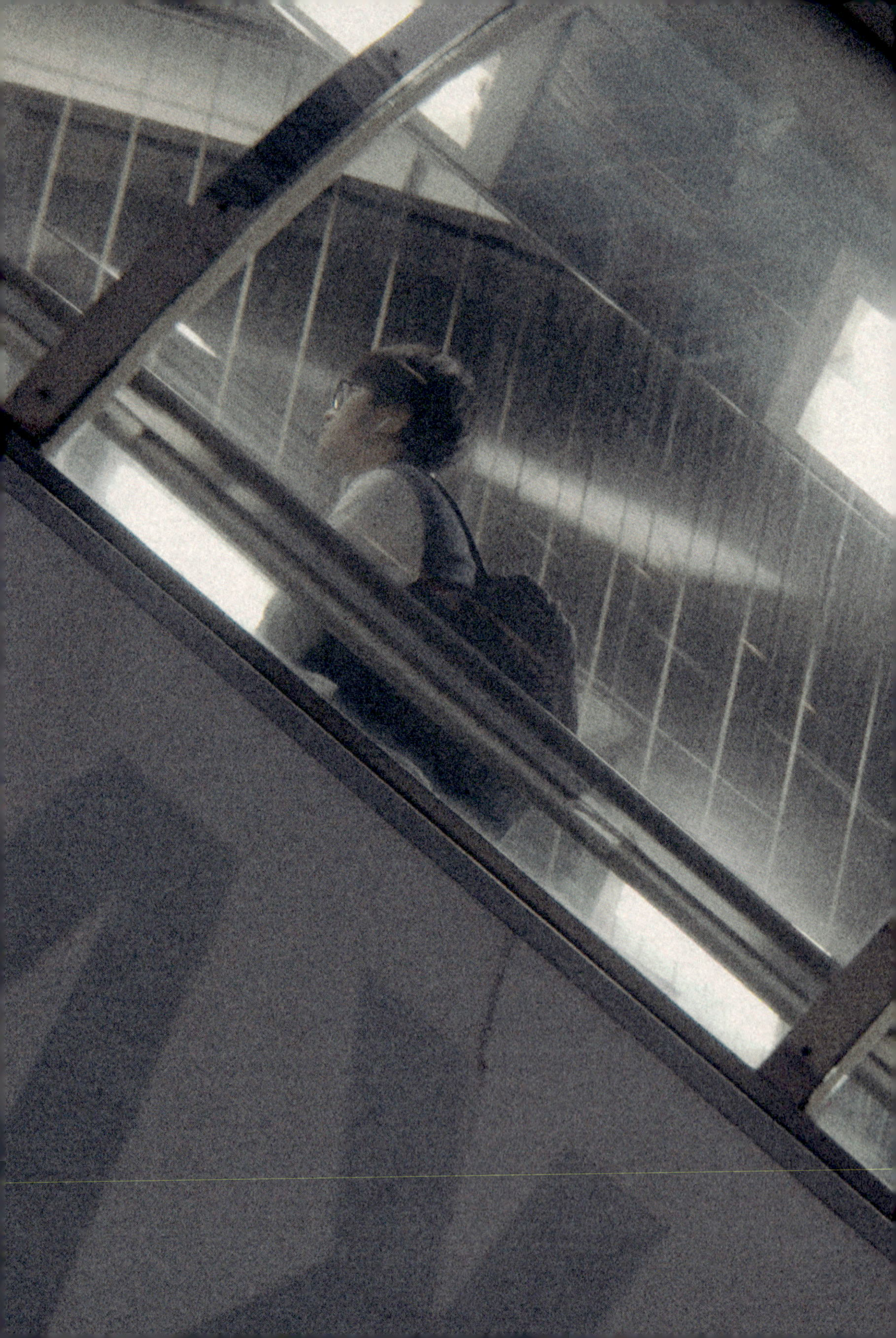

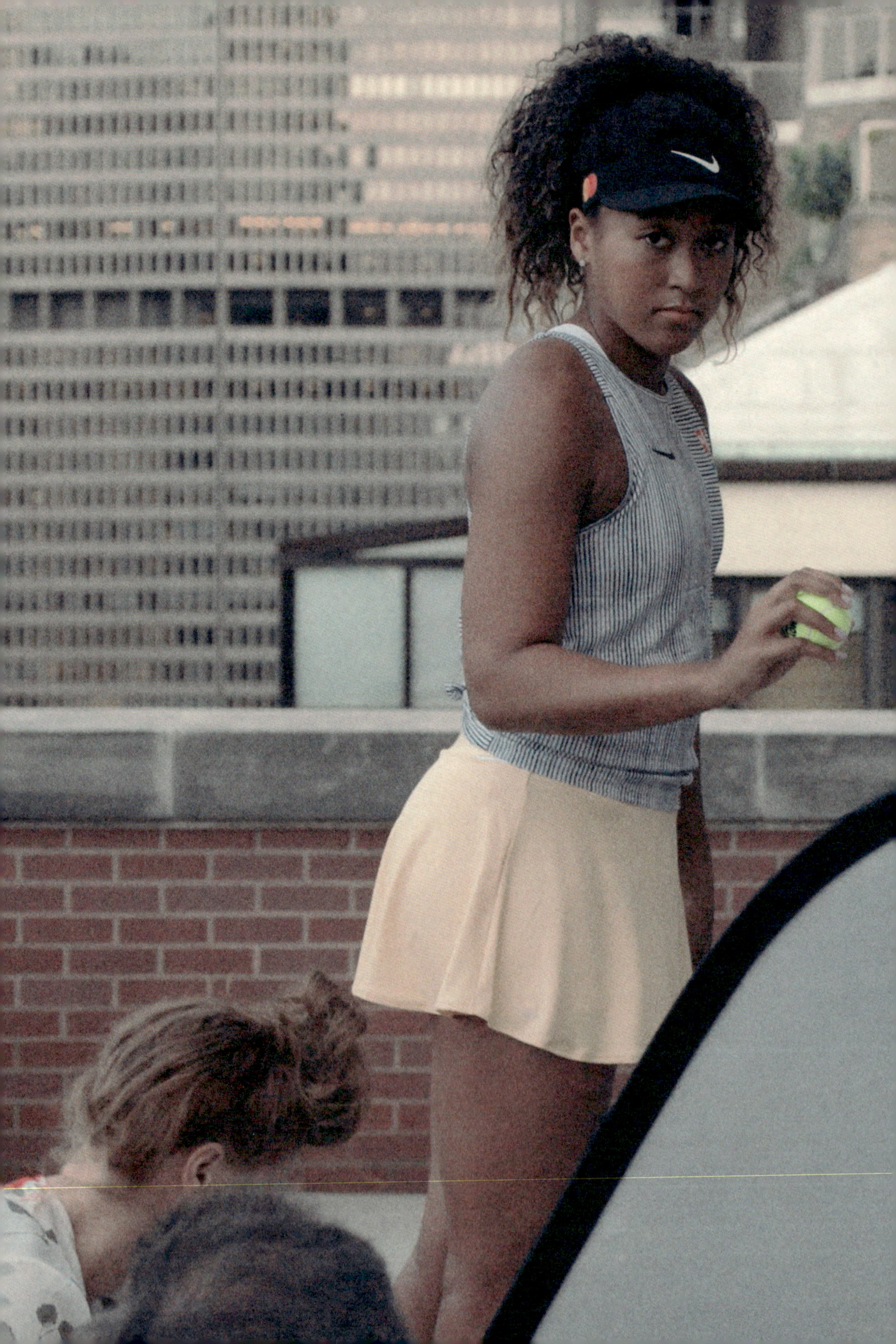

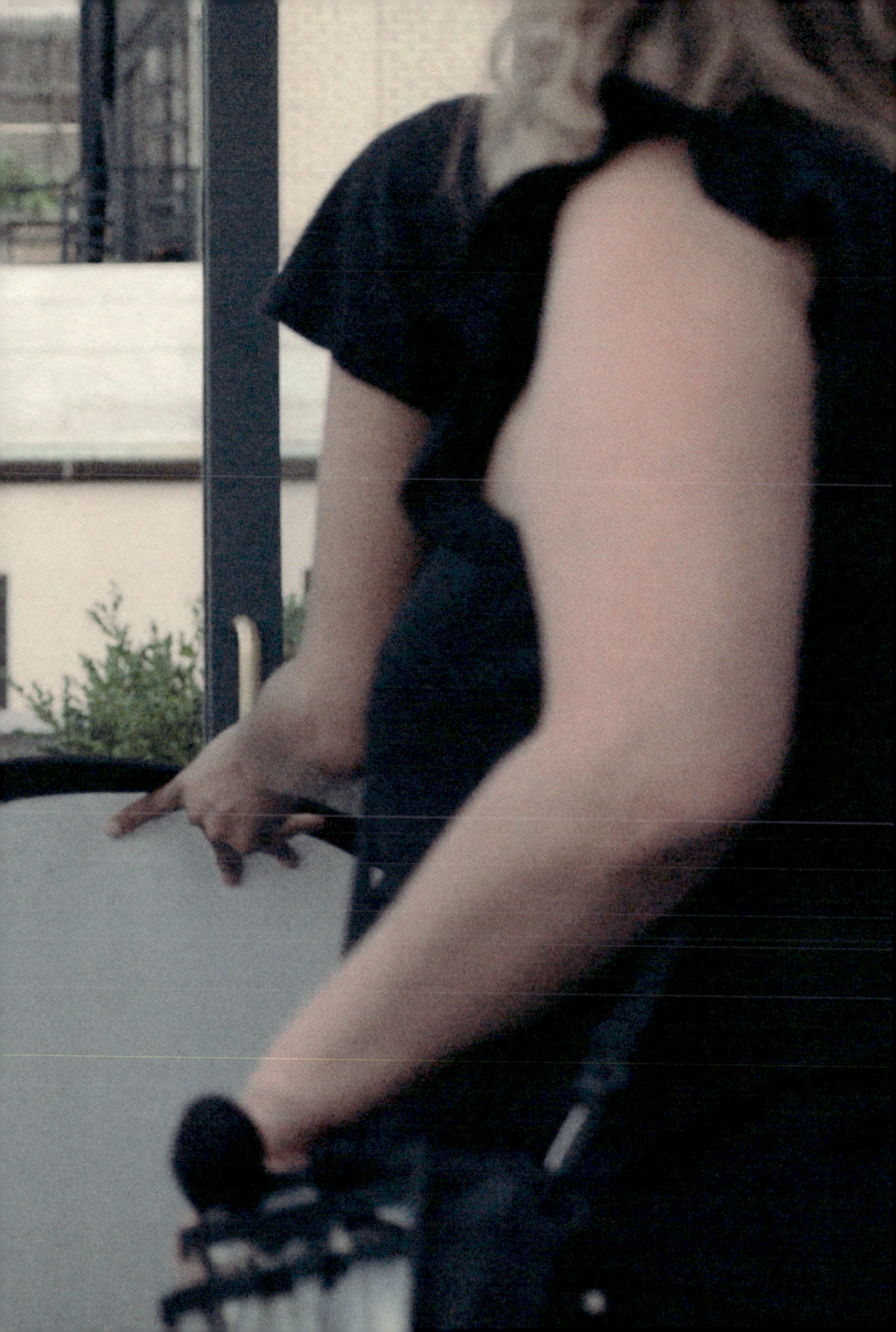

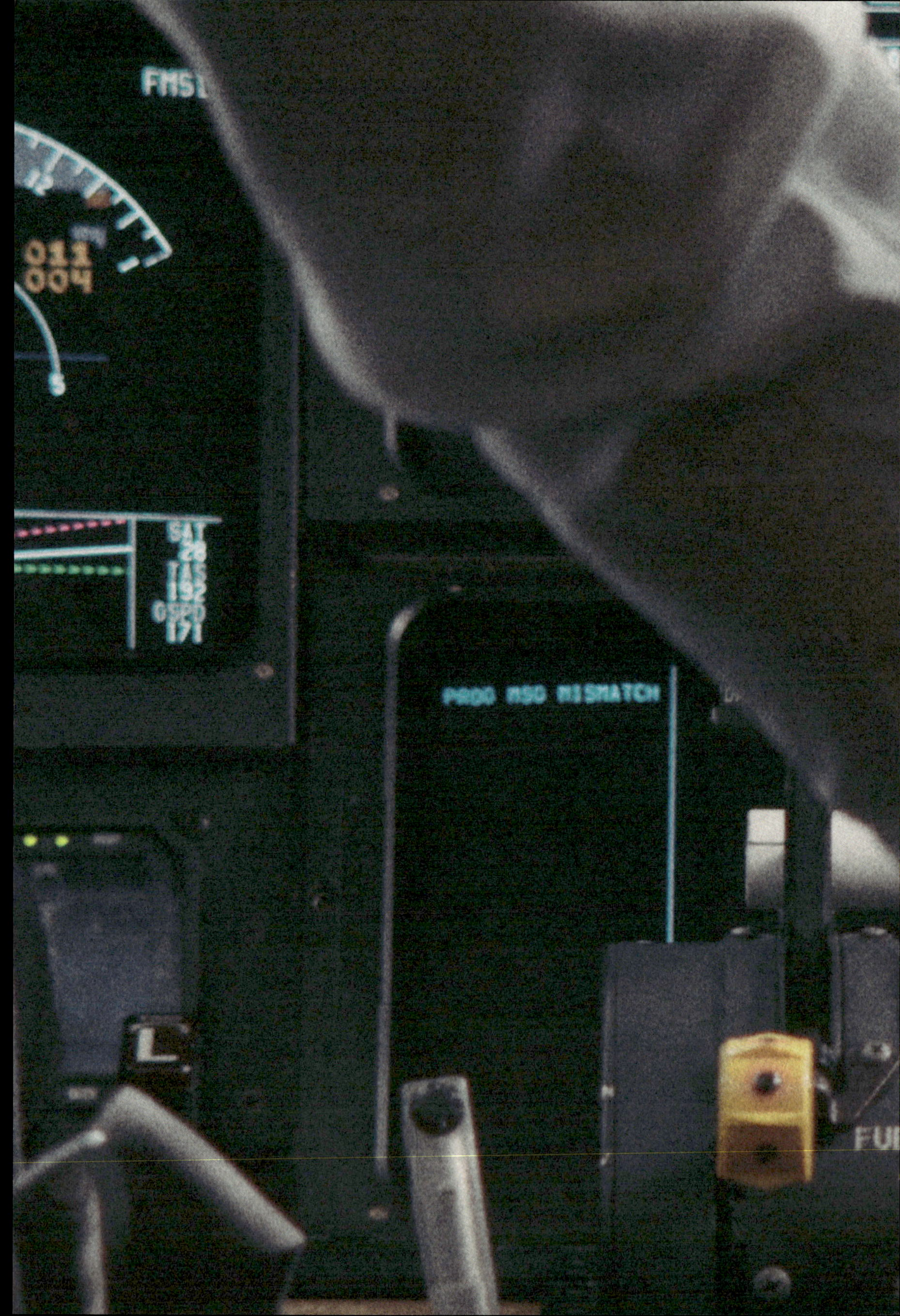
FMS1
011
004
SAT
28
TAS
192
GSPD
171
PROG MSG MISMATCH
L

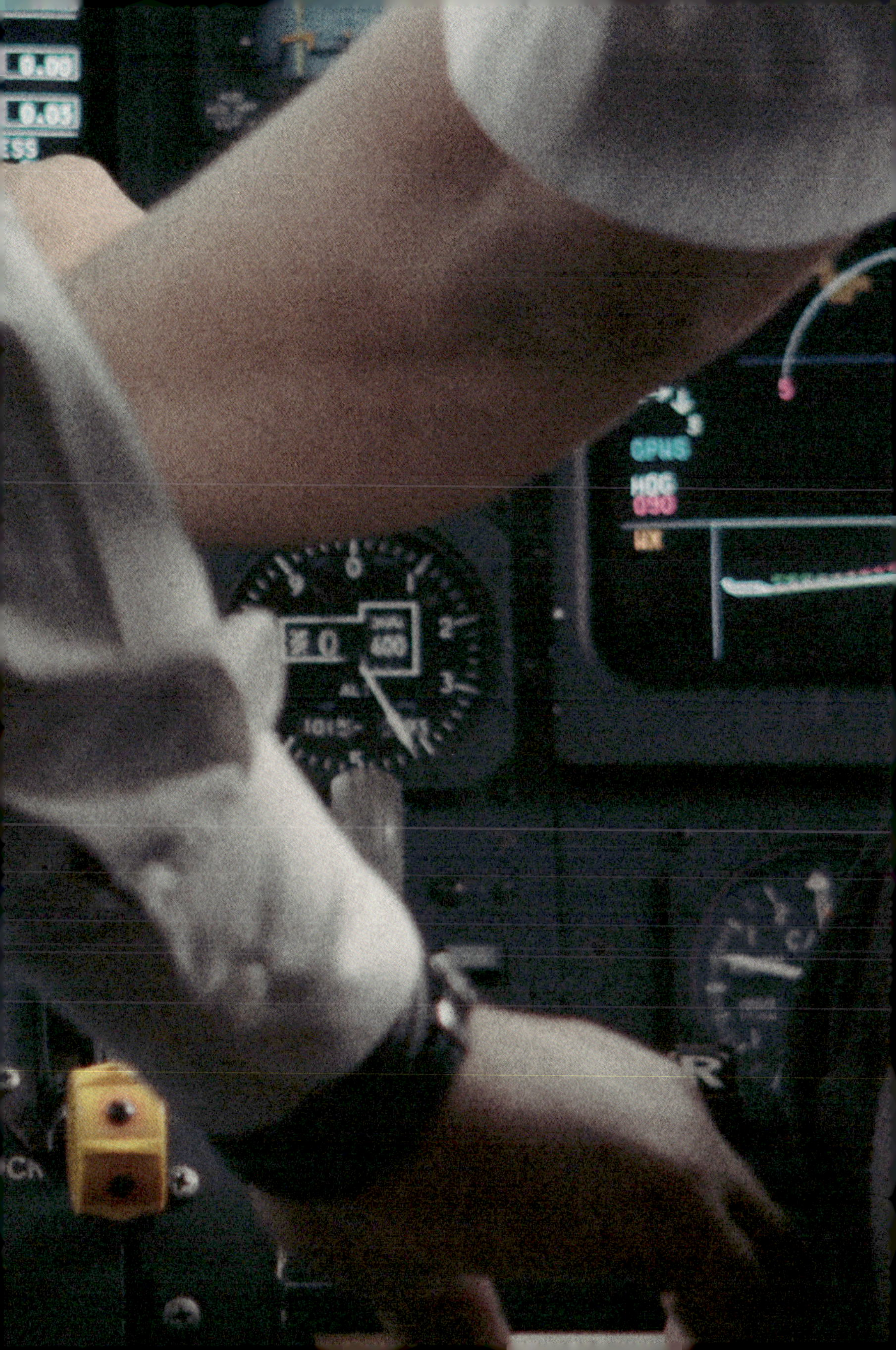
GPWS
HDG

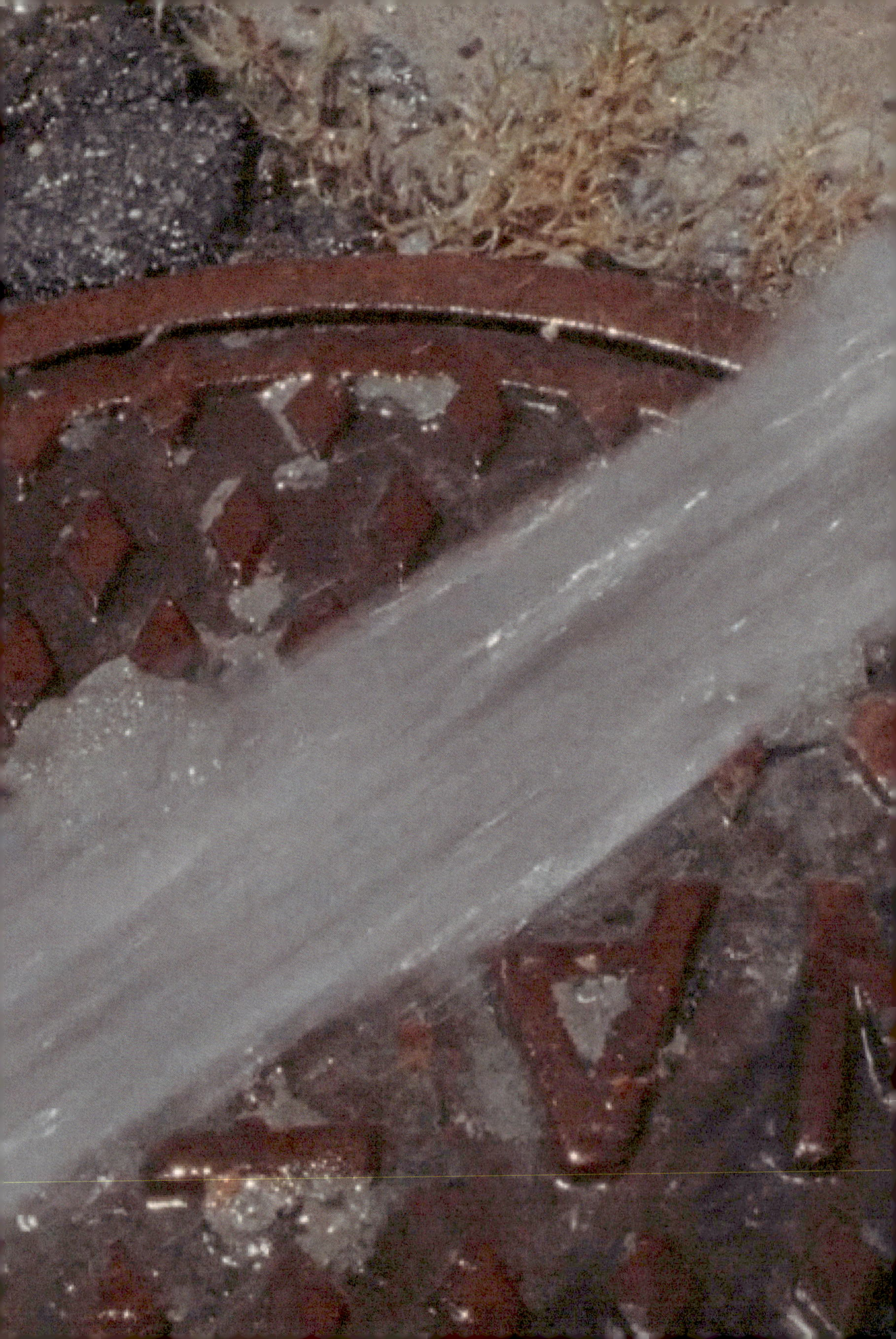

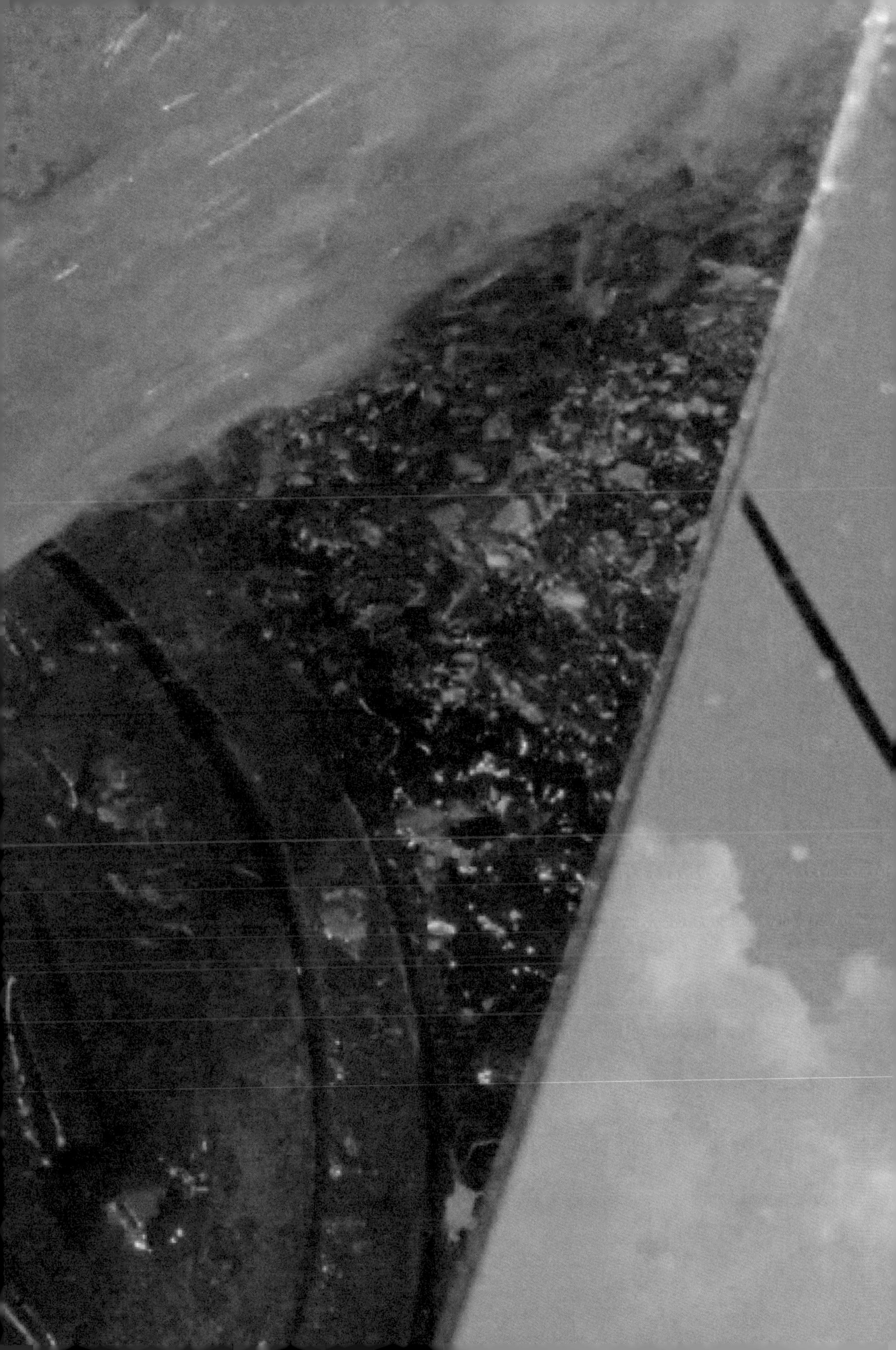

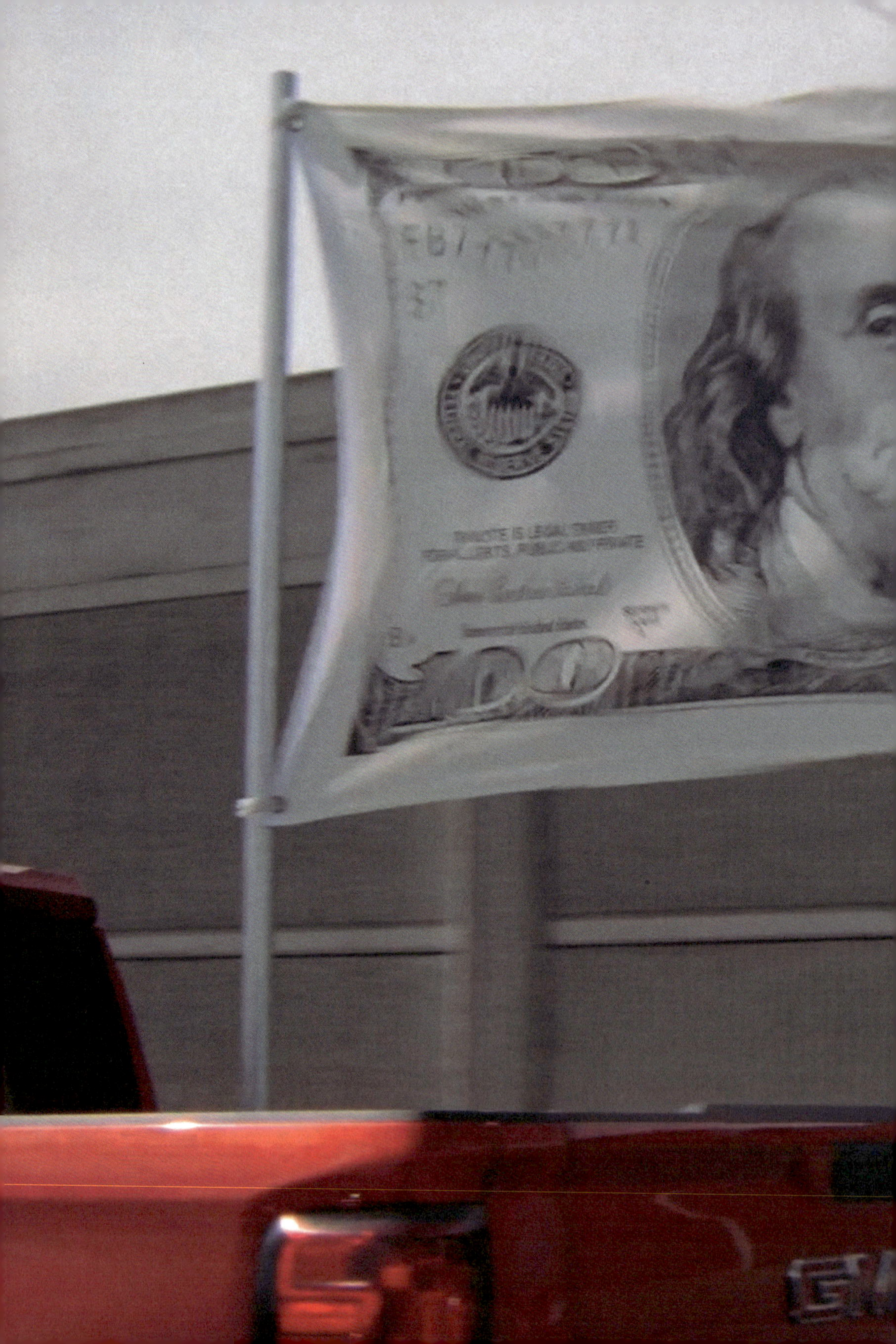

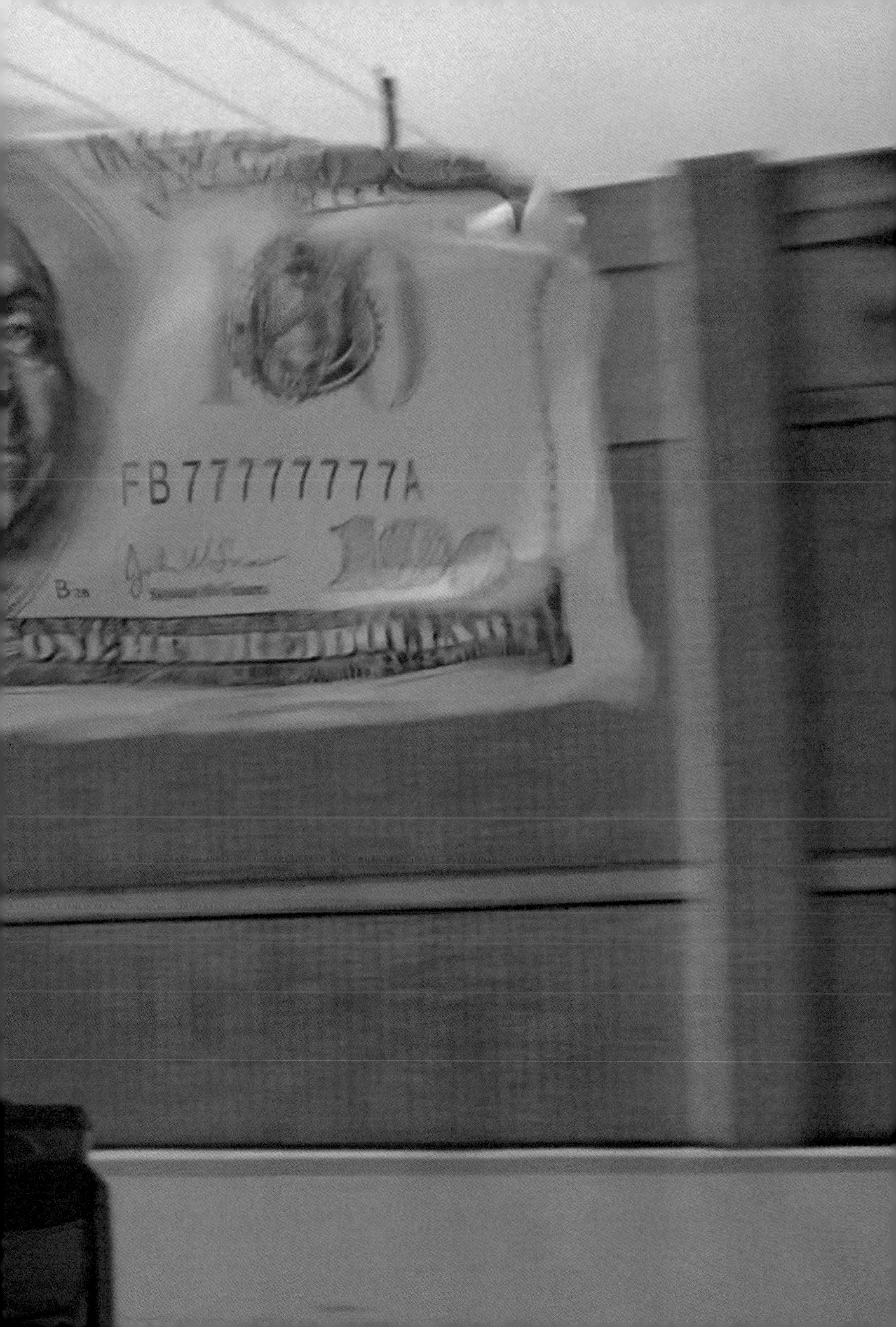
FB77777777A

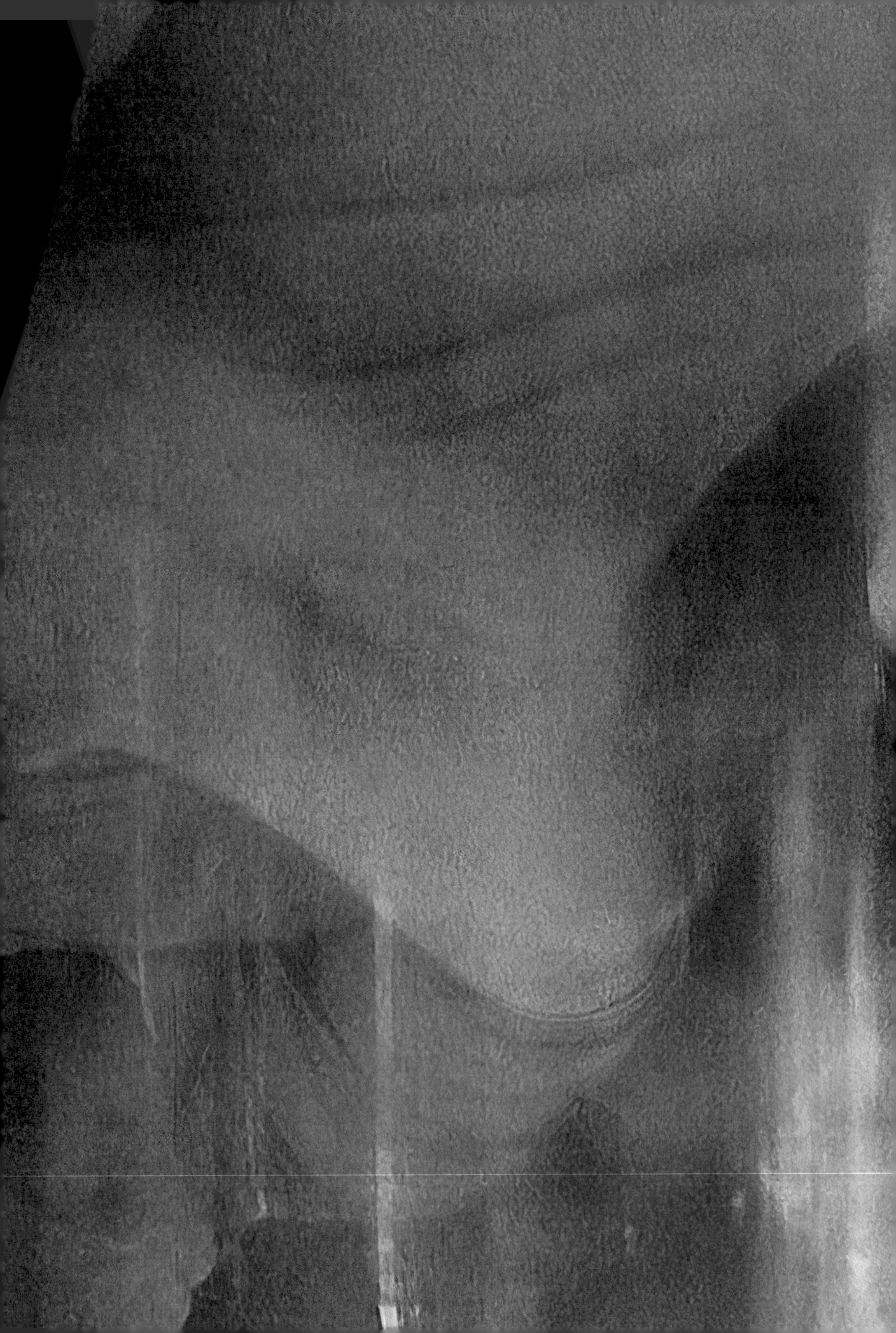

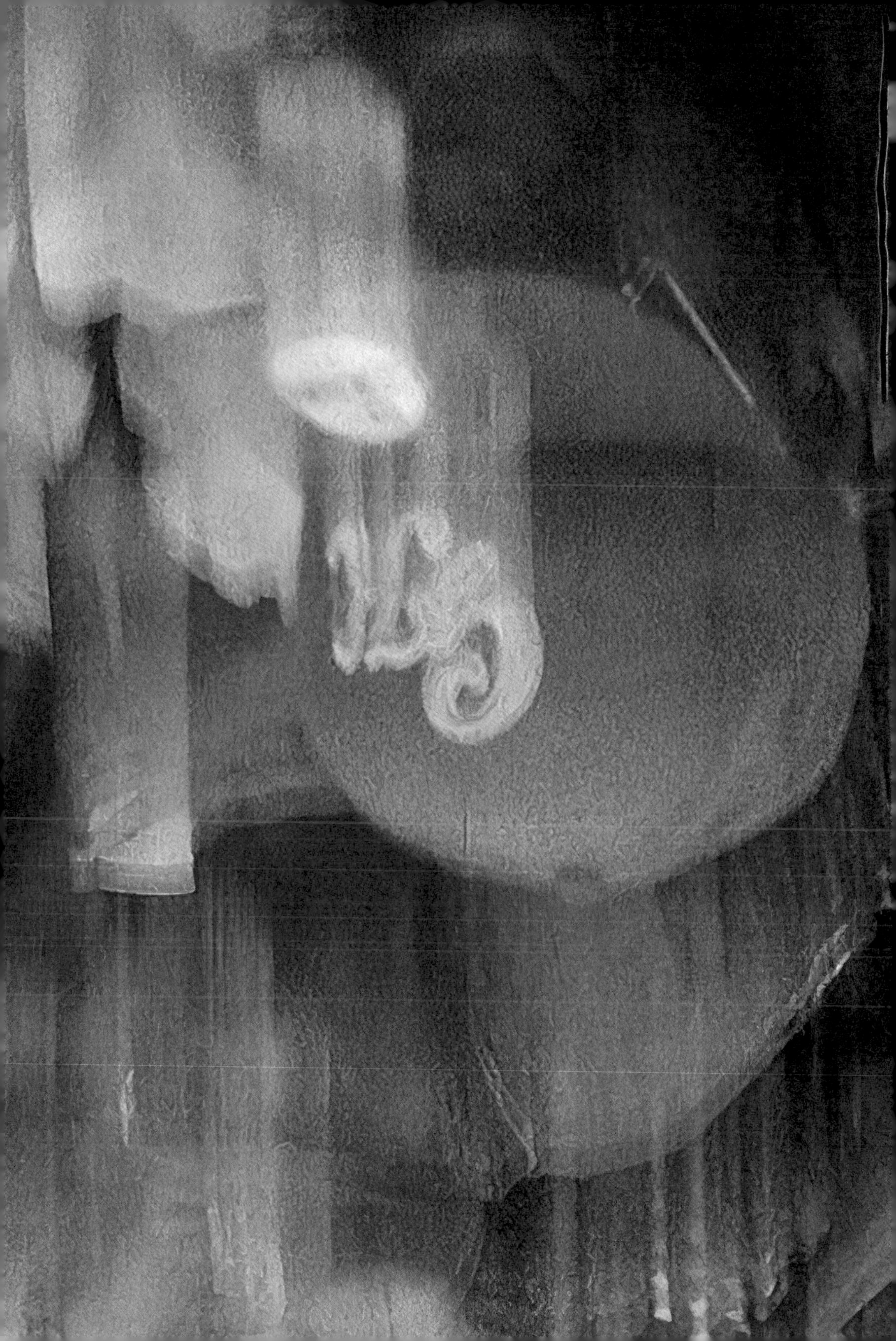

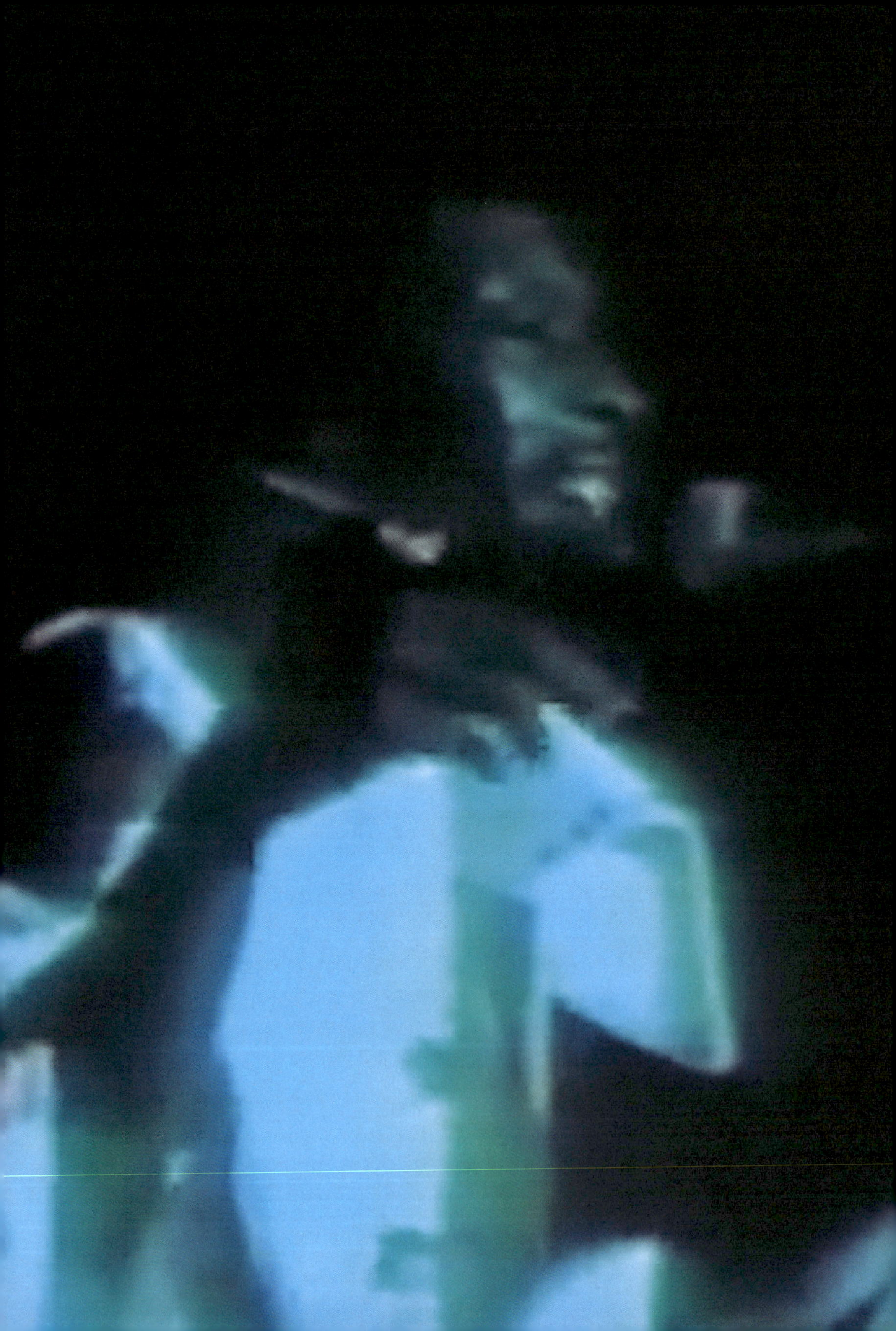

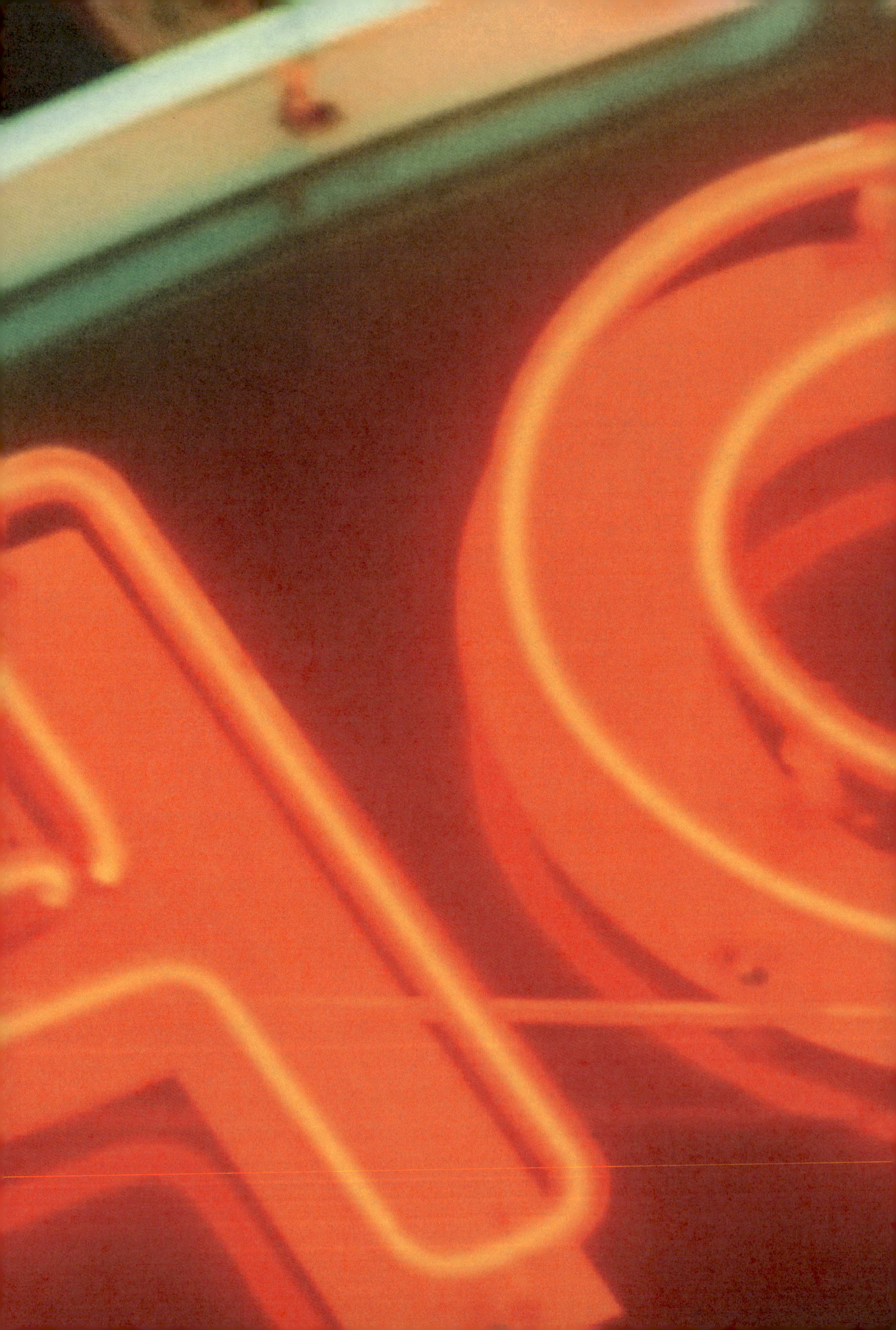

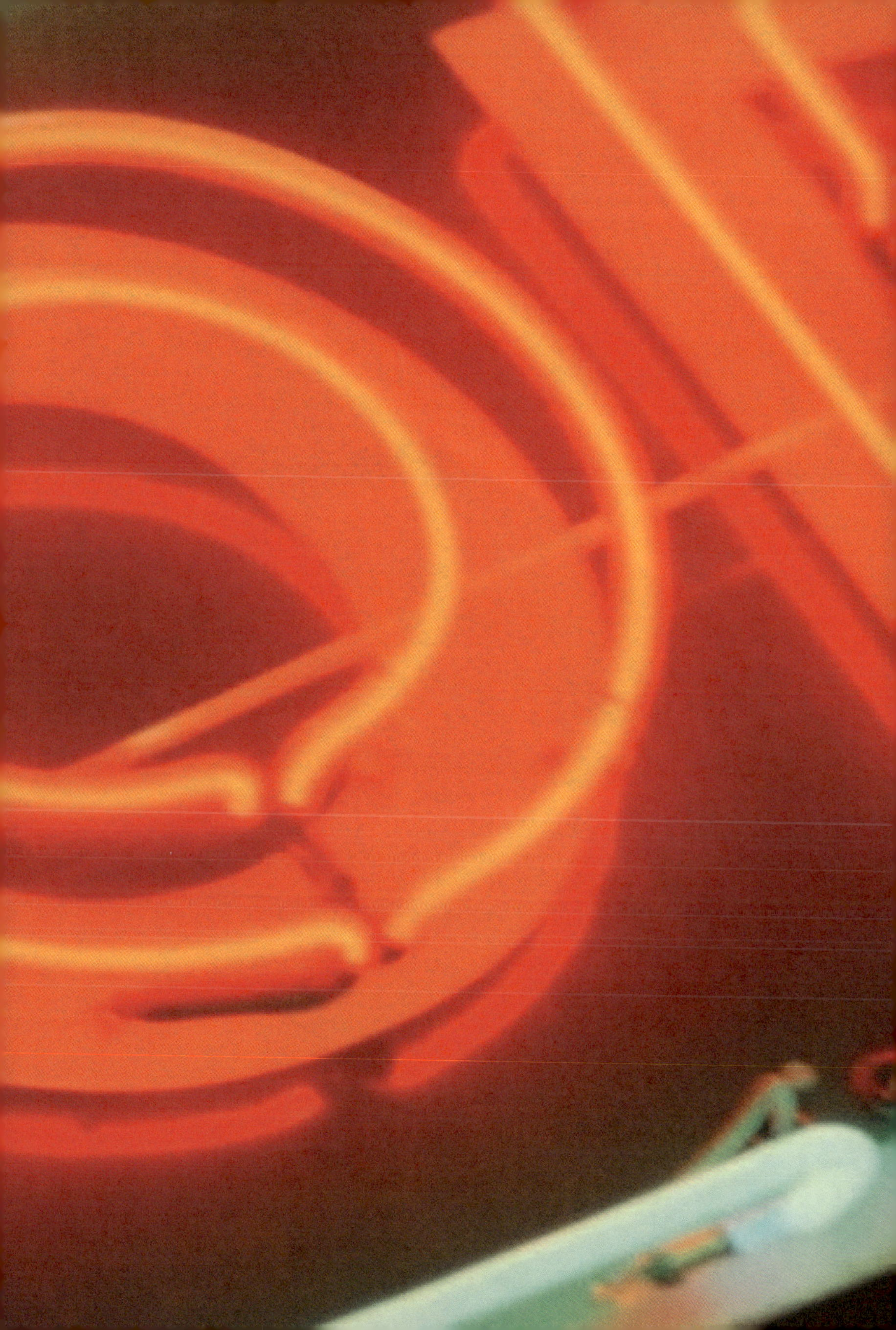

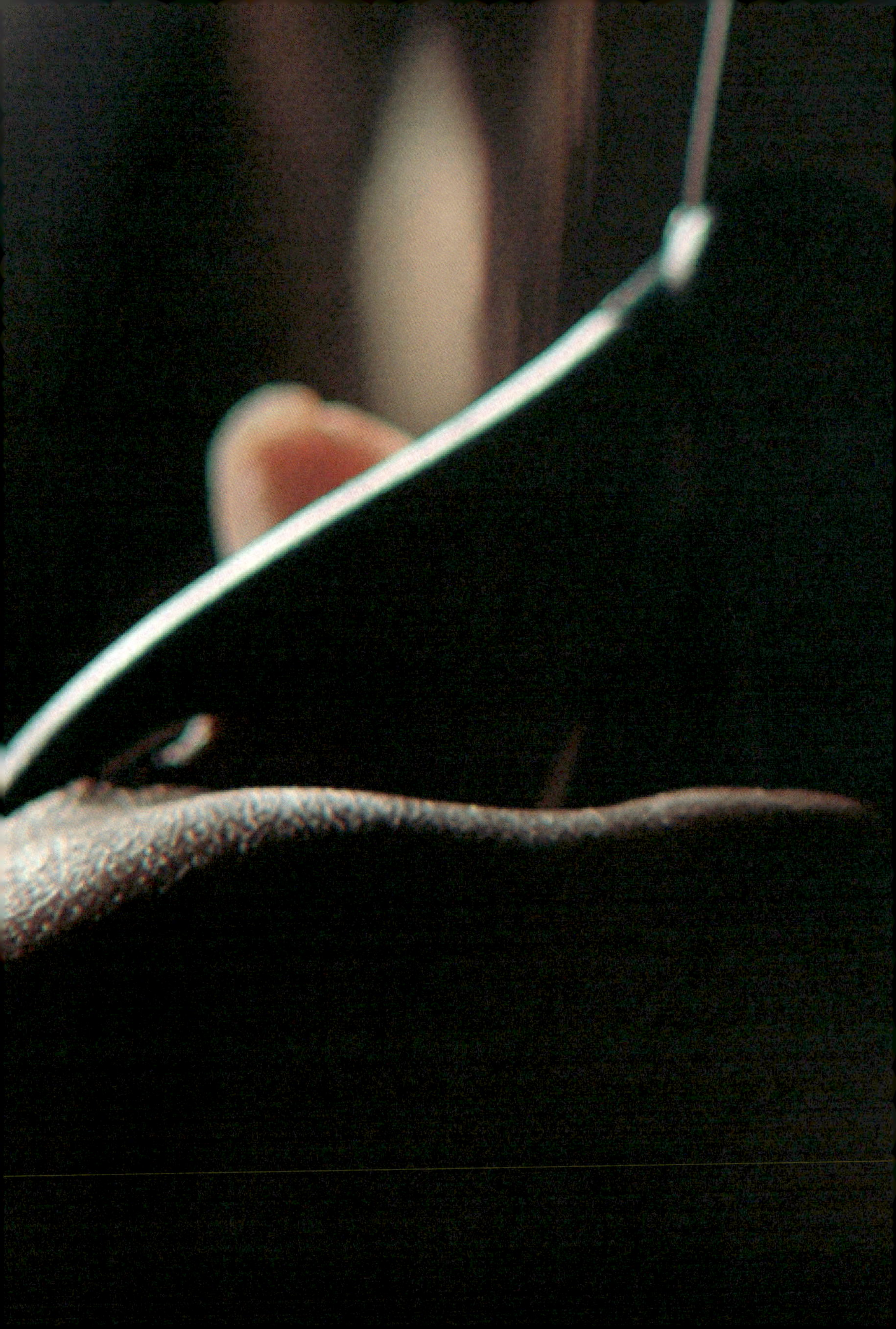

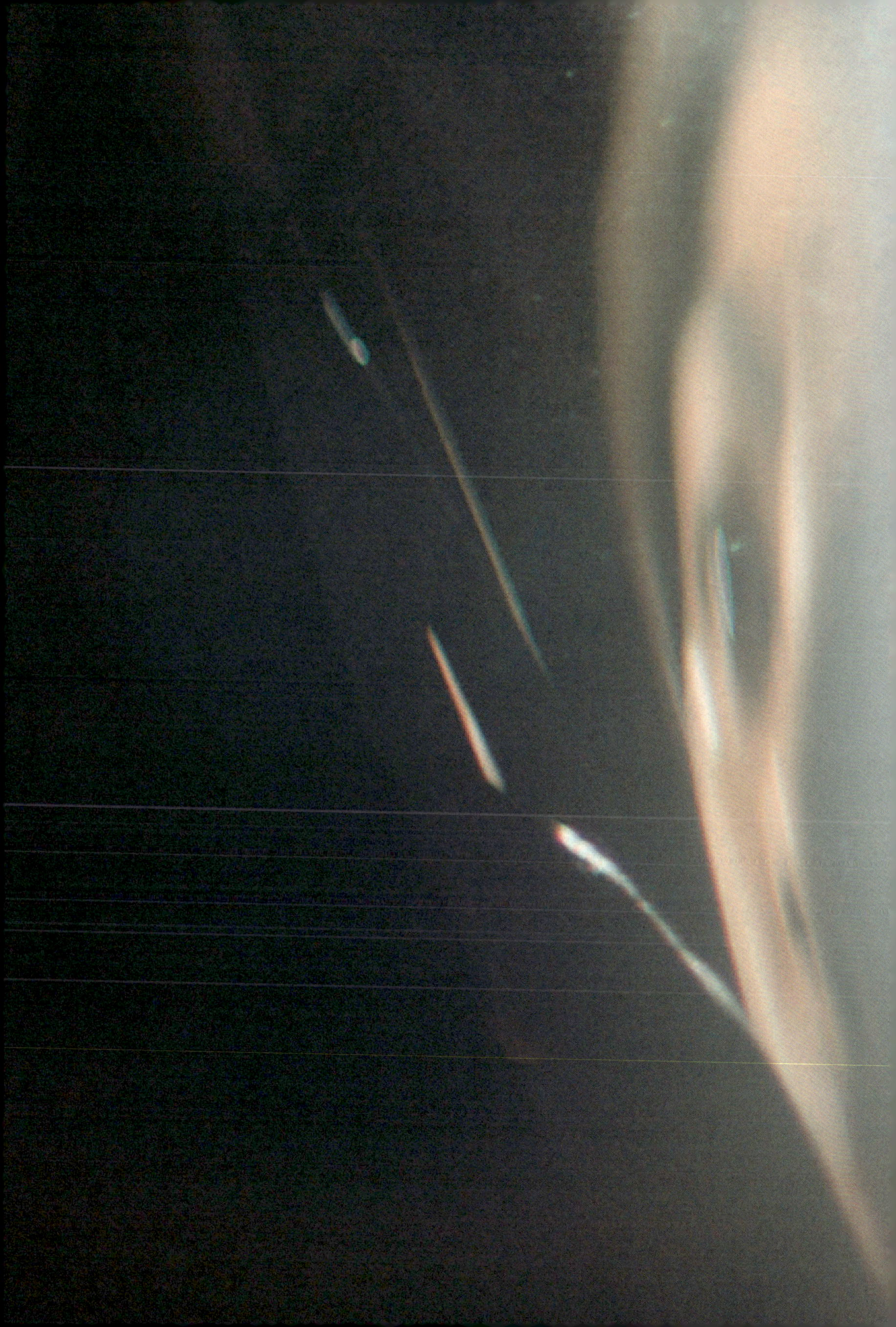

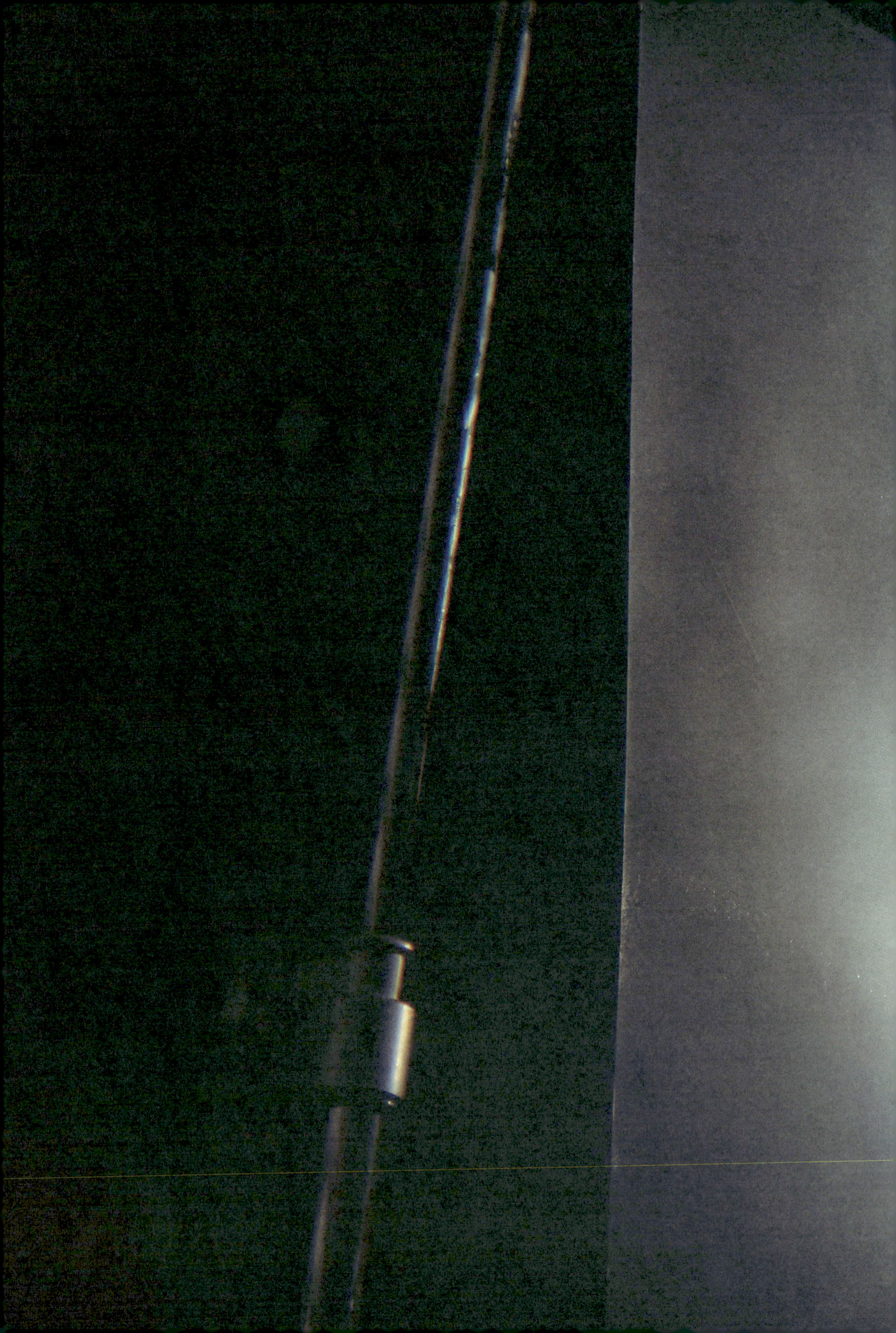

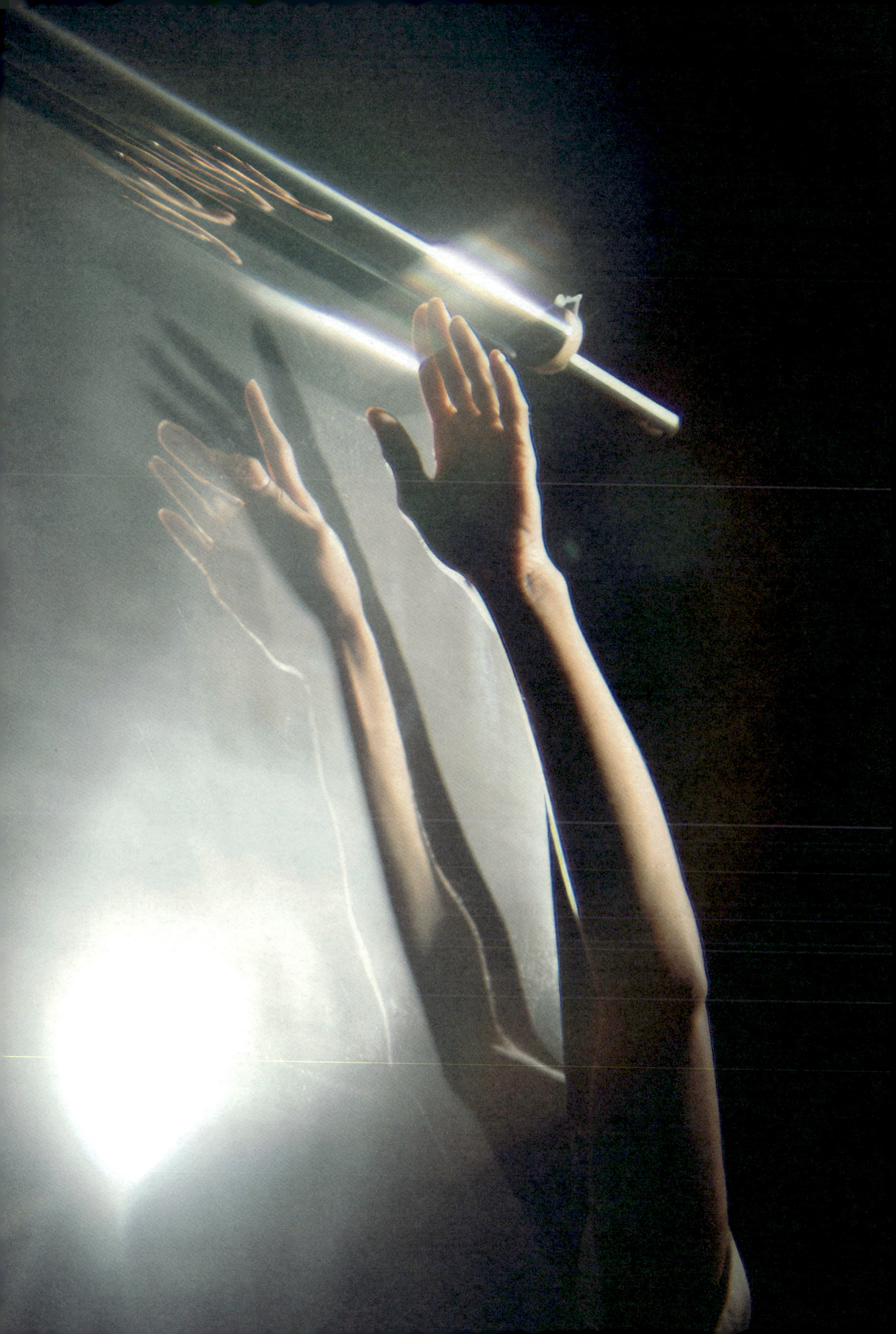

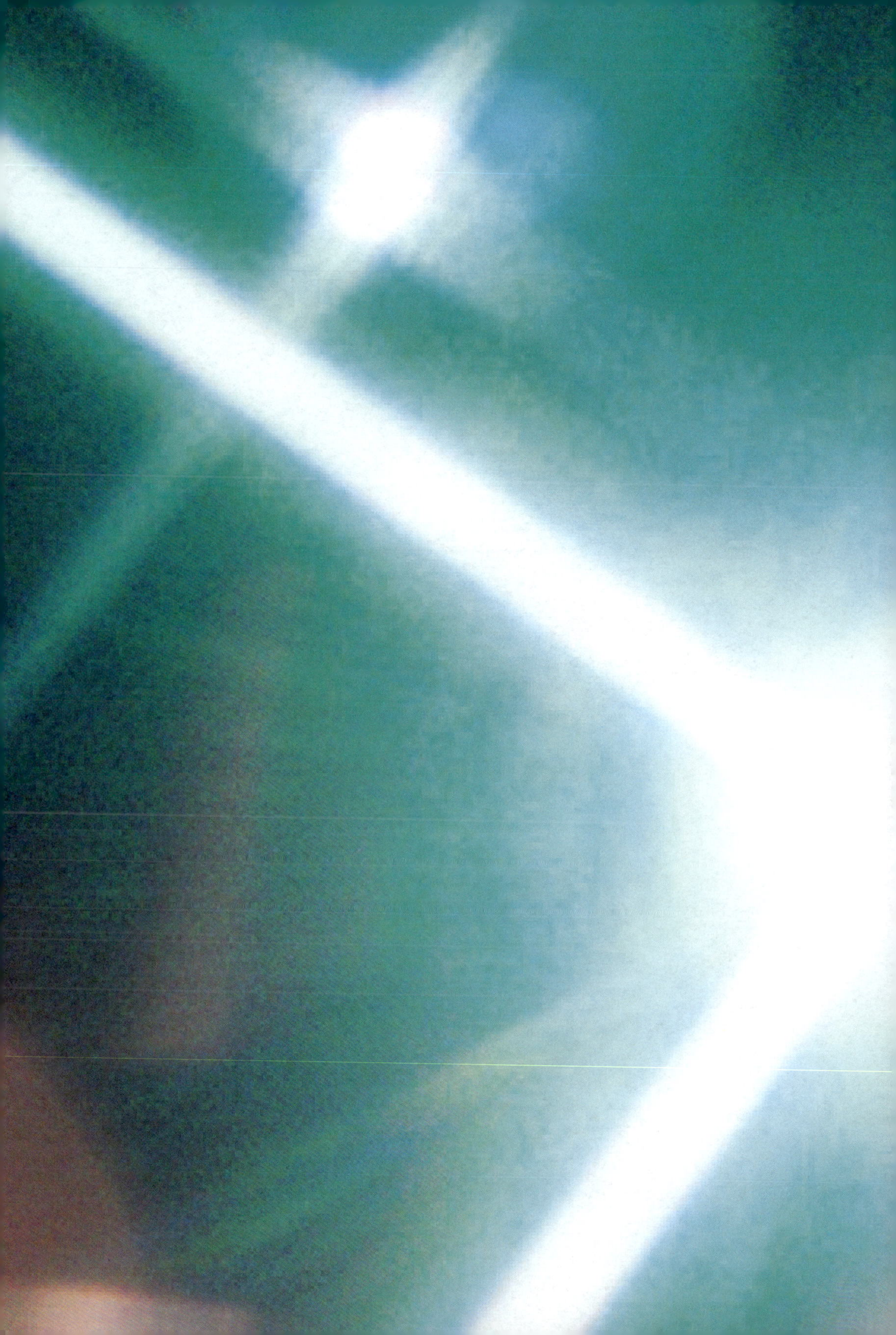

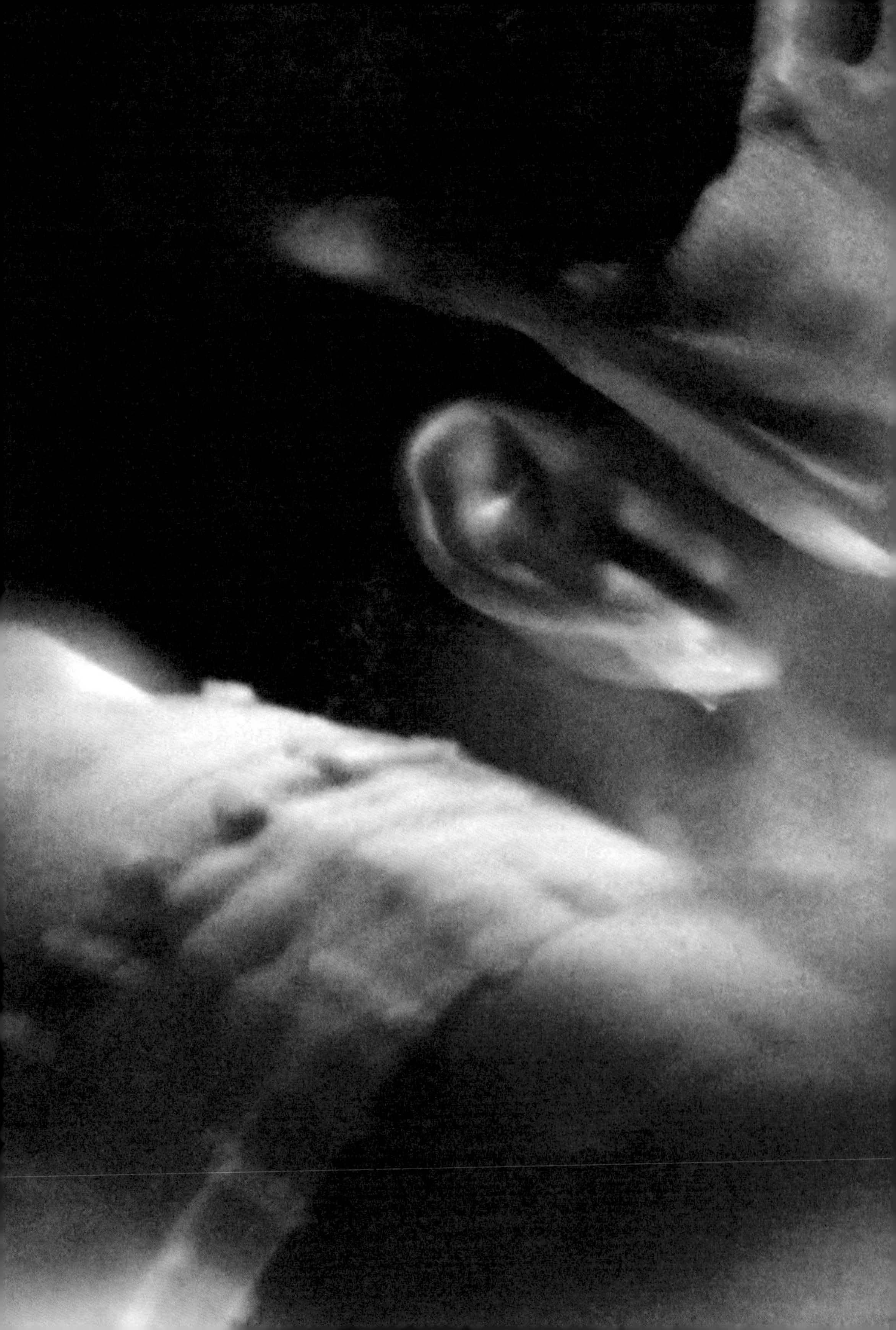

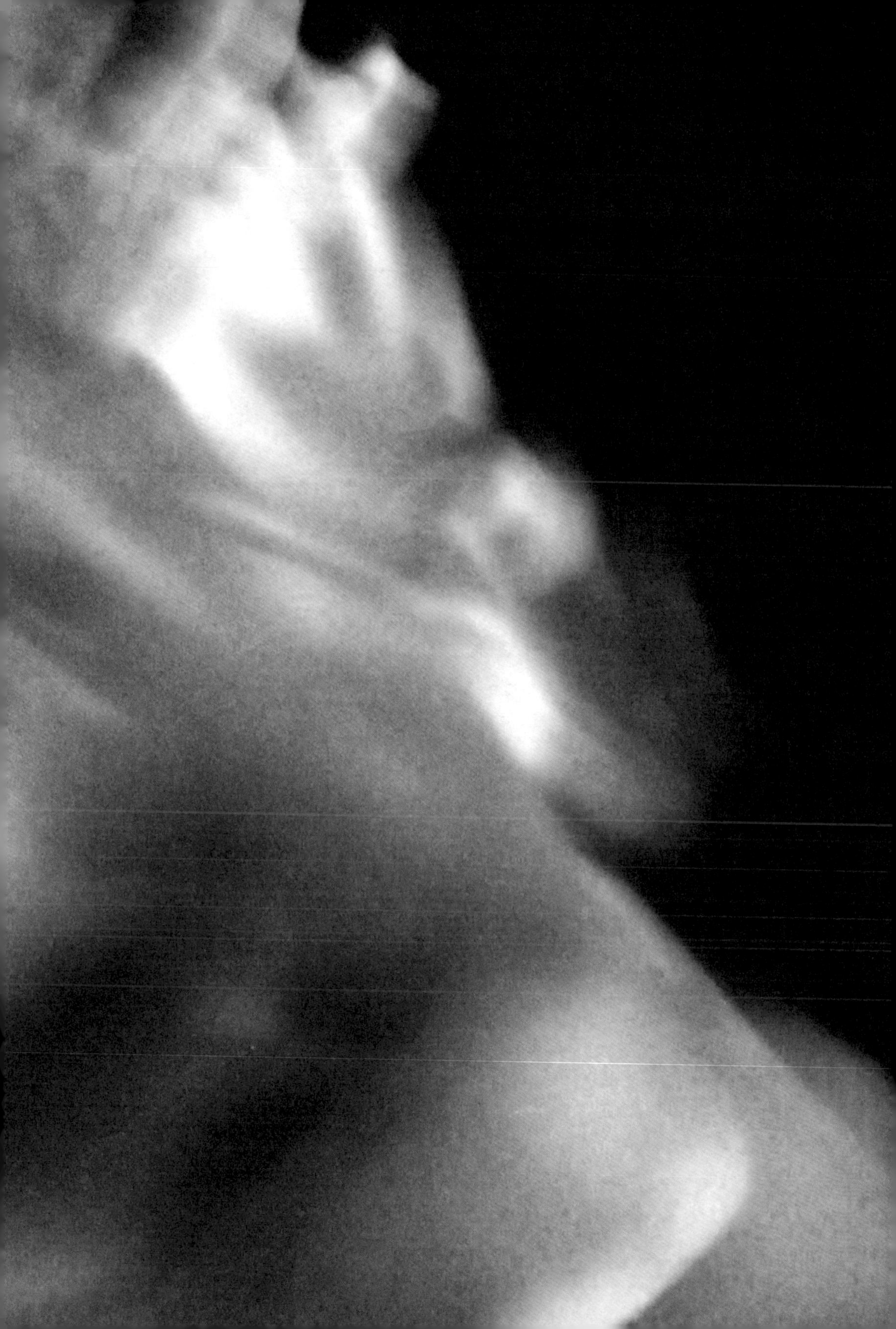

Re:

ASHLEY CLARK

BACK TO BLACK: *LIME KILN CLUB FIELD DAY*

In January 2019, at the Sundance Film Festival, I first saw Garrett Bradley's America. *I was captivated and deeply moved by the film, which imagines a rich counter-history of Black American life and on-screen representation. On the spot, I decided that I wanted to build a program around the film, and set about collaborating with Garrett to create Garrett Bradley's* America*: A Journey Through Race and Time, which ran at Brooklyn Academy of Music from October 11-19, 2019. The program opened with a screening of the silent film* Lime Kiln Club Field Day *(1913), which stars the vaudevillian entertainer Bert Williams, and which Garrett poignantly references in* America. *Though unfinished, the film is thought to be among the very first attempts to make a feature-film comedy with a majority-Black cast. Just over four years earlier in late 2014, I had attended the premiere presentation of* Lime Kiln Club Field Day *at New York's Museum of Modern Art. What follows is my report from this historic event.*

"[Bert Williams] was the funniest man I ever saw—and the saddest man I ever knew"
—W.C. Fields

"You haven't the faintest conception of the difficulties which we must overcome, of the prejudices which must be left slumbering, of the things we must avoid whenever we write or sing a piece of music, put on a play or a sketch, walk out in the street or land in a new town."
—Aida Overton Walker, *Indianapolis Freeman*, October 6, 1900

"I would like it to go viral, to tour the world. It needs to get out there," says Ronald S. Magliozzi, associate film curator at New York's Museum of Modern Art (MoMA). We've just met, and our conversation is seconds old, but his eyes are already wide with excitement. "We would like to give it back to the community, the Black artists. I had a vision of giving it to important Black artists and have them edit it, and sample from it, and do whatever they want to it."

He's animatedly referring to the next potential stage of a project which has kept him busy for a decade: the discovery of seven reels of previously unidentified, 101-year-old film footage, the earliest known surviving feature film with a cast of Black actors, among them legendary vaudevillian Bert Williams.[1]

The film, which Magliozzi and team have sculpted from the rushes, is a precious visual depiction of middle-class Black characters from an era when lynchings and racial stereotypes were rife. It came untitled, so the curators have dubbed it *Bert Williams Lime Kiln Club Field Day*, a reference to a fictional comedy club which repeatedly surfaced in their research. (A few weeks after our conversation, the film is added to the US Library of Congress's National Film Registry, where works are selected for preservation on account of their cultural, historic or aesthetic qualities.)

Magliozzi explains that the unedited, silent, non-intertitled daily rushes—multiple takes captured each day during production—were found among a hoard of 900 negatives that had been acquired from the pioneering Biograph studio by MoMA's founding film curator, Iris Barry, in 1939; ironically, she'd been scouring for work by D.W. Griffith, the director of virulently racist epic *The Birth of a Nation* (1915). Barry got there just in time: the rushes were on the brink of destruction, for Biograph's facilities in the Bronx had recently closed for business.

Later, in the 1970s, the rushes were printed onto safety film stock, and in the 1980s underwent the process of restoration. Magliozzi began the process of assemblage in 2004. It was at this point he realized the unique nature of Barry's unearthing. Though a few other films from that period featured Black casts, including Alice Guy-Blaché's *A Fool and his Money* (1912), and a smattering of micro-budget efforts by Black independent directors like William Foster and Hunter C. Haynes, they're all now considered lost.

Even more extraordinarily, hidden within the material were nearly a hundred stills depicting the Black cast and white crew happily mingling on set, several frames of Williams interacting with white extras on location during a filming break—remarkable considering established narratives about the Jim Crow era's poisonous racial dynamics—and startling images of Williams having his blackface applied by a valet. Williams, a major Broadway star by this juncture, was replicating the established stage tradition of blacking up, yet was the only cast member to do so. ("A sop to the white audience," says Magliozzi, explaining this bizarre contrivance. "The fact that the lead wore blackface allowed the rest of the cast not to wear blackface before white audiences.")

The rushes also include almost eight minutes of documentary footage—a sort of proto "making-of" depicting the cast and crew at the New York studio sets and suburban New Jersey locations. This compelling material makes up the vast majority of the exhibition, which is sequenced, elegantly and austerely, across two gallery floors.

Magliozzi characterizes the process of researching the exhibition as a "detective story"—very little information about the production and its history was obvious from the raw material. The identification of the cast, which he estimates comprising between fifty and one hundred performers, began with comparing frames of the film with images of sheet music and old

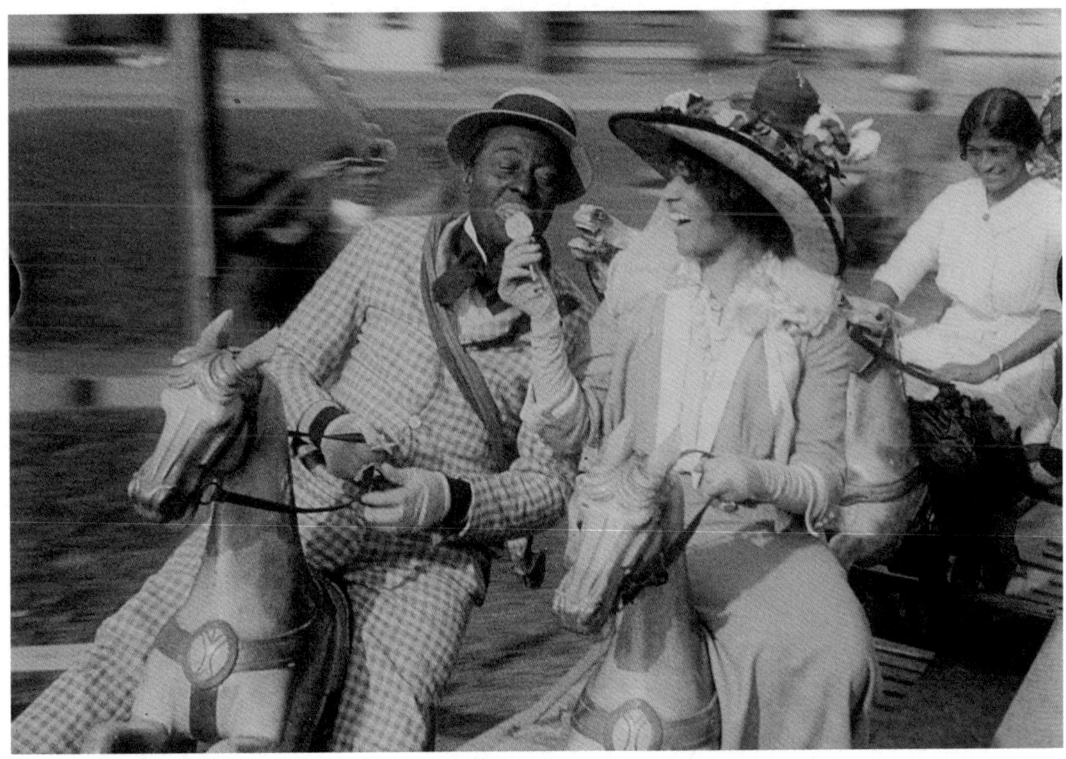

Lime Kiln Club Field Day, 1914/2014

press photos, which were often to be found in the pages of Harlem's Black newspaper *New York Age*. One was J. Leubrie Hill, who ran the Darktown Follies stage company. Another was the regal female lead Odessa Warren Grey, who, as a number of later trade ads confirmed, became a successful businesswoman in fashion, and a known associate of proto-Black feminist and stage performer Aida Overton Walker.

It eventually transpired that much of the cast had emerged from a little-known group of Harlem artists who, for years, had their events (concerts, carnivals, exhibitions) covered in the *Age*. The curator finds this particularly exciting, with good reason: "It brings to the world's attention this ... small community that's pre–Harlem Renaissance, and before the blues and jazz were officially identified as that. We're talking about the ragtime period." The process of discovering all the cast members remains ongoing.

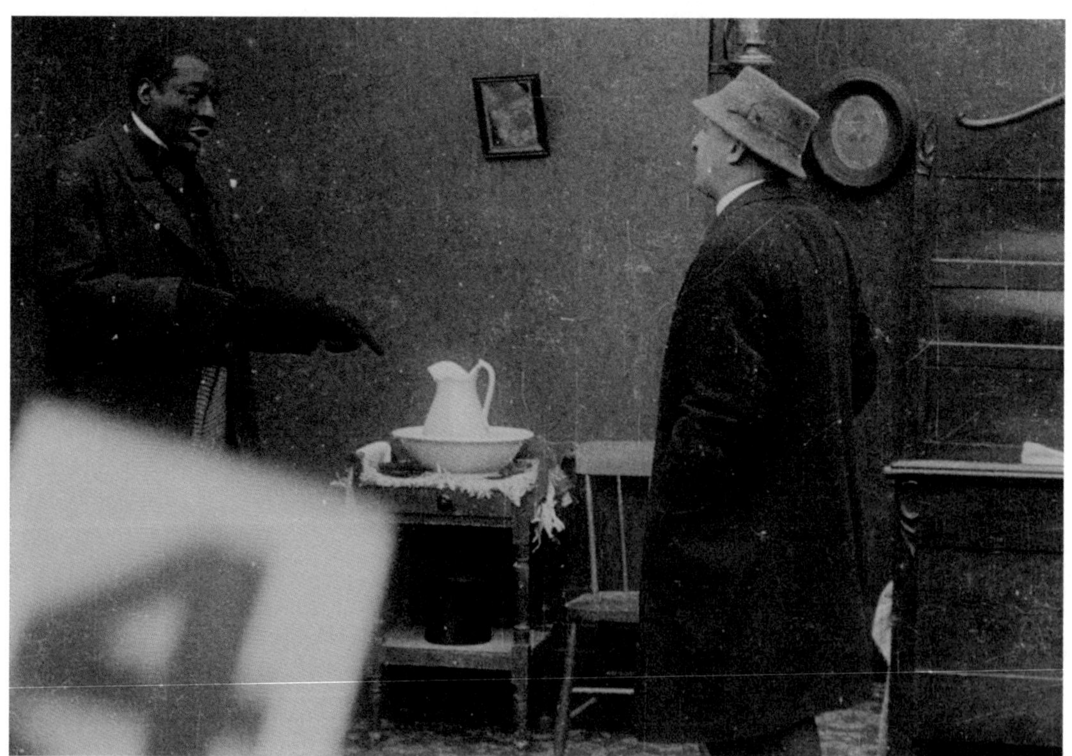

Magliozzi and his team were able to discern that the film was shot in 1913 from three distinct threads of research. The last films shot with Biograph's trademark "one-hole" camera—as this one was—were all made near the end of the year; a perusal of Williams's 1913-14 recording and performance schedule suggested he was both free and in New York in August that year; and an August 1914 obituary for production team member Sam Corker Jr., who is believed to have perished after falling off a ladder, provided the sole concrete written reference to the film: "Last fall [Corker Jr.] employed a large group of colored performers for the 'Lime Kiln Club' series of motion pictures ... in which Bert A. Williams was featured."

The obituary has been enlarged, and printed in full, near the entrance of the exhibition, and it struck me as a particularly powerful statement of intent—a strong reminder of the importance of Black behind-the-scenes involvement to complement the top-line attraction of the charismatic Williams. It also includes the line: "Corker Jr. was a fitting representative for that branch of theatricals with which few members of the race are identified or conversant—the business end." These sentiments resonate today, when issues around a lack of industry diversity, particularly at executive level, remain depressingly pertinent. Elsewhere, Magliozzi and co. were able to discern the involvement of white producers T. Hayes Hunter from prolific New York company Klaw and Erlanger, and Edwin Middleton from Biograph—these men strike a host of grandly authoritative poses in the behind-the-scenes snaps.

Though Bert Williams's story required less in-depth research—Magliozzi suggests that "he and Booker T. Washington were the two most famous Black men of their day"—it's no less fascinating. Following the premature death of his long-term performance partner George Walker in 1911, Williams went on to break the color barrier as a Black lead in the otherwise white-only casts of the Ziegfeld Follies from 1910 to 1919, where he was widely lauded for his expressive performance style, even as he was criticized in some quarters for his participation in art which reinforced negative racial stereotypes.[2]

Williams's intermittent dalliances with film, for example, were not to everybody's taste. Fascinatingly, MoMA's exhibition includes looped footage from two Biograph shorts named *Fish* and *A Natural Born Gambler* (both 1916), which locked Williams into more overtly stereotyped roles of the era.[3] A wall-mounted caption in the exhibition republishes a critique of Williams by an African American reviewer for the *Chicago Reader*: "The great ability of Bert Williams loses its charm on the screen [and] ... again demonstrates that moving picture directors know very little about what to do with the 'brother' on celluloid." This summation seems to reveal less frustration with Williams than it does with the mainstream white forces attempting to harness his talents. It also reveals the presence of a lively critical discourse within the Black press of the age.

The premiere public screening of the rushes (digital moving-image excerpts from the 35mm camera negative, including multiple takes, assembled in a semblance of narrative order) took place on the evening of Saturday, November 8 as part of the institution's twelfth annual To Save and Project festival of film preservation. The MoMA's Roy and Niuta Titus auditorium—an impressive 400-seater—was full, and buzzing with a mixture of races and ages: my screening neighbor, for example, was an excitable septuagenarian gent from Mumbai who regaled me at length with tales of a recent MoMA event about Iris Barry. A sizeable chunk of the lengthy standby queue was left disappointed, although an encore performance in January 2015 was swiftly announced.

Before the screening, Magliozzi and MoMA film preservation officer Peter Williamson further contextualized the film and its participants. One of the most chilling images in their slideshow depicted Williams in a print advertisement which championed him as an exclusive Columbia Records artist. In it, Williams sits in the foreground, free of the burnt cork, smiling gently. High in a mirror in the background, however, we see an image of Williams's blackface alter-ego looming down. The juxtaposition is clearly intended as an innocuous reference to his widely loved comic creations, but the effect today is horrifying—it's the ghoul in the reflection from whom Williams could never escape.[4]

In a contrasting register, Magliozzi drew a huge collective belly laugh by revealing that a lip-reader hired to glean the film's dialogue emerged with more contemporary-style findings than anyone had imagined: "Get the fuck out of here!", and "Where the fuck is my money?" were among the pearls deciphered.

The men discussed the potential reasons for the film's incomplete state, citing production delays and funding issues. Magliozzi argued that the 1915 release of Griffith's *Birth of a Nation* had a disastrous effect on American race relations, effectively poisoned the well for progressive filmmakers, and calcified a template for negative Black character types. Historian Donald Bogle explains: "With *Birth*, all the major screen types had been introduced. Literal and unimaginative as some types may now appear, the naive and cinematically untutored audiences of the early part of the century responded to the character types as if they were the real thing."

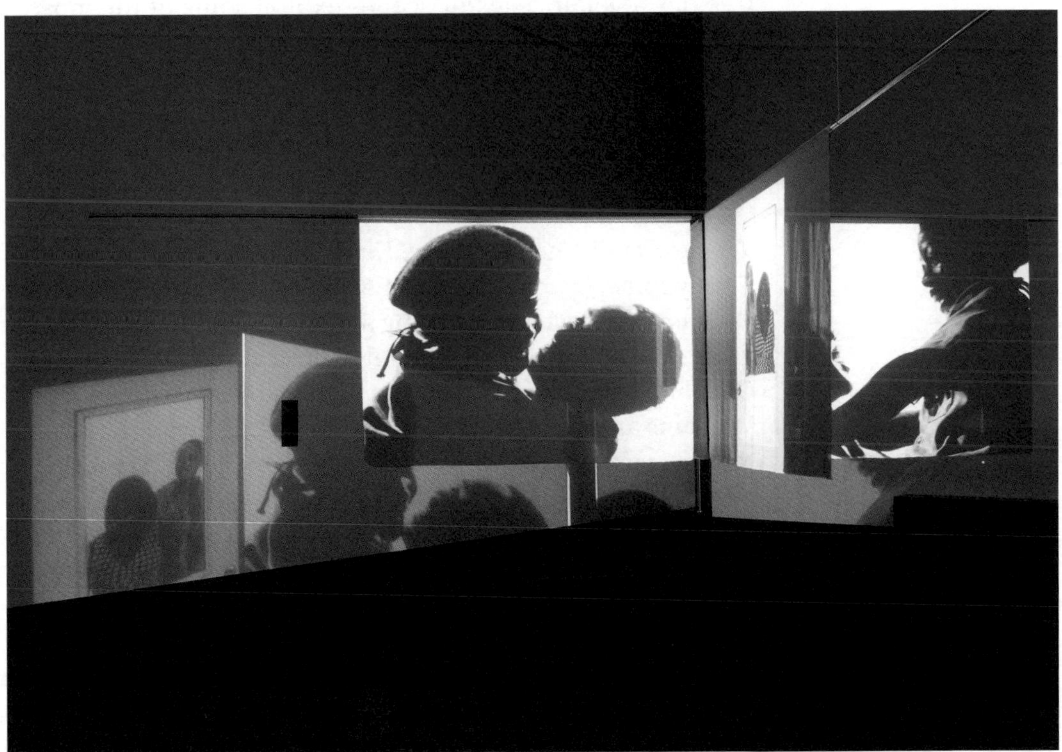

Garrett Bradley, *America*, 2019. Installation view at the Museum of Modern Art, New York, 2020

In the light of this, it seems the *Lime Kiln Club* film simply wasn't overtly racist enough. As a canny prelude to the screening, in order to contrast the rank perversion of *Birth*'s portrayal of Black characters with the forthcoming main attraction, the curators ran an infamous clip from Griffith's film: the shocking Congressional session, in which the freed Negro legislators are depicted as lustful, incompetent and arrogant.[5]

The film itself, accompanied here by a jaunty live piano score from Donald Sosin, humorously follows the travails of a top-hatted dandy and perennial schemer (Williams) who vies with two other suitors—one a dead ringer for a young Denzel Washington—for an elegant lady (Grey). Williams's character's chief obstacles seem to be his own bungling ineptitude, and his would-be paramour's disapproving mother.

The film features a host of dryly amusing domestic scenes, gatherings at a social club, a long comic set piece about Williams's "discovery" of a gin well and, at great length, a carefree day at a fair. The fair scenes exhibit some of the most jarringly regressive stereotypes associated with Black performers, including an ululating throng wrestling for loose shoes and a greased pig, a watermelon eating contest and a hundred-yard dash in which Williams clownishly bests his pint-sized competitor.

Yet the overall tone is restrained and measured, and the laughs mostly come organically, from the carefully seeded setups, and Williams's expert comic timing and hilariously precise facial expressions—he seems a clear influence on the likes of Charlie Chaplin and Harold Lloyd. In one transcendent scene featuring Williams and Grey flying around and flirting on a merry-go-round, I was temporarily able to forget completely the vexing context of Williams's blackface. The film is also notable for featuring a joyous, two-minute-long, full-cast cakewalk, the traditional African American dance which was popularized as early as 1900 by Williams, Walker and Aida Overton Walker.

One striking result of the curators' choice to include multiple takes is to render the film's ostensible simplicity a tantalizingly enigmatic slice of experimenta in its own right. Scenes pile up in layers, changing imperceptibly from moment to moment, hinting at a host of might-have-beens. Borderline subliminal, split-second flashes of an out-of-character Williams smiling warmly at the camera meanwhile carry a hauntological quality, as though there are ghosts in the fabric of the film talking to us today.

This sense of alternate pasts and futures mingling is most apparent in the gorgeous final sequence(s), when Williams may or may not get his girl—three competing takes make it unclear whether the long, tender kisses the couple share are a work of Williams's character's imagination. Even so, the effect is mightily stirring. "There's so much joy that we rarely ever see in films about Black people," Deborah Willis, the NYU chair of photography and imaging, told National Public Radio. "To see a Black man and Black woman kissing—it's an intimacy that we rarely see in Black film again during that time period." Arguably, it's the sort of vision we don't see enough of today.

Indeed, it was that final image of Williams and Grey—smiling, lips pressed together, caught in some ineffable locked groove between performance, reality, romance and laughter—which stayed with me long after I left the auditorium and disappeared into the midtown Manhattan bustle.

NOTES

1. Williams was, in fact, born in Nassau, Bahamas, to Danish and West Indian parents in 1874, meaning that he was mixed-race. MoMA's press notes refer to Williams's onstage persona as "a 'mask' he wore throughout his performing career, even in the 80 very popular recordings he made for Columbia Records." Referring to Williams as 'Black' simply illustrates the sheer complexity of discussing race and representation, yet the use of this terminology is a hedge that must do for the purposes of discussing this exhibition: Williams would have been considered 'Black' by the era's audiences, and perhaps would widely be considered so today.

2. Williams's name is invoked on a number of occasions in Spike Lee's contemporary blackface satire *Bamboozled* (2000), and appears in the closing montage of blackface performers. Magliozzi tells me that he was a little irritated by what he felt to be the film's overly negative viewpoint of Williams.

3. The title of Donald Bogle's classic book *Toms, Coons, Mulattoes, Mammies and Bucks* succinctly delineates these core, enduring stereotypes. In the shorts, Williams, despite his evidently excellent comic timing and remarkable range of facial expressions, displays the clownish bearing of the "Coon," and, particularly in *Fish*, the accommodationist impulse of the "Tom." To underscore their authenticity as compared to white men in blackface, Williams and Walker were earlier known to bill themselves as "Two Real Coons."

4. *Village Voice* theater critic Michael Feingold wrote of Williams in 2008: "Melancholy was his stock in trade. All his songs deal with misery, pain, and violence, usually visited on him. His primary activity in performance consisted of being lured from one hideous situation into a worse one. Onstage, his melancholy made audiences laugh immeasurably; offstage, a deeply inward soul, he carried it with him."

5. MoMA itself temporarily shelved *Birth of a Nation* in 1946 "[T]he potency of its anti-Negro bias ..." read the museum's press announcement, "exhibiting it at this time of heightened social tensions cannot be justified."

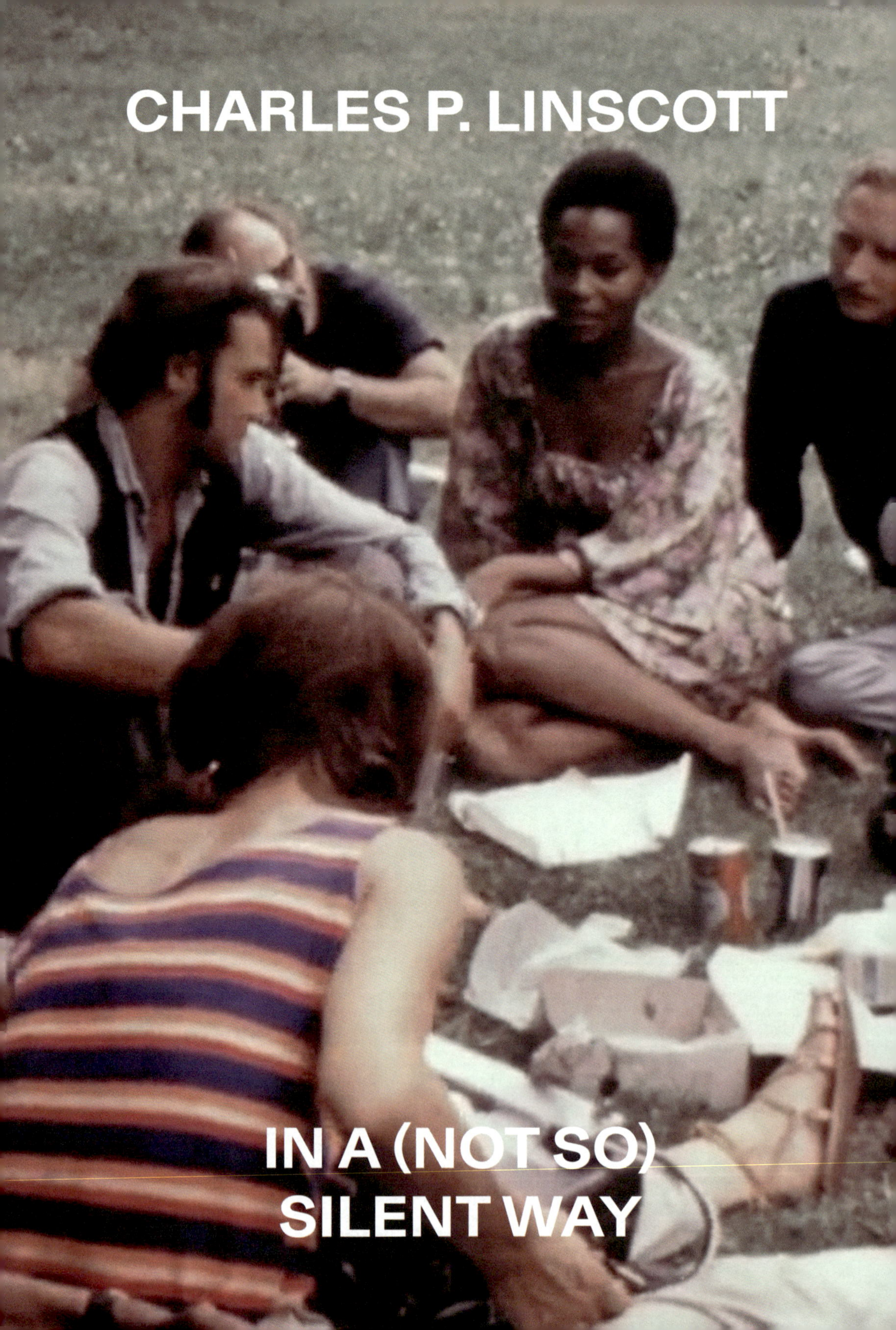
CHARLES P. LINSCOTT
IN A (NOT SO)
SILENT WAY

Listening Past Black Visuality in *Symbiopsychotaxiplasm*

Is silence simply a matter of not playing?
—John Mowitt, *Sounds: The Ambient Humanities*[1]

I always listen to what I can leave out.
—Miles Davis

But now ... let me hear your ... let me hear the sound.
—William Greaves, *Symbiopsychotaxiplasm*

Improvisation, in its divergence from the given, frequently will not allow us not to hear noise, the creaking of categorization, the noise categorization suppresses and the noise, not admitting doing so, it makes.
—Nathaniel Mackey, *Paracritical Hinge*[2]

Music in its own right is frequently considered generative and connective. Under such terms, music is a social force with the power to foster relations among people and groups and to spur social and political change. Going further, it is often argued that jazz itself is neither music nor genre but rather a critical and social practice—even a mode of being—that opens dialogue and, as Ajay Heble writes, "reinvigorates public life" and "builds purposeful communities of interest and involvement."[3] Jazz may in fact be particularly good at creating new forms of relation due to its group improvisatory nature and its emphasis on collective listening and coextension, if not cooperation.[4] When jazz happens, it is sometimes dissonant, noisy, and even disorganized—none of which are necessarily undesirable traits. The refusal of standardized form, melody, and harmony has flourished in jazz since Monk, Miles, and 1960s free music, but the potential for chaos, instability, and irreverence exists wherever groups of people spontaneously create anything. At times proximate with jazz but irreducible to it, Blackness itself can be a disruptive, performative, and critical intervention—a noisy and fecund ground rather than a sociological inevitability or a priori visual fact.[5] Moreover, there is also no doubt that jazz is Black, though not exclusively so. In the interest of such issues, I offer *Symbiopsychotaxiplasm: Take One* (dir. William Greaves, 1968), which, among other things, is a film that troubles the visual and discursive predicates of

Blackness while engaging sonic relations in ways that open both sound and race to audiovisual practices of improvisation, jazz, noise, and even remixing.[6]

In order to parse these issues, it is necessary to listen, just as improvising ensembles must listen. To listen is not to observe or perceive so much as it is to engage in a conversation; when we listen, we often involve ourselves in a relation with distinct elements of reciprocity. To listen is sometimes to diminish the primacy of vision, but it is also to augment vision. Thus, it is possible to hear (and see, more clearly) Blackness as performative, as disruptive, as relational, as noisy, as improvised, as available for reappropriation and remixing. In other words, *Symbio* distresses visuality, even as it acknowledges that the fictive essentialisms of race emerge in large part through processes of looking. The film does not ignore the objectifying processes of racialization through visuality, but as with everything in this singular work the arguments are presented

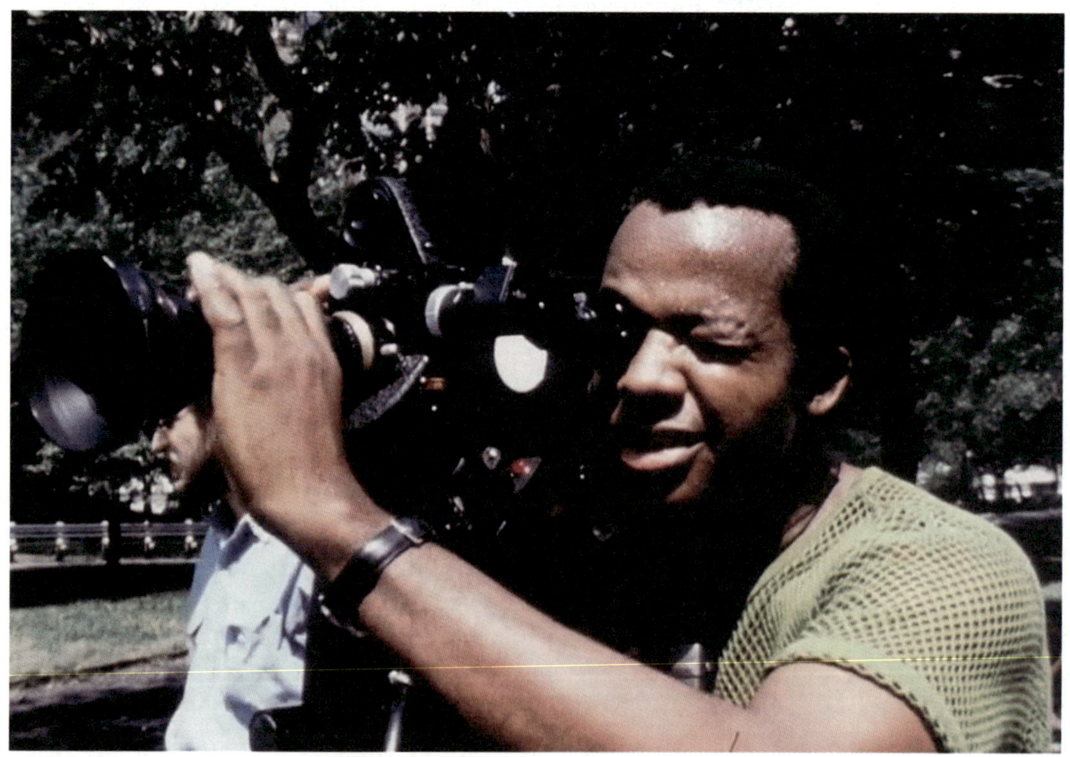

William Greaves, *Symbiopsychotaxiplasm: Take One*, 1968

in ways both labyrinthine and enigmatic—easily seen, but usually overlooked or unheard.[7] What follows is a consideration of *Symbio* in light of the common expectation that Blackness is a readily available visual fact. I argue here that a seemingly oblique or absent engagement with Blackness is foundational to the film's overarching strategies of misdirection and leads to explicit epistemological and ontological explorations of race made through sound. This approach allows me to explore the problematic nature of Black visuality, but it also provides an opportunity to explore the idea that *Symbio* lacks any perspicuous engagement with race, a common claim in critical discourses surrounding the film.[8] The film despoils essentially every standard of normative filmmaking practice and concomitantly destabilizes a priori Blackness alongside a variety of other categorical inadequacies. Ultimately, since the visual is clearly the dominant contemporary mode of engagement with Blackness, *Symbio* elides this Black visuality by figuring Blackness differently; it sounds, sings, and performs Blackness instead of strictly visualizing it.

Historically, one of the more consequential areas in which the visual is predominant is race. Throughout its rather short history, race has been defined principally by both subjective judgments of what humans look like—and therefore how they might be categorized—and by the authority to look. Regarding the latter, Nicholas Mirzoeff argues that "visuality," which he defines as "the exclusive claim to be able to look," is "part of how the 'West' historicizes and distinguishes itself from its others."[9] Regarding the former, W.J.T. Mitchell argues, in his recent provocative formulation of race as "medium," that race is not exclusively visual "but engages all the senses and signs that make human cognition, and especially *re*cognition, possible."[10] In contradistinction to the scopic capture enacted by Black visuality, many Black critical theorists offer sound as a productive ground for Black expressivity, struggle, and resistance. This critical tradition engages Black sound and music as "expressive alternatives" to vision.[11] Lindon Barrett's important theorization of the "singing voice" versus the "signing voice," or the "racialized opposition" present in "the reciprocal interests of the scopic and the phonic [as] indices of unequal cultural positions and resources," is emblematic of such thinking.[12] Paul Gilroy's arguments are also pivotal. He argues that music, as an organized subset of sound, forms a principal element of the unique expressive culture of the Black Atlantic. The system of chattel slavery predicated on epidermality indelibly marked post-slavery Black culture, Gilroy argues, concluding that a performative, embodied emphasis on orality and the musical are necessary Black-cultural counterbalances to visual apparatuses.[13] This theoretical trajectory is a significant influence on my argument, yet, to insist upon the visual as always racially circumscribing—to reduce vision to visuality—is to risk foreclosing the visual field to any challenge from Black subjectivities.[14] Thus, I ask the following: How can sound be used to dislodge the sedimented layers of racial discourses that work to define and restrict subjects coded as Black? How do some cultural productions, like *Symbio*, use sound, image, and performance to intervene in racial epistemes? Ultimately, varieties of sound—musical, vocal, noisy, silent, recombinant, aleatory, environmental, improvisational—and practices of sounding work to trouble the visual and discursive regimes that circulate and attach Blackness to subjects. While these sounds and sonic techniques are often connected to or partially embedded within visual fields, I argue that the sonic may nevertheless arouse dissonance, consonance, or harmony with the visual in matters of race; moreover, this sonic troubling of racist scopic regimes is an oft-overlooked but paradoxically highly conspicuous process deployed by objects such as *Symbio*.

Introduction and Synopsis

The film begins with a noise.[15] The director hired a heterogeneous crew—diverse in gender, ethnicity, and nationality—to shoot a film in Central Park. The fiction film they are ostensibly shooting, *Over the Cliff*, consists chiefly of a melodramatic argument between a wife and husband with serious relationship issues. Various actors portray the couple, but Patricia Ree Gilbert and Don Fellows are the most prominent pair in *Symbio*. The wife, Alice, accuses the husband, Freddie, of being closeted and having multiple gay affairs. Freddie argues that Alice has sexual hang-ups and is projecting. Alice is increasingly fed up with Freddie's cheating and wants to have a baby, citing the trauma caused by numerous abortions performed at his behest.[16] That is the extent of the fictional mise en abyme, but the real substance of the film is found outside the lovers' quarrel.

Over the Cliff is largely a ruse designed to rile up the actors and crew in the interest of exploring human relationships, group dynamics, authority, and so on. The crew are tasked with keeping three sets of cameras and portable sound recording equipment going at once, essentially forming three units: one filming the fiction scenes, the next filming that crew in a sort of behind-the-scenes fashion, and the third filming the first and second crews, along with anything else that might happen around the park. Greaves sometimes operated yet another camera himself, leading to exponential takes on many scenes, which the film often represents using split screen. The melodrama has only the barest skeleton of a script, and the crew is forced to watch multiple actors repeat the same scenes endlessly. As dozens of hours of footage pile up and the film fails to take shape, cast and crew grow increasingly frustrated with what they see as a pointless production and Greaves's variously haughty and hapless incompetence. These frustrations ultimately lead to a mutiny or palace revolt wherein the crew appropriate several rolls of film and retire to an indoor location to smoke and gripe thoughtfully about Greaves and his performance.

It seems that this is precisely how the director wants it, and the revolt scenes are some of the film's most reflexive moments. During this happening, one of the leaders of the production, Bob Rosen, turns to the camera to remark, "We may all be acting, and the director may be right outside the door right now." The indeterminacy and doubt engendered in such scenes are crucial to the film's overarching strategies. In any case, the crew is instructed to keep rolling at all costs, so the footage captures the accidents of the everyday: passersby, police, random drunks, malfunctioning equipment, and internecine strife. In a fortuitous accident, a penultimate moment of reflexivity occurs when a homeless man, Victor, wanders into the production. He has a vague French accent, carries his shoes and clothes slung over his shoulder, and rants colorfully to the crew while panhandling. He is a memorable figure, injecting a necessarily overt bit of class-consciousness into the film, and the director and crew are stunned to find that Victor and many others live in the bushes of Central Park.[17] Indeed, his commentary could hardly be more apt if it were scripted: "A movie? Who's moving whom?" he wonders.

This sort of polyphony—in the musical sense as well as the Bakhtinian sense of the term—and cacophony make *Symbio* highly complex and ripe with meaning, allowing the form to match the complexity of the film's concerns.[18] Take, for example, the multiple uses of split screen (image below). This set of images features a shot of the production crew, as it is bookended by both shot and reverse-shot simultaneously. The audio comes from multiple microphones at once. We thus hear the actors working their lines as well as various conversations among the crew, who express their frustration with errors

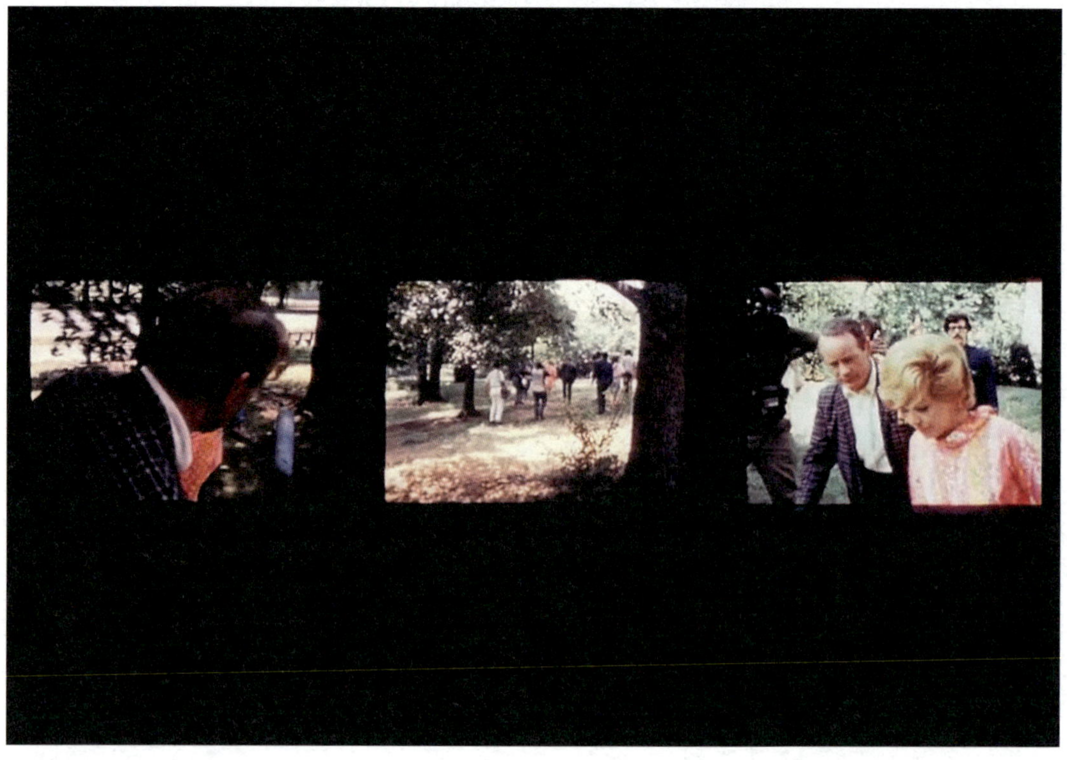

and mislaid equipment. This diversity of perspectives creates confusion, or even cacophony, and a sort of complex interplay among the various parts of the film (mise en abyme, documentary, behind-the-scenes footage, public location footage) that rewards repeated viewings, just as jazz often demands close listening. The film opens as many cinematic givens as possible to reinterpretation and rearrangement, if not complete ruin: it has no real script, the director feigns incompetence, multiple actors play the same characters, endless hours of footage are shot by three simultaneous crews, the cast and crew mutiny, the film only begins to make sense during editing, and so on. In other words, both industry-standard production practices and popular expectations of what a film should be are largely obliterated here, but there is a granular retention of the basics—acting, filming, editing—that is reconfigured into a new whole, all founded on improvisational dynamism, with a heavy and explicitly acknowledged debt to jazz. Indeed, Greaves always referred to the film as "cinematic jazz."[19] Jazz, however, can mean myriad different things.

Jazz, Improvisation, Noise, and Remixing

Here, jazz is specifically Miles Davis's *In a Silent Way*, which the film foregrounds as both a score and a formal, if not ontological, model. *Symbio* is obviously improvisational, but it engages *In a Silent Way*'s montagic improvisational jazz expressly to focalize the potential interventions of improvisational praxis itself.[20] Davis's music is a suggestive choice, as both the film and the album are composed of improvisation recorded from multiple vantages, heavily edited, and later reconstructed. *In a Silent Way* and the subsequent album *Bitches Brew* were somewhat infamously spliced together out of numerous free-form jam sessions loosely led by Miles, who provided rough ideas for his world-class combos to improvise upon, with the various takes then mixed together into a whole by producer Teo Macero. This is dangerously close to contemporary remixing practice and remains largely outside most jazz work. Not coincidentally, *Symbio* is put together in much the same way.[21] In short, the film and its music are nearly ontologically identical in their status as collective improvisation, remixed.

Notably, both *Symbio* and *In a Silent Way* accentuate the power of marginally directed group improvisation that is compiled and collated in a search for meaning.[22] In a sense, these two pioneering objects roughly envision and then create their own counter-archives, which may then be repeatedly scoured and reconfigured in enduring processual attempts to make meaning. The film, like the music, is composed of innumerable takes, and it makes meaning both during and after the act through editing. This is meaning as improvisational relation, but it is also meaning remixed.

Following this complex set of formal practices is the film's nearly unpronounceable title. The word "symbiotaxiplasm," without the "psycho," reflects Greaves's eclectic inspirations, including the work of Arthur F. Bentley, a contemporary of John Dewey who attempted to formulate a theory of the social that included micro-interactions among the socius, groups, and surrounding materiality. Greaves draws on Bentley's "symbiotaxiplasm," which in turn drew upon turn-of-the-century physiologist Michael A. Lane's "symbiotaxiosis."[23] The "psycho" represents Greaves's interest in psychoanalysis and human psychological states. Ultimately, Greaves's experiment was an attempt to set up and record, before finally editing down and analyzing, the incredible complexity of human's interactions with one another and the surrounding environment. This interactivity—the semi-scripted extemporization of the actors and the quotidian relations among the crew and between the crew and park patrons—is foundationally improvisational. Thus, improvisation forms the raw material of the film and even extends into the postproduction process of editing, where Greaves cuts and mixes the footage together in whatever ways feel right to him at the time—thus, multiple takes. It is this ontological modality of edited group improvisation, so rarely employed in most other filmmaking, that helps get to some of the difficult answers in the film.[24] As Nathaniel Mackey has said, improvisation insists "that the given is only the beginning, that arrangements as we find them are subject to change, rearrangement."[25] For jazz musicians, as for the trained actors and film crew Greaves hired, improvisation is not necessarily a fracas entered into without preparation—which is not to say that all improvisation, especially of the vital quotidian sort, requires education.[26] Careful study and refined skills are focalized during improvisation, especially in jazz playing. In improvisation, something unique emerges out of a shared performative temporality, something that precedes normative judgments and that could not be composed in advance. As it is in jazz, so it is in this film. *Symbio* understands improvisation as both the potential for the creation of the new and the equally powerful potential for everything to fall apart, for chaos to reign. This does not necessarily imply that order is normative, but rather that large groups being spontaneous together always holds the potential for a variety of responses, many of which are not necessarily harmonious. In short, improvisation can be very noisy, and varying subjectivities, by definition, bring difference to the process and constantly modulate the outcomes, regardless of the predetermined boundaries and idealized expectations. If there is a leader, the leader's expectations and boundaries are, as a matter of practice, met, strained, exceeded, or torpedoed by the improvisational practice. In this way, the improvisational is sometimes the noisy and is often the unexpected—or even and especially the response to the unexpected—and the noisy is also the political, and it is also the Black.[27]

Prior critical discourse tends to emphasize the contextual importance of Greaves as a Black auteur at a time where there were so few; in other words, the outside of the film impinges on its inside. This is by no means a controversial or even questionable stance to take as a critic: the anti-Blackness that (con)founds Western modernity makes Greaves and his work all the more important, but it proves the point: in its initiatory context, its critical-historical reception, and the present milieu, Greaves's Blackness is remarkable even when it remains unremarked upon, yet the fact of his Blackness foisted upon him neither requires nor prohibits that his art be Black. Still, I believe that the film engages Blackness in highly original, oblique (yet noisy) fashion, just as it does nearly everything else.

Nevertheless, a recent spate of scholarship attempts to parse why race is seemingly absent from *Symbio* when it is an overriding concern of most of Greaves's other films.[28] The overt racial politics of Greaves's previous work are of deep significance here: take, for example, a contemporaneous two-page *New York Times* piece wherein Greaves referred to himself as "Furious Black" and advocated a Black social and mediatic revolution in a powerfully written and strident denunciation of structural and ideological anti-Black racism.[29] To say nothing of strong denunciations regarding the "obligations" of Black artists to produce Black art, where is Greaves's strident Blackness in *Symbio*? Again, I suggest that it is in the sound, in the improvisation, in the performance, in the jazz, in the oppositionality, and in the noise. Not incidentally, there is a precedent here in Miles, who famously used flubbed notes, noises, and so-called non-musical sounds throughout his career, a fact that a number of critics have cited as his tragic flaw. Yet, other writers like David Ake and Ted Gioia argue that Miles Davis's music engages an "aesthetics of imperfection" that not only incorporates mistakes, voices, flubbed notes, and noises, but in so doing, returns an awareness of the body to jazz recordings.[30] Sometimes, sounds are better than words; noises are better than speech, and the oblique is precisely the point. Put differently, Blackness is regularly sonic, noisy, and performative, and is very much in line with the dynamic that Greaves endeavors to create in *Symbio*, from the film's title to its very last image and sounds.

Indeed Blackness, like so many other things in the film, is subjected to misdirection rather than absence. Blackness is absent here only as an aporia constructed in part by visual regimes that configure it as a lack. In this sense, Blackness is always absent, even when it is present, which is a key point the film makes through a voice that withholds visual signification and direct address of Blackness in favor of more subtle cues that are easily detected—with the right ear. Greaves did not simply abandon his passionate engagement with racial politics, but it would make no sense, in a film that goes to great pains to refuse the stentorian announcement of anything, to proclaim Blackness in starkly literal terms. A work as singular and enigmatic and complex as *Symbio* must offer a singular and enigmatic and complicated approach to Blackness. *Symbio* does not straightforwardly address race through a frontal turn toward the camera by the famously "furious Black" director. Instead, the film refracts race, breaking off pieces and sending them flying; it does this for two reasons: because the film is deliberately unobvious about most things and because race itself is never straightforward. Sometimes, to turn away says more than speaking out. Put differently, when looking relations are constructed in such a way as to code subjects as raced, the ontological resistance of those subjects is denied or broken down.[31] The film presumes an audience that perceives race through an uncritically habituated visuality. Thus, the film need not loudly proclaim matters of race because the culture in which the film exists and in which it is exhibited perpetually *sees through race* without bothering to trouble Black visuality. Since the culture of looking in which *Symbio* emerges is constantly thinking and talking about race *for* William Greaves, albeit not in the ways he would like, he takes this highly experimental opportunity to find other ways of saying things, other ways of *singing* things.

Take the opening credit sequence. Maria San Filippo has likened the extended opening credit sequence to Dziga Vertov in that editing is used to chronicle the cycles of human reproduction in linear order, from birth to death.[32] At the end of this sequence, there is a sound. Clearly, there are sounds throughout the film, but this one stands out. It is a strange, high-pitched tone that gradually increases in volume until it is nearly intolerable. While it is mixed in with the funky jazz of the film's score and ambient sounds from the park, somehow this sound *feels* different.[33] It seems to be separate from many of the other sounds. It is discernible but inarticulate, eluding easy identification. It is a bit grating. It is persistent. Perhaps it is a noise. Perhaps it should not be there. But this is hard to say: amid the busy, near-cacophony of the diegetic sounds from Central Park, plus the boisterous fusion music of the soundtrack, the source of this potentially unpleasant sound is obscured, just as its propriety within the audible portion of the sensorium is obscured. Do the filmmakers or scoring musicians want this sound there? Is it coming from the many ambient sounds of the park, or from the music, or from some sort of malfunctioning filmmaking equipment, or from some malfunctioning playback equipment with which we, the audience, are watching and listening to *Symbio*? Listening closely, this sound—this squeal or screech—becomes part of the music. It might be from a 1960s-era synthesizer, or a theremin, or electric guitar feedback, or from electrical interference coming through a speaker; it might be composed and played purposefully, or it might be a malfunction, accidental.

As this sequence winds down, and the music fades along with it, Greaves hears the squeal too, as do other crew members. We realize that he is hearing what we hear. He does not seem to like it (image below). The director asks to hear the sound coming through the headphones that monitor the recording. As he places headphones on his head, he pronounces what he hears "dreadful." He appears shocked by its unpleasantness. But things are still somewhat oblique, as so much is in this film. Is Greaves actually hearing what the film's audience is hearing? Is the squeal we hear coming through his headphones? Is the noise what sounds dreadful to him, or is it something else entirely? Or, perhaps Greaves likes that sound, and it is

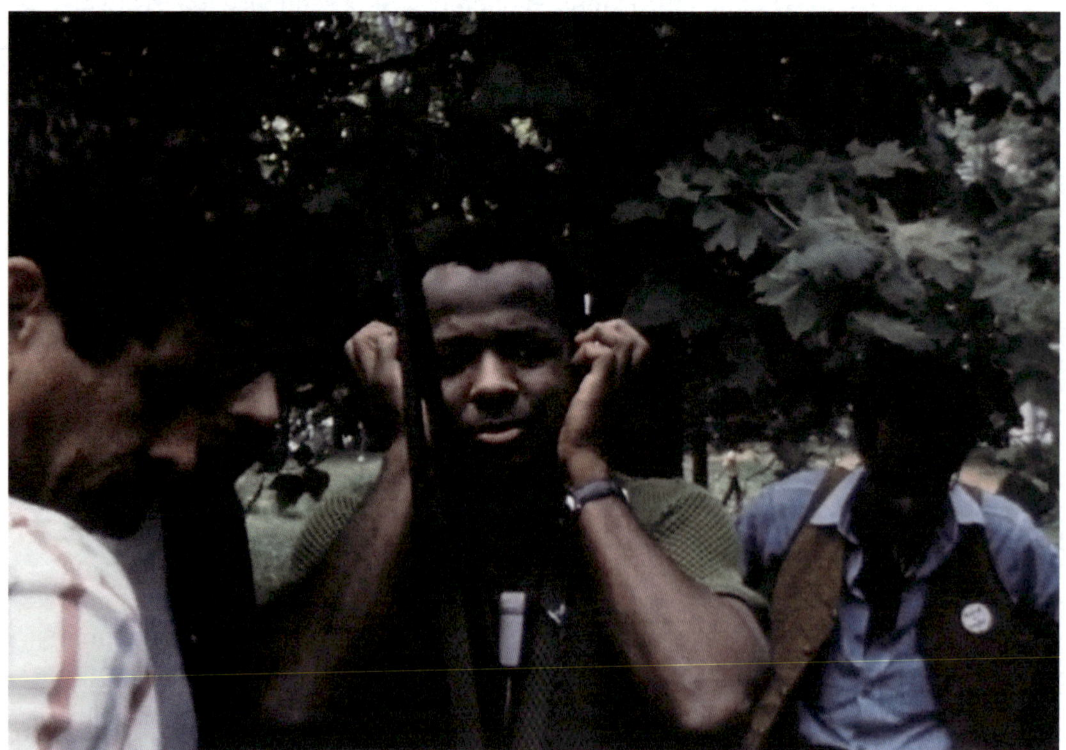

everything else that he hears that sounds terrible. Does he also hear the jazz music, with which the noise has been so expertly synced on the soundtrack? On the other hand, maybe the director does not hear anything at all, just dead air in the headphones, and that is what is distressing—his deprivation of sound, his lack of hearing. Or, perhaps Greaves is just acting. It is all just acting, in the end, is it not? Of course, *Symbio* is a performance and an improvisation. It comes together as a series of intertwining improvisational interactions coaxed from an eclectic ensemble by a charismatic, if recalcitrant and mysteriously taciturn (band) leader—a man with a rough string of ideas (not a chart or script, just some provocative notes) who lets things roll endlessly, seeing and hearing what occurs, only to try to mix all the noise together into something coherent later on. But as the squeal moves across scenes from which it likely did not originate, it blends in with the score; it is remixed into the music. This noise seems to be both within and outside of the narrative—it is *transdiegetic*.[34] And it forms the very last moment of the film as well—the noise in *Symbio* is alpha and omega, and it is of a piece with the heavily edited improvisations of *In a Silent Way*.

This is some of the Blackness of *Symbio*: a Blackness that disrupts, that unsettles, that is not settled; a Blackness that surprises, that mediates, that criticizes; a Blackness that is not determinate but is also not inessential; a Blackness that is accented and accentual; a Blackness that is troubling but not untroubled; a *noisy Blackness that sings*. In singing Blackness, *Symbio* implies that traditional methods of talking about Blackness have been exhausted. Greaves attempted to convey his points in a variety of mediums, from film to television to print, before finally concluding in the *Times*—wherein he identified himself as "Furious Black"—that "100 Madison Avenues" could not help resist white hegemony.[35] What was left to say via conventional modes? In this fashion, *Symbio* is a "break" in Fred Moten's varied sense of the term: a splitting, a cut, a tear, a departure, a solo. And, like all solos, the ride ends, and the soloist steps back into the group; Greaves would never again attempt anything so radically experimental, perhaps because so few people could hear the music he was making.

In any case, halfway through the film, amid the diverse chatter of various production units and an intense face-to-face conversation between Greaves and his two lead actors, we hear an offscreen crew member (Jonathan Gordon, the sound engineer) lament, "Ah, there's no mic on Bill, man! Where's that mic?" The failure of recording technologies is an insistent trope in the film. As the audible dialogue fades out completely, another sort of hectic conversation, "It's about That Time," from *In a Silent Way*, fades in. Talking is supplanted by music. The actors and director are still speaking; however, the dialogue is inaudible—we see this—but we hear it *in a silent way*. Their lips keep moving, but Miles Davis's music is doing all the talking (image below). The music becomes the focal point of communication through a ventriloquial substitution. This is but one instance leading to the realization that the film tells us things that it does not necessarily say using words, that it speaks languages of misdirection and singing, voicing ideas about race that transcend the immediate

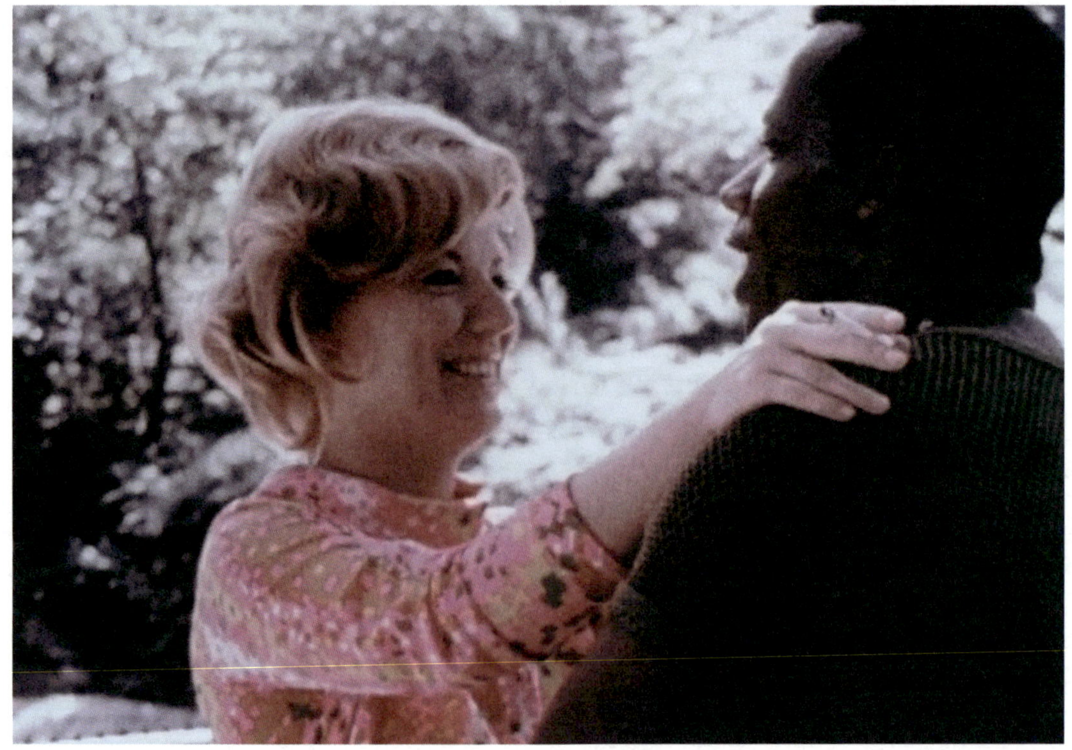

accessibility preferred by a culture dominated by racist scopic regimes. "It's about That Time" is busy music. To be sure, it is collective, funky improvisation among diverse electronic and acoustic instrumentalists, with a strong bass vamp and very little precomposed before recording, and it "interrupts" the equally busy location-based audio (ambient sounds and dialogue) of the film. Diegetic audio and nondiegetic music quite regularly bleed into each other throughout *Symbio*, with the nearly cacophonous dialogue of the production and the ambient sounds of the park (captured simultaneously by the three mobile audio recording rigs) fading out as the music fades in, and vice versa.

This use of sound reveals the lexical as merely a single source of language among many.[36] Polyphony tempting cacophony is thus a founding move of *Symbio*. The uninhibited group improvisational music often comes in just when things seem to be falling apart in the film shoot. The music plays and the noises get louder when speech will no longer suffice. This constant flirtation with dissolution, a collective improvisation that is loosely proctored by a leader with an elastic set of expectations, is very much like jazz. As David P. Brown writes, jazz reflects "the tenuous balance between object and action by which such borders maintain their tentative relations with the forces they organize, and how they are inherently subject to change, capable of resisting closure and objectification by acknowledging and engaging noise."[37] In other words, the apparent disorder of improvisation embraces change and indeterminacy through its assignation with noise, the spontaneous, and the aleatory. While it is important not to fetishize noise nor to grant it utopian powers, the (re)organization of forces against closure and objectification that is the hallmark of improvisatory praxis implies precisely the sort of confounding of normative Black visuality that *Symbio* works to achieve.[38] Again, as Greaves makes a film that breaks all the rules, it should not be surprising that Blackness will also be deconstructed—not absent, but reconfigured, challenged, and upended. As Moten points out, improvisation is a performative necessity for Blackness.[39] And, following the epigraph from Mackey at the beginning of this essay, we must recall that improvisation is a divergence from the given that refuses to allow the integral noise of categorization to be suppressed.[40] In terms of information theory, to remix may be to introduce noise into a system through appropriation and reconfiguration, so to remix from an improvisationally founded counter-archive is doubly, even exponentially, noisy.

Oppositional Performance and Anamnesis

Greaves inserts noise into the production of his film and into the lives and work of his crew in a variety of ways. Perhaps the most visible are his seeming incompetence and directionless leadership, but these foibles and failures all appear to be part of the plan. Greaves here performs the character of a director without a clue, but this is a ruse, as the director is in actuality highly accomplished and technically expert.[41] This stance, and all of the film, reflects what W.T. Lhamon calls "the optic black, or the widespread refusal to fit"; Lhamon contends that "performers who underwrite these propositions [of the optic black] drive the machine inside the machine of American vernacular art. They open spaces in public where an alternative to optic whiteness can do its oppositional work. That work is chiefly the display of a widespread refusal to fit."[42] In other words, the unsettling of expectation and the radical refusal to conform are foundational to a certain sort of Blackness that has in turn been fundamental to American (and, by turns, global) popular culture.[43] Greaves's oppositional film and his oppositional performance within that film refuse to comply with most expectations, including the expectation that Blackness be a facilely conceptualized and overtly proclaimed theme of the production.

So much of the scholarship on this film explores the limits of its reflexivity: whether or not Greaves's character in the film is genuine, how much was scripted, how much was planned, how much was a happy accident. All of this contributes to contextualization and certainly adds depth to the understanding of a historically important and tragically neglected film, yet I think it misses a crucial point that I have been driving at herein and that Lhamon articulates as well. To wonder who Greaves really is in the film is to simultaneously accept and reject the fundamentally performative character of his character; it is to meet, but then overlook, the performativity of not just Greaves as Greaves but also of Blackness itself. If the "optic black" is the vernacular refusal to fit, then Greaves effects an ambiguous posture in part to confound notions of authorship but also to confound notions of race. Greaves is signifyin', but that does not make Blackness absent, just differently directed.[44] This different direction for Blackness is plain to hear (and see) but sometimes gets lost in the mix. In this way, *Symbio* is nothing less than a redirection of the furious kinetic energies of Blackness through Greaves's performativity.[45]

The tensions surrounding Greaves's failures as a director come to a head during the aforementioned mutiny scene that is cut up and interspersed throughout the film. The scene is the apotheosis of the political and aesthetic promises and perils of a certain sort of loosely directed improvisation. In the scene, the heterogeneous crew debates the merits and perils of Greaves's leadership and the deceptive possibilities inherent in the potential failure of the film. Some see it as a disaster, some a put-on, but all have something to say. Here in life, as in art, each player longs for a chance to play; each speaker wants to use her voice, which can be a noisy, difficult, but politically essential process. Greaves is the leader, but his players are playing what they feel as they feel it. This is a very jazzy happening—a series of collective improvisational moments where everyone gets a break. In a brief introduction to his exploration of duende (following Lorca's monumental "Play and Theory of the Duende," from 1933), Nathaniel Mackey sees an opportunity to uncover both musical and poetic aspirations to a speaking beyond the possible in the frustration of voicelessness and the pursuit of a different, augmentary, or metavoice.[46] Mackey gestures toward "musical practices that achieve rending and dialogic effects and to poetry's cultivation of the bivocality or polyvocality of multiple meaning," extending all the way to "intermedia supplementation, the alternate voice one medium affords another or proffers the model of to another ... raising questions of translation or translatability and collaboration between media."[47] This is a signal part of what noise, improvisation, performativity, and jazz do in *Symbio*: provide an augmentary voice that speaks beyond the possible, figuring Blackness differently in order to obviate the "commonsensical" notion that Blackness is something that can be plainly seen.

The transpositional capacities of noise, the power of jazz, and the free response of spontaneous, improvised group performance are imperative here. When the screeching sound that begins the film appears at the end of *Symbio*, it is yet again mixed with Miles Davis's "It's about That Time." There is still confusion among the crew over the source of the squeal, and the director once again dons the headphones, as he did in the beginning: he wants to *listen* as closely as he can. When the noise dissipates in the beginning of the film, birds are heard chirping in the park. At the end of the film, a siren overlaps the squealing, but unlike at the beginning, the noise does not end until the film does. Noise is the very last thing we hear, and throughout, sounds are everywhere. Not coincidentally, the last image of the film is a zoom-in to extreme close-up

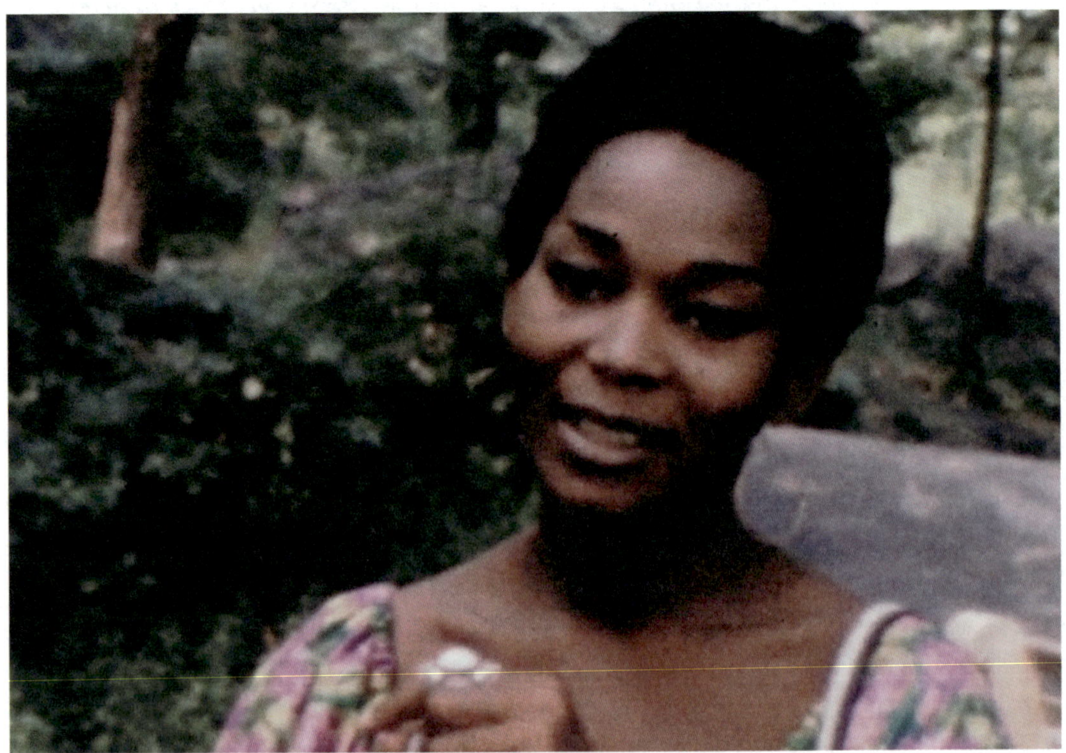

on a freeze frame of the face of Black actress Audrey Henningham, who portrays Alice in both films, but much more in *Take 2 1/2* than in *Symbio*. When the striking, squealing noise and the jazz music come together once again, along with the frozen face of Henningham, anamnesis—"the often involuntary revival of memory caused by listening and the evocative power of sounds ... reconnecting past mental images to present consciousness" is triggered, and the film's take on Blackness finally begins to coalesce.[48]

The combined effect of beginning and end is anamnestic and transpositional: we cannot fully understand the film until its end, after everything has passed, and whereupon earlier enigmas—in particular, the mysterious recurrent noise that bookends the film—make more sense.[49] All this is to say that where *Symbio* arrives at an enforced remembered connection between a beginning and an end, it does so in a less direct fashion than many audiences expect. Where frantic linear movement through the human lifespan provided images for the jazzy, noisy sounds in the beginning of the film, the stridently frozen image of a Black woman's face is yoked to the noise and then silence (the absence of all soundtrack whatsoever) along with a fade to different kind of black at the end of the film.

In essence, Greaves has provided the keys to deciphering an initially cryptic engagement with Blackness by placing an establishing shot as the finale of his film. When this final shot is connected to the jazzy, noisy establishing shots of the credit sequence and the repeated irruptions of noise and jazz throughout the film, Greaves's confounding creation may at last be decrypted. In this way, the film sings its arguments more than it directly signs them, which is why critics so often overlook these points, watching instead for a stentorian announcement of Blackness when Blackness is being performed right in front of them.[50] In *Symbio*, the beginning and end and all in between are similarly noisy and spontaneous but are shunted through the filter of the editor's mix, just as is Miles's music. Like existence itself, this is noise of which we endeavor to make sense, both as it occurs immediately and as we recall it later.

In the end, the mysterious and repeated failure of technology in *Symbio* draws attention to the similarly aligned positivistic faith in the ready visual legibility and empirical existence of Blackness.[51] Contra such empiricism, Blackness brings the noise into systems like racialization that only appear fixed. Each time technology fails in the film, Greaves listens closely and is satisfied. This is because, in many ways, *Symbio* is an extended and intricate allegorical meditation on the perils of looking at race and the possibilities of listening to it and spontaneously riffing upon it. Like Blackness, improvisation is not monolithic, uniform, or universalizable. Improvisation, noise, and Blackness are formed through diverse sets of culturally, historically, and individually variable practices that move and make meaning in innumerable, yet still specific, ways. But we must listen in order to hear.[52] When we do listen carefully, we hear that many things sound Black, but how Black sounds is often surprising.

NOTES

1. John Mowitt, *Sounds: The Ambient Humanities* (Oakland: University of California Press, 2015), 106.

2. Nathaniel Mackey, "Paracritical Hinge," *in Paracritical Hinge: Essays, Talks, Notes, Interviews* (Madison: University of Wisconsin Press, 2005), 209.

3. Ajay Heble, *Landing on the Wrong Note: Jazz, Dissonance, and Critical Practice* (New York: Routledge, 2000), xi.

4. James Tobias, *Sync: Stylistics of Hieroglyphic Time* (Philadelphia: Temple University Press, 2010), 149. Jazz, Tobias writes "works as a historical resource extensible across media."

5. Fred Moten, *In the Break: The Aesthetics of the Black Radical Tradition* (Durham, NC: Duke University Press, 2003), 255n1. Michael B. Gillespie, "Reckless Eyeballing: *Coonskin*, Film Blackness and the Racial Grotesque," in *Contemporary Black American Cinema: Race, Gender, and Sexuality at the Movies*, ed. Mia Mask (New York: Routledge, 2012), 56. Moten argues that "Blackness is always a disruptive surprise moving in the rich non-fullness of every term it modifies ... [s]uch mediation suspends neither the question of identity nor the question of essence" but is manifested through the "inscriptional events of a set of performances" that insist upon a rethinking of identity and essence. Gillespie argues for the "multi-accentual quality of Blackness as critical mediation and practice rather than ontological or biological determinate." These are but a few examples.

6. Greaves's film runs roughly seventy-five minutes; it is composed of heavily edited footage culled from many more hours of raw material and was shot outdoors in Central Park (the palace revolt scenes, during which the crew mutinies, were shot indoors). The director intended to produce up to five feature-length takes edited from the original shoot but shelved the project when distribution for the first take proved elusive. I focus only on *Symbiopsychotaxiplasm: Take One*. A sequel of sorts, *Symbiopsychotaxiplasm: Take 2 1/2* (Greaves, 2003) incorporates some of the original unused footage and is included on Criterion's DVD release. Steve Buscemi and Steven Soderbergh supported the new film, while also helping the original achieve renewed attention on the festival circuit in the 1990s. Personally, I do not find *Take 2 1/2* as compelling as *Symbiopsychotaxiplasm: Take One*.

7. The yoking of visual difference to ideological notions of racial essence may variously be called epidermality (particularly where the visual difference is based on skin color), Black visuality, and so on.

8. Paul Arthur, *A Line of Sight: American Avant-Garde Film since 1965* (Minneapolis: University of Minnesota Press,

2005). Franklin Cason Jr. and Tsitsi Jaji, "Symbiopsychotaxiplasticity," *Cultural Studies* 28, no. 4 (2014): 576: Akiva Gottlieb, "Just Another Word for Jazz: The Signifying Auteur in William Greaves's *Symbiopsychotaxiplasm: Take One*," *Black Camera* 5, no. 1 (2013). Charles Musser and Adam Knee, "William Greaves, Documentary Filmmaking, and the African American Experience," in *Cinemas of the Black Diaspora: Diversity, Dependence, and Oppositionality*, ed. Michael T. Martin (Detroit: Wayne State University Press, 1995), 389–404. Scholarship on the film tends to place its Blackness into two categories—missing or contextual—or some combination thereof. Gottlieb is chief among those who find the film largely empty of Black politics or aesthetics (he claims Blackness is a "structuring absence" in *Symbio*). Arthur discusses Greaves's importance to Black independent filmmaking. Cason and Jaji, much like Knee and Musser, situate the film in terms of Greaves's extensive and important oeuvre, which consists principally of film and television productions that overtly address Black history and culture. In addition, Cason and Jaji compare *Symbio* and *Take 2 1/2* in an effort to reveal the films' political engagements within a continuum of Greaves's work. This latter (contextual) approach may be seen as something of an answer to the question of wherein the film's Blackness exists, if it does so at all. Clearly, I am arguing something rather different: that a complex, conscious, and vital sort of Blackness is very much present in *Symbio* itself, even if it appears absent on the surface.

9. Nicholas Mirzoeff, *The Right to Look: A Counterhistory of Visuality* (Durham, NC: Duke University Press, 2011), 2, xiv.

10. W.J.T. Mitchell, *Seeing through Race* (Cambridge, MA: Harvard University Press, 2012), xii–xiii, emphasis in the original. Mitchell's thesis is contentious, as he argues for the usefulness of race as a concept following decades of work revealing race as a destructive mythology. He does not renaturalize race, though.

11. The intersections of Blackness and sound might be referred to as "Black sonicity."

12. Lindon Barrett, *Blackness and Value: Seeing Double* (Cambridge: Cambridge University Press, 1999), 216.

13. Paul Gilroy, *The Black Atlantic: Modernity and Double Consciousness* (Cambridge, MA: Harvard University Press, 2003), 75.

14. Nicole Fleetwood, *Troubling Vision: Performance, Visuality, and Blackness* (Chicago: University of Chicago Press, 2011), 16–18. Despite the use of visual apparatuses and scopic regimes for the circumscription, definition, and subjugation of Black subjects, Fleetwood argues that totalizing vision through equivalence between looking and racial repression is a trap from which Black identities cannot escape. As Fleetwood argues, the Black body may provide a critical, constructively "troubling presence to the very scopic regimes that define it" as a disquieting figuration.

15. I say that the film begins with noise, but, strictly speaking, that is incorrect. There are roughly four minutes of pre-credit sequences that establish the primary conceit of the film, namely, that it is a melodramatic and heated lovers' quarrel acted out by several different diverse pairs of actors. Once these scenes from the melodrama are finished, the true heft of the film begins to emerge, as we see the production crews and the director in the process of making a film. Also after these four minutes, the music plays, and the music, as I have said, is crucial.

16. There is a distinct current of homophobia in the scenes that discuss or depict Freddie's alleged queerness. Both the film's crew and the characters in *Over the Cliff* call Freddie a "faggot." Thus, the homophobia occurs within the diegesis of the melodrama and outside it, in the so-called documentary. I suspect this slur was common parlance in the sexual and gender politics of the time, yet, as with everything else in the film, we must recall the tendency to trouble sedimented categories. For example, when Greaves makes a misogynist remark about a woman's "tits" later in the film, he immediately follows it up with a reflexive turn, breaking the fourth wall and directly addressing the camera: "I'm kidding. Don't take me seriously."

17. Scott MacDonald, *The Garden in the Machine: A Field Guide to Independent Films about Place* (Berkeley: University of California Press, 2001), 242.

18. Musically, polyphony describes the simultaneous coexistence of multiple unique melodies within the same musical piece. While the parts often harmonize with one another, each melody is distinct and of roughly equal prominence. In *Symbio*, for example, the screeching noise and the jazz music are musically polyphonic as they co-occur. For Bakhtin, polyphony means the presence of many voices within every individual voice. In other words, Bakhtin shows that every seemingly discrete notion is composed of a multiplicity of other influential notions. This applies to people, ideas, art, and so on. See note 36, below.

19. Scott MacDonald, *A Critical Cinema 3: Interviews with Independent Filmmakers* (Berkeley: University of California Press, 1998), 59.

20. Attempting to define jazz is a losing proposition. Indeed, many of its most renowned practitioners have disavowed the word, going so far as to sneer or insult interviewers and critics who dared to label their music with the seemingly innocuous title. Again, Greaves often described the film as a sort of "audiovisual jazz" or "cinematic jazz," drawing attention both to Blackness and to the potential for the unexpected to emerge out of group and individual spontaneity. So, whether a musician plays something she prefers to simply call music, or American classical music (following Baraka), or jass, or refuses generic classification altogether, it is safe to say that jazz, for both Greaves and many musicians, has a core of improvisation. But not all improvisational music is jazz. Jazz probably has to *swing*, another term with various denotations, and thus the difficulty.

21. Cason and Jaji, "Symbiopsychotaxiplasticity," 590. The authors momentarily examine the use of Miles's music in *Symbio* and make brief mention of the important formal resonances between the film and *In a Silent Way*. They go on to contrast this with Greaves's use of Ron Carter's music in *Take 2 1/2*.

22. As I have noted, while the music was played by Davis's ensemble, the editing for *In a Silent Way* was famously performed by Teo Macero, who would achieve renown and criticism working with Miles in this fashion on a number of classic albums. For *Symbio*, Greaves was the primary force in the editing room, but the raw material was provided by the cast, crew, public, and so on.

23. James F. Ward, *Language, Form, and Inquiry: Arthur F. Bentley's Philosophy of Social Science* (Amherst: University of Massachusetts Press, 1984), 110.

24. MacDonald, *The Garden in the Machine*, 244.

25. Nathaniel Mackey, "Introduction: Door Peep (Shall Not Enter)," in *Paracritical Hinge*, 8–9.

26. Stefano Harney and Fred Moten, *The Undercommons: Fugitive Planning and Black Study* (Wivenhoe, England: Minor Compositions, 2013), 50. As Moten and Harney argue, improvisation is "something not but almost nothing other than the spontaneous."

27. Following my argument through, I want to reiterate the resonances among Blackness, jazz, noise, and improvisation. These relationships are not simply a matter of historical origination and artistic accreditation—not simply jazz as reduced to Blackness, nor vice versa. On the contrary, I am proposing that *Symbio* readily engages the same forces, perils, and potentials as the improvising jazz ensemble. Again, jazz is adept at creating new relations through improvisation, collective listening, and coextension. Such relations are not necessarily harmonious, though. Jazz may be dissonant, chaotic, noisy, and diffuse—often desirously so—and the potential for disruption, variability, and ingenuity exists wherever groups of people spontaneously create anything. In other words, jazz and improvisation abet the potential Blackness of everyday life, and this is a Blackness that is mobile and available for reappropriation and remixing. Once more, this leads to a consideration of Blackness itself as a disruptive, noisy, performative, relational, and critical intervention rather than a sociological determinant or a priori visual certainty.

28. As delineated above, Gottlieb ("Just Another Word for Jazz") and Cason/Jaji ("Symbiopsychotaxiplasticity") have published most recently on the film. Gottlieb considers Blackness a "structuring absence" in *Symbio*, and he addresses the contextual significance of Black directorial control in a white industry during a period of pronounced racial and political unrest. Cason and Jaji find Greaves's *Symbio* films (the first and its sequel) to be of a piece with his more overt, politically engaged works, although they also see Blackness, excepting the jazz influence, as largely outside *Symbio*'s purview. Part of what I am arguing is that the jazziness of the film and its score/soundtrack, far from being merely referential, are explicit and foundational engagements with Blackness.

29. William Greaves, "100 Madison Avenues Will Be of No Help," *New York Times*, August 9, 1970. So far as I know, Gottlieb is responsible for bringing this article into the critical discourse, which is a great service to scholarship on Greaves and the film.

30. David Ake, *Jazz Matters: Sound, Place, and Time since Bebop* (Berkeley: University of California Press, 2010), 37–53. Ted Gioia, *The Imperfect Art* (New York: Oxford University Press, 1988), 56.

31. Frantz Fanon, *Black Skin, White Masks*, trans. Richard Philcox (New York: Grove Press, 2008), 90. Fanon unpacks the connections between ontology and skin color throughout chapter 5 of the book. See, most famously, Fanon's incident on the train with the white French child: "The black man has no ontological resistance in the eyes of the white man."

32. Maria San Filippo, "What a Long, Strange Trip It's Been: *Symbiopsychotaxiplasm: Take One*," *Film History* 13, no. 2 (2001): 216–25.

33. In scholarship on the film, this particular opening credit music is almost always referred to as part of Miles Davis's *In a Silent Way*. I strongly suspect it is not Miles Davis, and it is definitely not part of that particular album. I cannot locate the track on any released version, including the *Complete In a Silent Way*, which includes hours of alternate takes. Other superb musicians—including Miles's keyboard player, Joe Zawinul, who also composed the track "In a Silent Way"—contributed music to the soundtrack. I believe this track comes from one of those artists, not Davis, which is why I do not identify it.

34. Transdiegesis refers to sounds or other elements that are both within the fictional world of the film and outside of it, or that seem to extend through different incongruous parts of a film's fictional world. Film scores are principally extradiegetic in that they exist for the audience but not for the film's characters. There are exceptions—transdiegetic elements—and such exceptions are often imbued with complex and weighty, if not ambiguous, significations.

35. Greaves, "100 Madison Avenues Will Be of No Help."

36. Mikhail M. Bakhtin, *Problems of Dostoevsky's Poetics*, trans. Caryl Emerson (Minneapolis: University of Minnesota Press, 1984); Mikhail M. Bakhtin, *The Dialogic Imagination: Four Essays*, trans. Caryl Emerson and Michael Holquist (Austin: University of Texas Press, 1981). This is polyphony and heteroglossia, two key Bakhtinian concepts. Polyphony (many voices) refers to the idea that each individual "voice" (a subjectivity, concept, artwork, etc.) actually contains the influences of many other voices. Heteroglossia—literally, "the speech of the other"—is closely connected. Dialogism, a third interrelated Bakhtinian concept, indicates the import of all voices through time as they "speak" to each other across past, present, and future.

37. David P. Brown, *Noise Orders: Jazz, Improvisation, and Architecture* (University of Minnesota Press, 2006), xxvi.

38. Hillel Schwartz, *Making Noise: From Babel to the Big Bang & Beyond* (New York: Zone Books, 2011), 22. Schwartz provides a helpful cautionary note against either overtly dystopian or excessively utopian conceptions of noise: "common are polemics urging us either to act against a mounting cacophony or to applaud noise as ground and guidepost to political, artistic, or cultural transfiguration. Aroused by the peals of resurgent environmentalism or the quavers of postmodernism, such polemics quickly shift from an ill defined past to an unrefined present."

39. Fred Moten, "The Subprime and the Beautiful," *African Identities* 11, no. 2 (2013), 239. "Preservation [of blackness/ black life] is . . . improvisation," Moten tells us.

40. Mackey, "Paracritical Hinge," 209.

41. The repeated failure of sound technology is all the more unlikely given the contextual fact that Greaves worked as a professional sound recordist on dozens of film and television productions.

42. W.T. Lhamon Jr., "Optic Black: Naturalizing the Refusal to Fit," in *Black Cultural Traffic*, ed. Harry J. Elam Jr. and Kennell Jackson (Ann Arbor: University of Michigan Press, 2005), 112.

43. Significantly, one need not actually be Black to effect the "optic black." Although Lhamon does not mention him, think Eminem, for instance.

44. Gottlieb discusses Greaves's use of signifyin' practices but leaves the Blackness of said practices largely unexamined.

45. Put differently, "Furious Black" is still furious, he is simply no longer screaming.

46. Mackey, "Introduction: Door Peep," 13–14.

47. Ibid., 14–15.

48. Jean-François Augoyard and Henry Torgue, eds., *Sonic Experience: A Guide to Everyday Sounds*, trans. Andra McCartney and David Paquette (Montreal: McGill-Queen's University Press, 2005), 21.

49. The use of sonic anamnesis as alpha and omega in a film is rare, but not unprecedented. In the film *Vidas secas / Barren Lives* (dir. Nelson Pereira dos Santos, 1963), for example, the screeching noise that begins and ends the film reoccurs several times throughout, sometimes non-diegetically. (The film is based on Graciliano Ramos's groundbreaking novel of the same name, from 1938.) Eventually, the diegesis reveals to the audience that the screech emanates from a barely functioning wagon wheel used by the destitute family of laborers who eke out a bare existence in the arid Brazilian *sertão*. This revelation triggers anamnesis, attaching the noise of the wheel to both the remembered sound heard earlier and the images of the hobbled cart. Further, this noise is now also attached to the *idea* of the exploitation of the *lumpenproletariat* and their starkly barren lives ("vidas" means lives, and "secas" means dry or barren in Portuguese) in the desolate Brazilian backlands. *Vidas secas* and *Symbiopsychotaxiplasm* are interesting when thought together due to their common affinities, most particularly their shared connections to the production practices of neorealism and cinema verité. An obvious point of departure lies in editing; *Vidas secas*, like Cinema Novo more broadly, tends to minimize editing and emphasize long takes. Greaves, inspired by Eisensteinian montage, obviously used editing to the fullest.

50. Jean-Jacques Nattiez, *Music and Discourse: Toward a Semiology of Music*, trans. Carolyn Abbate (Princeton, NJ: Princeton University Press, 1990); Naomi Cumming, *The Sonic Self: Musical Subjectivity and Signification* (Bloomington: Indiana University Press, 2000); Kofi Agawu, *Music as Discourse: Semiotic Adventures in Romantic Music* (Oxford: Oxford University Press, 2009). There is a sense in which musical semiotics has something to say here, but concerns of space and focus prevent me from pursuing this angle. There are a number of interesting texts on musical semiotics, many of which take fairly divergent approaches to their formulations of semiosis. I find these three of particular note. Nattiez is the "godfather" of musical semiotics.

51. Essentially, the film is focalized through an "aesthetics of imperfection," or even an "aesthetics of failure," but not failure in the colloquial or vernacular sense. This is an imperfection as celebrated by jazz (Gioia, Ake) and a failure as understood by noise (Hegarty) and through the lens of what Jack Halberstam calls "the queer art of failure." As technologies fail to "capture" the complex realities of human interactions and relationships; as political and dialogical encounters fail to arrive at concrete, lasting solutions; as heteronormative marriage fails to become the apotheosis of romantic and sexual partnerships; as a director and his cast and crew fail to make a "real" movie; as sound recordings fail into noise; as celluloid runs out, and surveillance fails in its aspirations toward ubiquitous capture; as auteurism, that typically reliable interpretive grid, fails as a hermeneutic, if not in practice; as cinematic distribution networks tragically, yet reliably, fail; then radical possibilities emerge. If *Symbiopsychotaxiplasm* fails, it fails up, as the saying goes. If *Take One* is difficult to categorize, cacophonous, strange, singular, oppositional, and provides no "easy answers," that is precisely as it should be. It fails because it must fail in order to succeed.

52. R. Murray Schafer, *The Soundscape: Our Sonic Environment and the Tuning of the World* (Rochester, VT: Destiny Books, 1993). As usual, some terminological clarification is in order. The most important distinction is perhaps between "hearing" and "listening." R. Murray Schafer popularized this distinction within sound studies in his work *The Soundscape*, but it has been made many times, by many others. Hearing means using one's auditory sense; it is a function of perception by which our ears receive a sound and send it to the brain. Listening means to use one's auditory senses carefully, to concentrate in order to hear something vigilantly, perhaps with an added level of understanding.

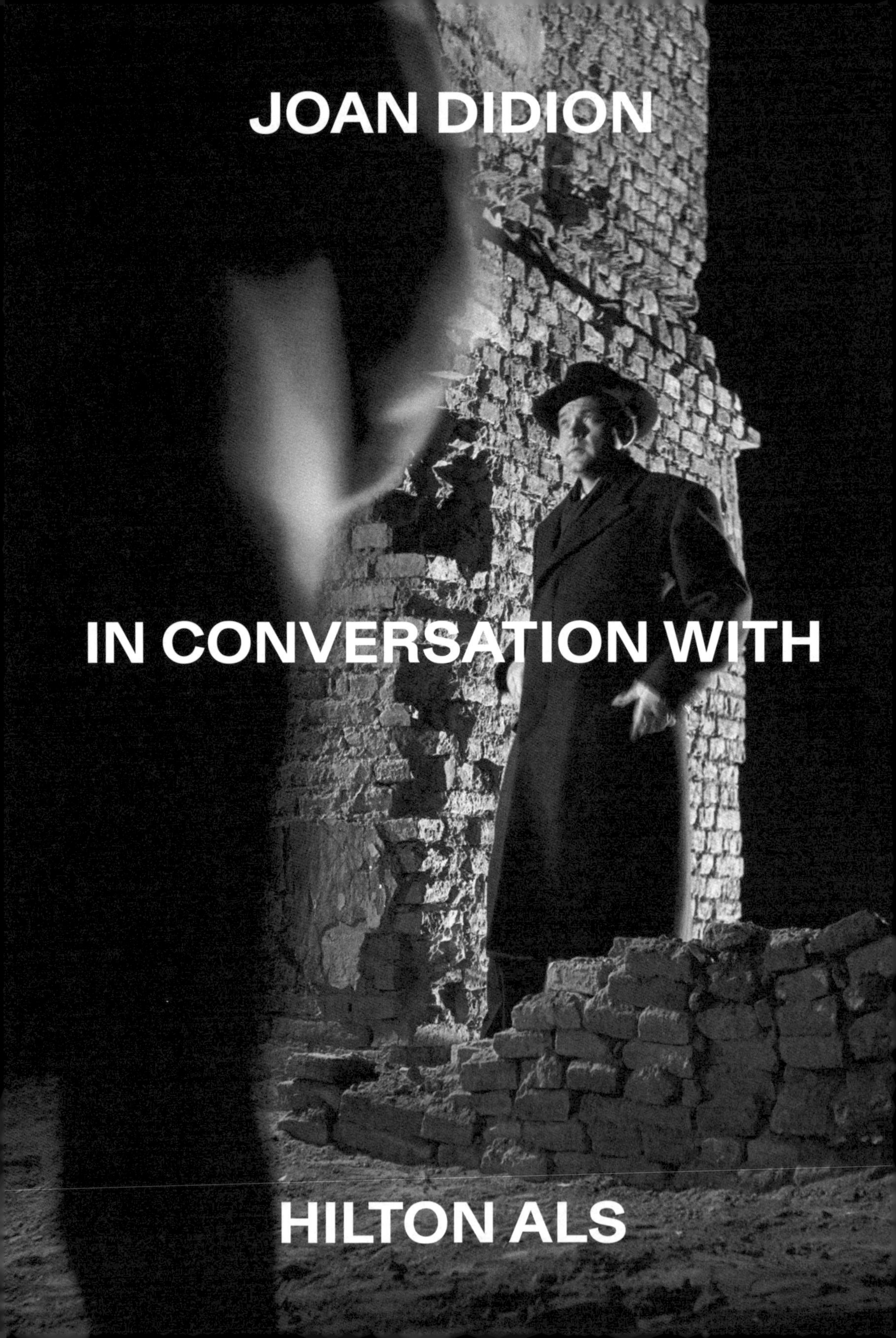

JOAN DIDION

IN CONVERSATION WITH

HILTON ALS

The Art of Nonfiction No. 1

Our conversation took place over the course of two afternoons in the Manhattan apartment Didion shared with her husband, John Gregory Dunne. On the walls were many photos of Didion, Dunne, and their daughter. Daylight flooded the book-filled parlor. "When we got the place, we assumed the sun went all through the apartment. It doesn't," Didion said, laughing. Her laughter was the additional punctuation to her precise speech.

Hilton Als: By now you've written at least as much nonfiction as you have fiction. How would you describe the difference between writing the one or the other?

Joan Didion: Writing fiction is for me a fraught business, an occasion of daily dread for at least the first half of the novel, and sometimes all the way through. The work process is totally different from writing nonfiction. You have to sit down every day and make it up. You have no notes—or sometimes you do, I made extensive notes for *A Book of Common Prayer*—but the notes give you only the background, not the novel itself. In nonfiction the notes give you the piece. Writing nonfiction is more like sculpture, a matter of shaping the research into the finished thing. Novels are like paintings, specifically watercolors. Every stroke you put down you have to go with. Of course you can rewrite, but the original strokes are still there in the texture of the thing.

HA: Do you do a lot of rewriting?

JD: When I'm working on a book, I constantly retype my own sentences. Every day I go back to page 1 and just retype what I have. It gets me into a rhythm. Once I get over maybe a hundred pages, I won't go back to page 1, but I might go back to page 55, or 20, even. But then every once in a while I feel the need to go to page 1 again and start rewriting. At the end of the day, I mark up the pages I've done all the way back to page 1. I mark them up so that I can retype them in the morning. It gets me past that blank terror.

HA: Did you do that sort of retyping for *The Year of Magical Thinking*?

JD: I did. It was especially important with this book because so much of it depended on echo. I wrote it in three months, but I marked it up every night.

HA: The book moves quickly. Did you think about how your readers would read it?

JD: Of course, you always think about how it will be read. I always aim for a reading in one sitting.

HA: At what point did you know that the notes you were writing in response to John's death would be a book for publication?

JD: John died December 30, 2003. Except for a few lines written a day or so after he died, I didn't begin making the notes that became the book until the following October. After a few days of making notes, I realized that I was thinking about how to structure a book, which was the point at which I realized that I was writing one. This realization in no way changed what I was writing.

HA: Was it difficult to finish the book? Or were you happy to have your life back—to live with a lower level of self-scrutiny?

JD: Yes. It was difficult to finish the book. I didn't want to let John go. I don't really have my life back yet, since Quintana died only on August 26.

HA: Since you write about yourself, interviewers tend to ask about your personal life; I want to ask you about writing and books. In the past you've written pieces on V.S. Naipaul, Graham Greene, Norman Mailer, and Ernest Hemingway—titanic, controversial iconoclasts whom you tend to defend. Were these the writers you grew up with and wanted to emulate?

JD: Hemingway was really early. I probably started reading him when I was just eleven or twelve. There was just something magnetic to me in the arrangement of those sentences. Because they were so simple—or rather they appeared to be so simple, but they weren't.

Something I was looking up the other day, that's been in the back of my mind, is a study done several years ago about young women's writing skills and the incidence of Alzheimer's. As it happens, the subjects were all nuns, because all of these women had been trained in a certain convent. They found that those who wrote simple sentences as young women later had a higher incidence of Alzheimer's, while those who wrote complicated sentences with several clauses had a lower incidence of Alzheimer's. The assumption—which I thought was probably erroneous—was that those who tended to write simple sentences as young women did not have strong memory skills.

HA: Though you wouldn't classify Hemingway's sentences as simple.

JD: No, they're deceptively simple because he always brings a change in.

HA: Did you think you could write that kind of sentence? Did you want to try?

JD: I didn't think that I could do them, but I thought that I could learn—because they felt so natural. I could see how they worked once I started typing them out. That was when I was about fifteen. I would just type those stories. It's a great way to get rhythms into your head.

HA: Did you read anyone else before Hemingway?

JD: No one who attracted me in that way. I had been reading a lot of plays. I had a misguided idea that I wanted to act. The form this took was not acting, however, but reading plays. Sacramento was not a place where you saw a lot of plays. I think the first play I ever saw was the Lunts in the touring company of *O Mistress Mine*. I don't think that that's what inspired me. The Theater Guild used to do plays on the radio, and I remember being very excited about listening to them. I remember memorizing speeches from *Death of a Salesman* and *Member of the Wedding* in the period right after the war.

HA: Which playwrights did you read?

JD: I remember at one point going through everything of Eugene O'Neill's. I was struck by the sheer theatricality of his plays. You could see how they worked. I read them all one summer. I had nosebleeds, and for some reason it took all summer to get the appointment to get my nose cauterized. So I just lay still on the porch all day and read Eugene O'Neill. That was all I did. And dab at my face with an ice cube.

HA: What you really seem to have responded to in these early influences was style—voice and form.

JD: Yes, but another writer I read in high school who just knocked me out was Theodore Dreiser. I read *An American Tragedy* all in one weekend and couldn't put it down—I locked myself in my room. Now that was antithetical to every other book I was reading at the time because Dreiser really had no style, but it was powerful.

And one book I totally missed when I first read it was *Moby-Dick*. I reread it when Quintana was assigned it in high school. It was clear that she wasn't going to get through it unless we did little talks about it at dinner. I had not gotten it at all when I read it at her age. I had missed that wild control of language. What I had thought discursive were really these great leaps. The book had just seemed a jumble; I didn't get the control in it.

HA: After high school you wanted to go to Stanford. Why?

JD: It's pretty straightforward—all my friends were going to Stanford.

HA: But you went to Berkeley and majored in literature. What were you reading there?

JD: The people I did the most work on were Henry James and D.H. Lawrence, who I was not high on. He irritated me on almost every level.

HA: He didn't know anything about women at all.

JD: No, nothing. And the writing was so clotted and sentimental. It didn't work for me on any level.

HA: Was he writing too quickly, do you think?

JD: I don't know, I think he just had a clotted and sentimental mind.

HA: You mentioned *Moby-Dick*. Do you do much rereading?

JD: I often reread *Victory*, which is maybe my favorite book in the world.

HA: Conrad? Really? Why?

JD: The story is told thirdhand. It's not a story the narrator even heard from someone who experienced it. The narrator seems to have heard it from people he runs into around the Malacca Strait. So there's this fantastic distancing of the narrative, except that when you're in the middle of it, it remains very immediate. It's incredibly skillful. I have never started a novel—I mean except the first, when I was starting a novel just to start a novel—I've never written one without rereading *Victory*. It opens up the possibilities of a novel. It makes it seem worth doing. In the same way, John and I always prepared for writing a movie by watching *The Third Man*. It's perfectly told.

HA: Conrad was also a huge inspiration for Naipaul, whose work you admire. What drew you to Naipaul?

JD: I read the nonfiction first. But the novel that really attracted me—and I still read the beginning of it now and then—is *Guerillas*. It has that bauxite factory in the opening pages, which just gives you the whole feel of that part of the world. That was a thrilling book to me. The nonfiction had the same effect on me as reading Elizabeth Hardwick—you get the sense that it's possible simply to go through life noticing things and writing them down and that this is OK, it's worth doing. That the seemingly insignificant things that most of us spend our days noticing are really significant, have meaning, and tell us something. Naipaul is a great person to read before you have to do a piece. And Edmund Wilson, his essays for *The American Earthquake*. They have that everyday-traveler-in-the-world aspect, which is the opposite of an authoritative tone.

HA: Was it as a student that you began to feel you were a writer?

JD: No, it began to feel almost impossible at Berkeley because we were constantly being impressed with the fact that everybody else had done it already and better. It was very daunting to me. I didn't think I could write. It took me a couple of years after I got out of Berkeley before I dared to start writing. That academic mind-set—which was kind of shallow in my case anyway—had begun to fade. Then I did write a novel over a long period of time, *Run River*. And after that it seemed feasible that maybe I could write another one.

HA: You had come to New York by then and were working at *Vogue*, while writing at night. Did you see writing that novel as a way of being back in California?

JD: Yes, it was a way of not being homesick. But I had a really hard time getting the next book going. I couldn't get past a few notes. It was *Play It as It Lays*, but it wasn't called that—I mean it didn't have a name and it wasn't what it is. For one, it was set in New York. Then, in June of 1964, John and I went to California and I started doing pieces for the *Saturday Evening Post*. We needed the money because neither one of us was working. And during the course of doing these pieces I was out in the world enough that an actual story for this so-called second novel presented itself, and then I started writing it.

HA: What had you been missing about California? What were you not getting in New York?

JD: Rivers. I was living on the East Side, and on the weekend I'd walk over to the Hudson and walk back to the East River. I kept thinking, All right, they are rivers, but they aren't California rivers. I really missed California rivers. Also the sun going down in the West. That's one of the big advantages to Columbia-Presbyterian hospital—you can see the sunset. There's always something missing about late afternoon to me on the East Coast. Late afternoon on the West Coast ends with the sky doing all its brilliant stuff. Here it just gets dark.

The other thing I missed was horizons. I missed that on the West Coast, too, if we weren't living at the beach, but I noticed at some point that practically every painting or lithograph I bought had a horizon in it. Because it's very soothing.

HA: Why did you decide to come back east in 1988?

JD: Part of it was that Quintana was in college here, at Barnard, and part of it was that John was between books and having a hard time getting started on a new one. He felt it was making him stale to be in one place for a long time. We had been living in Brentwood for ten years, which was longer than we had ever lived in any one place. I think he just thought it was time to move. I didn't particularly, but we left. Even before moving, we had a little apartment in New York. To justify having it, John felt that we had to spend some periods of time there, which was extremely inconvenient for me. The apartment in New York was not very comfortable, and on arrival you would always have to arrange to get the windows washed and get food in ... It was cheaper when we stayed at the Carlyle.

HA: But when you finally moved to New York, was it a bad move?

JD: No, it was fine. It just took me about a year, maybe two years all told. The time spent looking for an apartment, selling the house in California, the actual move, having work done, remembering where I put things when I unpacked—it probably took two years out of my effective working life. Though I feel that it's been the right place to be after John died. I would not have wanted to be in a house in Brentwood Park after he died.

HA: Why not?

JD: For entirely logistical reasons. In New York I didn't need to drive to dinner. There wasn't likely to be a brush fire. I wasn't going to see a snake in the pool.

HA: You said that you started writing for the *Saturday Evening Post* because you and John were broke. Is that where the idea of working for movies came from—the need for cash?

JD: Yes it was. One of the things that had made us go to Los Angeles was we had a nutty idea that we could write for television. We had a bunch of meetings with television executives, and they would explain to us, for example, the principle of *Bonanza*. The principle of *Bonanza* was: break a leg at the Ponderosa. I looked blankly at the executive and he said, Somebody rides into town, and to make the story work, he's got to break a leg so he's around for two weeks. So we never wrote for *Bonanza*. We did, however, have one story idea picked up by *Chrysler Theatre*. We were paid a thousand dollars for it.

That was also why we started to write for the movies. We thought of it as a way to buy time. But nobody was asking us to write movies. John and his brother Nick and I took an option on *The Panic in Needle Park* and put it together ourselves. I had read the book by James Mills and it just immediately said *movie* to me. I think that the three of us each put in a thousand dollars, which was enormous at the time.

HA: How did you make it work as a collaboration? What were the mechanics?

JD: On that one, my memory is that I wrote the treatment, which was just voices. Though whenever I say I did something, or vice versa, the other person would go over it, run it through the typewriter. It was always a back-and-forth thing.

HA: Did you learn anything about writing from the movie work?

JD: Yes. I learned a lot of fictional technique. Before I'd written movies, I never could do big set-piece scenes with a lot of different speakers—when you've got twelve people around a dinner table talking at cross-purposes. I had always been impressed by other people's ability to do that. Anthony Powell comes to mind. I think the first book I did those big scenes in was *A Book of Common Prayer*.

HA: But screenwriting is very different from prose narrative.

JD: It's *not* writing. You're making notes for the director—for the director more than the actors. Sydney Pollack once told us that every screenwriter should go to the Actors Studio because there was no better way to learn what an actor needed. I'm guilty of not thinking enough about what actors need. I think instead about what the director needs.

HA: John wrote that Robert De Niro asked you to write a scene in *True Confessions* without a single word of dialogue—the opposite of your treatment for *The Panic in Needle Park*.

JD: Yeah, which is great. It's something that every writer understands, but if you turn in a scene like that to a producer, he's going to want to know where the words are.

HA: At the other end of the writing spectrum, there's the *New York Review of Books* and your editor there, Robert Silvers. In the seventies you wrote for him about Hollywood, Woody Allen, Naipaul, and Patty Hearst. All of those essays were, broadly speaking, book reviews. How did you make the shift to pure reporting for the *Review*?

JD: In 1982, John and I were going to San Salvador, and Bob expressed interest in having one or both of us write something about it. After we'd been there a few days, it became clear that I was going to do it rather than John, because John was working on a novel. Then when I started writing it, it got very long. I gave it to Bob, in its full length, and my idea was that he would figure out something to take from it. I didn't hear from him for a long time. So I wasn't expecting much, but then he called and said he was going to run the whole thing, in three parts.

HA: So he was able to find the through-line of the piece?

JD: The through-line in "Salvador" was always pretty clear: I went somewhere, this is what I saw. Very simple, like a travel piece. How Bob edited "Salvador" was by constantly nudging me toward updates on the situation and by pointing out weaker material. When I gave him the text, for example, it had a very weak ending, which was about meeting an American evangelical student on the flight home. In other words it was the travel piece carried to its logical and not very interesting conclusion. The way Bob led me away from this was to suggest not that I cut it (it's still there), but that I follow it—and so ground it—with a return to the political situation.

HA: How did you decide to write about Miami in 1987?

JD: Ever since the Kennedy assassination, I had wanted to do something that took place in that part of the world. I thought it was really interesting that so much of the news in America, especially if you read through the assassination hearings, was coming out of our political relations with the Caribbean and Central and South America. So when we got the little apartment in New York, I thought, Well that's something useful I can do out of New York: I can fly to Miami.

HA: Had you spent time down south before that?

JD: Yes, in 1970. I had been writing a column for *Life*, but neither *Life* nor I was happy with it. We weren't on the same page. I had a contract, so if I turned something in, they had to pay me. But it was soul-searing to turn things in that didn't run. So after about seven columns, I quit. It was agreed that I would do longer pieces. And I said that I was interested in driving around the Gulf Coast, and somehow that got translated into "The Mind of the White South." I had a theory that if I could understand the South, I would understand something about California, because a lot of the California settlers came from the Border South. So I wanted to look into that. It turned out that what I was actually interested in was the South as a gateway to the Caribbean. I should have known that at the time because my original plan had been to drive all over the Gulf Coast.

We began that trip in New Orleans and spent a week there. New Orleans was fantastic. Then we drove around the Mississippi Coast, and that was fantastic too, but in New Orleans, you get a strong sense of the Caribbean. I used a lot of that week in New Orleans in *Common Prayer*. It was the most interesting place I had been in a long time. It was a week in which everything everybody said was astonishing to me.

HA: Three years later you started writing for the *New York Review of Books*. Was that daunting? In your essay "Why I Write" you express trepidation about intellectual, or ostensibly intellectual, matters. What freed you up enough to do that work for Bob?

JD: His trust. Nothing else. I couldn't even have imagined it if he hadn't responded. He recognized that it was a learning experience for me. Domestic politics, for example, was something I simply knew nothing about. And I had no interest. But Bob kept pushing me in that direction. He is really good at ascertaining what might interest you at any given moment and then just throwing a bunch of stuff at you that might or might not be related, and letting you go with it.

When I went to the political conventions in 1988—it was the first time I'd ever been to a convention—he would fax down to the hotel the front pages of the *New York Times* and the *Washington Post*. Well, you know, if there's anything you can get at a convention it's a newspaper. But he just wanted to make sure.

And then he's meticulous once you turn in a piece, in

terms of making you plug in all relevant information so that everything gets covered and defended before the letters come. He spent a lot of time, for example, making sure that I acknowledged all the issues in the Terri Schiavo piece, which had the potential for eliciting strong reactions. He's the person I trust more than anybody.

HA: Why do you think he pushed you to write about politics?

JD: I think he had a sense that I would be outside it enough.

HA: No insider reporting—you didn't know anyone.

JD: I didn't even know their names!

HA: But now your political writing has a very strong point of view—you take sides. Is that something that usually happens during the reporting process, or during the writing?

JD: If I am sufficiently interested in a political situation to write a piece about it, I generally have a point of view, although I don't usually recognize it. Something about a situation will bother me, so I will write a piece to find out what it is that bothers me.

HA: When you moved into writing about politics, you moved away from the more personal writing you'd been doing. Was that a deliberate departure?

JD: Yes, I was bored. For one thing, that kind of writing is limiting. Another reason was that I was getting a very strong response from readers, which was depressing because there was no way for me to reach out and help them back. I didn't want to become Miss Lonelyhearts.

HA: And the pieces on El Salvador were the first in which politics really drive the narrative.

JD: Actually it was a novel, *Common Prayer*. We had gone to a film festival in Cartagena and I got sick there, some kind of salmonella. We left Cartagena and went to Bogotà, and then we came back to Los Angeles and I was sick for four months. I started doing a lot of reading about South America, where I'd never been. There's a passage by Christopher Isherwood in a book of his called *The Condor and the Cows*, in which he describes arriving in Venezuela and being astonished to think that it had been down there every day of his life. That was the way that I felt about South America. Then later I started reading a lot about Central America because it was becoming clear to me that my novel had to take place in a rather small country. So that was when I started thinking more politically.

HA: But it still didn't push you into an interest in domestic politics.

JD: I didn't get the connection. I don't know why I didn't get the connection, since I wasn't interested in the politics of these countries per se, but rather in how American foreign policy affected them. And the extent to which we are involved abroad is entirely driven by our own domestic politics. So I don't know why I didn't get that.

I started to get this in *Salvador*, but not fully until *Miami*. Our policy with Cuba and with exiles has been totally driven by domestic politics. It still is. But it was very hard for me to understand the process of domestic politics. I could get the overall picture, but the actual words people said were almost unintelligible to me.

HA: How did it become clearer?

JD: I realized that the words didn't have any actual meaning, that they described a negotiation more than they described an idea. But then you begin to see that the lack of specificity is specific in itself, that it is an obscuring device.

HA: Did it help you when you were working on *Salvador* and *Miami* to talk to the political figures you were writing about?

JD: In those cases it did. Though I didn't talk to a lot of American politicians. I remember talking to the then president of El Salvador, who was astounding. We were talking about a new land reform law and I explained that I couldn't quite understand what was being said about it. We were discussing a provision—Provision 207—that seemed to me to say that landowners could arrange their affairs so as to be unaffected by the reform.

He said, 207 always applied only to 1979. That is what no one understands. I asked, Did he mean that 207 applied only to 1979 because no landowner would work against his interests by allowing tenants on his land after 207 took effect? He said, Exactly, no one would rent out land under 207. They would have to be crazy to do that.

Well, that was forthright. There are very few politicians who would say exactly.

HA: Was it helpful to talk with John about your experiences there?

JD: It was useful to talk to him about politics because he viscerally understood politics. He grew up in an Irish Catholic family in Hartford, a town where politics was part of what you ate for breakfast. I mean, it didn't take *him* a long time to understand that nobody was saying anything.

HA: After *Salvador*, you wrote *Democracy*. It seems informed by the reporting you were doing about America's relationship to the world.

JD: The fall of Saigon, though it takes place offstage, was the main thing on my mind. Saigon fell while I was teaching at Berkeley in 1975. I couldn't get those images out of my head, and that was the strongest impulse behind *Democracy*. When the book came out, some people wondered why it began with the bomb tests in the Pacific, but I think those bomb tests formed a straight line to pushing the helicopters off the aircraft carriers when we were abandoning Saigon. It was a very clear progression in my mind. Mainly, I wanted to show that you could write a romance and still have the fall of Saigon, or the Iran-Contra affair. It would be hard for me to stay with a novel if I didn't see a very strong personal story at the center of it.

Democracy is really a much more complete version of *Common Prayer*, with basically the same structure. There is a narrator who tries to understand the character who's being talked about and reconstruct the story. I had a very clear picture in my mind of both those women, but I couldn't tell the story without standing way far away. Charlotte, in *Common Prayer*, was somebody who had a very expensive dress with a seam that was coming out. There was a kind of fevered carelessness to her. *Democracy* started out as a comedy, a comic novel. And I think that there is a more even view of life in it. I had a terrible time with it. I don't know why, but it never got easy.

In Brentwood we had a big safe-deposit box to put manuscripts in if we left town during fire season. It was such a big box that we never bothered to clean it out. When we were moving, in 1988, and I had to go through the box, I found I don't know how many different versions of the first ninety pages of *Democracy*, with different dates on them, written over several years. I would write ninety pages and not be able to go any further. I couldn't make the switch. I don't know how that was solved. Many of those drafts began with Billy Dillon coming to Amagansett to tell Inez that her father had shot her sister. It was very hard to get from there to any place. It didn't work. It was too conventional a narrative. I never hit the spot where I could sail through. I never got to that point, even at the very end.

HA: Was that a first for you?

JD: It was a first for a novel. I really did not think I was going to finish it two nights before I finished it. And when I did finish it, I had a sense that I was just abandoning it, that I was just calling it. It was sort of like Vietnam itself—why don't we say just we've won and leave? I didn't have a real sense of completion about it.

HA: Your novels are greatly informed by the travel and reporting you do for your nonfiction. Do you ever do research specifically for the fiction?

JD: *Common Prayer* was researched. We had someone working for us, Tina Moore, who was a fantastic researcher. She would go to the UCLA library, and I would say, Bring me back anything on plantation life in Central America. And she would come back and say, This is really what you're looking for—you'll love this. And it would not be plantation life in Central America. It would be Ceylon, but it would be fantastic. She had an instinct for what was the same story, and what I was looking for. What I was looking for were rules for living in the tropics. I didn't know that, but that's what I found. In *Democracy* I was more familiar with all the places.

HA: The last novel you wrote was *The Last Thing He Wanted.* That came out in 1996. Had you been working on it for a long time?

JD: No. I started it in the early fall or late summer of 1995, and I finished it at Christmas. It was a novel I had been thinking about writing for a while. I wanted to write a novel about the Iran-Contra affair, and get in all that stuff that was being lost. Basically it's a novel about Miami. I wanted it to be very densely plotted. I noticed that conspiracy was central to understanding that part of the world; everybody was always being set up in some way. The plot was going to be so complicated that I was going to have to write it fast or I wouldn't be able to keep it all in my head. If I forgot one little detail it wouldn't work, and half the readers didn't understand what happened in the end. Many people thought that Elena tried to kill Treat Morrison. Why did she want to kill him? they would ask me. But she didn't. Someone else did, and set her up. Apparently I didn't make that clear.

I had begun to lose patience with the conventions of writing. Descriptions went first; in both fiction and nonfiction, I just got impatient with those long paragraphs of description. By which I do not mean—obviously—the single detail that gives you the scene. I'm talking about description as a substitute for thinking. I think you can see me losing my patience as early as *Democracy*. That was why that book was so hard to write.

HA: After *Democracy* and *Miami*, and before *The Last Thing He Wanted*, there was the nonfiction collection *After Henry*, which strikes me as a way of coming back to New York and trying to understand what the city was.

JD: It has that long piece "Sentimental Journeys," about the Central Park jogger, which began with that impulse. We had been in New York a year or two, and I realized that I was living here without engaging the city at all. I might as well have been living in another city, because I didn't understand it, I didn't get it. So I realized that I needed to do some reporting on it. Bob and I decided I would do a series of short reporting pieces on New York, and the first one would be about the jogger. But it wasn't really reporting. It was coming at a situation from a lot of angles. I got so involved in it that, by the time I finished the piece, it was too long. I turned it in and Bob had some comments—many, many comments, which caused it to be even longer because he thought it needed so much additional material, which he was right about. By the time I'd plugged it all in, I'd added another six to eight thousand words. When I finally had finished it, I thought, That's all I have to do about New York.

HA: Although it is about the city, "Sentimental Journeys" is really about race and class and money.

JD: It seemed to me that the case was treated with a lot of contempt by the people who were handling it.

HA: How so?

JD: The prosecution thought they had the press and popular sentiment on their side. The case became a way of expressing the city's rage at being broke and being in another recession and not having a general comfort level, the sense that there were people sleeping on the streets—which there were. We moved here six months after the '87 stock market crash. Over the next couple of years, its effect on Madison Avenue was staggering. You could not walk down Madison Avenue at eight in the evening without having to avoid stepping on people sleeping in every doorway. There was a German television crew here doing a piece on the jogger, and they wanted to shoot in Harlem, but it was late in the day and they were losing the light. They kept asking me what the closest place was where they could shoot and see poverty. I said, Try Seventy-Second and Madison. You know where Polo is now? That building was empty and the padlocks were broken and you could see rats scuttling around inside. The landlord had emptied it—I presume because he wanted to get higher rents—and then everything had crashed. There was nothing there. That entire block was a mess.

HA: So from California you had turned your attention to the third world, and now you were able to recognize New York because of the work you had done in the third world.

JD: A lot of what I had seen as New York's sentimentality is derived from the stories the city tells itself to rationalize its class contradictions. I didn't realize that until I started doing the jogger piece. Everything started falling into place on that piece. Bob would send me clips about the trial, but on this one I was on my own, because only I knew where it was going.

HA: In some of your early essays on California, your subject matter was as distinctively your own as your writing style. In recent decades, though, it's not so much the story but your take on the story that makes your work distinctive.

JD: The shift came about as I became more confident that my own take was worth doing. In the beginning, I didn't want to do any stories that anyone else was doing. As time went by, I got more comfortable with that. For example, on the Central Park jogger piece I could not get into the courtroom because I didn't have a police pass. This forced me into another approach, which turned out to be a more interesting one. At least to me.

HA: Wasn't it around the same time that you were doing "Letter from Los Angeles" for Robert Gottlieb at the *New Yorker*?

JD: Yes. Though I wasn't doing more than two of those a year. I think they only ran six to eight thousand words, but the idea was to do several things in each letter. I had never done that before, where you just really discuss what people are talking about that week. It was easy to do. It was a totally different tone from the *Review*. I went over those *New Yorker* pieces when I collected them. I probably took out some of the *New Yorker*'s editing, which is just their way of making everything sound a certain way.

HA: Can you characterize your methods as a reporter?

JD: I can't ask anything. Once in a while if I'm forced into it I will conduct an interview, but it's usually pro forma, just to establish my credentials as somebody who's allowed to hang around for a while. It doesn't matter to me what people say to me in the interview because I don't trust it. Sometimes you do interviews where you get a lot. But you don't get them from public figures.

When I was conducting interviews for the piece on Lakewood, it was essential to do interviews because that was the whole point. But these were not public figures. On the one hand, we were discussing what I was ostensibly there doing a piece about, which was the Spur Posse, a group of local high school boys who had been arrested for various infractions. But on the other hand, we were talking, because it was the first thing on everyone's mind, about the defense industry going downhill, which was what the town was about. That was a case in which I did interviewing and listened.

HA: Did the book about California, *Where I Was From*, grow out of that piece, or had you already been thinking about a book?

JD: I had actually started a book about California in the seventies. I had written some of that first part, which is about my family, but I could never go anywhere with it for two reasons. One was that I still hadn't figured out California. The other was that I didn't want to figure out California because whatever I figured out would be different from the California my mother and father had told me about. I didn't want to engage that.

HA: You felt like you were still their child?

JD: I just didn't see any point in engaging it. By the time I did the book they were dead.

HA: You said earlier that after *The White Album* you were tired of personal writing and didn't want to become Miss Lonelyhearts. You must be getting a larger personal response from readers than ever with *The Year of Magical Thinking*. Is that difficult?

JD: I have been getting a very strong emotional response to *Magical Thinking*. It's not a crazy response; it's not demanding.

It's trying to make sense of a fairly universal experience that most people don't talk about. So this is a case in which I have found myself able to deal with the response directly.

HA: Do you ever think you might go back to the idea of doing little pieces about New York?

JD: I don't know. It is still a possibility, but my basic question about New York was answered for me: it's criminal.

HA: That was your question?

JD: Yes, it's criminal.

HA: Do you find it stimulating in some way to live here?

JD: I find it really comfortable. During the time we lived in California, which lasted twenty-four years, I didn't miss New York after the first year. And after the second year I started to think of New York as sentimental. There were periods when I didn't even come to New York at all. One time I realized that I had been to Hong Kong twice since I had last been to New York. Then we started spending more time in New York. Both John and I were really happy to have been here on 9/11. I can't think of any place else I would have rather been on 9/11, and in the immediate aftermath.

HA: You could have stayed in Sacramento forever as a novelist, but you started to move out into the worlds of Hollywood and politics.

JD: I was never a big fan of people who don't leave home. I don't know why. It just seems part of your duty in life.

HA: I'm reminded of Charlotte in *A Book of Common Prayer*. She has no conception of the outside world but she wants to be in it.

JD: Although a novel takes place in the larger world, there's always some drive in it that is entirely personal—even if you don't know it while you're doing it. I realized some years after *A Book of Common Prayer* was finished that it was about my anticipating Quintana's growing up. I wrote it around 1975, so she would have been nine, but I was already anticipating separation and actually working through that ahead of time. So novels are also about things you're afraid you can't deal with.

HA: Are you working on one now?

JD: No. I haven't felt that I wanted to bury myself for that intense a period.

HA: You want to be in the world a bit.

JD: Yeah. A little bit.

CLAUDIA RANKINE

II

CITIZEN:
AN AMERICAN LYRIC

Hennessy Youngman aka Jayson Musson, whose *Art Thoughtz* take the form of tutorials on YouTube, educates viewers on contemporary art issues. In one of his many videos, he addresses how to become a successful Black artist, wryly suggesting Black people's anger is marketable. He advises Black artists to cultivate "an angry nigger exterior" by watching, among other things, the Rodney King video while working.

Youngman's suggestions are meant to expose expectations for Blackness as well as to underscore the difficulty inherent in any attempt by Black artists to metabolize real rage. The commodified anger his video advocates rests lightly on the surface for spectacle's sake. It can be engaged or played like the race card and is tied solely to the performance of Blackness and not to the emotional state of particular individuals in particular situations.

On the bridge between this sellable anger and "the artist" resides, at times, an actual anger. Youngman in his video doesn't address this type of anger: the anger built up through experience and the quotidian struggles against dehumanization every brown or Black person lives simply because of skin color. This other kind of anger in time can prevent, rather than sponsor, the production of anything except loneliness.

You begin to think, maybe erroneously, that this other kind of anger is really a type of knowledge: the type that both clarifies and disappoints. It responds to insult and attempted erasure simply by asserting presence, and the energy required to present, to react, to assert is accompanied by visceral disappointment: a disappointment in the sense that no amount of visibility will alter the ways in which one is perceived.

Recognition of this lack might break you apart. Or recognition might illuminate the erasure the attempted erasure triggers. Whether such discerning creates a healthier, if more isolated, self, you can't know. In any case, Youngman doesn't speak to this kind of anger. He doesn't say that witnessing the expression of this more ordinary and daily anger might make the witness believe that a person is "insane."

And insane is what you think, one Sunday afternoon, drinking an Arnold Palmer, watching the 2009 Women's US Open semifinal, when brought to full attention by the suddenly explosive behavior of Serena Williams. Serena in HD before your eyes becomes overcome by a rage you recognize and have been taught to hold at a distance for your own good. Serena's behavior, on this particular Sunday afternoon, suggests that all the injustice she has played through all the years of her illustrious career flashes before her and she decides finally to respond to all of it with a string of invectives. Nothing, not even the repetition of negations ("no, no, no") she employed in a similar situation years before as a younger player at the 2004 US Open, prepares you for this. Oh my God, she's gone crazy, you say to no one.

What does a victorious or defeated Black woman's body in a historically white space look like? Serena and her big sister Venus Williams brought to mind Zora Neale Hurston's "I feel most colored when I am thrown against a sharp white background." This appropriated line, stenciled on canvas by Glenn

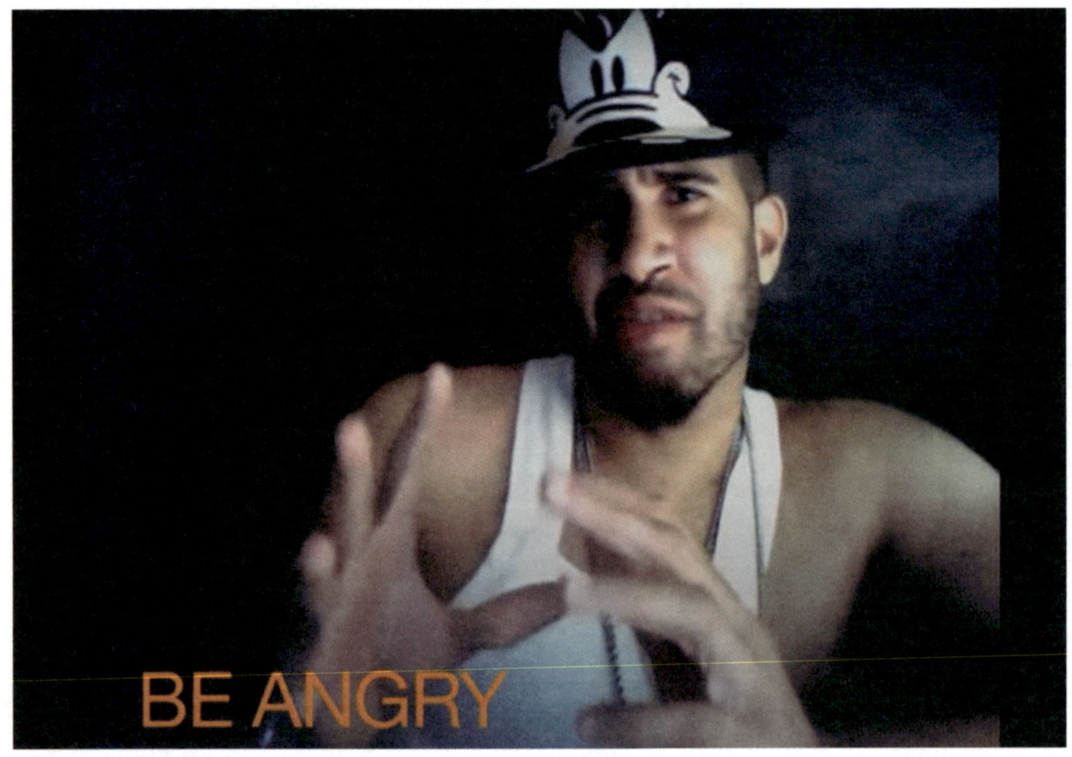

Jayson Musson, *ART THOUGHTZ: How to Be a Successful Black Artist*, 2010-12

Ligon, who used plastic letter stencils, smudging oil sticks, and graphite to transform the words into abstractions, seemed to be ad copy for some aspect of life for all Black bodies.

Hurston's statement has been played out on the big screen by Serena and Venus: they win sometimes, they lose sometimes, they've been injured, they've been happy, they've been sad, ignored, booed mightily, they've been cheered, and through it all and evident to all were those people who are enraged they are there at all—graphite against a sharp white background.

For years you attribute to Serena Williams a kind of resilience appropriate only for those who exist in celluloid. Neither her father nor her mother nor her sister nor Jehovah her God nor NIKE camp could shield her ultimately from people who felt her Black body didn't belong on their court, in their world. From the start many made it clear Serena would have done better struggling to survive in the two-dimensionality of a Millet painting, rather than on their tennis court—better to put all that strength to work in their fantasy of her working the land, rather than be caught up in the turbulence of our ancient dramas, like a ship fighting a storm in a Turner seascape.

The most notorious of Serena's detractors takes the form of Mariana Alves, the distinguished tennis chair umpire. In 2004 Alves was excused from officiating any more matches on the final day of the US Open after she made five bad calls against Serena in her quarterfinal matchup against fellow American Jennifer Capriati. The serves and returns Alves called out were landing, stunningly unreturned by Capriati, inside the lines, no discerning eyesight needed. Commentators, spectators, television viewers, line judges, everyone could see the balls were good, everyone, apparently, except Alves. No one could understand what was happening. Serena, in her denim skirt, black sneaker boots, and dark mascara, began wagging her finger and saying "no, no, no," as if by negating the moment she could propel us back into a legible world. Tennis superstar John McEnroe, given his own keen eye for injustice during his professional career, was shocked that Serena was able to hold it together after losing the match.

Though no one was saying anything explicitly about Serena's Black body, you are not the only viewer who thought it was getting in the way of Alves's sight line. One commentator said he hoped he wasn't being unkind when he stated, "Capriati wins it with the help of the umpires and the lines judges." A year later that match would be credited for demonstrating the need for the speedy installation of Hawk-Eye, the line-calling technology that took the seeing away from the beholder. Now the umpire's call can be challenged by a replay; however, back then after the match Serena said, "I'm very angry and bitter right now. I felt cheated. Shall I go on? I just feel robbed."

And though you felt outrage for Serena after that 2004 US Open, as the years go by, she seems to put Alves, and a lengthening list of other curious calls and oversights, against both her and her sister, behind her as they happen.

Yes, and the body has memory. The physical carriage hauls more than its weight. The body is the threshold across which each objectionable call passes into consciousness—all the unintimidated, unblinking, and unflappable resilience does not erase the moments lived through, even as we are eternally stupid or everlastingly optimistic, so ready to be inside, among, a part of the games.

And here Serena is, five years after Alves, back at the US Open, again in a semifinal match, this time against Belgium's Kim Clijsters. Serena is not playing well and loses the first set. In response she smashes her racket on the court. Now McEnroe isn't stunned by her ability to hold herself together and is moved to say, "That's as angry as I've ever seen her." The umpire gives her a warning; another violation will mean a point penalty.

She is in the second set at the critical moment of 5–6 in Clijsters's favor, serving to stay in the match, at match point. The line judge employed by the US Open to watch Serena's body, its every move, says Serena stepped on the line while serving. What? (The Hawk-Eye cameras don't cover the feet, only the ball, apparently.) What! Are you serious? She is serious; she has seen a foot fault, one no one else is able to locate despite the numerous replays. "No foot fault, you definitely do not see a foot fault there," says McEnroe. "That's overofficiating for certain," says another commentator. Even the ESPN tennis commentator, who seems predictable in her readiness to find fault with the Williams sisters, says, "Her foot fault call was way off." Yes, and even if there had been a foot fault, despite the rule, they are rarely ever called at critical moments in a Grand Slam match because "You don't make a call," tennis official Carol Cox says, "that can decide a match unless it's flagrant."

As you look at the affable Kim Clijsters, you try to entertain the thought that this scenario could have played itself out the other way. And as Serena turns to the lineswoman and says, "I swear to God I'm fucking going to take this fucking ball and shove it down your fucking throat, you hear that? I swear to God!" As offensive as her outburst is, it is difficult not to applaud her for reacting immediately to being thrown against a sharp white background. It is difficult not to applaud her for existing in the moment, for fighting crazily against the so-called wrongness of her body's positioning at the service line.

She says in 2009, belatedly, the words that should have been said to the umpire in 2004, the words that might have snapped Alves back into focus, a focus that would have acknowledged what actually was happening on the court. Now Serena's reaction is read as insane. And her punishment for this moment of manumission is the threatened point penalty resulting in the loss of the match, an $82,500 fine, plus a two-year probationary period by the Grand Slam Committee.

Perhaps the committee's decision is only about context, though context is not meaning. It is a public event being watched in homes across the world. In any case, it is difficult not to think that if Serena lost context by abandoning all rules of civility, it could be because her body, trapped in a racial imaginary, trapped in disbelief—code for being Black in America—is being governed not by the tennis match she is participating in but by a collapsed relationship that had promised to play by the rules. Perhaps this is how racism feels no matter the context—randomly the rules everyone else gets to play by no longer apply to you, and to call this out by calling out "I swear to God!" is to be called insane, crass, crazy. Bad sportsmanship.

Two years later, September 11, 2011, Serena is playing the Australian Sam Stosur in the US Open final. She is expected to win, having just beaten the number-one player, the Dane Caroline Wozniacki, in the semifinal the night before. Some speculate Serena especially wants to win this Grand Slam because it is the tenth anniversary of the attack on the Twin Towers. It's believed that by winning she will prove her red-blooded American patriotism and will once and for all become beloved by the tennis world (think Arthur Ashe after his death). All the bad calls, the boos, the criticisms that she has made ugly the game of tennis—through her looks as well as her behavior—that entire cluster of betrayals will be wiped clean with this win.

One imagines her wanting to say what her sister would say a year later after being diagnosed with Sjögren's syndrome and losing her match to shouts of "Let's go, Venus!" in Arthur Ashe Stadium: "I know this is not proper tennis etiquette, but this is the first time I've ever played here that the crowd has been behind me like that. Today I felt American, you know, for the first time at the US Open. So I've waited my whole career to have this moment and here it is."

It is all too exhausting and Serena's exhaustion shows in her playing; she is losing, a set and a game down. Yes, and finally she hits a great shot, a big forehand, and before the ball is safely past Sam Stosur's hitting zone, Serena yells, "Come on!" thinking she has hit an irretrievable winner. The umpire, Eva Asderaki, rules correctly that Serena, by shouting, interfered with Stosur's concentration. Subsequently, a ball that Stosur seemingly would not have been able to return becomes Stosur's point. Serena's reply is to ask the umpire if she is trying to screw her again. She remembers the umpire doing this to her before. As a viewer, you too, along with John McEnroe, begin to wonder if this is the same umpire from 2004 or 2009. It isn't—in 2004 it was Mariana Alves and in 2009 it was Sharon Wright; however, the use of the word "again" by Serena returns her viewers to other times calling her body out.

Again Serena's frustrations, her disappointments, exist within a system you understand not to try to understand in any fair-minded way because to do so is to understand the erasure of the self as systemic, as ordinary. For Serena, the daily diminishment is a low flame, a constant drip. Every look, every comment, every bad call blossoms out of history, through her, onto you. To understand is to see Serena as hemmed in as any other Black body thrown against our American background. "Aren't you the one that screwed me over last time here?" she asks umpire Asderaki. "Yeah, you are. Don't look at me. Really, don't even look at me. Don't look my way. Don't look my way," she repeats, because it is that simple.

Yes, and who can turn away? Serena is not running out of breath. Despite all her understanding, she continues to serve up aces while smashing rackets and fraying hems. In the 2012 Olympics she brought home two of the three gold medals the Americans would win in tennis. After her three-second celebratory dance on center court at the All England Club, the American media reported, "And there was Serena ... Crip-Walking all over the most lily-white place in the world. You couldn't help but shake your head ... What Serena did was akin to cracking a taste-less, X-rated joke inside a church. What she did was immature and classless."

Before making the video *How to Be a Successful Black Artist*, Hennessy Youngman uploaded to YouTube *How to Be a Successful Artist.* While putting forward the argument that one needs to be white to be truly successful, he adds, in an aside, that this might not work for Blacks because if "a nigger paints a flower it becomes a slavery flower, flower de *Amistad*," thereby intimating that any relationship between the white viewer and the Black artist immediately becomes one between white persons and Black property, which was the legal state of things once upon a time, as Patricia Williams has pointed out in *The Alchemy of Race and Rights*: "The cold game of equality staring makes me feel like a thin sheet of glass. I could force my presence, the real me contained in those eyes, upon them, but I would be smashed in the process."

Interviewed by the Brit Piers Morgan after her 2012 Olympic

victory, Serena is informed by Morgan that he was planning on calling her victory dance "the Serena Shuffle"; however, he has learned from the American press that it is a Crip Walk, a gangster dance. Serena responds incredulously by asking if she looks like a gangster to him. Yes, he answers. All in a day's fun, perhaps, and in spite and despite it all, Serena Williams blossoms again into Serena Williams. When asked if she is confident she can win her upcoming matches, her answer remains, "At the end of the day, I am very happy with me and I'm very happy with my results."

Serena would go on to win every match she played between the US Open and the year-end 2012 championship tournament, and because tennis is a game of adjustments, she would do this without any reaction to a number of questionable calls. More than one commentator would remark on her ability to hold it together during these matches. She is a woman in love, one suggests. She has grown up, another decides, as if responding to the injustice of racism is childish and her previous demonstration of emotion was free-floating and detached from any external actions by others. Some others theorize she is developing the admirable "calm and measured logic" of an Arthur Ashe, who the sportswriter Bruce Jenkins felt was "dignified" and "courageous" in his ability to confront injustice without making a scene. Jenkins, perhaps inspired by Serena's new comportment, felt moved to argue that her continued boycott of Indian Wells in 2013, where she felt traumatized by the aggression of racist slurs hurled at her in 2001, was lacking in "dignity" and "integrity" and demonstrated "only stubbornness and a grudge." (Serena lifted her boycott in 2015, and Venus lifted hers in 2016.)

Watching this newly contained Serena, you begin to wonder if she finally has given up wanting better from her peers or if she too has come across Hennessy's *Art Thoughtz* and is channeling his assertion that the less that is communicated the better. Be ambiguous. This type of ambiguity could also be diagnosed as dissociation and would support Serena's claim that she has had to split herself off from herself and create different personae.

Now that there is no calling out of injustice, no yelling, no cursing, no finger wagging or head shaking, the media decides to take up the mantle when on December 12, 2012, two weeks after Serena is named WTA Player of the Year, the Dane Caroline Wozniacki, a former number-one player, imitates Serena by stuffing towels in her top and shorts, all in good fun, at an exhibition match. Racist? CNN wants to know if outrage is the proper response.

It's then that Hennessy's suggestions about "how to be a successful artist" return to you: be ambiguous, be white. Wozniacki, it becomes clear, has finally enacted what was desired by many of Serena's detractors, consciously or unconsciously, the moment the Compton girl first stepped on court. Wozniacki (though there are a number of ways to interpret her actions—playful mocking of a peer, imitation of the mimicking antics of the tennis player known as the joker, Novak Djokovic) finally gives the people what they have wanted all along by embodying Serena's attributes while leaving Serena's "angry nigger exterior" behind. At last, in this real, and unreal, moment, we have Wozniacki's image of smiling blond goodness posing as the best female tennis player of all time.

GARRETT BRADLEY

IN CONVERSATION WITH

HUEY COPELAND

Huey Copeland: I'd like to begin by talking about the ways you're engaging the archive in your work, recruiting a range of different materials, even outtakes from your own films. Your process—mixing and working on different projects simultaneously—seems to resonate with but also exceed what scholar Saidiya Hartman calls "critical fabulation" in terms of posing the question "How do we return to and engage the archive in order to reframe it with all of its liabilities and possibilities"?[1] In this sense, your work also resonates with what I've recently called "black auto-citational practice," a modality that you can see in Hartman's work, in Arthur Jafa and Carrie Mae Weems's work, or in Glenn Ligon's work—which, in many ways, is *all* about returning to aspects of one's own production, to those things that ultimately weren't included in a final project, and saying, "Well, this material continues to have a life and can have a life of its own."[2] It's a mode of working that suggests a particular kind of ethical relationship or stance to archives, both institutional and personal ones. I wonder if you could talk about how you've been moving toward that approach and what's been inspiring you or informing you as you try to develop relationships to the material and to the visual that honor both your engagements with communities and your sense of yourself as both a filmmaker and a facilitator?

Garrett Bradley: Yeah, okay. Cool. I guess I'll start off specifically with *America* (2019), which I started in 2014 and for which I did a lot of archival research, including spending days watching films at the Black Film Archives in the Library of Congress. It was inspired by an article that a friend, the artist Byron Kim, had sent me about the Museum of Modern Art, New York's discovery of what they thought to be the very first film with an all-Black cast and integrated production: *Lime Kiln Club Field Day* (1913), starring Bert Williams and Odessa Warren Grey.[3] They started restoring it in 2004 and finally released it a hundred years after it had been shot as a series of unassembled outtakes. *America* is very much, for me, connected to the discovery of this film. It is also connected to a survey I had read that the Library of Congress had done in 2013 which stated that 70 percent of the feature-length films made between 1912 and 1929 had gone missing.[4] If we know that this one film that does exist, out of the 7,500 [or so] that are missing, is extremely progressive, what would it mean to make the assumption that there is a whole body of work, lost to the archive, that is equally as progressive? And that's what *America* is. It's a chronology, a series of vignettes rooted in Black and "American" history that function as visual illustrations and exist as a physical timeline.

As a person who works in the world with people, who's making work often inspired by personal and peripheral experiences, by observing the things that are around me, I am always thinking, Where can I help? I think of myself as a facilitator and, right now, the best way that I can take action is through the communal and collaborative effort involved in making personal films about issues of relevance to me and the communities I interact with. With *America*, I actually started off thinking about the work in a physical way because I was digging through a timeline, I was digging through a chronology, a history that had gaps. And that felt really counterintuitive to two-dimensional space. It felt actually harder to translate that research, that chronology within a single screen than to actually create an accordion-like installation of a series of screens in physical space that people could move through and around. It was less about trying to make "art" or be in an art space and more about asking, What is the clearest and most efficient way of dealing with the subject matter that actually makes sense, you know? How do we construct a chronology that is not necessarily linear? On a technical or formal level, we did this by using chiffon, which is highly transparent, as the material for the screens, creating a layering effect.

HC: That's totally fascinating. Hearing you say that, I think, "Well, of course that makes sense!" Because with *America*, even if you're watching it on a laptop or on a big-screen TV as a single-channel work, there's a way in which each moment within the film holds a multiplicity of other moments within it. Being able to actually physicalize the multiplicity of the film's unfolding and to have these moments spatially held in relationship to each other seems to really make sense in terms of the experience you're trying to generate.

It's also very interesting to think about you as a filmmaker. I love that you emphasize that it's a practice that has to do with engaging bodies and space, with working and moving in between sites and subjects and communities. Your language, in other words, underlines that the practice of filmmaking is always deeply corporeal and interpersonal. But I think there's a way in which we train ourselves to receive films without thinking about the behind-the-scenes, the apparatus, the structural conditions of a film's construction, because, of course, we want to immerse ourselves in the mirage that's before us, to have this moment of suturing to the fantasmatic.[5] Even the choice of clips and stills from *Lime Kiln Club Field Day* that you use in *America* often seem motivated by a desire to reveal the actualities of production as well as the kinds of aesthetic and political engagements they represent. Though you're not necessarily showing us how every shot of either film was framed and produced, there's still this kind of indexical cue that asks us to examine how we think about cinema and film as fitting in with larger social apparatuses and the ways in which we can read with and against what is ultimately given us to see, so that we can begin to understand, to borrow a phrase from Jacqueline Goldsby, "the larger social construction or organization of the world at a given moment."[6]

GB: Going back to Hartman and her term, critical fabulation, which I just love so much, leads to another question that you had prompted, which is the question of *possibilities versus liabilities* and how the different spaces of "traditional cinema" and visual art intersect, how they present different ways of moving through those two issues. I think, on one hand, filling gaps is a natural part of the human experience. I think our minds naturally create a narrative around the things that we don't know. Part of what the practice of meditation, in some cases, really forces us to do is to move away from the narratives we formulate in the absence of information. Of course, there's this other type of meditation that's really mantra-based, which is, in some ways, about doing the exact opposite—filling that space up with new narratives rather than emptying it out. "Things will always work for my highest good." "Everything is going to be okay." I think as I've gotten older, I've learned how to be more conscious of filling gaps and how to use that tool in a more crafted way in my work, in a material and in a physical way. And I think that as I've moved through my work, again going back to possibilities versus liabilities, it's become more and more clear that these two things are always interconnected, they are never separate from each other.

When I make a movie and I send it to the company that's funding the film for their review, they may not understand or value X, Y or Z. It's my job to find a way to both approach form and storytelling in the way I want while also giving people—funders, audiences, etc.—the things that they feel they need. At times, it's about making compromises. But a part of my soul would die, frankly, if I felt that just because this one space—the traditional film world—doesn't understand the more experimental modes and models I am working in, that those aspects of my practice need to disappear. There's another space for it, there are other possibilities for it.

HC: I think that describes, in such poetic, political, and tactical terms, the way in which one moves with and against different kinds of platforms and institutional frames in order to carve out provisional spaces of autonomy. Of course, those spaces are always already compromised, but they still might allow you to actually speak to the connective communities that you want to in these direct ways that maybe just sticking with one kind of platform or medium wouldn't allow.

And perhaps that relates to this idea of you as a kind of facilitator, which I love, and which very much makes me think of how Arthur Jafa describes the importance of his godmother's work as a church usher to his aesthetic practice, because it was her role—and subsequently, his—to point out those possessed by the spirit. In his practice, I think there's a certain Black feminist ethos that undergirds many of his choices and decisions. At the same, I think there's a whole range of Black feminist cultural practitioners, from Meg Onli to Martine Syms to Toni Morrison, who have been interested in reframing everyday experience from a Black feminist perspective. I wonder if you could talk about how that lands for you and animates your work or doesn't?

GB: I think part of working in the mundaneness of the everyday makes a lot of sense because it's what we're closest to. On some level, it's the most universal and relatable space to start from. Where Martine's work or Toni's work and mine meet is perhaps in understanding how abstract and fantastical even the mundane is. I think for me the interest in the everyday is also an attempt to understand the connection between the personal and intimate, the internal and external. I'm interested in bridging these spaces, above and below, inside and outside. Writing in particular is probably one of the only art forms that really, truly on some level does balance exactly the internal and the external. If someone asked me, "What is the one object that represents these two spaces," it would have to be a book. But as a facilitator, that's exactly what I'm interested in doing, bridging these two worlds, above and below together into one space.

HC: That's fantastic! I think the question that naturally follows is about your real investment in engaging particular locations and populations, especially in New Orleans, whose history takes on a much larger significance when we think about the unfolding of life across the modern world and Black life across the diaspora. Given the focus of your film work—where it takes place, who the subjects are—how do you imagine speaking to audiences in a range of different contexts as the work circulates and appears in different locations? It is very specific but also has this expansive quality precisely because of its engagement with questions of the everyday.

GB: Yes, exactly! I think the question of the everyday and of the unfolding of Black life across time could apply to all the work that I've been doing lately, but in particular this project *AKA* (2019), which is about upward mobility as it exists between women, between mothers and daughters. *AKA* came to me by way of looking back on films that I had watched as a child and trying to sift through those narratives and the questions they presented and what they mean in a contemporary context.

I got a grant to develop an adaptation of a famous twentieth-century race film, which I've been thinking about making for years. I tried to put together a more traditional pitch and it was so flat and lacking substance. I was really having a hard time articulating my ideas—both *why* it was significant and *how* it would be told. But it wasn't coming together. Then I got an invitation to make a new work for the Whitney Biennial last spring, which offered me a space to think about this larger project in a new and more experimental way, not as a pitch but as a series of screen tests that might leave more room for discovery.

The process of making *AKA* started with a series of questions. My first question was, okay, are these classic race films at all still relevant? Or, to be more specific, how do we think about the relationship between white women and Black women across generations in a way that is contemporary, but that may have also been touched on in these older films. How do we think about love? How do we think about upward mobility? How do we think about the way we see ourselves and the way we think others see us?

In order for me to make an adaptation of a classic American film, even if it's a Hollywood film, I needed to understand how

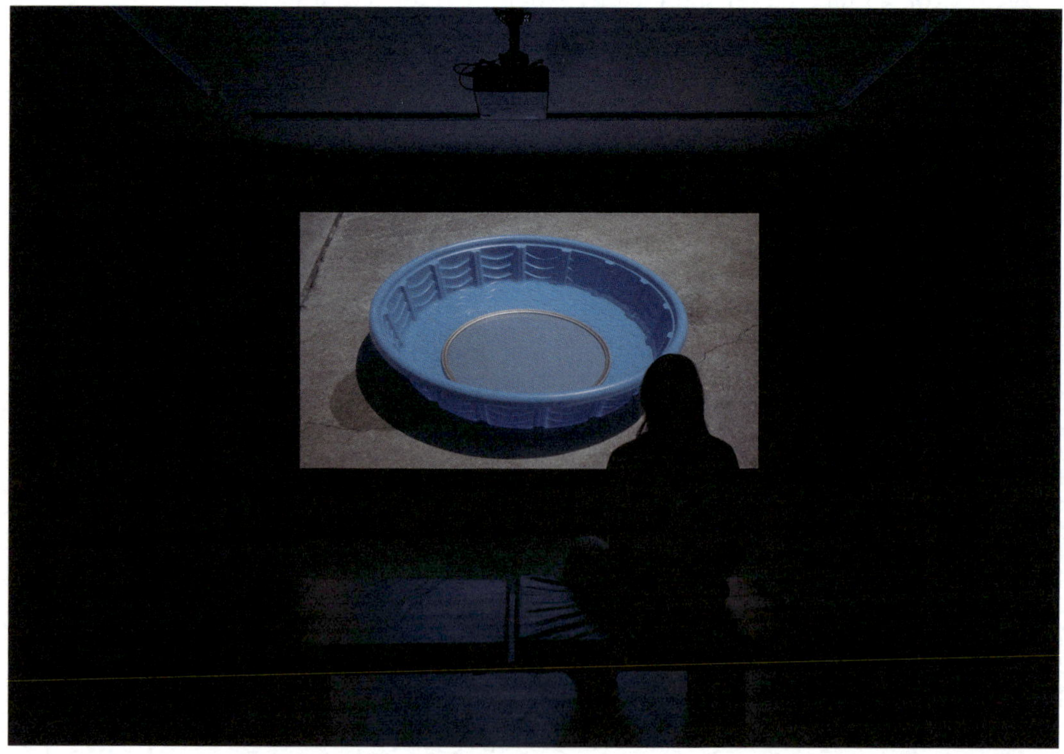

Garrett Bradley, *AKA*, 2019. Installation view at COMA in Sydney, Australia, 2023

it was going to be relevant in contemporary space in a contemporary moment. And the only way to do that was to talk to people who might feel in any kind of way directly connected to or reflected in that narrative. So, I went to family members, I went to friends, and I went on social media—which has been an ongoing resource for me. I always start off with a series of questions that are no different from the questions that I would ask an audience in a panel once the work is done. I think that language is really important for me as a way of creating an ethical bridge between the process and where the work ends up going, because oftentimes they're so separate from one another.

What becomes more complex is the visual illustration of the feedback that I get. So, I had mothers and daughters coming together. I interviewed each of them separately. They were mothers and daughters who self-identified as being in a mixed-race household or in houses where everyone was the same race but had really different skin tones and felt like they could speak to feeling like they were treated differently than their mother, for instance, or differently than their daughter.

I just started off with questions: How do you see yourself? How do you think the world sees you? What did these older films get right, what did they get wrong? I'd send links to the films so they could re-watch them. What ended up happening was a series of dialogues and transcripts, and a lot of conversations, probably 12 one-hour-long conversations. I would pull certain pieces of dialogue out of those conversations. Then I would do what we were kind of talking about earlier in terms of filling gaps. This one woman in particular, Lindsay, she kept asking her mother, "Are you color struck?" "Are you color struck?" And she kept asking it over and over and over again.

To me, that one phrase, color struck, became the premise for the whole visual landscape of the piece.[7] What does color struck mean when you visualize it? How could I work with analog filtrations so that when the light hit the lens, you've got rainbows and stars across the screen, layered over everyday spaces? It's just this trippy, weird piece. I think that my process is to always be open. It always starts with questions and it's open to what those answers might be. The work comes from those answers and it doesn't change when it's brought out into the world. The meaning of it and the purpose of it doesn't change in terms of how I talk about it. How people interpret it, maybe that's different.

HC: That's really interesting, especially as it underlines your critical relationship to the normative structures of contemporary filmmaking, whether it be the process of casting or trying to think about the location. In your work, if I'm following, it's not about imposing a predetermined structure that "content" is set into, but instead about simultaneously generating an understanding of what the content and the form are through conversations with this larger set of communities and interlocutors who are sometimes in the films and sometimes the audiences for the films. It gives us a sense that your work is coming from a particular place that is not being shoehorned into the world that a Hollywood production company imagines a film from New Orleans needs to look like or fit into.

As such, I think your process also interestingly puts pressure on the notion of auteur cinema. It's not as if you're imposing "the Bradley optic," but more like you're really trying to think carefully about how you're visually and sonically constructing a material world that is connected to and an emanation from the place it was made.

GB: I love this idea of challenging the notion of the auteur in cinema. And as you say, in many ways, my work is very much directed and dictated by the specific communities I engage—by specific places and specific people.

I would also say that yes, my work is about Black life. It is also a series of love stories, I think. My love for the people that I work with and my love and compassion for circumstance. And my hope that in making something, it will induce the same level of compassion and imagination—the ability to imagine being somebody besides yourself, for the viewer, and then to bridge gaps. It isn't just for Black folks, it's for all of us. It's for us to think about how we can work within existing spaces and how to illuminate the beauty that we are and bring it on a mass scale to people so that they can connect with it.

I think you can see this in a feature-length documentary that I'm working on right now which is about a woman who

I met in the process of making *Alone* (2017) and who I have been filming for the past two years. *Alone* was about my friend, Aloné Watts, and her having to deal with feelings of extreme loneliness and isolation as a result of her partner's incarceration. I don't know if you remember, but there's a lady at the very end of the film who makes this analogy between slavery and incarceration, and you see her very briefly.

HC: Yeah, like a little flash.

GB: A little flash. While I was making *Alone* I contacted this organization called Families and Friends of Louisiana's Incarcerated Children, and they connected me with a series of women that had gone through this process and could give advice to Aloné based on their own experiences navigating the intentionally complex prison system in the US. So this was how I met Fox Rich, who robbed a bank with her husband in the '90s. She served two years because she took the plea deal. But her husband was coaxed into not taking the deal and ended up getting a numerical life sentence—sixty years—for a first-time offense. He served twenty-one, and when I met Fox it had been 20 years at that point. She was selling Cadillacs. She is an incredible human being. She started these "Power Parties" when she was in prison where she would get all the women to circle around her and she would talk about what it meant to be empowered and how to find the right partner for yourself.

HC: Amazing.

GB: Ninety percent of my experience filming Fox was watching her on the phone. Her whole life is on the phone, maneuvering the bureaucracy of the prison system. I started thinking about how when you're making more traditional films, or you have financiers behind you, they have certain expectations for how stories are going to be told. I feel like there's no reason why that should, in any kind of way, eclipse the possibilities for other, more nuanced, even more essentialist ways of telling the same story. What would it look like to just take every single moment that we have of her on her phone, in her office, for the past two years and just have each one of those shots back to back, right? However long that string-out ends up being. Maybe it's two hours of her on the phone. That, to me, says just as much as an hour-and-an-half narratively crafted documentary that has all these other expectations on it in terms of its form and structure and how the audience is going to understand it.

HC: That sounds incredible. I love the way you're pushing against certain filmic structures or avoiding them, but still invested in a kind of visually rhythmic propulsion, so that there is a logic to the film, though not at all the one through which we usually think of cinematic or imagistic moving-image works as captivating. Does that make sense?

GB: Totally.

HC: It's liberatory, I think, in terms of moving us away from certain kinds of forms we've come to rely upon without critically interrogating what those forms are, what their limitations might be, or how they are caught up in heteronormative, patriarchal, white, masculinist presumptions. Your tack seems to be to develop a form from a different positionality and with a different set of concerns and subjects and audiences in mind.[8]

GB: A part of the failure of Hollywood is that they are so eager to compartmentalize identity—to differentiate between Black audiences, or Hispanic audiences, or queer audiences, for example. I think we're so much more sophisticated than that. Film viewers, like the population, are incredibly diverse and there is no reason why the work we do shouldn't reflect that.

HC: I think that's right. I was in Paris in May where I saw the exhibition *Le modèle noir: De Géricault à Matisse* [The Black Model: From Géricault to Matisse] at Musée d'Orsay, which is the French version of *Posing Modernity: The Black Model from Manet and Matisse to Today*, a show originally presented in New York. It was wonderful to see so many Black folks at the Orsay, in particular Black Americans. There was a Black woman from New York looking at a painting and she said to me, totally unsolicited, "Aren't we beautiful?" I said, "Yeah, but did you need some nineteenth-century French painter to tell you that?" And maybe some of us do need to find ways of telling ourselves that and communicating that within hegemonic frames. Because not only are we dealing with the onslaught and historicity of a certain visual regime intent on emptying Black people of interiority and producing us as a species of stereotype, but it's a regime that also impoverishes everyone and makes us not able to see precisely those connections that might otherwise link us—connections that I think your work is really trying to stage and to offer as a proposition or a spur for a set of conversations that can happen and perhaps have different kinds of outcomes and take us to different places.

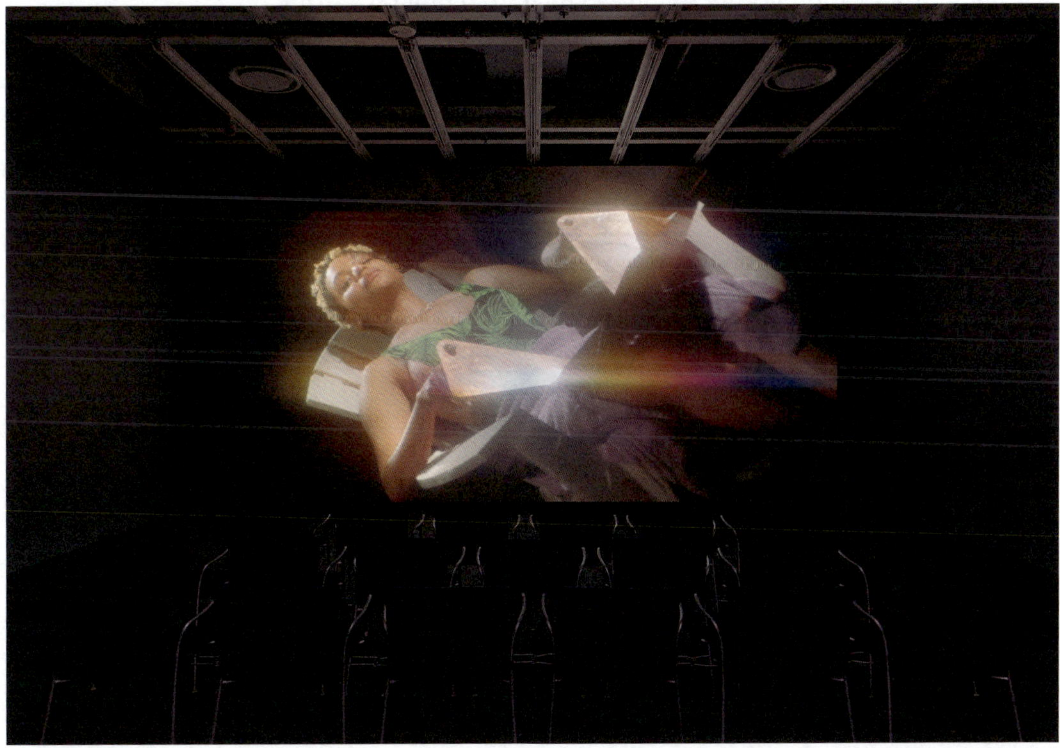

Garrett Bradley, *AKA*, 2019. Installation view of Whitney Biennial 2019

GB: Right, exactly. Yeah, I think with *Alone*, that was definitely the goal. But to go back to *America*, this makes me think of the trauma that existed around the material from *Lime Kiln Club Field Day* and what it meant to go through it frame by frame and try to find these moments that were beautiful, despite seeing Bert Williams in blackface. There was something really powerful in that process. Those films are 17 frames a second, and so there's all this nuance that we can miss. For me, I thought that was a powerful lesson in my own work as well, which is that I would like to think that it can't rely on the holistic nature of cinema, meaning it can't rely on the durational quality of it, on the music, on the sound. It has to also work as an image, as a still image, if you pause it will it still say the same things? I hope so.

HC: I think what's amazing about *America* is that you give us these moments of joy that you're able to find, but it's not as if you're saying the terror doesn't exist. But even within the terror, there's something that exceeds it, that emerges from it, and that there's also something in the visual that exceeds any singular ideologically motivated attempt to script it in one way. And I think in this moment when we have so many people trying to think about Black visuality, your work holds out a really exciting model because for so long, I think there's been a way in which the visual, to its core, has been this "problem space" within African American culture.[9] Your work says, "No, we can own this visuality and inhabit it *and* have an understanding of the ways in which it's been deployed as a weapon against us. We can't give up on visuality as something that still helps us produce ourselves, but we can do it in other terms." And that, to me, is incredibly inspiring. As someone who has often thought, "I don't know about representational imagery, we might have to just let that go," now, I'm like, oh no, Garrett Bradley has shown me we can hold onto it!

NOTES

1. On "critical fabulation," see Saidiya Hartman, "Venus in Two Acts," *Small Axe* 12, no. 2 (2008): 1–14.

2. See, respectively, Huey Copeland, "A Seat at the Table: Notes of an Institutional Creature," *October* 168 (Spring 2019): 63–78; and Huey Copeland, "Love Is the Message, The Message Is Death," *ASAP Journal*, June 4.

3. Felicia R. Lee, "Coming Soon, a Century Late: A Black Film Gem," the *New York Times*, September 20, 2014.

4. David Pierce, *The Survival of American Silent Feature Films: 1912–1929* (Washington, DC: Council on Library and Information Resources Library of Congress, 2013).

5. In film theory, suturing describes a cinematic effect, imposed by a system of editing techniques, that structures a viewer's suspension of disbelief and results in an identification between the viewer and the camera eye that maintains the illusion of the filmic narrative. See Stephen Heath, "On Suture," in *Questions of Cinema* (Bloomington: Indiana University Press, 1982), 76–112.

6. Jacqueline Goldsby, *A Spectacular Secret: Lynching in American Life and Literature* (University of Chicago Press, 2006), 26–27.

7. *Color Struck* (1925) is a play by Zora Neale Hurston that explores the notion of "colorism," which describes discrimination based on the color of one's skin. In Hurston's play, she examines the internalization of racism among and between African Americans of varying skin tones. *Color Struck* is reproduced in this volume from its original source.

8. See Huey Copeland, "Photography, the Archive, and the Question of Feminist Form: A Conversation with Zoe Leonard," *Camera Obscura* 28, no. 2 (2013): 176–89; and "The Fae Richards Photo Archive: A Panel with Garrett Bradley, Huey Copeland, Lanka Tattersall, and Rebecca Matalon," panel discussion at the Museum of Contemporary Art, Los Angeles, February 27, 2019.

9. On the notion of "problem space," see David Scott, *Conscripts of Modernity: The Tragedy of Colonial Enlightenment* (Durham, NC: Duke University Press, 2004); and Michele Wallace, "Modernism, Postmodernism and the Problem of the Visual in Afro-American Culture," in *Dark Designs and Visual Culture* (Durham, NC: Duke University Press, 2004).

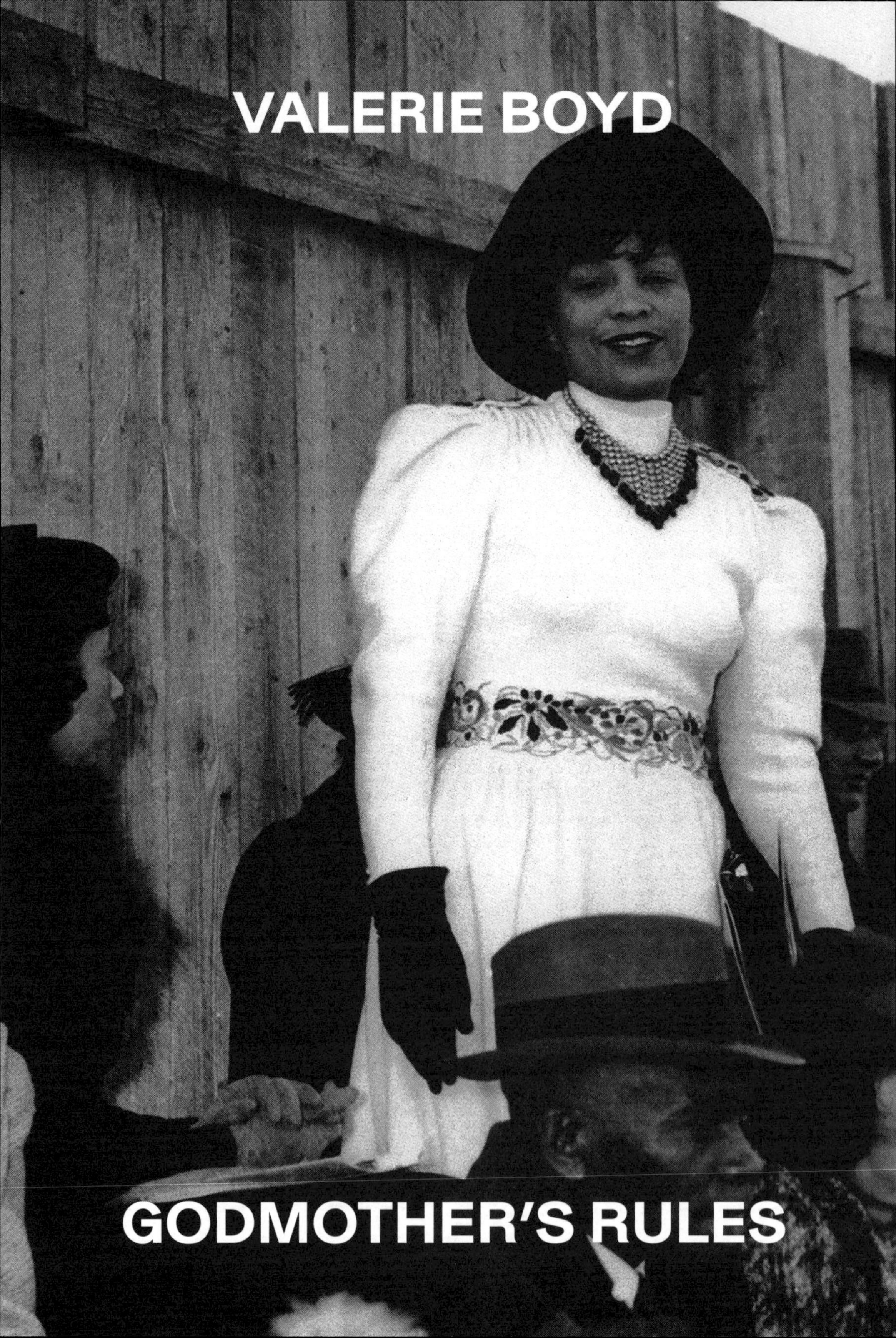

VALERIE BOYD

GODMOTHER'S RULES

Godmother was kind enough to extend Hurston's employment contract through 1929, but not without a price: The "hazy dreams" of the Negro theater that Zora had spoken of with Langston Hughes and Alain Locke must be abandoned at once, Godmother demanded. "She trusts her three children to never let those words pass their lips again," a rebuked Hurston informed Locke, "until the gods decree that they shall materialize."

After a brief winter visit to New York to seal the extended deal with Godmother, Hurston returned to New Orleans to finish her conjure work. Her last night there, she gave a talk on poetry at the University of New Orleans and read six poems by *Fire!!* contributor Helene Johnson, a few from Hughes's *Weary Blues*, and *Fine Clothes to the Jew* from cover to cover. Though the frank language of *Fine Clothes* almost gave one old matron a heart attack, Zora told Langston, the students "et it up."

By the first week of April 1929, Zora had returned to her beloved Florida, where she stayed with her brother John and his wife, Blanche, on Evergreen Avenue in Jacksonville. "I am sitting down to sum up and I am getting on very well at it," Hurston apprised Hughes. "I am feeling full of my subjects," she added, but admitted she wasn't sure how established folklore scholars—the Odums and Johnsons and Pucketts of the world—would respond to her work. In fact, Hurston expected to hear "lots of hollering as various corns get stepped on."

After a couple of weeks in Jacksonville, Zora motored 170 miles downstate to Eau Gallie. Slap on the Indian River, this village near Melbourne was too tiny to warrant a pin on most maps, but it was just what Zora wanted: a beautiful and quiet place to sort through all the material she'd collected. She rented a small cabin there and hunkered down.

Some days, Zora felt swamped by the voluminosity of her material—and by the extraordinary task that lay ahead of her: to make sense of it all for the reading public. "I have more than 95,000 words of story material, a collection of children's games, conjure material, and religious material with a great number of photographs," she wrote to Franz Boas. Hurston then peppered her mentor with questions that would help to ensure her ethnographic accuracy: "Is it safe for me to say that baptism is an extension of water worship as a part of pantheism just as the sacrament is an extension of cannibalism? Isn't the use of candles in the Catholic church a relic of fire worship?" she wanted to know. "May I say that the decoration in clothing is an extension of the primitive application of paint (coloring) to the body?" Then—in direct defiance of her just-renewed contract with Godmother—Hurston promised Boas: "As soon as I can get the typing done, I shall send you the carbons."

Hurston knew the material she'd collected—and the conclusions she hoped to draw—could be academically contentious, as Boas suggested in his reply. That was exactly why she wanted his input. He could provide the anthropological perspective and expertise Hurston needed but could not get from Hughes, Locke, or Godmother, her trio of armchair collaborators. Zora told none of the three—not even best friend Hughes—of her correspondence with Boas, but she was careful to keep them in the loop otherwise. Offering Hughes a stake in all that she did, Zora wrote: "Really I think our material is going to be grand, Langston." At the end of April, she surveyed her progress. "I am just beginning to hit my stride. At first I tried to do too much in a day. Now I am satisfied with a few pages if they say what I want. I have to rewrite a lot as you can understand," she told Hughes. "For I not only want to present the material with all the life and color of my people. I want to leave no loop-holes for the scientific crowd to rend and tear us."

Sensing that Godmother was getting anxious, Zora sent her some of the collected stories in raw form, with hopes of receiving the material back, along with Godmother's comments, by early June. Locke's place in the loop was a lesser concern for Hurston, who believed the professor merely "approves anything that has already been approved." Elaborating, she judged Locke severely, if soundly: "The trouble with Locke is that he is intellectually dishonest. He is too eager to be with the winner... He wants to autograph all successes, but is afraid to risk an opinion first hand."

By the end of May, Zora had received a tentative thumbs-up from Godmother—parroted by Locke—on the material she'd sent to Park Avenue so far. She also was wrapping up first drafts of her volumes on lore and religion, the latter featuring an entire Baptist church service, rendered word for word and note for note. "I shall now set it aside to cool till it grows inside me," Hurston decided.

On a roll now, Zora spent part of the early summer working on the musical play she still hoped to cowrite with Hughes, despite Godmother's nixing of their plans for a Negro theater. Zora suggested they call their play "Jook." She already had worked out a filling-station skit, she reported, and had plenty of jook songs to include.

Hurston also suggested another collaboration of sorts with Hughes: She wanted to buy a tract of land on the Indian River, she told him, and build a Negro art colony—for "you, and Wallie, and Aaron Douglas and Bruce and me and all our crowd." The plat Zora had in mind, about three miles from Eau Gallie proper, would give the artists sufficient privacy while affording them a view of "the most beautiful river in the world," as well as the Atlantic. It would be "a lovely place to retire and write on occasion," she judged. At $4,000, she thought it was a good buy and felt it was "absolutely safe" from rednecks, though their group would be the first Negroes allowed to buy Indian River property. Zora didn't expect Hughes to contribute financially, she said; she just wanted his opinion. Did he think the wealthy A'Lelia Walker might like the idea enough to help with the $1,500 down payment? "We don't need too many. No big society stuff. Just a neat little colony of kindred souls," Zora fantasized. "I'm crazy to build me a house that looks something like an African king's menage. More elaborate, of course."

Zora's dream of becoming a homeowner, however, soon took a backseat to more fundamental concerns. On a foray to St. Augustine in July, she was attacked by severe abdominal pains. Fearing she might need a stomach operation, Zora rushed to Flagler Hospital, a public facility occupying an elegant, new three-story building in the heart of the nation's oldest city. Her stomach was fine, doctors there said, but her liver was out of order—and had been dragging on her health for the past two years. Zora had to be hospitalized immediately. By July 23, though, she felt well enough to begin planning her drive down the coast to collect more lore and conjure in South Florida.

Zora spent all of August and early September in Miami, which she found pleasant and conducive to her work and her recovery. While waiting for her slowpoke stenographer to finish typing the work she'd given her, Zora collected more material and also started to develop new skit ideas for her folk opera with Hughes. By mid-August, she had seven skits completed and was beginning to try her hand at writing music. Her health and appetite were fully recovered: "I am getting on fine now," she reported, "and eating plenty." In early September, though, she hit a snag. Her collecting was "going at a rapid rate," she noted, but she felt a "little depressed spiritually." Around the same time, in Miami's Liberty City, Zora heard some Bahamian music and saw a "jumping dance" that enthralled her. This spirit-elevating music struck her as "more original, dynamic and African" than the songs of American Negroes. Wanting to know more about Bahamian culture, Zora quickly convinced herself that a jaunt across the water to the island nation was just what she needed to permanently chase away her ennui. "Without giving Godmother a chance to object," Zora sailed for Nassau on September 12.

Hurston fell in love with the place before her feet even touched the ground. Her first night there, she stretched out in bed and listened to a rustling coconut palm whisper sweet nothings just outside her window. Then, she was delighted to hear a small chorus of male voices break into song. It was a lovely, melodious folk song about a rum-running boat called *Bellamina*. The next day, Zora met her serenaders, who gave her a hint at what prolific song makers they were. "You do anything, we put you in sing," they told her in lilting voices that hinted of Africa. Some Bahamians actually knew the African tribes from which they'd descended, Hurston soon discovered, and a few even spoke the dialects of their ancestors. She immediately realized she needed to collect Bahamian folklore to contrast it with the lore of Black Americans—and to track its influence, since so many Bahamians lived in South Florida. Before the end of September, Hurston had collected twenty Bahamian songs and learned how to "jump"—that is, how to dance in the way of the folk; she also had recorded three reels of Bahamians performing their native folk dances, including an impressive "Fire Dance." In addition, she had acquired a Bahamian conga drum, called a gimbay, to take home with her.

At one point, however, Zora thought she'd never make it home. On September 28, Nassau was bashed by a devastating hurricane. Traveling on the fierce wings of a 150-mph wind, the storm lingered for five days. "It was horrible in its intensity and duration," recalled Hurston, who was living with a Bahamian family. The second night, as the tempest howled on, Zora had a premonition. Having learned to trust the veracity of her visions—and having been told that the Spirit would speak to her through storms—she leapt from her bed and insisted that everyone in the house get out. Moments after they heeded her warning, the building collapsed.

Zora temporarily joined the ranks of Bahamians who'd been rendered homeless by the storm, which blew down more than three hundred houses in Nassau alone and also ripped through outlying areas. In the days that followed, Zora found shelter, along with dozens of Bahamians, at a local police station. Growing hungry, she gave a man fifty cents to go out and bring back whatever food he could find. He returned with a large bunch of bananas, about fifteen rolls and a slab of bologna. Others at the shelter mobbed the man for the food, despite the police presence, and Zora managed to get only a couple of rolls and a banana. She was happy to have her life, though. At least seven Bahamians lost theirs in the hurricane. "I saw dead people washing around on the streets when it was over," Hurston remembered. "You could smell the stench from dead animals as well."

Despite the death and destruction, Zora stayed in Nassau for several more days and collected some fragmented information on Bahamian hoodoo, or obeah, as it was most commonly called there. The day before she was scheduled to leave, she met a man who she'd been told was the greatest of the island conjure doctors, but she didn't have sufficient time to spend with him. She did have time, though, to get the obeah man "favorably worked up" to her, as she put it. She then promised she'd return to study with him before the end of the year. "I had only my return ticket and 24 cents," she later explained, "so I had to come on."

When Zora returned to Miami and checked her post office box, Number 24, at the Lemon City Station, she found a pile of mail awaiting her. One piece in the stack was a wire from Hughes, responding to her early September complaint of feeling down. So much had happened in the month since she'd sent that SOS, what with her trip to the Bahamas and all, but Hurston still was cheered by Hughes's encouraging, if tardy, reply. "Well, honey, your wire did me so much good," she wrote back. "Gee, I felt forlorn. Too tired. Been working two years without rest, & behind that all my school life with no rest. No peace of mind. But the Bahamas trip did me a world of good. I got rested while working hard."

Zora had been leaning heavily on Hughes during her exhausting two years of collecting. Langston's letters suggesting new angles of looking at her work—and ways to keep Godmother happy—were Zora's pillars during her time in the field. And she used her letters to him as sounding boards. "You know I depend on you so much," she often told him. Her reliance on Hughes was understandable: Hurston had not yet published a book; Hughes, on the other hand, had published two volumes of poetry that were well received among the proletariat, whose opinions mattered most to both writers. Hughes also had known Godmother longer than Hurston had, and he was geographically close to her—close enough, Zora figured, to gauge her moods. Now, Zora wanted to make sure Langston could read and edit the collection of stories—many from the Polk County lying contests—that she'd sent to Park Avenue. Godmother already had insisted that the stories' dirty words had to be toned down, Zora pointed out. "Can you not take them & edit them and indicate changes and generally touch up?" she asked her friend. "I want to close out all the volumes as soon as I can. When it is all in you and I can take plenty of time to edit it. Locke will be a great help too," she conceded, "but I am afraid he will not see it just as we do." Hurston suggested Hughes consult the original stories, in Godmother's safety deposit box, and make notes to send to her. Then she added a sisterly postscript: "Do you need some money?"

While Zora routinely offered to help Langston financially, she knew she could turn to him for something more valuable: emotional support. "You are my mainstay in all crises," she told him in October. "No matter what may happen, I feel you can fix it."

Another piece of mail awaiting Zora was from Locke, suggesting that she had not been specific enough about some of her religious material from New Orleans. She took his criticism constructively: As soon as she finished her collecting in Miami, around the end of October, she would simply go back to New Orleans to correct any oversights.

That settled, Zora slogged through the rest of her mail, then wrote a long-overdue letter to Franz Boas, responding to a job offer he'd extended her back in May. The anthropology department at Columbia University was embarking on a study of the "mental characteristics" of various ethnic groups, he told her. He and the study's director, Otto Klineberg, were particularly interested in "the special ability of the Negroes" in music. Boas wanted Hurston to join the Columbia investigation in New Orleans, and offered her a salary of $150 a month, plus reasonable expenses.

Hurston was enthusiastic about the idea, citing "a new birth of creative singing among Negroes" that she'd observed in New Orleans and elsewhere during her southern travels. "The old songs are not sung so much. New ones are flooding everywhere," Hurston advised Boas. She also updated him on her own work: She'd finished compiling her volume of folktales and was still wrestling with second drafts of the manuscripts on conjure and religion. "I have not quite located all that I want," she admitted. Even so, Hurston hoped soon to send Boas the volume of folktales for his scientific review. "I have tried to be as exact as possible. Keeping to the exact dialect as closely as I could, having the story teller to tell it to me word for word as I write it. This after it has been told to me off hand until I know it myself. But the writing down from the lips is to insure the correct dialect and wording so that I shall not let myself creep in unconsciously," she reported, detailing her fidelity to accuracy. Since she planned to return to New Orleans in November anyway, Hurston concluded, she would be happy to meet with Klineberg and offer her assistance with the Columbia study.

Hurston had not yet spoken with Charlotte Mason about Boas's promising job offer, but she knew her amended contract with Godmother was due to expire shortly, at the end of 1929. She assumed she'd be free then to take on other work, and believed Godmother might encourage her career independence—and welcome the chance to remove her from her payroll. Hurston was wrong. An aggravated Mason upbraided her young folklorist, letting her know she was not to take on any assignments for Boas or anyone else until she had completed the work at hand. She also reminded Hurston that she, Godmother, still had legal control over all the collected material.

Hurston's hands were tied—in a slipknot, it seemed, and Godmother was tightening the twine. Sensitive to rope burn, Hurston realized that if she ever wanted to see the fruits of her two years of labor published—under her name—she had to play by Godmother's rules. Embarrassed, Hurston wrote to Boas at once: "I find that I am restrained from leaving the employ of my present employers... I cannot tell you how sorry I am, but I cannot say anything more... I thought I could do it. I felt very sure," she apologized.

This news threw Boas and Klineberg into a tizzy. Although Hurston's apologetic dispatch included a list of potential contacts for Klineberg in New Orleans, America's leading anthropologist believed the project was doomed without Hurston's active participation. Boas immediately began making plans for Klineberg to launch a study of South Dakota Indians instead. Not warmed by the thought of a Dakota winter, Klineberg was relieved to receive a copy of Hurston's subsequent letter to Boas, explaining herself more fully.

"I am in a trying situation," she wrote from Miami. "If Dr. Klineberg will come on, I will give him all the assistance possible. Perhaps just as much as if I were entirely at liberty. But I wanted you to understand what I am up against." Without ever divulging her employer's identity, Hurston told Boas she had figured out a solution to her dilemma: She would tell Mason she was going to New Orleans to collect more conjure, which was true. Godmother never had to know she also was helping with the Columbia study. Hurston assured Boas: "I shall see to it that Dr. K. has the proper openings, help, contacts and whatever else you want... Really things will work out better than they sound. I pray that you trust me and send Dr. K. along."

Boas did, and in early November, Hurston and Klineberg met each other in the city of brass bands and beignets. The very next day, Hurston persuaded Klineberg to inaugurate his palate with some famous New Orleans oysters. The social scientist got a bad half dozen and was sick and shut in for the next week. When he finally recovered enough to write, Klineberg told Boas he was favorably impressed with Hurston, despite her dubious dining choice. "Miss Hurston strikes me as an extremely interesting and intelligent person," he wrote. "I think she will be a great help, and she seems to have a considerable amount of time for me." Relieved that all had turned out well, Boas wrote back to approve Klineberg's proposed new research direction: a study, "together with Miss Hurston," of the racial makeup, educational history, and mystical background of New Orleans Creoles. Boas was especially excited about the prospect of comparing the Creoles to the other Negroes of New Orleans. But he offered Klineberg a caveat: "Please be sure to check Miss Hurston in regard to accuracy. I have no reason to doubt her, but temperamently, she is so much more artistic rather than scientific that she has to be held down." No problem, Klineberg responded after another week in the field with Hurston. "She continues to be very active and very valuable," Klineberg assured Papa Franz.

Well into December, Hurston also was enjoying the collaboration: "Dr. Klineberg is very fine to work with," she told Boas. Her own work was proceeding smoothly, too, she added. She was now collecting conjure stories—"all the miraculous tales the people tell me about conjure and witchcraft"—to add to the actual ceremonies she'd recorded for her volume on hoodoo. "I want to make this conjure work very thorough and inclusive," she explained to Boas. "As soon as I have the latest material assembled in some order, I shall let you have it."

This promise would have been unremarkable had it not been a clear violation of Hurston's contract with Mason. Hurston flouted Godmother's ban against showing anyone her collected material because she believed, rightly, that exposing her work to Boas's scrutiny would make it better. And, she bargained, what Godmother didn't know couldn't possibly hurt her.

Deception, however, often takes a toll on the deceiver, Hurston found out. "I am simply wasting away with fear," she soon whispered to Hughes from New Orleans. Her fear, however, was not related to her dealings with Boas, which even Hughes knew nothing about. She was now fretting over the crucial matter of transportation. Because of all the miles she'd logged on the once-shiny Chevrolet, Zora had to have a new car. "Just HAD to," she told Hughes. When she mentioned her need to Godmother, the old woman exploded, insinuating that Zora was extravagant or "took her for a good thing." Neither accusation, Hurston noted, "was soothing to my self-respect." The next time the car gave her trouble, mechanics told Zora she would have to spend ninety-five dollars to get it back on the road. Instead, she took it upon herself to haggle for a new one, she wrote, "and keep my big mouth shut." But Godmother learned of the transaction when the car dealer checked Zora's references. Predictably, Godmother was livid. "She wrote me a letter that hurt me thru and thru," Zora told Langston. "Why couldn't Negroes be trusted?" Godmother demanded to know.

Rather than challenge the old woman on her bigoted view—indicting the whole race for one person's mistake—Zora dissembled to protect her cash flow and the research that it financed. But the episode left her feeling "half ill," she confided to Hughes. A cooled-down Godmother later sent the $400 to pay for the car. But now there was another problem. The used car that Zora had purchased—"as is"—started knocking before she had driven it a hundred miles. Without consulting Godmother, Zora immediately traded it in for a newer model—and, though she got some credit for the trade-in, she now had a balance of $300, which she planned to pay out of her monthly salary. "I am just praying that she won't find out what I have done," Zora worried. "I don't feel that I have done wrong for nobody knows what inconvenience I have suffered fooling with old cars. Always something to fix. Money I ought to spend on my work is spent on the old can and keeping me strapped," she grumbled. Then, more to the point, Hurston added: "I just feel that she ought not to exert herself to supervise every little detail. It destroys my self-respect and utterly demoralizes me for weeks. I know you can appreciate what I mean. I do care for her deeply, don't forget that. That is why I can't endure to get at odds with her. I don't want anything but to get at my work with the least possible trouble."

Hughes certainly could appreciate Hurston's perspective, for he had begun to have his own run-ins with Godmother over what seemed to be her growing list of rules. Now that he had completed his studies at Lincoln University, for instance, Godmother did not want him living in Harlem because it harbored too many distractions, she said. Instead, she put him up in Westfield, New Jersey, an hour from Manhattan. Renting a room from a quiet, elderly Black couple, Hughes was hard at work on his first novel, *Not Without Laughter*. Zora cheered his efforts from afar: "A poet should turn out marvelous prose," she nudged him. But Godmother—sometimes through Locke—was serving as Hughes's unwanted editor, admonishing him not to submerge the novel's beauty beneath a wave of propaganda.

Despite his own troubles with their shared patron, Hughes advised Hurston that the best thing to do was to be honest with Godmother about the car. She might explode again, he conceded, but explosions were part of the business. Besides, he assured Zora, Godmother loved her too much to cut her off completely.

Langston's words of advice, Zora told him, "comforted my soul like dreamless sleep." And he was right. Godmother's car conniption soon blew over. "Well, I tell you, Langston, I am nothing without you," Zora wrote. "That's no flattery either.

We will talk a lot when I get there."

Zora spent much of December 1929 running about New Orleans, as she reported, "with my tongue hanging out to get everything I see." At Christmastime, she returned to the Bahamas for carnival season. After catching up with the noted conjure doctor with whom she'd promised to study, Hurston prepared to return to New York. She tarried a bit more in the Bahamas and Florida, however, before finally making her way North in early March.

When Zora returned to New York from more than two solid years in the South, she found the Big Apple (as the jazzmen had begun to call it) slightly bruised. The Wall Street crash of October 1929 had left some noticeable scars. "People were sleeping in subways or on newspapers in office doors, because they had no homes," Hughes would recall. "And in every block a beggar appeared." Hurston was disconcerted by this public poverty, as well as by the haggard faces of her friends in Harlem. "Some of my friends are all tired and worn out—looking like death eating crackers," she commented.

Still, Zora was heartened to be back among her old pals, who immediately informed her that she had a new dance to learn. The Lindy hop—named for Charles Lindbergh's famous transcontinental flight—had become all the rage at the Savoy Ballroom. No sooner had Zora learned the lively steps than Charlotte Mason summoned her to 399 Park Avenue to do a different dance.

When Zora arrived at the penthouse apartment, she found Godmother largely untouched by the Depression that was swelling all around her. Sitting at her dining room table in her high, thronelike chair, "over capon, caviar and gleaming silver," Mason exhorted Zora to tell the tales, sing the songs, and do the dances she'd picked up during her southern expedition. With the reels of film she'd shot as visual aids, Zora assented to the show-and-tell.

Hurston's footage showed deeply Black children in Florida playing games and dancing like no one was watching. At one point, Hurston formed the children in a circle and slowly panned her camera around the ring, lingering lovingly on each child's face. Sometimes, she filmed them in extreme close-ups, as their wide eyes peered inquisitively into the lens. In another reel, a woman walked off her porch toward the camera; Zora zoomed in frankly on her face for a candid shot that showed both beauty and sorrow, curiosity and wariness. In the next scene, the woman and a friend, both wearing simple housedresses, lounged comfortably on the porch. Zora also had footage of Cudjo Lewis, showing him to be handsome, active, and courtly. Another reel recorded Hurston's visit to the cypress swamp with the men at the Loughman sawmill camp. All of the footage—of the Black men, women, and children—said as much about Hurston as it did about her subjects: Whoever recorded these images knew Black people intimately, the footage insinuated, and loved them intensely.

The passion of Hurston's cinematic eye could not have been lost on Mason, and she did not wish to give the ardor a moment to cool. Ignoring Zora's obvious need for rest, and for some playtime, Godmother insisted she get to work immediately. And New York was no place to engage in the serious task of preparing her manuscripts. So Godmother set Zora up in villagelike Westfield, too, just a few doors from Langston Hughes's room at 514 Downer Street.

From the outset, the arrangement suited Zora well. She and Hughes were happy to be reunited, and neighbors, too. They talked constantly, and Langston, as promised, helped Zora to edit her stacks and stacks of collected material, which she was anxious to publish so she could return to a more creative groove. "I am stuffed with things I'd like to write now, and I shall get down hard at it as soon as I clear this work up," she vowed.

In their idyllic colony of two, Langston and Zora frequently had company: Louise Thompson, a bright and attractive young woman hired by Godmother the previous September to work as Hughes's secretary. Now that Zora was also in Westfield, Godmother decided, the two writers would share Thompson's services. Godmother had amply prepared Louise for Zora's arrival: “She used to talk about Zora, about this wonderful child of nature who was so unspoiled, and what a marvelous person she was,” Thompson later recalled. “And Zora did not disappoint me. She was a grand storyteller.”

Zora had not been similarly prepped to meet Louise, but she’d heard a little about her in a gossipy letter from Langston: Louise had been briefly, and disastrously, married to Wallace Thurman, who everyone knew was a homosexual—except, apparently, his bride. “Poor Wallie! I wish he might get a divorce,” Zora had sympathized. Now, meeting Thompson, Hurston didn’t think she was so bad after all. In fact, Hurston, Thompson, and Hughes got on famously. Zora entertained Langston and Louise with stories from her southern travels, and Louise’s large apartment in the city, at 435 Convent Avenue, became a second home for the trio.

All the while, Hurston continued her efforts to organize her field notes. Now, the goal was to produce one comprehensive volume that would include folktales and conjure. “I am urged to do things as quickly as possible and so at present I am working furiously,” Hurston reported to Boas in mid-April. On the sixteenth, she “received a word from headquarters” telling her to come over the following Friday at three o’clock, and to bring materials for discussion. Consequently, she told Boas, she would have to stop by his office to retrieve the essay he was secretly reading for her.

Several days after the penthouse appointment, Locke assured Hurston that Godmother remained pleased with her. “I thought it would cheer you at this critical stage of your work that she really thinks you have done well and is eagerly looking forward to pushing the book,” he wrote. Even so, Godmother thought the material might be too unwieldy. Her new idea—which Locke fully supported, of course—was to pare down the manuscript by selecting only the best material. “She thinks it would be a mistake even to have a scientific tone to the book, so soft pedal all notion of too specific documentation and let loose on the things that you are really best equipped to give—a vivid dramatizing of your material and the personalities back of it,” Locke recommended. His implication that she was not "best equipped" to provide scientific documentation must have galled the anthropologist in Hurston. But Locke was not finished; he was to insult Hurston the writer as well: "You can do this in a feverish two or three days," he presumed, "and then it will be all over, but the shouting." Locke then would be happy to edit the manuscript, he offered. It would be grand to present Godmother with the finished document on her birthday, May 18. Didn't Zora agree? "I think we can whip it into shape by then," Locke asserted.

Hurston largely ignored Locke's ivory-towered advice. "It has been very hard to get the material in any shape at all," she complained; wrapping up the whole enterprise in a few days was impossible.

In lieu of a completed manuscript, then, Zora presented Godmother with a long, fawning letter for her birthday. "You are God's flower," Zora purred to Godmother, "and my flower and Miss Chapin's flower and Langston's flower and the world's blossom." This birthday epistle was both cloying and comic—though Godmother no doubt believed it utterly sincere. "Oh, my lovely just-born flower, if back there when you fluttered pink into this drab world—if they had but known how much joy and love you should bring! How much of the white light of God you would diffuse into soft radiance for the eyes of the primitives, the wise ones would have stood awed before your cradle and brought great gifts from afar." Hurston's references to Mason's pink skin and to "the white light of God" were almost certainly tongue-in-cheek, but she cleverly concealed her mocking words under a sugary sheen. And the joke, Hurston boldly wagered, was above Godmother's head. Or, perhaps more accurately, it was beneath her—just below the reach of her condescension.

Like Langston Hughes and Louise Thompson, Hurston sometimes felt uncomfortable with Godmother's obsession with the "primitive," but she knew how to play the wealthy widow like a guitar. This is not to say that Hurston did not care for Godmother. She did, genuinely. But in their remarkably complex relationship, Hurston certainly did not care for everything Godmother said or did—usually under the influence of her zealous devotion to "primitivism." Once, for example, Godmother sent an excessively exotic dress to Westfield for Zora to wear. On the phone to Park Avenue, Zora reported that the dress looked fabulous on her. Then she hung up and shared a laugh with Thompson about the gaudiness of the dress, which she would never dream of wearing. But what would have been the benefit of telling Godmother the dress was hideous? Perhaps it would have given Hurston a fleeting feeling of racial victory and, in the best possible scenario, it might have influenced Godmother to adopt a more realistic racial outlook. Yet that kind of bluntness was not what Godmother wanted—and certainly not something she would have continued to finance. True honesty, across racial lines, was possible and acceptable in relationships with some white people, Hurston found. With Carl Van Vechten, for instance, both Hurston and Hughes felt free to speak their minds. But he was their friend. Godmother was their patron. And Hurston understood the difference. So she usually told Godmother what she wanted to hear, which kept the checks coming—and enabled her to do the work she felt called to do.

In this regard, Zora's birthday missive was written for the express purpose of stroking Godmother's outsize ego, not to mention her Messianic complex: "I really should not extend my congratulations to you on this day, but to all those who have been fortunate enough to touch you," Zora wrote, the molasses practically dripping from her pen. "It is you who gives out life and light and we who receive."

Hurston's flattery got her nowhere, however, when she asked Godmother to consider funding her for graduate studies at Columbia. Boas had been impressed enough with the material Hurston had shared with him to write to Trevor Arnett, director of the General Education Board, recommending her for a graduate fellowship. "She is an unusually gifted person with a good deal of literary skill," Boas wrote, and "well fitted" for graduate work in anthropology. But the General Education Board, which had been founded by John D. Rockefeller in 1902, could not help; its policy was to assist scholars already teaching at one of the Negro colleges. Perhaps the Julius Rosenwald Fund might be of some use, Boas was advised.

Papa Franz suggested Zora ask her current employer to support her academic ambitions. "The 'Angel' is cold towards the degrees, but will put up more money for further research," Hurston reported back. Perhaps her patron might allow her to combine the degree program with her research, Boas offered, still unaware of the identity of Hurston's "angel." "Make it clear to her that your research work under the direction of a university would be much more profitable than without it and that she will further your own welfare considerably by making the combination," he counseled. The argument was useless, Hurston knew: "I have broached the subject from several angles," she told Boas, "but it got chill blains no matter how I put it."

Late that spring, the blains threatened to erupt, and both of Mason's godchildren in Westfield felt the pain. Without warning, Godmother's temper flared. Somehow, probably from Locke, she had gotten the impression that her Westfield pair was having too much fun—and not doing enough work. When Hurston and Hughes tried to calm Mason, she snubbed them both. Finally her hackles were smoothed by a letter of atonement from Langston, followed by a longer apology, for what he wasn't certain.

The most likely reason for Godmother's tantrum was her discovery of a secret that Hurston and Hughes had tried to keep from her. Back in March, the two had begun working on a play together, without Mason's consent. She was particularly upset with Zora over this, because she feared the play would pilfer time from her efforts to complete her folklore manuscript—the work Godmother was still paying her to do. Godmother's worry was unwarranted, though. The play, to be called *Mule Bone*, did not significantly slice into the time Hurston spent on her folklore work. *Mule Bone* would, however, have a sundering effect that no one could have anticipated—not even Godmother, the self-proclaimed clairvoyant. In the end, the play would rip the Hurston-Hughes friendship apart.

ZORA NEALE HURSTON

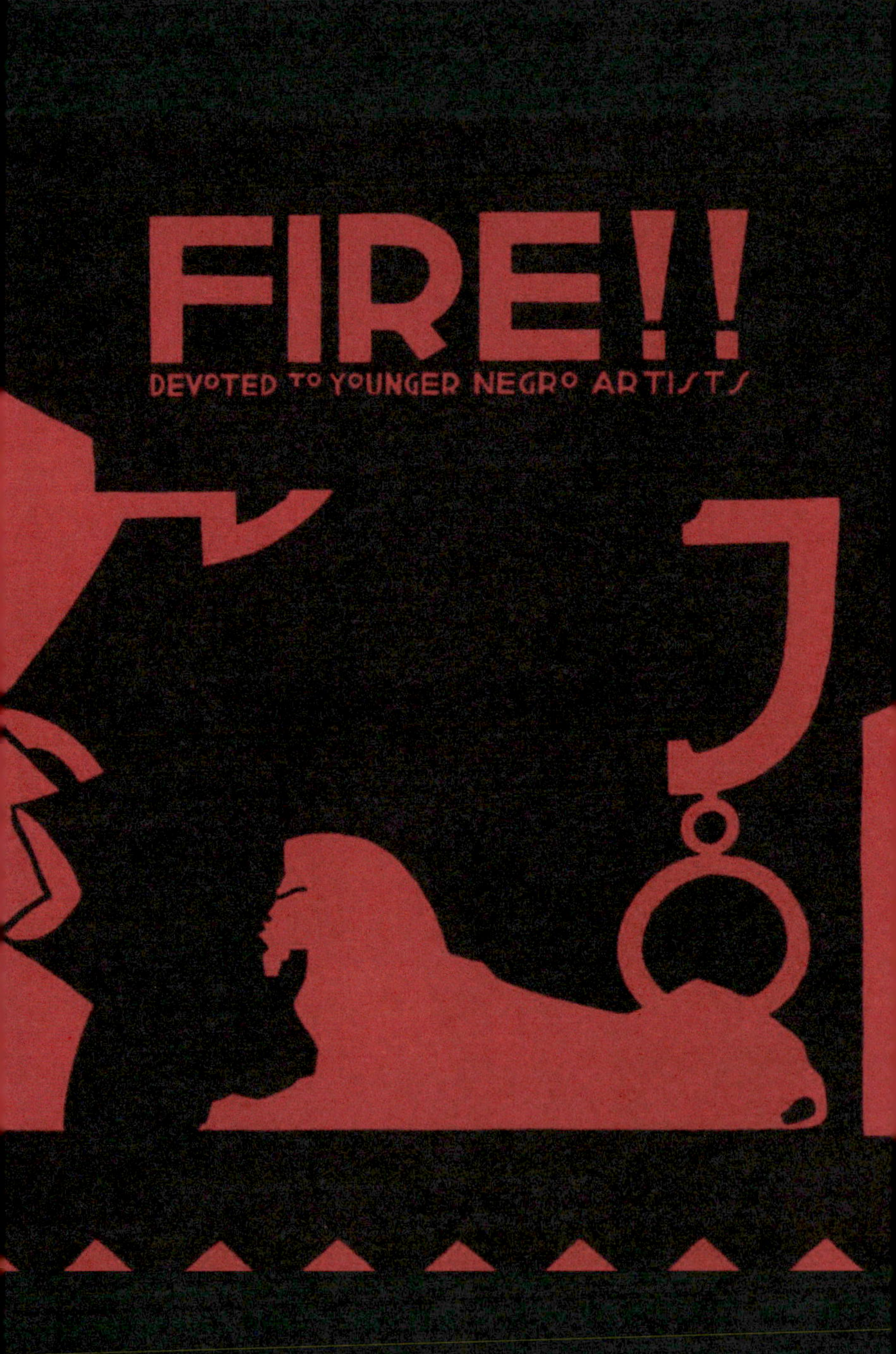

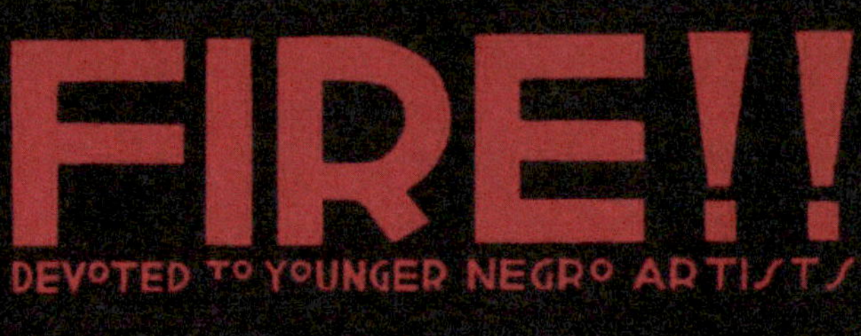

COLOR STRUCK

FIRE!!

A Quarterly Devoted to the Younger Negro Artists

Premier Issue Edited by

WALLACE THURMAN

In Association With

Langston Hughes
Gwendolyn Bennett
Richard Bruce
Zora Neale Hurston
Aaron Douglas
John Davis

Table of Contents

Volume One   Number One

EDITORIAL OFFICES

314 West 138th Street, New York City

Price $1.00 per copy   Issued Quarterly

Foreword

FIRE . . . *flaming, burning, searing, and penetrating far beneath the superficial items of the flesh to boil the sluggish blood.*

FIRE . . . *a cry of conquest in the night, warning those who sleep and revitalizing those who linger in the quiet places dozing.*

FIRE . . . *melting steel and iron bars, poking livid tongues between stone apertures and burning wooden opposition with a cackling chuckle of contempt.*

FIRE . . . *weaving vivid, hot designs upon an ebon bordered loom and satisfying pagan thirst for beauty unadorned . . . the flesh is sweet and real . . . the soul an inward flush of fire. . . . Beauty? . . . flesh on fire—on fire in the furnace of life blazing. . . .*

"Fy-ah,
Fy-ah, Lawd,
Fy-ah gonna burn ma soul!"

Color Struck

A Play in Four Scenes

Time: Twenty years ago and present. *Place: A Southern City.*

PERSONS

JOHN	*A light brown-skinned man*
EMMALINE	*A black woman*
WESLEY	*A boy who plays an accordion*
EMMALINE'S DAUGHTER	*A very white girl*
EFFIE	*A mulatto girl*

A RAILWAY CONDUCTOR A DOCTOR

Several who play mouth organs, guitars, banjos.
Dancers, passengers, etc.

SETTING.—*Early night. The inside of a "Jim Crow" railway coach. The car is parallel to the footlights. The seats on the down stage side of the coach are omitted. There are the luggage racks above the seats. The windows are all open. They are exits in each end of the car—right and left.*

ACTION.—*Before the curtain goes up there is the sound of a locomotive whistle and a stopping engine, loud laughter, many people speaking at once, good-natured shreiks, strumming of stringed instruments, etc. The ascending curtain discovers a happy lot of Negroes boarding the train dressed in the gaudy, twdry best of 1900. They are mostly in couples—each couple bearing a covered-over market basket which the men hastily deposit in the racks as they scramble for seats. There is a litle friendly pushing and shoving. One pair just miss a seat three times, much to the enjoyment of the crowd. Many "plug" silk hats are in evidence, also sun-flowers in button holes. The women are showily dressed in the manner of the time, and quite conscious of their finery. A few seats remain unoccupied.*

Enter Effie (left) above, with a basket. ONE OF THE MEN (*standing, lifting his "plug" in a grand manner*). Howdy do, Miss Effie, you'se lookin' jes lak a rose.

(*Effie blushes and is confused. She looks up and down for a seat.*) Fack is, if you wuzn't walkin' long, ah'd think you wuz a rose—(*he looks timidly behind her and the others laugh*). Looka here, where's Sam at?

EFFIE (*tossing her head haughtily*). I don't know an' I don't keer.

THE MAN (*visibly relieved*). Then lemme scorch you to a seat. (*He takes her basket and leads her to a seat center of the car, puts the basket in the rack and seats himself beside her with his hat at a rakish angle.*)

MAN (*sliding his arm along the back of the seat*). How come Sam ain't heah—y'll on a bust?

EFFIE (*angrily*). A man dat don't buy me nothin tuh put in *mah* basket, ain't goin' wid *me* tuh no cake walk. (*The hand on the seat touches her shoulder and she thrusts it away*). Take yo' arms from 'round me, Dinky! Gwan hug yo' Ada!

MAN (*in mock indignation*). Do you think I'd look at Ada when Ah got a chance tuh be wid you? Ah always wuz sweet on you, but you let ole Mullet-head Sam cut me out.

ANOTHER MAN (*with head out of the window*). Just look at de darkies coming! (*With head insite coach.*) Hey, Dinky! Heah come Ada wid a great big basket.

(*Dinky jumps up from beside Effie and rushes to exit right. In a moment they re-enter and take a seat near entrance. Everyone in coach laughs. Dinky's girl turns and calls back to Effie.*)

GIRL. Where's Sam, Effie?

EFFIE. Lawd knows, Ada.

GIRL. Lawd a mussy! Who you gointer walk de cake wid?

EFFIE. Nobody, Ah reckon. John and Emma gointer win it nohow. They's the bestest cake-walkers in dis state.

ADA. You'se better than Emma any day in de week. Cose Sam cain't walk lake John. (*She stands up and scans the coach.*) Looka heah, ain't John an' Emma going? They ain't on heah!

(*The locomotive bell begins to ring.*)

EFFIE. Mah Gawd, s'pose dey got left!

MAN (*with head out of window*). Heah they come, nip and tuck—whoo-ee! They'se gonna make it! (*He waves excitedly.*) Come on Jawn! (*Everybody crowds the windows, encouraging them by gesture and calls. As the whistle blows twice, and the train begins to move, they enter panting and laughing at left. The only seat left is the one directly in front of Effie.*)

DINKY (*standing*). Don't y'all skeer us no mo' lake dat! There couldn't be no cake walk thout y'all. Dem shad-mouf St. Augustine coons would win dat cake and we would have tuh kill 'em all bodaciously.

JOHN. It was Emmaline nearly made us get left. She says I wuz smiling at Effie on the street car and she had to get off and wait for another one.

EMMA (*removing the hatpins from her hat, turns furiously upon him*). You wuz grinning at her and she wuz grinning back jes lake a ole chessy cat!

JOHN (*positively*). I wuzn't.

EMMA (*about to place her hat in rack*). You wuz. I seen you looking jes lake a possum.

JOHN. I wuzn't. I never gits a chance tuh smile at nobody—you won't let me.

EMMA. Jes the same every time you sees a yaller face, you *takes* a chance. (*They sit down in peeved silence for a minute.*)

DINKY. Ada, les we all sample de basket. I bet you got huckleberry pie.

ADA. No I aint, I got peach an' tater pies, but we aint gonna tetch a thing tell we gits tuh de hall.

DINKY (*mock alarm*). Naw, don't do dat! It's all right tuh save the fried chicken, but pies is *always* et on trains.

ADA. Aw shet up! (*He struggles with her for a kiss. She slaps him but finally yields.*)

JOHN (*looking behind him*). Hellow, Effie, where's Sam?

EFFIE. Deed, I don't know.

JOHN. Y'all on a bust?

EMMA. None ah yo' bizness, you got enough tuh mind yo' own self. Turn 'round!

(*She puts up a pouting mouth and he snatches a kiss. She laughs just as he kisses her again and there is a resounding smack which causes the crowd to laugh. And cries of* "Oh you kid!" "Salty dog!")

(*Enter conductor left calling tickets cheerfully and laughing at the general merriment.*)

CONDUCTOR. I hope somebody from Jacksonville wins this cake.

JOHN. You live in the "Big Jack?"

CONDUCTOR. Sure do. And I wanta taste a piece of that cake on the way back tonight.

JOHN. Jes rest easy—them Augustiners aint gonna smell it. (*Turns to Emma.*) Is they, baby?

EMMA. Not if Ah kin help it.

Somebody with a guitar sings: "Ho babe, mah honey taint no lie."

(*The conductor takes up tickets, passes on and exits right.*)

WESLEY. Look heah, you cake walkers—y'all oughter git up and limber up yo' joints. I heard them folks over to St. Augustine been oiling up wid goose-grease, and over to Ocala they been rubbing down in snake oil.

A WOMAN'S VOICE. You better shut up, Wesley, you just joined de church last month. Somebody's going to tell the pastor on you.

WESLEY. Tell it, tell it, take it up and smell it. Come on out you John and Emma and Effie, and limber up.

JOHN. Naw, we don't wanta do our walking steps—nobody won't wanta see them when we step out at the hall. But we kin do something else just to warm ourselves up.

(*Wesley begins to play "Goo Goo Eyes" on his accordian, the other instruments come in one by one and John and Emma step into the aisle and "parade" up and down the aisle—Emma holding up her skirt, showing the lace on her petticoats. They two-step back to their seat amid much applause.*)

WESLEY. Come on out, Effie! Sam aint heah so you got to hold up his side too. Step on out. (*There is a murmur of applause as she steps into the aisle. Wesley strikes up "I'm gointer live anyhow till I die." It is played quite spiritedly as Effie swings into the pas-me-la—*)

WESLEY (*in ecstasy*). Hot stuff I reckon! Hot stuff I reckon! (*The musicians are stamping. Great enthusiasm. Some clap time with hands and feet. She hurls herself into a modified Hoochy Koochy, and finishes up with an ecstatic yell.*)

There is a babble of talk and laughter and exultation.

JOHN (*applauding loudly*). If dat Effie can't step nobody can.

EMMA. Course you'd say so cause it's her. Everything she do is pretty to you.

JOHN (*caressing her*). Now don't say that, Honey. Dancing is dancing no matter who is doing it. But nobody can hold a candle to you in nothing.

(*Some men are heard tuning up—getting pitch to sing. Four of them crowd together in one seat and begin the chorus of "Daisies Won't Tell." John and Emma grow quite affectionate.*)

JOHN (*kisses her*). Emma, what makes you always picking a fuss with me over some yaller girl.

What makes you so jealous, nohow ? I don't do nothing.

(*She clings to him, but he turns slightly away. The train whistle blows, there is a slackening of speed. Passengers begin to take down baskets from their racks.*)

EMMA. John! John, don't you want me to love you, honey?

JOHN (*turns and kisses her slowly*). Yes, I want you to love me, you know I do. But I don't like to be accused o' ever light colored girl in the world. It hurts my feeling. I don't want to be jealous like you are.

(*Enter at right Conductor, crying "St. Augustine, St. Augustine." He exits left. The crowd has congregated at the two exits, pushing good-naturedly and joking. All except John and Emma. They are still seated with their arms about each other.*)

EMMA (*sadly*). Then you don't want my love, John, cause I can't help mahself from being jealous. I loves you so hard, John, and jealous love is the only kind I got.

(*John kisses her very feelingly.*)

EMMA. Just for myself alone is the only way I knows how to love.

(*They are standing in the aisle with their arms about each other as the curtain falls.*)

SCENE II

SETTING.—*A weather-board hall. A large room with the joists bare. The place has been divided by a curtain of sheets stretched and a rope across from left to right. From behind the curtain there are occasional sounds of laughter, a note or two on a stringed instrument or accordion. General stir. That is the dance hall. The front is the ante-room where the refreshments are being served. A "plank" seat runs all around the hall, along the walls. The lights are kerosene lamps with reflectors. They are fixed to the wall. The lunch-baskets are under the seat. There is a table on either side upstage with a woman behind each. At one, ice cream is sold, at the other, roasted peanuts and large red-and-white sticks of peppermint candy.*

People come in by twos and three, laughing, joking, horse-plays, gauchily flowered dresses, small waists, bulging hips and busts, hats worn far back on the head, etc. People from Ocala greet others from Palatka, Jacksonville, St. Augustine, etc.

Some find seats in the ante-room, others pass on into the main hall.

Enter the Jacksonville delegation, laughing, pushing proudly.

DINKY. Here we is, folks—here we *is*. Gointer take dat cake on back tuh Jacksonville where it belongs.

MAN. Gwan! Whut wid you mullet-head Jacksonville Coons know whut to do wid a cake. It's gointer stay right here in Augustine where de *good* cake walkers grow.

DINKY. Taint no 'Walkers' never walked till John and Emmaline prance out—you mighty come a tootin'.

Great laughing and joshing as more people come in. John and Emma are encouraged, urged on to win.

EMMA. Let's we git a seat, John, and set down.

JOHN. Sho will—nice one right over there. (*They push over to wall seat, place basket underneath, and sit. Newcomers shake hands with them and urge them on to win.*)

(*Enter Joe Clarke and a small group. He is a rotund, expansive man with a liberal watch chain and charm.*)

DINKY (*slapping Clarke on the back*). If you don't go 'way from here! Lawdy, if it aint Joe.

CLARKE (*jovially*). Ah thought you had done forgot us people in Eatonville since you been living up here in Jacksonville.

DINKY. Course Ah aint. (*Turning.*) Looka heah folks! Joe Clarke oughta be made chairman uh dis meetin'—Ah mean Past Great-Grand Master of Ceremonies, him being the onliest mayor of de onliest colored town in de state.

GENERAL CHORUS. Yeah, let him be—thass fine, etc.

DINKY (*setting his hat at a new angle and throwing out his chest*). And *Ah'll* scorch him to de platform. Ahem!

(*Sprinkling of laughter as Joe Clarke is escorted into next room by Dinky.*)

(*The musicians are arriving one by one during this time. A guitar, accordian, mouth organ, banjo, etc. Soon there is a rapping for order heard inside and the voice of Joe Clarke.*)

JOE CLARKE. Git yo' partners one an' all for de gran' march! Git yo' partners, gent-mens!

A MAN (*drawing basket from under bench*). Let's we all eat first.

(*John and Emma go buy ice-cream. They coquettishly eat from each other's spoons. Old Man Lizzimore crosses to Effie and removes his hat and bows with a great flourish.*)

LIZZIMORE. Sam ain't here t'night, is he, Effie.

EFFIE (*embarrassed*). Naw suh, he aint.

LIZZ. Well, you like chicken? (*Extends arm to her.*) Take a wing!

(*He struts her up to the table amid the laughter of the house. He wears no collar.*)

JOHN (*squeezes Emma's hand*). You certainly is a ever loving mamma—when you aint mad.

EMMA (*smiles sheepishly*). You oughtn't to make me mad then.

JOHN. Ah don't make you! You makes yo'self mad, den blame it on me. Ah keep on tellin' you Ah don't love nobody but you. Ah knows heaps uh half-white girls Ah could git ef Ah wanted to. But (*he squeezes her hard again*) Ah jus' wants *you!* You know what they say! De darker de berry, de sweeter de taste!

EMMA (*pretending to pout*). Oh, you tries to run over me an' keep it under de cover, but Ah won't let yuh. (*Both laugh.*) Les' we eat our basket!

JOHN. Alright. (*He pulls the basket out and she removes the table cloth. They set the basket on their knees and begin to eat fried chicken.*)

MALE VOICE. Les' everybody eat—motion's done carried. (*Everybody begins to open baskets. All have fried chicken. Very good humor prevails. Delicacies are swapped from one basket to the other. John and Emma offer the man next them some supper. He takes a chicken leg. Effie crosses to John and Emma with two pieces of pie on a plate.*

EFFIE. Y'll have a piece uh mah blueberry pie—it's mighty nice! (*She proffers it with a timid smile to Emma who "freezes" up instantly.*)

EMMA. Naw! We don't want no pie. We got cocoanut layer-cake.

JOHN. Ah—Ah think ah'd choose a piece uh pie, Effie. (*He takes it.*) Will you set down an' have a snack wid us? (*He slides over to make room.*)

EFFIE (*nervously*). Ah, naw, Ah got to run on back to mah basket, but Ah thought maybe y'll mout' want tuh taste mah pie. (*She turns to go.*)

JOHN. Thank you, Effie. It's mighty good, too. (*He eats it. Effie crosses to her seat. Emma glares at her for a minute, then turns disgustedly away from the basket. John catches her shoulder and faces her around.*)

JOHN (*pleadingly*). Honey, be nice. Don't act lak dat!

EMMA (*jerking free*). Naw, you done ruint mah appetite now, carryin' on wid dat punkin-colored ole gal.

JOHN. Whut kin Ah do? If you had a acted polite Ah wouldn't a had nothin' to say.

EMMA. Naw, youse jus' hog-wile ovah her cause she's half-white! No matter whut Ah say, you keep carryin' on wid her. Act polite? Naw Ah aint gonna be deceitful an' bust mah gizzard fuh nobody! Let her keep her dirty ole pie ovah there where she is!

JOHN (*looking around to see if they are overheard*). Sh-sh! Honey, you mustn't talk so loud.

EMMA (*louder*). Ah-Ah aint gonna bite mah tongue! If she don't like it she can lump it. Mah back is broad—(*John tries to cover her mouth with his hand*). She calls herself a big cigar, but *I* kin smoke her!

(*The people are laughing and talking for the most part and pay no attention. Effie is laughing and talking to those around her and does not hear the tirade. The eating is over and everyone is going behind the curtain. John and Emma put away their basket like the others, and sit glum. Voice of Master-of-ceremonies can be heard from beyond curtain announcing the pas-me-la contest. The contestants, mostly girls, take the floor. There is no music except the clapping of hands and the shouts of "Parse-me-lah" in time with the hand-clapping. At the end Master announces winner. Shadows seen on curtain.*)

MASTER. Mathilda Clarke is winner—if she will step forward she will receive a beautiful wook fascinator. (*The girl goes up and receives it with great hand-clapping and good humor.*) And now since the roosters is crowin' foah midnight, an' most of us got to git up an' go to work tomorrow, The Great Cake Walk will begin. Ah wants de floor cleared, cause de representatives of de several cities will be announced an' we wants 'em to take de floor as their names is called. Den we wants 'em to do a gran' promenade roun' de hall. An' they will then commence to walk fuh de biggest cake ever baked in dis state. Ten dozen eggs—ten pounds of flour—ten pounds of butter, and so on and so forth.

Now then—(*he strikes a pose*) for St. Augustine—
Miss Lucy Taylor, Mr. Ned Coles.

(*They step out amid applause and stand before stage.*)

For Daytona—
Miss Janie Bradley, Enoch Nixon
(*Same business.*)
For Ocala—
Miss Docia Boger, Mr. Oscar Clarke
(*Same business.*)
For Palatka—
Miss Maggie Lemmons, Mr. Senator Lewis
(*Same business.*)

And for Jacksonville the most popular "walkers" in de state—
Miss Emmaline Beazeby, Mr. John Turner.

(*Tremendous applause. John rises and offers his arm grandiloquently to Emma.*)

EMMA (*pleadingly, and clutching his coat*). John let's we all don't go in there with all them. Let's we all go on home.

JOHN (*amazed*). Why, Emma?

EMMA. Cause, cause all them girls is going to pulling and hauling on you, and—

JOHN (*impatiently*). Shucks! Come on. Don't you hear the people clapping for us and calling our names? Come on!

(*He tries to pull her up—she tries to drag him back.*)

Come on, Emma! Taint no sense in your acting like this. The band is playing for us. Hear 'em? (*He moves feet in a dance step.*)

EMMA. Naw, John, Ah'm skeered. I loves you —I—.

(*He tries to break away from her. She is holding on fiercely.*)

JOHN. I got to go! I been practising almost a year—I—we done come all the way down here. I can walk the cake, Emma—we got to—I got to go in! (*He looks into her face and sees her tremendous fear.*) What you skeered about?

EMMA (*hopefully*). You won't go it—You'll come on go home with me all by ourselves. Come on John. I can't, I just can't go in there and see all them girls—Effie hanging after you—.

JOHN. I got to go in—(*he removes her hand from his coat*)—whether you come with me or not.

EMMA. Oh—them yaller wenches! How I hate 'em! They gets everything they wants—.

VOICE INSIDE. We are waiting for the couple from Jacksonville—Jacksonville! Where is the couple from—.

(*Wesley parts the curtain and looks out.*)

WESLEY. Here they is out here spooning! You all can't even hear your names called. Come on John and Emma.

JOHN. Coming. (*He dashes inside. Wesley stands looking at Emma in surprise.*)

WESLEY. What's the matter, Emma? You and John spatting again? (*He goes back inside.*)

EMMA (*calmly bitter*). He went and left me. If we is spatting we done had our last one. (*She stands and clenches her fists.*) Ah, mah God! He's in there with her—Oh, them half whites, they gets everything, they gets everything everybody else wants! The men, the jobs—everything! The whole world is got a sign on it. Wanted: Light colored. Us blacks was made for cobble stones. (*She muffles a cry and sinks limp upon the seat.*)

VOICE INSIDE. Miss Effie Jones will walk for Jacksonville with Mr. John Turner in place of Miss Emmaline Beazeley.

SCENE III—*Dance Hall*

Emma springs to her feet and flings the curtains wide open. She stands staring at the gay scene for a moment defiantly, then creeps over to a seat along the wall and shrinks into the Spanish Moss, motionless.

Dance hall decorated with palmetto leaves and Spanish Moss—a flag or two. Orchestra consists of guitar, mandolin, banjo, accordian, church organ and drum.

MASTER (*on platform*). Couples take yo' places! When de music starts, gentlemen parade yo' ladies once round de hall, den de walk begins. (*The music begins. Four men come out from behind the platform bearing a huge chocolate cake. The couples are "prancing" in their tracks. The men lead off the procession with the cake—the contestants make a grand slam around the hall.*)

MASTER. Couples to de floor! Stan' back, ladies an' gentlemen—give 'em plenty room.

(*Music changes to "Way Down in Georgia." Orchestra sings. Effie takes the arm that John offers her and they parade to the other end of the hall. She takes her place. John goes back upstage to the platform, takes off his silk hat in a graceful sweep as he bows deeply to Effie. She lifts her skirts and curtsies to the floor. Both smile broadly. They advance toward each other, meet midway, then, arm in arm, begin to "strut." John falters as he faces her, but recovers promptly and is perfection in his *style. (Seven to nine minutes to curtain.) Fervor of spectators grows until all are taking part in some way—either hand-clapping or singing the words. At curtain they have reached frenzy.)*

QUICK CURTAIN

(It stays down a few seconds to indicate ending of contest and goes up again on John and Effie being declared winners by Judges.)

MASTER *(on platform, with John and Effie on the floor before him).* By unanimous decision de cake goes to de couple from Jacksonville! *(Great enthusiasm. The cake is set down in the center of the floor and the winning couple parade around it arm in arm. John and Effie circle the cake happily and triumphantly. The other contestants, and then the entire assembly fall in behind and circle the cake, singing and clapping. The festivities continue. The Jacksonville quartet step upon the platform and sing a verse and chorus of "Daisies won't tell." Cries of "Hurrah for Jacksonville! Glory for the big town," "Hurrah for Big Jack.")*

A MAN *(seeing Emma).* You're from Jacksonville, aint you? *(He whirls her around and around.)* Aint you happy? Whoopee! *(He releases her and she drops upon a seat. She buries her face in the moss.)*

(Quartet begins on chorus again. People are departing, laughing, humming, with quartet cheering. John, the cake, and Effie being borne away in triumph.)

SCENE IV

Time—present. The interior of a one-room shack in an alley. There is a small window in the rear wall upstage left. There is an enlarged crayon drawing of a man and woman—man sitting cross-legged, woman standing with her hand on his shoulder. A center table, red cover, a low, cheap rocker, two straight chairs, a small kitchen stove at left with a wood-box beside it, a water-bucket on a stand close by. A hand towel and a wash basin. A shelf of dishes above this. There is an ordinary oil lamp on the center table but it is not lighted when the curtain goes up. Some light enters through the window and falls on the woman seated in the low rocker. The door is center right. A cheap bed is against the upstage wall. Someone is on the bed but is lying so that the back is toward the audience.

ACTION—*As the curtain rises, the woman is seen rocking to and fro in the low rocker. A dead silence except for the sound of the rocker and an occasional groan from the bed. Once a faint voice says "water" and the woman in the rocker arises and carries the tin dipper to the bed.*

WOMAN., No mo' right away—Doctor says not too much. *(Returns dipper to pail.—Pause.)* You got right much fever—I better go git the doctor agin.

(There comes a knocking at the door and she stands still for a moment, listening. It comes again and she goes to door but does not open it.)

WOMAN. Who's that?

VOICE OUTSIDE. Does Emma Beasely live here?

EMMA. Yeah—*(pause)*—who is it?

VOICE. It's me—John Turner.

EMMA *(puts hands eagerly on the fastening).* John? did you say John Turner?

VOICE. Yes, Emma, it's me.

(The door is opened and the man steps inside.)

EMMA. John! Your hand *(she feels for it and touches it).* John flesh and blood.

JOHN *(laughing awkwardly).* It's me alright, old girl. Just as bright as a basket of chips. Make a light quick so I can see how you look. I'm crazy to see you. Twenty years is a long time to wait, Emma.

EMMA *(nervously).* Oh, let's we all just sit in the dark awhile. *(Apologetically.)* I wasn't expecting nobody and my house aint picked up. Sit down. *(She draws up the chair. She sits in rocker.)*

JOHN. Just to think! Emma! Me and Emma sitting down side by each. Know how I found you?

EMMA *(dully).* Naw. How?

JOHN *(brightly).* Soon's I got in town I hunted up Wesley and he told me how to find you. That's who I come to see, you!

EMMA. Where you been all these years, up North somewheres? Nobody round here could find out where you got to.

JOHN. Yes, up North. Philadelphia.

EMMA. Married yet?

JOHN. Oh yes, seventeen years ago. But my wife is dead now and so I came as soon as it was decent to find *you.* I wants to marry you. I couldn't die happy if I didn't. Couldn't get over you—couldn't forget. Forget me, Emma?

EMMA. Naw, John. How could I?

JOHN (*leans over impulsively to catch her hand*). Oh, Emma, I love you so much. Strike a light honey so I can see you—see if you changed much. You was such a handsome girl!

EMMA. We don't exactly need no light, do we, John, tuh jus' set an' talk?

JOHN. Yes, we do, Honey. Gwan, make a light. Ah wanna see you.

(*There is a silence.*)

EMMA. Bet you' wife wuz some high-yaller dickty-doo.

JOHN. Naw she wasn't neither. She was jus' as much like you as Ah could get her. Make a light an' Ah'll show you her pictcher. Shucks, ah gotta look at mah old sweetheart. (*He strikes a match and holds it up between their faces and they look intently at each other over it until it burns out.*) You aint changed none atall, Emma, jus' as pretty as a speckled pup yet.

EMMA (*lighter*). Go long, John! (*Short pause*) 'member how you useter bring me magnolias?

JOHN. Do I? Gee, you was sweet! 'Member how Ah useter pull mah necktie loose so you could tie it back for me? Emma, Ah can't see to mah soul how we lived all this time, way from one another. 'Member how you useter make out mah ears had done run down and you useter screw 'em up agin for me? (*They laugh.*)

EMMA. Yeah, Ah useter think you wuz gointer be mah husban' then—but you let dat ole—.

JOHN. Ah aint gonna let you alibi on me lak dat. Light dat lamp! You cain't look me in de eye and say no such. (*He strikes another match and lights the lamp.*) Course, Ah don't wanta look too bossy, but Ah b'lieve you got to marry me tuh git rid of me. That is, if you aint married.

EMMA. Naw, Ah aint. (*She turns the lamp down.*)

JOHN (*looking about the room*). Not so good, Emma. But wait till you see dat little place in Philly! Got a little "Rolls-Rough," too—gointer teach you to drive it, too.

EMMA. Ah been havin' a hard time, John, an' Ah lost you—oh, aint nothin' been right for me! Ah aint never been happy.

(*John takes both of her hands in his.*)

JOHN. You gointer be happy now, Emma. Cause Ah'm gointer make you. Gee Whiz! Ah aint but forty-two and you aint forty yet—we got plenty time. (*There is a groan from the bed.*) Gee, what's that?

EMMA (*ill at ease*). Thass mah chile. She's sick. Reckon Ah bettah see 'bout her.

JOHN. You got a chile? Gee, that great! Ah always wanted one. but didn't have no luck. Now we kin start off with a family. Girl or boy?

EMMA (*slowly*). A girl. Comin' tuh see me agin soon, John?

JOHN. Comin' agin? Ah aint gone yet! We aint talked, you aint kissed me an' nothin', and you aint showed me our girl. (*Another groan, more prolonged.*) She must be pretty sick—let's see. (*He turns in his chair and Emma rushes over to the bed and covers the girl securely, tucking her long hair under the covers, too—before he arises. He goes over to the bed and looks down into her face. She is mulatto. Turns to Emma teasingly.*) Talkin' 'bout *me* liking high-yallers—*yo* husband musta been pretty near *white*.

EMMA (*slowly*). Ah, never wuz married, John.

JOHN. It's alright, Emma. (*Kisses her warmly.*) Everything is going to be O.K. (*Turning back to the bed.*) Our child looks pretty sick, but she's pretty. (*Feels her forehead and cheek.*) Think she oughter have a doctor.

EMMA. Ah done had one. Course Ah cain't git no specialist an' nothin' lak dat. (*She looks about the room and his gaze follows hers.*) Ah aint got a whole lot lake you. Nobody don't git rich in no white-folks' kitchen, nor in de washtub. You know Ah aint no school-teacher an' nothin' lak dat.

(*John puts his arm about her.*)

JOHN. It's all right, Emma. But our daughter is bad off—run out an' git a doctor—she needs one. Ah'd go if Ah knowed where to find one—you kin git one the quickest—hurry, Emma.

EMMA (*looks from John to her daughter and back again.*) She'll be all right, Ah reckon, for a while. John, you love me—you really want me sho' nuff?

JOHN. Sure Ah do—think Ah'd come all de way down here for nothin'? Ah wants to marry agin.

EMMA. Soon, John?

JOHN. Real soon.

EMMA. Ah wuz jus' thinkin', mah folks is away now on a little trip—be home day after tomorrow—we could git married tomorrow.

JOHN. All right. Now run on after the doctor—we must look after our girl. Gee, she's got a full suit of hair! Glad you didn't let her chop it off. (*Looks away from bed and sees Emma standing still.*)

JOHN. Emma, run on after the doctor, honey. (*She goes to the bed and again tucks the long braids of hair in, which are again pouring over the side of *the bed by the feverish tossing of the girl.*) What's our daughter's name?

EMMA. Lou Lillian. (*She returns to the rocker uneasily and sits rocking jerkily. He returns to his seat and turns up the light.*)

JOHN. Gee, we're going to be happy—we gointer make up for all them twenty years (*another groan*). Emma, git up an' gwan git dat doctor. You done forgot Ah'm de boss uh dis family now—gwan, while Ah'm here to watch her whilst you're gone. Ah got to git back to mah stoppin'-place after a while.

EMMA. You go git one, John.

JOHN. Whilst Ah'm blunderin' round tryin' to find one, she'll be gettin' worse. She sounds pretty bad—(*takes out his wallet and hands her a bill*)—get a taxi if necessary. Hurry!

EMMA (*does not take the money, but tucks her arms and hair in again, and gives the girl a drink*). Reckon Ah better go git a doctor. Don't want nothin' to happen to *her*. After you left, Ah useter have such a hurtin' in heah (*touches bosom*) till she come an' eased it some.

JOHN. Here, take some money and get a good doctor. There must be some good colored ones around here now.

EMMA (*scornfully*). I wouldn't let one of 'em tend my cat if I had one! But let's we don't start a fuss.

(*John caresses her again. When he raises his head he notices the picture on the wall and crosses over to it with her—his arm still about her.*)

JOHN. Why, that's you and me!

EMMA. Yes, I never could part with that. You coming tomorrow morning, John, and we're gointer get married, aint we? Then we can talk over everything.

JOHN. Sure, but I aint gone yet. I don't see how come we can't make all our arrangements now.

(*Groans from bed and feeble movement.*)

Good lord, Emma, go get that doctor!

(*Emma stares at the girl and the bed and seizes a hat from a nail on the wall. She prepares to go but looks from John to bed and back again. She fumbles about the table and lowers the lamp. Goes to door and opens it. John offers the wallet. She refuses it.*)

EMMA. Doctor right around the corner. Guess I'll leave the door open so she can get some air. She won't need nothing while I'm gone, John. (*She crosses and tucks the girl in securely and rushes out, looking backward and pushing the door wide open as she exits. John sits in the chair beside the table. Looks about him—shakes his head. The girl on the bed groans,* "water," "so hot." *John looks about him excitedly. Gives her a drink. Feels her forehead. Takes a clean handkerchief from his pocket and wets it and places it upon her forehead. She raises her hand to the cool object. Enter Emma running. When she sees John at the bed she is full of fury. She rushes over and jerks his shoulder around. They face each other.*)

EMMA. I knowed it! (*She strikes him.*) A half white skin. (*She rushes at him again. John staggers back and catches her hands.*)

JOHN. Emma!

EMMA (*struggles to free her hands*). Let me go so I can kill you. Come sneaking in here like a pole cat!

JOHN (*slowly, after a long pause*). So this is the woman I've been wearing over my heart like a rose for twenty years! She so despises her own skin that she can't believe any one else could love it!

(*Emma writhes to free herself.*)

JOHN. Twenty years! Twenty years of adoration, of hunger, of worship! (*On the verge of tears he crosses to door and exits quietly, closing the door after him.*)

(*Emma remains standing, looking dully about as if she is half asleep. There comes a knocking at the door. She rushes to open it. It is the doctor. White. She does not step aside so that he can enter.*

DOCTOR. Well, shall I come in?

EMMA (*stepping aside and laughing a little*). That's right, doctor, come in.

(*Doctor crosses to bed with professional air. Looks at the girl, feels the pulse and draws up the sheet over the face. He turns to her.*)

DOCTOR. Why didn't you come sooner. I told you to let me know of the least change in her condition.

EMMA (*flatly*). I did come—I went for the doctor.

DOCTOR. Yes, but you waited. An hour more or less is mighty important sometimes. Why didn't you come?

EMMA (*passes hand over face*). Couldn't see.

(*Doctor looks at her curiously, then sympathetically takes out a small box of pills, and hands them to her.*) Here, you're worn out. Take one of these every hour and try to get some sleep. (*He departs.*)

(*She puts the pill-box on the table, takes up the low rocking chair and places it by the head of the bed. She seats herself and rocks monotonously and stares out of the door. A dry sob now and then. The wind from the open door blows out the lamp and she is seen by the little light from the window rocking in an even, monotonous gait, and sobbing.*)

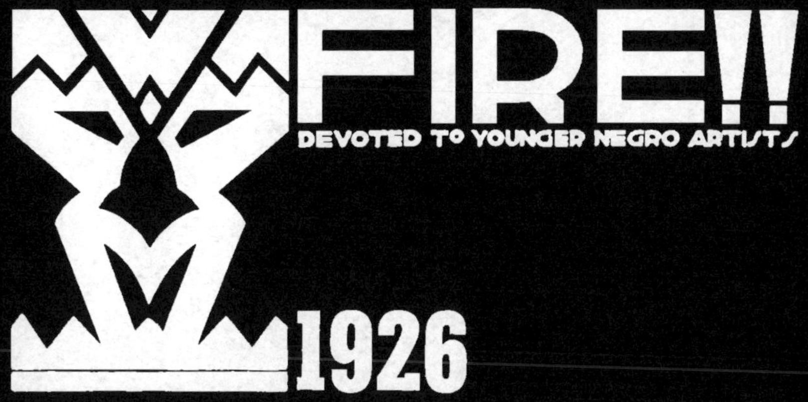

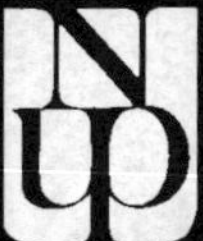

NEGRO UNIVERSITIES PRESS
WESTPORT, CONNECTICUT
1970

JOSIE ROLAND HODSON

REST NOTES: ON BLACK SLEEP AESTHETICS

In sleep I am looking
for poems in the shape of open
V's of birds flying in formation,
or open arms saying, I forgive you, all.
—Elizabeth Alexander, "Blues" (1996)

At the annual San Francisco Antiquarian Book, Print and Paper Fair in 2016, I was probing around in worn and mothball-scented plastic bins containing outdated maps, confessional postcards that may have never been answered, anonymous family portraits mounted in weathered cardboard frames, and other forsaken paper inheritances now for sale by passionate hobbyist collectors. Among the disarray I pulled out a small vintage photograph of a young Black woman, her eyes closed, lying in sensuous and solitary repose on the earthen ground. The photograph's idle subject appeared to be sleeping. The woman's apparent insouciance made her indifferent, perhaps unwitting in her slumber, to the camera trained on her. I was both minorly discomfited and enticed by my encounter with the photograph, feeling as though in looking I had breached an intimate boundary, exposing a subject engaged in a private and vulnerable act never intended for my consumption: sleep. As I reflect on the encounter now, it also occurs to me that the conditions of her restful state remain unknowable to me a half-century later, not simply because of the decontextualized nature of an antiquarian paper fair, which leaves one with few evidentiary traces, but also because the subject's recumbence could just as well be a convincing and agential performance *for* the camera—a coy invitation to witness a vision of restfulness—as much as an unconscious act subjected to its voyeuristic lens. My own projection of vulnerability onto the sleeping Black subject might say more about the ways in which I have metabolized notions around the conditions of Black sleep than it does about the reality of this subject's condition. Whether it is performance or documentation, it occurred to me that I had never seen a photograph like this before: a spontaneous image of a Black woman's sleep. My own nightly encounter with the reality of Black sleep, my awareness of my mother's days spent in bed recovering from terrible insomnia and of my great-grandmother, whose recent stroke has consigned her to a mostly recumbent life, could not temper the impact of witnessing such sleepy vulnerability, or the performance of it, captured here on film.

In a society so inured to images of Black trauma, I wondered, was it plausible that I had seen more images of Black people lying in death than in rest? It is precisely because images of Black death circulate with such facility and perverse demand that some Black artists have emphasized representing emphatic Black life, eyes wide open. These works importantly perform a potent rejection of the reproducibility of Black death, but they are not my interest here. My present pursuit, conversely, is to introduce a speculative sketch of what I am calling Black sleep aesthetics: a visual poetics of somnolence that acts as a refusal of and reparation for the enduring myths of Black sleeplessness or nonsomnia,[1] indolence, and extraordinary industry.

Christina Sharpe has written that wakefulness is the condition of consciousness.[2] She deploys the metaphor of the wake—powerfully invested with many meanings, including the wake of a ship and a funerary wake, as well as the state of wakefulness—to diagnose the condition of modern Black life in the aftermath of the transatlantic slave trade, which forcibly brought ten million Africans to the Americas. The second half of her analytical formation—the "work" of "wake work"—describes the labors that contemporary writers, visual artists, and musicians pursue in the afterlife of slavery in the Americas, insisting on other possibilities of being in the world against and despite practices of ontological negation. It is not my intention here to write in opposition to Sharpe's illuminating and capacious analytic of "wake work," but rather to think with contemporary artists who theorize the other side of consciousness, elaborating the knowledge to be found in the modest event that is Black sleep. I am interested in Black sleep as a quiet gesture cast against tropes of Black idleness and the rationalization of the Black (non)human as a laboring, nonsomniac machine. Confronting the expectation of laborious endurance and resilience that defines racial capitalism's infinite extortions, artists visualizing or producing new conditions for Black sleep advocate something other than "work" entirely: a submission to the liberatory space of the Black unconscious and a fugitive withdrawal from the present terms of engagement. It is my contention, however, that despite the inherently solitary nature of sleep, conditions for Black sleep cannot be produced by individual acts of reclamation, and thus I emphasize projects that are produced through modes of collaboration. The artists discussed act out the productive sociality to be found in Black sleep, delivering new possibilities for the intimate act of "sleeping together." Consequently, I am concerned with how reclamations of Black sleep operate at the thorny threshold of the interior, subjective space of the self and the sense of belonging to be found in the collective.

While scientific sleep research in the United States began in the first half of the twentieth century, it is only more recently that scientists have begun to consider the ways in which sleep can be a racialized phenomenon in spite of its biologically equalizing nature. Researchers have found that Black people in the United States sleep more poorly than their racial counterparts, with injurious health effects. According to a study published in 2019 that reviews recent sleep research, "Blacks have the highest risk and prevalence of poor sleep patterns across various dimensions of sleep health than any other racial/ethnic group"[3]—meaning Black people spend shorter periods asleep, spend less time in deep sleep, have a harder time staying asleep, and report more incidents of insomnia. When we sleep, easing our bodies and minds into a relaxed state of semiconsciousness, we move through REM and slow-wave cycles in which our brains consolidate memories from waking life and regenerative physiological functions kick in.[4] Poor sleep health, or the chronic disruption of these restorative capacities, is associated with myriad physiological and psychic conditions, including impaired cognition, increased risk of hypertension, diabetes, and stroke, as well as cardiovascular disease.[5] Taken together, poor sleep exposes Black people to what Saidiya Hartman has called "the vulnerability to premature death" that follows transatlantic chattel slavery and the subsequent constraints on fully lived Black life.[6]

Central to understanding the origins of this racial sleep gap, the authors of the study suggest, is "John Henryism," a phenomenon in which minoritized and racialized "populations may develop a strong work ethic as an attempt to combat/overcome negative stereotypes applied to their social identity group."[7] This coping mechanism was named by American epidemiologist Sherman James for John Henry, the Black "steel-driving man" of American folk legend and song who exhibited an extraordinary, superhuman aptitude for steel-driving, the laborious task of manually hammering a steel drill into rock, a necessary step in the construction of railroad tunnels.[8] As the song in its many variations recounts, John Henry's industrious nature is tested against the modern advances of a steam-powered rock-drilling machine. Though John Henry ultimately defeats his mechanical competition, his hardworking efforts are undone when his heart gives out from stress, causing him to die. John Henry's tale of heroism offers a profound parable for untangling the imbricated roles of modern capital's insatiable appetite (signified by the encroachment of the steel-driving machine) and the enduring myths about the ontological industry of Black people that play in the story of modern Black sleeplessness.

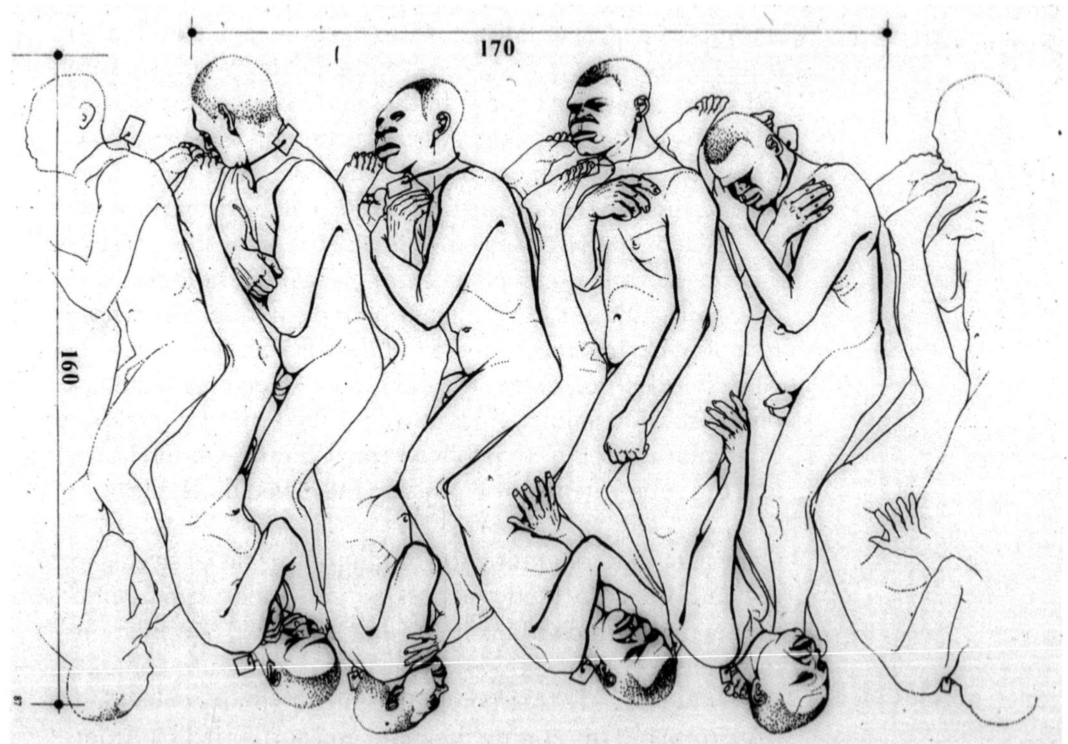

Sleeping Position of Africans on Slave Ship, 1857, *Illustrated London News*, June 20, 1857

Black nonsomnia is a myth that has traces in the hold of the slave ship. One illustrated reconstruction of *L'Aurore,*a ship that crossed the Atlantic to transport enslaved Africans to the Americas in 1784, depicts a diagram of the confined sleeping positions of those captive in the hold. As historian Stephanie Smallwood writes, space between captive bodies was minimized to ensure the "slave ship's profitability,"[9] further elucidating the perverse dialectic between capital accumulation and restrictions on sleep.[10] An illustration from the *Illustrated London News* in 1857 displays the "sleeping position of slaves in the pack." None of the seven enslaved people huddled in this image appear to actually be asleep—their eyes are wide open, as if to remind us of their surveilled condition.[11] In his *Notes on the State of Virginia*, Thomas Jefferson wrote of enslaved Black people that "they seem to require less sleep. A black, after hard labour through the day, will be induced by the slightest amusements to sit up till midnight, or later, though knowing he must be out with the first dawn of the morning."[12] While *Notes on the State of Virginia* is admittedly only one document in the vast array of antebellum American letters, its wide circulation and translation, along with Jefferson's prominent political influence, are enough to suggest that his fictive notions about Black people's ability to dispense with sleep were widely persuasive. Indeed, it has been documented that enslaved people endured extraordinarily brutal punishments on Southern plantations for expressions of fatigue, and that anti-sleep torture technologies such as weighty iron collars would be deployed to prevent the possibility of rest. Writing of these sleepless conditions in *Narrative of the Life of Frederick Douglass*, Frederick Douglass reports that on slave plantations, "no beds [are] given the slaves, unless one coarse blanket be considered such, and none but the men and women had these. This, however, is not considered a very great privation. They find less difficulty from the want of beds than from the want of time to sleep."[13] From this account, we learn that the very architecture of sleep—the bed—was rarely at the disposal of enslaved Black people. On the other hand, as scholars have noted, nineteenth-century legislation following the abolition of slavery in the United States such as the Vagrancy Act of 1866 sutured the emancipated Black subject to mythologies of his or her indolence by criminalizing vagrancy and joblessness.

No longer enslaved, Black people were reinvented in public mythology as lazy or idle.

As Hortense Spillers has shown, such early narratives as were inflicted on the bodies of Black people, specifically Black women, endure in contemporary discourse: "I am a marked woman," she writes.[14] For Spillers, these markings are evidenced in Daniel Patrick Moynihan's infamous report on the Black family, which he characterizes as a "tangle of pathology" that includes perennial Black unemployment and underemployment, shorthand for a lazy disposition. The specter of these narratives haunts present-day conceptions of Black racial ontology, as we see with the unfortunate durability of the trope of the slothful, gluttonous, and overdependent (Black) welfare queen, a transmutation of earlier racialized and gendered exclusions from normative (white) ideals. I have described both the scientific phenomenon of modern Black sleeplessness as well as the endurance of the double bind of contradictory narratives about Black people's indolence and nonsomnia at such length because it is on and against this biopolitical terrain that artists have produced aesthetics of Black sleep, works of art that resist the regulation of Black rest and the lethal expectation of perpetual industry.

A long view of African American and Black-diasporic artistic production reveals recurring themes of sleep and, notably, its discontents. Well-cited examples might include Olaudah Equiano's anguished narrative of his capture[15] and eventual enslavement both in the Caribbean and Colonial Virginia, first published in 1789, which became one of the earliest and most influential slave narratives in transatlantic circulation. In his narrative, Equiano writes that amid the trauma of capture, "our only relief was some sleep, which allayed our misfortune for a short time."[16] For Harriet Jacobs, conversely, forced to spend the night in her masters' quarters, sleep was defiled by the ongoing threat of sexual violence. However, in the cramped attic in which she hid for seven years, nearly immobile but nonetheless free from the brutality of enslavement, Jacobs "slept such sleep as the wretched may, when a tempest has passed over them,"[17] submitting that such slivers of somatic self-determination, however constrained by spaces of confinement and hemmed in by fear, nonetheless produced conditions for a more peaceful slumber.

A more persistent trope than mere sleep, however, is the presence of dreams across Black cultural imaginings, deployed both as metaphor for aspirational political possibility and as premonitory apparition. "What happens to a dream deferred?" Langston Hughes asked in 1951 in his influential poem "Harlem". Of course, in 1963 Martin Luther King Jr. spoke of his dream on the steps of the Lincoln Memorial to an audience of two hundred thousand people. In 1965, amid political turmoil, painter Jacob Lawrence rendered *Dreams #1*, two sleeping figures, in vibrant gouaches, enduring the torment of a nightmare. Meanwhile, the widespread circulation of dream books—which paired numbers with interpretations of dreams to be played in an illicit lottery circuit[18]—among African Americans throughout the twentieth century evinces a general belief in dreams' prophetic potential. Importantly, the preoccupation with the emancipatory and prophetic potential of dreams is not delimited by national borders that would isolate African Americans from the rest of the Black-diasporic globe; dreams play an important cultural role among Black-diasporic cultures around the world, too, such as in Voudou religious traditions practiced in Haiti, where communion with spirits occurs through oneiric activity.

Despite such abundant historical preoccupations with Black sleep and dreams, I concentrate here on contemporary artists engaging with these themes because I am interested in how the particular terrain of modern Black life makes investing in sleep a newly operable mode of pursuing Black liberation against practices of domination. Modern phenomena that circumscribe Black life and Black sleep include the incursion of constant technological surveillance, the explosion of incarceration and the criminalizing of everyday life, the extraordinary health disparities caused in part by environmental and medical racisms, homelessness and dispossession born of racist housing policies, and hyperexploitative labor conditions that require that Black people work more for less. These spectacularly quotidian acts of violence have not arisen spontaneously but are historically continuous, having been distorted and at times accelerated beyond recognition. Attending to contemporary artists observing predicaments of Black sleeplessness allows us to more keenly identify the shape of oppressive practices that constrain Black freedom today. The contemporary projects surveyed here mark engagements with Black sleep that are not out of history but in relation to it, surfacing important foundational myths and their present mutations while speculating on ways out of a living nightmare.

Artists Simone Leigh and Chitra Ganesh, working as a collaborative under the moniker Girl, partially explore dynamics of constraint and autonomy in their video work *my dreams, my works must wait till after hell* (2011). In this seven-minute-long video, titled after a Gwendolyn Brooks poem and set against a soundtrack of flutes by Kaoru Watanabe, the softly illuminated bare back of a Black woman's body lies recumbent on the ground, facing away from the viewer into the inky black that is the video's disorienting mise-en-scène. A pile of gravel buries the figure's head, obscuring it under the weighty accumulation and rendering the partial figure (played by the performance artist Kenya Robinson) anonymous. In an interview with performance scholar Tavia Nyong'o, Leigh said of the video: "There's a prehistory to the image. Something must have happened that had to do with war or labor,"[19] but the viewer is given no such insight here—we arrive in the middle of this event and leave before it is over, and so do not know how she got here, who placed the rocks, or why. The only evidence of movement, of life, is the nearly imperceptible, measured inhale and exhale of unencumbered sleep.

A nude feminine form in a recumbent posture situates the video in the visual idioms of European painting traditions beginning in the Western Renaissance. The reclining female nude appeared in early iconographic works that took up mythological tropes, such as Giorgione's *The Sleeping Venus*, painted in 1510, and Titian's *Venus of Urbino* of 1534, and is later transfigured by nineteenth-century French painters to depict the eroticized odalisque, as in Manet's *Olympia*. Collaborator Chitra Ganesh confirms this historical visual affinity, stating in an interview with Uri McMillan, "It was almost as if we had subconsciously responded to French painter Édouard

Manet's *Olympia* (1863),"[20] although here, critically, the visual script is flipped. In Manet's *Olympia*, the Black maid attends to the composition's languorous white protagonist; Lorraine O'Grady has written powerfully of this racialized dynamic: "Olympia's maid, like all other 'peripheral Negroes,' is a robot conveniently made to disappear into the background drapery."[21] Here, however, the Black figure is the embodiment of leisure, although under weighted constraint. Under such compression, the sleeping Black body becomes a mechanized organism, a human ventilation machine whose function is dismally reduced to the preservation of bare life. With an obscured head, the (non)subject evinces what Alexander G. Weheliye has characterized as the condition of Black life through his theory of "racializing assemblages," or the "set of sociopolitical processes that discipline humanity into full humans, not-quite-humans, and nonhumans,"[22] with Black people at the bottom of the schema. The sleeping Black body here, returning to O'Grady's characterization of *Olympia*'s Black maid, becomes roboticized, performing functionality without the privilege of a subjectivity. Like so many robots, the sleeping Black figure has been recruited to perform useless labor—without going anywhere, she endures the needless task of breathing, so gracefully, under pressure.

In his diagnostic of a modern "24/7 society," Jonathan Crary defines capitalism's present sleepless (dis)order as "a non-social model of machinic performance and a suspension of living that does not disclose the human cost required to sustain its effectiveness."[23] In other words, under capitalism's boot, we're *all* robots, living without really living at all. As if it couldn't get any worse, Crary reports that the Pentagon's research division (DARPA) is experimenting with sleeplessness techniques through the use of "neurochemicals, gene therapy, and transcranial magnetic stimulation" to eradicate human fatigue in the dystopic pursuit of absolute militaristic and capitalistic efficiency.[24] If we look at sustained practices of racialized sleep regulation, however, we see that such desires for a post-human, robotic, nonsomniac society are not new but rather can be located in the pervasive myths of Black nonsomnia and the disciplining of Black sleep in the interests of capital. Like so many of the conditions of our modern, globalized, capitalist society that are assumed to be universal, the Black laboring (and, here, gendered) body has been the proverbial canary in the coal mine. Indeed, as Afrofuturist Kodwo Eshun has written, "like the robot ... the slave was actually manufactured to fulfill a function: as a servomechanism, as a transport system, as furniture, as 3/5 of the human, as a fractional subject."[25] Under our present terms, should a world come to be where we eliminate the biological need for sleep, one can be certain that the effects of such an innovation would not be felt equitably.

Nevertheless, in *my dreams, my works must wait till after hell,* the sleeping figure's steady breath under the rocks' mass also visualizes the claims to autonomous life Black people create despite the constrictions of the present regime of anti-Blackness, white supremacy, and capitalism. One should be careful, however, to avoid an analysis of the work that would read the fact of the subject's slumber under duress as evidence of Black women's ontological resilience, which frames struggle as an individual project in which oppression might be outmaneuvered by a little personal effort, resourcefulness, or enterprise. Here, the sleeping figure's liberatory gesture is found in her

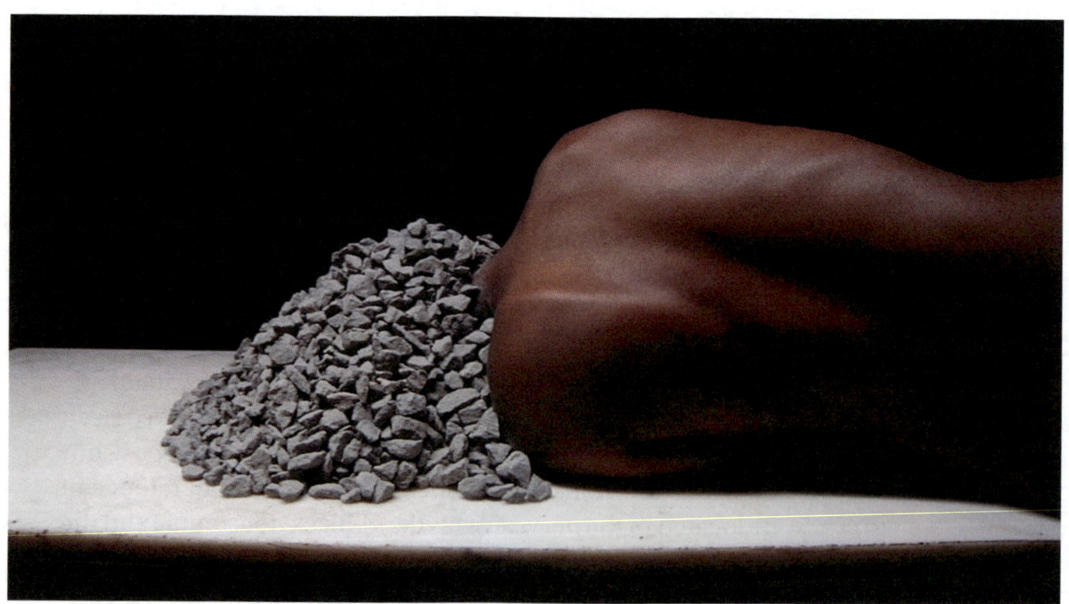

Girl (Simone Leigh and Chitra Ganesh), *my dreams, my works must wait till after hell,* 2011

found in her posture. Where Manet's Olympia gazes outward in direct confrontation with the viewer, the unnamed subject of *My Dreams, My Works Must Wait Till After Hell* refuses the viewer's gaze entirely by facing away from the camera trained on her, producing her own interior space inaccessible to us as viewers. In her interview with McMillan, Leigh muses, "While our exhibitions are not always welcome, the black performing body always is."[26] Against this invitation, the monotonous seven minutes of a slumbering Black body turned away from the camera's gaze enacts an anti-performance, a repudiation of Black spectacle, and a ritualized turn to the interior space of the self.

In his recent experimental meditation on the biopolitics of sleep, Matthew Fuller asserts that "sleep is the means by which people turn themselves into objects, or by means of which they become most object-like."[27] The notion of becoming-object is an awkward theoretical configuration for the Black human that has already been decreed an object by dominant discourses. Thinking with *my Dreams, my works must wait till after hell* and the gaze away from the viewer, I want to flip Fuller's notion of becoming-object to suggest that, possibly, it is precisely when the Black subject falls asleep that she reasserts her humanity. This humanity is emphatically not the Western bourgeois conception of the human ("Man") that underwrites modernity, the "overrepresented" human that Sylvia Wynter unsettles.[28] Nor is it the conception of the human as merely a biological category, clinging to bare life via the flow of oxygen into the lungs. This humanity, on the contrary, is defined by a quiet relationship to the self, or interiority. Here, "quiet" takes its primary meaning from Kevin Quashie's idiom, where quiet acts as "a metaphor for the full range of one's inner life—one's desires, ambitions, hungers, vulnerabilities, fears." Through enactments of quiet, Quashie writes, "the interior could be understood as the source of human action—that anything we do is shaped by the range of desires and capacities of our inner life."[29] A retreat into the unconscious territory of Black sleep, then, is a profound reclamation of such private interiority, and thus an embodied rejection of Western philosophical foundations that would render the Black subject into "not-quite-humans ... and nonhumans."

The Black experience has been described through the phenomenon of "double-consciousness," the sensation of self-awareness always through the prism of racial performance and reception, or the "sense of always looking at one's self through the eyes of others," as W.E.B. Du Bois originally described it. Sleep, on the other hand, might offer a fleeting emancipation from this psychic duality, processing experience instead through REM and slow-wave brain activity. In *my dreams, my works must wait till after hell,* the anonymous figure embodies an ethic of "looking away" to access a space of unconscious interiority. This is not to pretend that sleep transcends racial difference, or that it approaches some mythic post-raciality—we have seen it does not—but rather to propose that the Black sleeping subject, if only momentarily, escapes from the conscious weight of perpetual misrecognition and disengages from the awareness of *being* perceived. In this way, sleep is distinct from other acts of rest, leisure, or temporal reprieve, which remain above the surface of consciousness.

Jennifer Packer's paintings are lush and quiet imaginings of Black interior life. Many of her intimate portraits reveal subjects—friends of hers—in states of private repose, reclining on armchairs, mattresses, and couches. In some works, as in *Blessed Are Those Who Mourn (Breonna! Breonna!)* (2020), they are asleep. In this epic composition, a lithe Black man reclines on a yellow quilted sofa in the foreground, his head thrown back against the armrest, surrendered to a state best described by Léopold Senghor as "a deep Negro sleep."[30] The man is shirtless and wearing only blue shorts. Painterly clues suggest heat is the source of his lethargy: Three fans whir behind and above the figure, and watery yellow paint drips down the left flank of the composition as if it were melting. In the stale air of a hot summer day, awash in a honeysuckle glow, the figure has abandoned his tasks and sought the relief of sleep—an upturned iron remains ready to be used, and a forsaken game of chess floats impossibly behind him. A framed mantra on the wall, partially obscured, reads "TOO BLESSED TO BE STRESSED".

Surreal moments punctuate the painting's composition. On the right edge of the frame, three rectangles of abstracted color hover uncannily, as if on their own plane. The rectangles might be comic-book covers, or open portals to polychromatic worlds, but they are not here, not in the same room as the sleeping man. These portals are abstracted apertures at the threshold of the sleeper's dreams, where a midday nap's fantasy ineffably escapes waking legibility. In the top left corner, another such portal appears, although clearer here: an open window framing a black bird. This threshold, I imagine, is a visual rendering of the dreams Elizabeth Alexander describes in her poem "Blues", an ode to idleness; she writes, "In sleep I am looking / for poems in the shape of open / V's of birds flying in formation, / or open arms saying, I forgive you, all."[31] The sleeper's dream, these lines would suggest, is a sacred space where one finds momentary absolution from the pressure cooker of waking life. Although concerned primarily with dreams that occur during waking life—or our deep imaginative capacities—Alexander has written extensively about the "dream space" that flows through the African American artistic tradition, where dreams are a site of "complex and often unexplored interiority beyond the face of the social self,"[32] as she writes in *The Black Interior.* The internal "territory" of which she writes is evinced powerfully here in Packer's rendering of a deep sleep's dreams.

Conversely, the work's evocative title, *Blessed Are Those Who Mourn (Breonna! Breonna!),* introduces a new problematic curtailing sleep and thwarts a purely romantic or emancipatory reading of this dream space. It reminds the conscious viewer that sleep is also a state of profound vulnerability for the Black subject by invoking the name of Breonna Taylor, a twenty-six-year-old Black woman murdered by Louisville police officers on March 13, 2020. Taylor's home was raided by plainclothes police officers in the middle of the night, waking her from the unconsciousness of sleep to a confrontation with the terror of the state. Taylor's boyfriend, Kenneth Walker, reported to the news: "There was a loud bang at the door. ... She pops out of sleep, it scared her, me too. Like, who is that?"[33] Packer's memorial invocation of Breonna Taylor's name reminds the viewer that even in the quiet intimacy of sleepy repose, the threat of violence is never far off. "Blessed are those who mourn" is a fragmentary citation from Matthew 5:4, which continues, "for they shall be comforted." Against the ongoing incursion of state terror and the collective grief it produces, Packer paints dream spaces. These dream spaces propose that sleep is not merely a biological interregnum to the day's waking activities but also a potent space in which to glimpse worlds apart from our present one, possibilities suggested by the symbol of a solitary black swallow flitting by the window, a momentary pleasure.

For artistic collaborators Amara Tabor-Smith and Ellen Sebastian Chang, cultivating such speculative dream space is at the center of their practice. Working collectively as House/Full of Blackwomen, the artists have staged episodic "ritual performances" in the Bay Area over the course over a five-year period that respond, in their own words, to the imbricated crises of "displacement, well-being, and sex trafficking of black women and girls in Oakland." While the collaborative performance project takes shape over several thematic episodes,

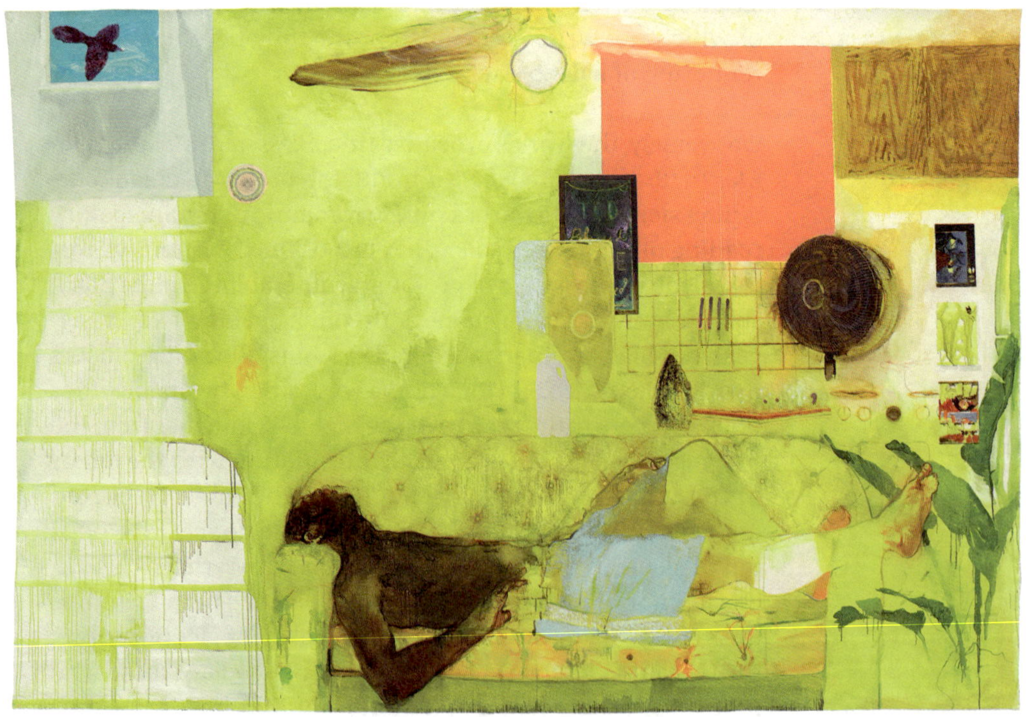

Jennifer Packer, *Blessed Are Those Who Mourn (Breonna! Breonna!)*, 2020.

I will focus here on *Black Womxn Dreaming*, a participatory work performed in 2017 and 2019 that invited Black women and femme-identified people to commune in rest and dream. By word-of-mouth invitation alone, over one hundred and fifty Black women were welcomed to an undisclosed location to engage in a ritual practice of a week of collective rest.

Black Womxn Dreaming takes as its animating legend Harriet Tubman's narcolepsy,[34] the legacy of a traumatic head injury suffered at the hands of her master while a child. Tubman, who returned to the South thirteen times to guide enslaved people to freedom, would fall into periods of unexpected sleep, during which time she received visions in her dreams that revealed where to move next; her passengers would simply have to wait until she woke up to proceed on their journey. The artists drew from the spirit of the Underground Railroad and its principle of freedom through fugitivity, in which no guiding map nor sanctioned geography was available: In order to find the destination, participants were guided only by landmarks.

Upon entering the space, participants were greeted by a group of "attendants" who also identified as Black women or with feminine genders. In an act revisioning Black women's conscription to the roles of servile mammy, maid, and caretaker, here Black women engaged as "attendants" in an act of willing reciprocity. The attendants were also asked to rest as a principle of their service. Iterative acts of rest and watchful vigilance shaped a social sculpture that demanded both space and time, a collaborative performance that evaded, if obliquely evoked, the more familiar embodied condition of durational works: endurance.

No documentation of the collective sleep was publicly circulated, a gesture of opacity working against the ubiquitous surveillance that compels Black women to sleep, proverbially, with one eye open. As Tabor-Smith stated, "Black women are not going to sleep when they are being gazed upon."[35] As with the slumbering figure in *My Dreams, My Works Must Wait Till After Hell* and her "look away," or the inscrutable abstractions in *Blessed Are Those Who Mourn (Breonna! Breonna!)* registered amidst violence, this collaborative work insists on privacy and produces a space of covert refuge for its participants. In doing so, it obstructs cultural hegemony's enduring fixation with representation, producing no graspable object for consumption or voyeurism and instead deploying Black privacy in an anti-Black society that desires to see the Black abject as fuel for its project.

Before turning to sleep, participants agreed to relinquish their cellphones to ensure rest free from the dings, alerts, and alarms of a hyperactive, restless modern world. In this way, *Black Womxn Dreaming* is an indictment of an overstimulatory capitalist society that divests Black people of the space to dream. This society is one Byung-Chul Han describes in his diagnosis of the source of "burnout" and collective exhaustion as a specifically modern phenomenon: "Today we live in a world that is very poor in interruption; 'betweens' and 'between-times' are lacking. Acceleration is abolishing all intervals,"[36] to the detriment of our collective creative capacities, which require such interregnums. Sleep is a period for somatic and psychic recuperation against a landscape of interminable grief and exhaustion. For Tabor-Smith and Sebastian Chang, similarly, the dreams to be found in sleep are vessels for creative visions of emancipatory futures. After the performance of *Black Womxn Dreaming*, participants were invited to record their dreams in a shared book, an artifactual document that physically manifests Saidiya Hartman's notion of "a dreambook for existing otherwise,"[37] an unfinished blueprint for new architectures of liberation.

Han identifies the source of our weary discontent—"burnout"—as an "achievement society," a hyperpositivist civilization in which "one exploits oneself" in the culture of perpetual can-do. "Today's society is no longer Foucault's disciplinary world of hospitals, madhouses, prison barracks, and factories," he writes. "It has long been replaced by another regime, namely a society of fitness studios, office towers, banks, airports, shopping malls, and genetic laboratories."[38] What attending to the Black (non)sleeping subject reveals, however, is that Han's "replacement" of one regime with another is insufficient to describe the ways in which modern society has maintained, if not aggravated, its disciplinary functions, disproportionately targeting Black people. Where sleep and dreaming are concerned, it is precisely *through* the acceleration and expansion of always racialized disciplinary and punitive practices, like the penalization of poverty through private-debt schemes, or the use of solitary confinement as a form of sleep deprivation, or the threat of the police at the door in the middle of the night—through the deregulation of corporate power and the amplified regulation of our bodies—that modern-day life bound by capitalism has constrained our capacities for dreaming. *Black Womxn Dreaming* thus provides reparatory dreaming space, demonstrating Robin D.G. Kelley's powerful contention, if more literally than he intended, that "it has been the poets—no matter the medium—who have succeeded in imagining the color of the sky, in rendering the kinds of dreams and futures social movements are capable of producing."[39] Calling on the uncharted geographies of Tubman's fugitive operations, *Black Womxn Dreaming* finds its power not by furnishing a clear or resolved guide out of reality's present sleeplessness but by dreaming that which remains inconceivable under present conditions, a speculative world where Black sleep is uncontroversial and collectively valued.

In a lecture at the Unitarian Universalist Association General Assembly in June 1966, Martin Luther King Jr. said, "There is nothing more tragic than to sleep through a revolution."[40] In a society that celebrates endurance, freedom dreams are still measured in units of industry and insomniac fortitude. Glimmers of new worlds might sound like the cacophonous din of the collective formed by marching bodies or look like the eruption of a riot that breaks free from stasis. It might be a late-night conversation that turns you all the way inside out. The works explored here show quieter approaches to imagining life outside of its present crises, alternative modes of being found in somnolent fugitivity: a reclamation of stolen time, returning collective freedom dreams to the space of the unconscious. Black sleep is, indeed, a mode of reparation against stolen time. Tracing lineages of sleep inequities faced by Black people—from practices of sleep deprivation of the enslaved to post-emancipation and present-day struggles against extractive labor practices and the everyday stress of discrimination—reveals that Black sleep is one variable in the calculus of what Michael Hanchard calls "racial time," defined as "the inequalities of temporality that result from power relations between racially dominant and subordinate groups."[41] Finding ways to reclaim sleep-time against the enduring impositions of racial time might be a mode of quiet rebellion. As Hanchard points out, however, these modalities of temporal reparation can exist "on both collective and individual levels."[42] The collaborative practices surveyed here—the artistic duo Girl, *Black Womxn Dreaming*'s private communion and even Jennifer Packer's practice, which observes the intimate relations between subject and painter—insist on principles of collectivity if we are to alter the conditions of our sleepless discontent. These works enact an ethos of mutuality that suggests that the recuperation of sleep is not revolutionary as an individual project. Where a singular stolen moment of rest may perform a fleeting denial of present constraints, it is ultimately in the service of the dominant ideology. Liberal individualism demands that everyone take matters into their own hands, but admonitions to "just rest" are the perversion of "be resilient," locating resistance at the site of the individual and obfuscating structural forces that produce such sleeplessness under duress. The project of overturning the precarious conditions of waking life that produce Black sleeplessness must, in the end, be undertaken by the collective.

NOTES

1. I use the word "nonsomnia" here and throughout the text as distinguished from "insomnia", a common sleep disorder that involves difficulty falling asleep. Nonsomnia has been used to describe a rare condition of extreme sleeplessness in which a person might not sleep for days at a time. For a fuller description of this disorder, see Peter Gray, *Psychology* (New York: Worth Publishers, 2007), 209. I've adopted nonsomnia to discuss the racialized presupposition of a condition of sleeplessness that has been mapped onto the Black body.

2. Christina Sharpe, *In the Wake: On Blackness and Being* (Durham, NC: Duke University Press, 2016), 4.

3. D.A. Johnson, C.L. Jackson, et al., "Are Sleep Patterns Influenced by Race/Ethnicity—A Marker of Relative Advantage or Disadvantage? Evidence to Date," *Nature and Science of Sleep* 11 (2019), 83.

4. Jürgen Zulley, "Without Sleeping, There Is No Waking: An Introduction to Sleep in Modern Society," in *Sleeping and Dreaming* (London: Black Dog Publishing, 2007), 29.

5. Ibid., 79.

6. Saidiya Hartman, "Venus in Two Acts," *Small Axe* 12 (2008), 4.

7. Johnson, Jackson, et al., "Are Sleep Patterns Influenced by Race/Ethnicity?," 83.

8. While there is no scholarly consensus as to the fact of John Henry's existence and the circumstances of his life, recent scholarship by Scott Reynolds Nelson suggests that he may be based on a Black inmate incarcerated at the Virginia State Penitentiary. See Scott Reynolds Nelson, *Steel Drivin' Man: John Henry, the Untold Story of an American Legend* (Oxford University Press, 2006).

9. Stephanie E. Smallwood, *Saltwater Slavery: A Middle Passage from Africa to American Diaspora* (Harvard University Press, 2007), 70.

10. While this paper focuses on conditions of sleeplessness endured by Black people primarily in the US, this diagram, which depicts a slave ship that traveled from the Loango coast of West Central Africa to Saint

Domingue (modern-day Haiti), testifies that the regulation of Black sleep and its productive myths are conditions experienced across the Black diaspora. For discussions of diasporic continuities around the mythologies of Black indolence, see, for example, Christine Jeske, "'They Don't Want to Work': The Laziness Myth," in *The Laziness Myth: Narratives of Work and the Good Life in South Africa* (Cornell University Press, 2020), pp. 26–54. Additionally, John Garrison Marks discusses white fears of "idleness" among formerly enslaved Black people in Caribbean Colombia; see John Garrison Marks, "Paths to Freedom," in *Black Freedom in the Age of Slavery: Race, Status, and Identity in the Urban Americas* (University of South Carolina Press, 2020), 36.

11. "Sleeping Position of Africans on Slave Ship, 1857," *Illustrated London News* (June 20, 1857), vol. 30, 595.

12. Thomas Jefferson, *Notes on the State of Virginia* (Boston: Lilly and Wait, 1832). PDF available at https://www.loc.gov/item/03004902/.

13. Frederick Douglass and William Lloyd Garrison, *Narrative of the Life of Frederick Douglass, an American Slave* (Boston: Anti-Slavery Office, 1849), 10. PDF available at https://www.loc.gov/ item/82225385/.

14. Hortense J. Spillers, "Mama's Baby, Papa's Maybe: An American Grammar Book," *Diacritics* 17, no. 2 (1987), 65.

15. While Equiano's narrative claims that he was born in the Kingdom of Benin, some scholars, notably Vincent Carretta, have suggested, based on the discovery of naval and baptismal records, that he may have been born in South Carolina. For a historiographical discussion of Equiano's birthplace, see Vincent Carretta, *Equiano the African: Biography of a Self-Made Man* (New York: Penguin, 2005); and Yael Ben-Zvi, "Equiano's Nativity: Negative Birthright, Indigenous Ethic, and Universal Human Rights," *Early American Literature* (2013), 399–423.

16. Olaudah Equiano, *The Interesting Narrative of the Life of Olaudah Equiano, or Gustavus Vassa, the African* (New York: W. Durell, 1791), 34, https://www.loc.gov/item/99199422/.

17. Harriet Jacobs and Lydia Maria Child, *Incidents in the Life of a Slave Girl* (Boston: Jacobs, 1861), 173.

18. Christopher W. Vandegrift, "Oneirocritica Afro-Americana," *Cabinet* 67 (Spring 2019–Winter 2020).

19. The Studio Museum in Harlem, "Simone Leigh, Kalup Linzy, and Jacolby Satterwhite: An Interview with Tavia Nyong'o," YouTube video, August 22, 2013.

20. Simone Leigh, Chitra Ganesh, and Uri McMillan, "Alternative Structures: Aesthetics, Imagination, and Radical Reciprocity: An Interview with Girl," *ASAP/Journal* 2, no. 2 (May 2017), 247.

21. Lorraine O'Grady, "Olympia's Maid: Reclaiming Black Female Subjectivity (1992/1994)," in *Writing in Space, 1973–2019*, ed. Aruna D'Souza (Durham, NC: Duke University Press, 2020), 97.

22. Alexander G. Weheliye, *Habeas Viscus: Racializing Assemblages, Biopolitics, and Black Feminist Theories of the Human* (Durham, NC: Duke University Press, 2014), 4.

23. Jonathan Crary, *24/7: Late Capitalism and the Ends of Sleep* (New York: Verso, 2013), 27.

24. Ibid., 12.

25. Kodwo Eshun, *More Brilliant Than the Sun: Adventures in Sonic Fiction* (London: Quartet Books, 1998), 113.

26. Leigh, Ganesh, and McMillan, "Alternative Structures: Aesthetics, Imagination, and Radical Reciprocity," 249.

27. Matthew Fuller, *How to Sleep: The Art, Biology and Culture of Unconsciousness* (London: Bloomsbury Academic, 2017), 14.

28. Sylvia Wynter, "Unsettling the Coloniality of Being/Power/Truth/Freedom: Towards the Human, After Man, Its Overrepresentation—An Argument," *CR: The New Centennial Review* 3, no. 3 (2003), 273.

29. Kevin Quashie, *The Sovereignty of Quiet: Beyond Resistance in Black Culture* (New Brunswick: Rutgers University Press, 2012), 8.

30. Léopold Sédar Senghor, "In New York," in *The Collected Poetry* (Charlottesville: University Press of Virginia, 1991).

31. Elizabeth Alexander, "Blues," in *Body of Life* (Sylmar: Tia Chucha Press, 1997).

32. Elizabeth Alexander, *The Black Interior* (Saint Paul, MN: Graywolf Press, 2004), 5.

33. Shay McAlister, "Piecing Together the Night of Breonna Taylor's Death," 13newsnow.com, July 30, 2020.

34. Tubman's episodic condition, described in scholarship as "sleeping spells" or "sleep attacks," has been variably attributed to both narcolepsy or epilepsy. See Chantal N. Gibson and Monique Silverman, "Sur/Rendering Her Image: The Unknowable Harriet Tubman," *RACAR: Revue d'Art Canadienne / Canadian Art Review* 30, nos. 1–2 (2005), 33.

35. Tabor-Smith in discussion with author, December 2020.

36. Byung-Chul Han, *The Burnout Society*, trans. Erik Butler (Stanford, CA: Stanford University Press, 2015), 22.

37. Saidiya Hartman, *Wayward Lives, Beautiful Experiments* (New York: Norton, 2019), xv.

38. Han, *The Burnout Society*, 8.

39. Robin D.G. Kelley, *Freedom Dreams: The Black Radical Imagination* (Boston: Beacon Press, 2002), 11.

40. Martin Luther King Jr., "1966 Ware Lecture: Don't Sleep Through the Revolution" (speech, Hollywood, Florida, May 18, 1966), Unitarian Universalist Association. I was first made aware of this famous dictum through Anna Della Subin's book-length essay about the cultural politics of sleeping, written in the wake of the 2011 Egyptian uprising. See Anna Della Subin, *Not Dead but Sleeping* (New York: Triple Canopy, 2016), 5.

41. Michael Hanchard, "Afro-Modernity: Temporality, Politics, and the African Diaspora," *Public Culture* 11, no. 1 (1999), 253.

42. Ibid., 265.

GARRETT BRADLEY

IN CONVERSATION WITH

TYLER MITCHELL

Garrett Bradley: There's some crazy heat wave in New Orleans. I am torn between AC and fresh air. The darkness and hum of machines starts to bring me down. Where are you?

Tyler Mitchell: I'm in my studio in Brooklyn, New York. I've been in Europe for the past few months. It's nice to be back and feel somewhat grounded.

GB: It occurred to me, right before we got talking that you and I kind of have this funny, reverse migration situation, right? You grew up in the South? Where did you grow up?

TM: Atlanta, Georgia. Yeah.

GB: And then you came North... I grew up in New York and found my home in the South. What pulled you North?

TM: To be honest, I suppose it was school and studies, because I had this maybe clichéd syndrome of not appreciating where you grew up until you leave. And maybe you have similar, but I couldn't appreciate Atlanta while I was there, I found it to be a politically regressive place. I felt the energies of past race relations and all of those ideas weighing on me very heavy and just wanting to get out ... I actually had more of a California fever as a teenager, that'll be the promised land, you know? And then I got accepted into film school at NYU. I think so much about Atlanta, and I love that you live in New Orleans, I envy it a little bit. New Orleans and Atlanta are like rival cities, but also friends, connected inextricably. I remember Hurricane Katrina happening and basically, suddenly, Atlanta was New Orleans. Many of my friends are from New Orleans, or migrated here from there post-Katrina. So, I really feel the energy of that city. And I love that you are based there as an artist. Do you feel like the South informs your work and your process?

GB: I've spent a good part of 2023 with the intention of listening, resting, making things quietly without a deadline, without an idea I can fully articulate yet to anyone. I was starting to feel a little bit like I was in an echo chamber and so I'm here sort of resetting everything. Living in one place, not traveling a lot, working quietly, which is unnerving and also liberating. But I am definitely thinking about how I got here and why I'm still here after thirteen years. Maybe the same reasons that my family left were those same reasons I wanted to return. I've been fortunate to find community in that pursuit. Whereas New York and Los Angeles have always felt like future cities, like their investment has always been in the future, somehow my instinct has been to seek the other side of history.

TM: There's so much to unpack there. I mean congrats to you for taking this year to just be in process. That's not talked about enough, you know, an artist's journey or just taking time to really think, to focus—not so much on output but on the in-betweens, and how that impacts your life and work. I'm curious, because I'm having quite the opposite year and so that sounds so nice. Do you want to talk about that for a bit?

GB: The way you phrased that idea of "the in-betweens," that's how Robert De Niro talks about acting, that it's really about the moments in between—not the lines or back and forth. It's how we come to things. The process. The outcome is the very last of it.

If we aren't in the world and taking time to really be a part of it, I'm not sure what we're making work about otherwise. I remember my mom saying to me, when I was looking at colleges, she said: "You can't go to film school." I knew I wanted to make films and I felt very fortunate to find that in high school, that I had a mode and way to communicate with the world. She was adamant: What was I going to make films about if I didn't know anything about the world? If I only knew about the medium itself?

TM: I didn't realize how aligned we were in that way. My reason for going to New York was to go to film school and I feel similar to you in that, in high school I felt lucky to find a calling and felt equally questioned by my parents. Just to zoom out a little bit, I have to say that I was so excited to talk to you, but I actually feel embarrassed that I didn't know about your work sooner. Kahlil Joseph introduced us three years ago, in the midst of the pandemic, and he said to me: "I think you should know this young filmmaker Garrett, I think you'd like the work". And my first exposure to your work was *America* and I've never seen a filmmaker's work that I felt so in tune with, connected to, inspired by and in awe of. And now hearing your story about film school and your relationship to that and your ideas around what you're going to be doing and how it's led you to this moment of beautiful pause, or reflection and living—I almost envy that! As my year has felt like nothing but go, go, go. I hope in between it all I'm finding space for pause and care.

And maybe it's important, if we're talking about process, also to take a moment to think about how filmmaking and art making are lifelong pursuits. These are such hyper-fast times that I often forget that my favorite filmmakers really took sometimes three, five or ten years between some of their best films. And in those three, five and ten years, they're really *living*. Those experiences craft beautiful work. It sounds like you're doing a bit of that for yourself, am I correct?

GB: Yes, I mean most of my work comes from being in it, identifying a paradox and wanting to work through it. I don't know anything about physics, but one of the principles, from my understanding, is that paradox is an indication of some kind of fundamental truth. There is, I have to admit, a particular kind of discomfort in not having your hands in anything concrete yet though, it's running in the dark a bit and just sensing things in the periphery. You feel like you're not doing anything, like you're being lazy or avoidant, but then it comes to you and continues to come to you, even in contradiction.

What I wanted to talk about too, was this distinction between commissioned projects and non-commissioned projects, because the media we work in, filmmaking especially, have been historically exclusionary in part because of their cost. When you work with a material that often requires a good amount of people and resources, one's process also can be forced and dictated to by an industry, right? So, how do you find your process is delineated, if at all, between that level of negotiation?

TM: For me, it's matured and undulated. It's ebbed and flowed over the years. Commissioned work is about operating within what I find to be healthy constraints. You get to work within a context and, of course, that comes with negotiations of how much of "yourself" is in the final result. I find that space to be potentially capacious and beautiful. Sometimes the boundaries, incentives and nudges of commissioned work can create a beautiful new combination, or a new process, or can unlock some sort of new way to approach making work, that you hadn't thought of before, if you were just by yourself in a vacuum.

For a few years, I had some kind of anxiety that was external, from other people asking me, "Well, are you an artist or a fashion photographer?" or "Are you focused on your commissioned work or your *personal* work right now?" What I felt they were asking me to do was *choose*. I've more recently accepted that I simply embody both sides. And I no longer have this internal struggle because I feel equal reverence for how my work lives on the printed pages of a magazine as I do seeing it in a gallery or museum. Those two things operate differently and yet, they excite me equally. So that's my own philosophy on it. In the end, commissioned or personal, art or fashion, what creates strong and impactful work is what you decide to make of it all.

I'll just add—and I think you know this—that I feel in a weird way cinema-*adjacent*. I went to film school, I'm definitely a cinephile, I have made all sorts of experimental and short films in the past and I have hopes and dreams of one day making narrative feature-length films. But for now, I'm primarily a photographic artist, and I have no problems with that. I'm someone who—in my school days—moved on from solely filmmaking primarily because of exactly what you said, which is how long these projects take. We're often talking about enormous budgets needed from big studios, large crews and long lead times. And while I'm very much prepared to go the distance to make films I love—somewhere along the way as a student I found photography a more immediate and autonomous way to go out and make work that I felt compelled by.

But what I'm saying is you are both a filmmaker and an artist, so can you talk a bit about the idea of commissioned versus personal for you? For example, the amazing Naomi Osaka piece you directed—how do you, as an artist, navigate that and keep it open?

GB: I didn't know Naomi before we went into it, which was a different experience for me. I felt like most "celebrity docs" are basically propaganda films—a highlight reel of things you've already seen in the news, with brief moments where the person can defend themselves on their own terms with the support of their team. Neither of us were interested in doing that. So protecting her, while also allowing there to be a real sense of what her life feels like—what's on her mind, what she cares about, what her challenges are. You know, like a real person? [Laughing.] I wanted to be sensitive to the stage of life that she was in and felt nothing should feel definitive or fixed so that the final outcome could reflect her—as all of us—in constant evolution. I felt that would create a framework that would protect her, also creating something people could relate to and connect with in a real way.

Naomi can also be a bit of an introvert, as well as someone with strong opinions, who observes and thinks deeply. Tennis itself, as you know, is a solo sport but also a uniquely mental one—once you're on the court, it's all you. You can't ask for help from a coach. In most cases, the headspace of a tennis player is just as important as where they are physically. I should say it's no coincidence that Black women have dominated the sport when you take this into account.

Building something within these parameters presented a series of questions: How could the work represent or visualize headspace? How could the series make the important connection between Naomi's performance and where she was emotionally on any given day? One solution was to balance the focus between Naomi and her immediate environment. So seeing the spaces she was in—placing the camera in situations where we could feel the context, the people and the energy of her surroundings. All the other cameras were looking at her and so I wanted to look back at them. And then there was just the extreme drama of filming from 2019 to 2021. Naomi was navigating the pressures of defending a world championship, personal and professional loss, environmental turmoil in Australia, a global pandemic, a global uprising in defense of Black life. A lot of this prompted her—and most of us—to relook at our lives and our world. The questions she brought to the table as result of that became the foundation for the series: How does one find balance in life? How does purpose change over time as one continues to meet milestones? As these questions started to dictate the highs and lows of her journey, on and off the court, they also expanded to the universal inquiry of life's purpose, of personal worth, and about the courage that it takes to allow one's personal values to inform their work and vice versa.

I think most of us have been raised to look at our heroes as being inaccessible—as if that's part of the appeal. The show evolved naturally, making a case for the power of empathy and to feel encouraged to take chances in life, perhaps especially in moments where the stakes can feel impossibly high. For these reasons, production was also really challenging. There was little consistency in terms of the crew I was working with, which, as you know, can present issues. I am used to having at least two DPs [directors of photography] working at once: *Below Dreams* had two, *America* had two, but *Time* had four, *Osaka* had four.

TM: I did not know that. I would say that that's certainly not a choice most people would make.

GB: I'm not really sure at what point I realized it was a process that suited me. It started by seeing different kinds of strength in different people and wanting to bring them together. And then another part of it was just logistics, right? Like one person can only be available for so long. With *Below Dreams*, you know, Milena Pastreich and Brian Richard shot that together. Milena has a very specific eye, and Brian has a very specific eye. And together, they provided multiple dimensions of the same city. But I want to go back really quickly to something you just said that reminds me of John Berger's *Ways of Seeing* I remember reading it in high school.

TM: Yeah, that's one of my favorite books.

GB: It's great and so simple. The basic premise that stayed with me was this idea that effective advertising is essentially allowing customers or people to see themselves within the product. Is there tension in that for you? The idea of overtness as an essential part of being seen?

TM: Yeah, it's like putting on different clothes on different days—sometimes I'm this, sometimes I'm that. We should be allowed that full range of expression. I'm really more open to making whatever it is that may service any given project or purpose that I'm focused on at that given moment. I'm trying to not limit myself. Ninety-nine percent of my work is portraiture, so it is representational, but I will say that as I'm growing, my ideas and taste are expanding. My ideas around what sort of work I enjoy are becoming more complex and varied. My last show in London [*Chrysalis*, Gagosian, Davies Street, October 6–November 12, 2022] welcomes more abstraction than I've ever done before. I made these images of bodies that you didn't quite fully know were there. Images of people wading through mud. Or just a left-behind trail of muddy footsteps on a wood-paneled surface, like traces of human life, but not always evidence of it.

GB: I loved those. Susan Sontag also is coming to mind right now in thinking about photography, nonintervention and this idea that the minute one takes a photograph, they're detaching themselves from the world. And I couldn't disagree with that more. I think it dismisses the fact that image making is the by-product of choices made. Her proposal was prophetic in one sense, however, in terms of what it means to take a photo of a sunset on your phone. Or anything on your phone. I can understand that feeling of detachment.

TM: Suddenly, you're no longer connected. But actually, as image makers, this sort of aspirational construction—making photographs versus taking them I guess—it makes me ask the question: Could constructing an image or a scene, as you've done in *America* so beautifully, potentially be more generative, more connective and connected? Could that be more true than the truth itself?

GB: Yes, totally. I do feel the process is just as important as the outcome. I don't know why this is making me think about AI. I'm sorry to be that person [laughing]. I'm simultaneously bored and obsessed with it. It's super scary when we think about its application and uses in institutional and law enforcement settings. But you know, the question around what it means for art? I don't feel like it's a threat to art making. It is a processing of materials which creates something "new," in one second or whatever, right? It's like *super-duper* fast.

But my feeling is that those shortcuts can not only be emotionally discerned by a viewer, but also rob us of the insights gained through the trouble that goes into making something. And the linearity of its goal is quite limiting for where the work can go. Is it not a cliché that the process leads us and informs us to what the work will become and be? When there is no time to pause and question the what and why, my feeling is it will only exacerbate a sense of loss and disconnection. In other words doubt is essential to making something good and worthy of revelation. AI has no doubt, so its confidence feels naive and without substance and that's something I think we, as humans, as viewers, need to feel in order to really connect with.

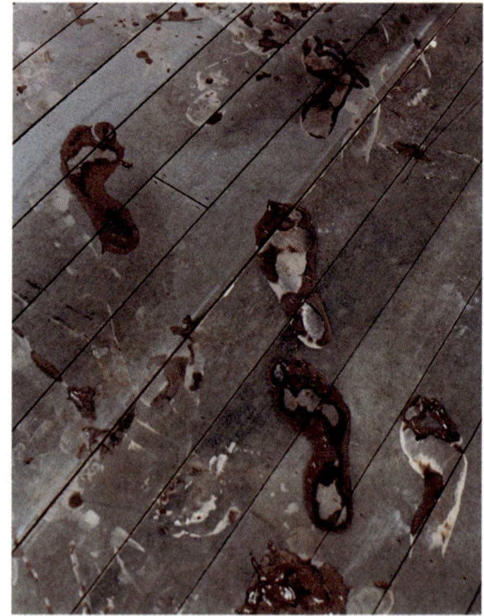

TM: I was listening to a podcast this morning about education and AI and whether students are using it to plagiarize or how we sort of view those lines anymore, how it affects the

Tyler Mitchell, *Tenderly*, 2022

educational system. What's the point of a university class if you have this other brain that can write your essays? Do you need to memorize things anymore? I guess I've just kept my blinders on a little bit. I'm a little bit in this space, where if it's just me making my little pictures and if someone else cares, then that's perfectly nice. But if it ends up being only me who cares, I'm fine with that too. There's a video I saw online of Saul Bass saying, "I want to make beautiful things, even if nobody cares." He talks about that being the leading principle by which he wants to live his life—without giving a damn if that matters to anyone else. I really feel that.

GB: Before we go, I'm curious, what are you most concerned about in life? What matters to you the most right now?

TM: What matters to me the most is making work that I feel in some way, shape or form, pushes this idea of interconnectedness or human groundedness as well. And not in a trite or righteous way, you know. I've always tried to lead with sincerity and then the other things fall into place. What concerns me is where we're headed, globally, like without getting heavy I do think about how you're in this heat wave and I'm in New York and it's becoming untenable to live here. It's not affordable. That sounds like I'm worried about some basic needs, but how can artists function here? There's nowhere to go. Maybe I'll end up in New Orleans with you, Garrett. I don't know.

GB: Yes, well you have a place to stay, always. And it's unfortunate but also a window of hope to think that our tendency is to both learn and forget, learn again and forget again. What's gotten us here is that perpetual amnesia but I do also think we are remembering, we're going back and awakening. Anyway …

TM: Right, wow.

GB: Yeah, too much for the end. Okay, be safe. Bye, Tyler.

JOY JAMES

TRAUMA, TIME THEFT, AND THE CAPTIVE MATERNAL

Meeting the Captive Maternal[1]

We are missing the stories of women who are keeping life going in the midst of war. —Zainab Salbi, 2016 [2]

The nature of this war assumes many different guises, sometimes overtly violent, sometimes economically restrictive, and still other times socially repressive ... modern wars of US imperialism waged against Third World people have not all been completely military campaigns, but have also included social pacification programs, economic aid to reactionary regimes, political police extermination of legitimate opposition.
—Message to the Black Movement: A Political Statement from the Black Underground (1976)[3]

Perspectives from an Arab feminist human rights refugee and an organization associated with a Black feminist revolutionary fugitive initiate this reflection on captivity and resistance. Raised during the 1980s war between Iran and Iraq (the United States secretly armed both sides),[4] Iraqi American Zainab Salbi notes how women in Middle East war zones forge resistance by maintaining pleasure in their children's lives and personal beauty in their own (one woman declares her desire to have contraband red lipstick so that when a sniper fires as she walks in public he will realize that he has just "killed a beautiful woman").[5] A former member of the Black Panther Party (BPP) and the Black Liberation Army (BLA), an activist in the Black Underground, Assata Shakur maintains her innocence in the shooting death of New Jersey State Trooper Werner Foerster. Her escape from prison rendered her a political fugitive and "refugee" in Cuba (the US normalized relations with the nation in 2016). The FBI engineered a counterintelligence program that hunted, imprisoned, and on occasion, assassinated radicals, such as Fred Hampton and Mark Clark in the December 1969 Chicago raid on BPP headquarters. That same federal police would place Shakur, with a two-million-dollar bounty on her head, on the 2014 terrorist list with Al-Qaeda, which suggests that ideological links have been formed in the policing of foreign and domestic threats.

Born in different generations and continents, under diverse political and cultural states of siege and violence, the narratives of Salbi and Shakur grapple with persecution, death, and grief. Pursuing fights and flights for justice, despite captivity and trauma, both women's narratives recognize the unrecoverable years stolen or spent surviving warfare and murder. One woman, Salbi, is elevated from subjugated female to free citizen in her adopted nation (that the United States intervened, invaded, and destabilized Iraq triggering genocidal violence is context that might be underscrutinized). Another woman, Shakur, is forced into mutating positions of enslavement: from engineering sickle cell testing and breakfast programs in Harlem, while threatened by police and Cointelpro, through survival in a militarist underground formation as a "slave" rebel, to being shot, captured, and tortured as a political prisoner who plans her escape into political exile as a "maroon." Democracy-seeking Salbi emigrates from a dictatorial state to become a sovereign citizen in the West. Democracy-fleeing Shakur in metamorphosis is in constant violent transitions, from that of a "slave" insurrectionist labeled, tortured, convicted, and imprisoned as a "common criminal" into a political prisoner-fugitive who survives a lethal, governmental war that killed or disappeared other Black radicals.[6] The anonymous counterparts to these women's public lives are the more typical "Captive Maternals"—those most vulnerable to violence, war, poverty, police, and captivity; those whose very existence enables the possessive empire that claims and dispossesses them.

Global dominance in economics, military, and cultural commodities allows the United States' imperial reach, despite the "blowback" of its devastating, unwinnable wars (alongside the genocidal violence the United States unleashed abroad, its interventionist warfare has resulted, in 2016, in twenty veteran suicides a day, trillions of dollars in military debt, and projected decades of warfare in the Middle East). However, the United States' longest war is with its domestic target: enslaved or captive Black women, a war that dates back to the Commonwealth of Virginia's 1658 attempts to (re)enslave Elizabeth Key, one of the first Captive Maternals to have her battles enter public record.

Captive Maternals can be either biological females or those feminized into caretaking and consumption. To better understand the meaning of Captive Maternals requires context.

Western theory or Womb Theory provides the historical context that married democracy with slavery. In transitioning a colony through a republic into a representative democracy with imperial might, the emergent United States grew a womb, it took on the generative properties of the maternals it held captive. Western democracy, based in American Exceptionalism, merged Enlightenment ideologies with Western theories to birth a new nation (a nascent empire) that fed on Black frames. Centuries later, Black Captive Maternals remain disproportionately disciplined, denigrated, and consumed for the greater democracy. Although Black males are most publicly policed, imprisoned, and executed by state violence and vigilantism, and remembering to call out the names or images of their female counterparts is an important additive in a Black death roll call and mobilization, this lens is shaped by paternal power, imagery, and desires. For Captive Maternals, the chitchat of the little cuts and ratlike gnawing is the norm; they face verbal slander and intimidation, physical violence, domestic violence, rape and sexual assault, and contempt, policing in schools, jobs, society, and prisons, from every sector. Still, it is not their victimization that marks them; it is their productivity and its consumption. Throughout history, Captive Maternals provided the reproductive and productive labor to stabilize culture and wealth. The Viking mercantile raiders survived and thrived because of slavery: agricultural work and reproductive work by the feminized or female enabled raiders to seek glory through pillage and rape. Even Thor required a Captive Maternal (although he would likely have denied the fact).

Captive Maternals work in and for governance, corporations, prisons, police, and the military. Their diversity—from CEOs and university presidents to attorney generals and janitors and the incarcerated—indicates ideological difference, economic need, and political desire within a democracy. The concept of the "Captive Maternal" is not fungible. There are distinctions between Salbi and Shakur because of the importance of their respective work for justice and against war. Venerated and employable by governance and nonprofits, Salbi is sovereign in a democracy that installed the dictator Saddam Hussein that terrorized her birth nation, levied deadly sanctions against

Hussein that led to the deaths of half a million children, deposed him through an invasion under the false pretext of weapons of mass destruction, an invasion that caused mass destruction. In order for Shakur's narrative to emerge in its own right, not as a perversion or pathological mutation of victimization or violence, one cannot ignore Shakur's structural relationship to propping up Western democracy, first as caretaker (Panther breakfast program supplementing for social services denied to the urban poor) and later as demonized criminal. Material conditions, refugee or immigrant status only slightly determine one's status as captive. The resolve and ability to resist captivity through the use of a fulcrum, even if leverage engenders disarray, is a form of politics, disparaged and punished by conventional politics.

Western theory or Womb Theory creates the template that makes predation of the Captive Maternal invisible, through consumptive relationships that provide the free theorist or citizen with plausible deniability. Today, Womb Theory accommodates critiques of feminism, antiracism, and heterosexism to some degree. Womb Theory co-opted genesis for democracy, idealized as the highest form of human self-governance. For centuries, patriarchal, enslaving Womb Theory normalized—as natural, universal, and befitting the diminished capacities of the captive—trauma and theft of labor and time, which legitimized the existence of Captive Maternals as inevitable, inconsequential, and invisible. Citizen and ruler benefit from reproductive labor to accrue leisure and space for theory, war, and power. Oral and written biographies[7] and treatises of captive females embattled against violence offer important perspectives.[8] As forms of theorizing,[9] such works allow Western theory to be viewed as the anti-soulmate of freedom.

Trauma and Time Theft

I am a Black revolutionary woman, and because of this I have been charged with and accused of every alleged crime in which a woman was believed to have participated.

—Assata Shakur[10]

In 1619, the British colony Jamestown, Virginia, marked its impoverished Africans, Europeans, and Native Americans as indentured servants; but it began to seek the mechanism through law and custom to turn a free indentured person of color into a slave. In 1658, Elizabeth Key, a "free woman of color," not a "Negro/African/Slave," petitioned the Virginia colony to end her captivity. Key argued that her deceased father had been a member of the Virginia House of Burgesses, had her baptized, and provided a guardianship under an indenture before his death. English common law ruled that children inherited the legal status of their fathers who must acknowledge and financially support them. Key successfully proved that, based on English ancestry, Christian status, and record of indenture, she was free.

Three years later, Virginia abandoned English common law and ruled that slave or free status would follow the status of the mother;[11] black women would be slaves and if a white mother chose to give birth with a black/African father, then slave status would follow the African bloodline. This split the Captive Maternal into distinct racial categories. The majority of bonded women as African could no longer follow the example set by Key.[12] Captivity followed Black Maternals—mothers and fathers. The paternal womb erased moral and financial obligations of the white father to the Black family but preserved his political agency. It erased these obligations of the Black father to the Black family by criminalizing his political agency. The augmented freedom for the white and diminished freedom for the Black father meant the negation of child and birth mother. Intimacy and bonding dissipated into the loss of "childhood" and "motherhood" as understood among the free. A slave child is a *slave*. A slave mother is a *slave*. Their social standing is obliterated by their captivity. Expressed in the concept of time means that there is no sacred or protected "time" of Black childhood under white governance, or colonialism, or occupation, or war. The time of captivity does not recognize "childhood" or "motherhood" as possessing unique rights other than those granted to the enslaved.

Centuries after Key's winning legal strategy and the subsequent changes in the law, Harriet Jacobs self-published her

1861 memoir (written under the pseudonym Linda Brent): *Incidents in the Life of a Slave Girl, Written by Herself.*[13] The work describes a society shaped by torture. Jacobs structures her own captivity into an active crawl space for nearly seven years until she stole her time and self into rebellion and flight. Tortured for years by her slave masters, Jacobs created an attic prison as a form of freedom: she damaged herself in order to minimize the violence of others. Jacobs's historical reality plays out in contemporary prisons and refugee camps and cellars, where there is no direct remedy given the function of government (police, education, health systems, employment) largely as managerial sectors not vectors for social justice (there is also the injustice that said agencies manufacture as they stabilize and maintain governance). Foucault argues that governance exceeds the scope of ideology. If so, then it also exceeds the capacity of on-continuum political paradigms insufficiently prepared for wartime analyses or full inspection of the ramifications of a Captive Maternal within Womb Theory.

In the theft and transferal of time to her consumers, Jacobs became a timekeeper and timepiece. With seven years of time as "moral measure" of her attic prison, she reminds one that mid-twentieth-century European genocide, while it is the apex of Western moral theory or contemporary Womb Theory, is not the height of human suffering and resistance. Jacobs was motivated by sacrifices for her children.[14] Such sacrifices are never repaid (activism does not bring back slain children; surviving children cannot repay the debt given for their lives). The time of the captive fugitive within the larger captivity of slavery is filtered today through notions of "Black time" and non-Black or "white time." In prison, hard time is Black time in both duration and duress shaped by longer sentences for similar offenses and harsher conditions during imprisonment and moral outrage at the injustice of justice. (In foster care and schools, a "harder" time relative to an "easier" time in confinement produces negative consequences.)

Even in resistance for freedom, differentiated time is tied to captivity. Captive Maternals organize mourners and protestors against police or vigilante violence that disproportionately kills sons and disproportionately often requires a female kin to mount public campaigns in memory and honor of the slain and in search for justice. The time and trauma of mothers, aunts, sisters, and daughters fill public political advocacy and private domestic duties (and political campaigns, if one notes Hillary Clinton's ability to incorporate the grief of Black women who lost children or siblings through police violence into her presidential campaign[15]). Entering the public realm of protest requires leaving to some extent the private realm of reproductive or domestic labor. Who will now pick up kids after school, get dinner on the table, oversee homework, and help family manage grief? Surrogate maternals, many times younger or older women, such that teenage daughters or grandmothers might be utilized to fill the void more than their masculine counterparts.

Trauma and time theft, including the loss of leisure to recover from fatigue and violence, altered markers on genomes in which African Americans allegedly share the intergenerational challenges of Native Americans,[16] and Hmong[17] who survived genocide.[18] Thus, time for health is shortened within the biological womb of the captive. Crunk Feminist perspectives on Black girls waiting for their verb extends through time,[19] as an expression of resistance in the face of a daunting recovery.

Time exists as and in slave status (the duration of the lives of one's owners), penal status (the duration of legal sentence until parole, pardon, escape, or death), and maternal status (the duration of the neediness of children, adults, and elders). Love appears to suspend time (a human fabrication) but cannot restore it. Time is lost, fragmented, broken in family terrors (that Sigmund Freud conveniently suppressed to resurrect his career), constant negotiations with whiteness-as-property owners (that structure the inequalities in schooling, employment, housing, and mental health),[20] and time is lost in memories of genocide.[21] To grapple with such phenomena requires sanctuary and vision. Suffering produces the conditions under which sanctuaries are imagined, and constructed within minds, at times extended into the physical world.

NOTES

1. This excerpt from "The Womb of Western Theory: Trauma, Time Theft, and the Captive Maternal" is part of a larger project entitled, "Fulcrum: Captive Maternals, Leverage, and a Theory of Democracy."

2. Zainab Salbi, "How Do People Live and Cope in the Midst of Violent Conflict?" *TED Radio Hour*, NPR, February 11, 2016.

3. From the perspective of the Black Liberation Army, its most prominent member was Assata Shakur. This was a reaction to lethal repression from the police and FBI Cointelpro. See Coordinating Committee, Black Liberation Army, "Message to the Black Movement: A Political Statement from the Black Underground" (1976), 12.

4. Seymour M. Hersh, "US Secretly Gave Aid to Iraq Early in Its War against Iran," *New York Times*, January 26, 1992.

5. Salbi, "How Do People Live and Cope in the Midst of Violent Conflict?"

6. Senate hearings on CIA/FBI illegal or extralegal warfare and malfeasance against the Black Panther Party and radical activists is public record. Most though are unfamiliar with the Department of Homeland Security and FBI maintaining surveillance files on Black Lives Matter. With Jeh Johnson, former counsel for the Department of Defense, as the Secretary of Homeland Security and Barack Obama as president, the government sought influence or control over Black political leadership in resistance to racist violence. Black Lives Matter activists also publicly critiqued FBI requests that Apple create software to compromise security on its devices following the December 2, 2015, San Bernardino mass killings by Syed Rizwan Farook and Tashfin Malik. *The Intercept* maintains that the FBI Joint Terrorism Task Force has also monitored Black Lives Matter. See the Senate Select Committee to Study Governmental Operations with Respect to Intelligence Activities (The Church Committee), 1976; George Joseph, "Feds Regularly Monitored Black Lives Matter since Ferguson," *The Intercept*, July 24, 2015.

7. Although possibly censored for icon respectability, the most well-known biographies or autobiographies of Black radical women in twentieth-century politics and movements include Shirley Chisholm, *Unbought and Unbossed* (Boston: Houghton Mifflin, 1970); Barbara Ransby, *Ella Baker and the Black Freedom Movement* (Chapel Hill: University of North Carolina Press, 2003); Chana Kai Lee, *For Freedom's Sake: The Life of Fannie Lou Hamer* (Champaign: University of Illinois Press, 2000); Angela Y. Davis, *Angela Y. Davis: An Autobiography* (New York: Random House, 1985); and Assata Shakur, *Assata: An Autobiography* (London: Zed Books, 1987).

8. The 1977 Combahee River Collective Statement is a manifesto that dissects predatory violence from multiple sectors. See https://wgs10016. commons.gc.cuny.edu/combahee-river-collective-black-feminist-statement/.

9. For a discussion of Black feminist theory's use of the term "theorizing," see Barbara Christian, "The Race for Theory," *Cultural Critique* 6 (Spring 1987): 51–63.

10. In the death of NJ trooper Werner Foerster, Assata Shakur was shot by troopers and partially paralyzed; her companions are alleged to have shot him. An analysis of Shakur and her legal counsel's perspectives are found in *Assata: An Autobiography*, 1987 (Chicago: Lawrence Hill Books, 2001). I offer my analysis in "Framing the Panther: Assata Shakur and Black Female Agency," in *Want to Start a Revolution?,* ed. Dayo Gore, Jeanne Theoharis, and Komozi Woodard (New York: New York University Press, 2009), 138–60.

11. See Pamela Barnes Craig, "Slavery and Indentured Servants," *American Women: A Library of Congress Guide for the Study of Women's History and Culture in the United States*, online edition (Library of Congress, 2001).

12. Sharon Block argues that while seventeenth-century British law made rape of women or girls a capital offense, American eighteenth-century law emphasized interracial rape to deflect from the sexual assaults of white men and to diminish their vulnerability to execution. According to Block, rape was racialized and politicized by whites in the eighteenth century, not the postbellum nineteenth-century society. Block also notes that Black and Native women raped by white males faced grotesque forms of sadistic violence not visited upon white rape victims. See Sharon Block, *Rape & Sexual Power in Early America* (Durham: University of North Carolina Press, 2006).

13. Harriet Jacobs (Linda Brent), *Incidents in the Life of a Slave Girl, Written by Herself* (Cambridge, MA: Harvard University Press, 1987).

14. Christian morality and religiosity are part of contemporary Western democracy. Blood sacrifice for the eradication of sins is understood to be heroic and divine as is the act of forgiveness. Theologian Delores Williams has written of the precariousness of Black women assuming the role of the crucified in order to sustain their churches (in which some are still under the sway of patriarchal leadership). See Delores Williams, *Sisters in the Wilderness: The Challenge of Womanist God-Talk* (Maryknoll, NY: Orbis Books, 2013). When family members of those slain by mass murderer, white supremacist Dylann Roof, publicly forgave him for the 2015 massacre in Charleston, South Carolina's Emanuel African Methodist Episcopal (AME) Church became a catalyst for retiring the Confederate flag from government buildings. That blood sacrifice in an AME church, linked to the nineteenth-century slave insurrectionist Denmark Vesey, also repudiated Vesey's bloody slave rebellion.

15. Shirley Chisholm's campaign for president in 1972 represented her refusal to disavow the Black Panther Party. In 2016, Bernie Sanders's gradual incorporation of Black Lives Matter analyses in his Racial Justice platform featured the "It's Not Over" video produced by Erica Garner. Erica Garner is the daughter of Eric Garner, whom NYPD killed by chokehold in 2014 (his mother Gwen Carr campaigned for Clinton), and her narrative incorporates the experiential activist theory of the Captive Maternal into her trauma and protest culture. Erica Garner identifies herself as an "activist" for a year, during which she protested weekly the killing of Eric Garner. Speaking as a mother of a six-year-old who misses her grandfather, someone that Erica Garner also mourns as a murder victim, Garner notes that Malcolm X died for the right to be free and she asserts that only Sanders seriously protests the killings of Black people by police. "It's Not Over | Bernie Sanders," YouTube video, 3:56, posted by "Bernie 2016," February 11, 2016.

16. When the Cherokee Nation expelled Black Freedmen in 2011, their former slaves included their relatives (counted by tabulators who listed all Blacks who survived the Trail of Tears as non-Indian and all whites as Indian. Black Freedmen protested before the Muskogee, Oklahoma, Bureau of Indian Affairs (BIA) office, led by Descendants of Freedmen Association President Marilyn Vann. BIA stated that the Freedmen's citizenship rights cannot be revoked due to an 1866 US treaty with the Cherokee for equal rights that it signed with the United States.

17. The US bombings of French Indochina, Cambodia, and Vietnam by Presidents Lyndon Johnson and Richard Nixon and Secretary of State Henry Kissinger opened the door to Khmer Rouge killing fields in the 1975–79 Cambodian genocide. Journalists also maintain that the United States enabled the genocide of Cambodians during the Carter, Reagan, and Bush administrations. Gregory Elich, "Who Supported the Khmer Rouge?," *Counterpunch* 16 (October 2014).

18. See Dan Hurley, "Grandma's Experiences Leave a Mark on Your Genes," *Discover*, May 2013; Judith Shulevitz, "The Science of Suffering," *New Republic*, November 16, 2016.

19. Brittney Cooper, "Black Girl Is a Verb: A New American Grammar Book," *Crunk Feminist Collective*, March 28, 2016.

20. Cheryl Harris, "Whiteness as Property," *Harvard Law Review* 106, no. 8 (June 1993): 1707–91.

21. After the ethnic cleansings and genocides in Yugoslavia and Rwanda, the UN created the International Criminal Court in 1998; the UN Security Council declared rape an act of war or a war crime in 2008. There has been more attention to race and less to rape in warfare. Civil war, despite its fratricidal mayhem, encompasses a recognizable fraternal humanity, one to be reconstructed from the ashes of genocidal violence. Non-European/American wars in which Hutus battle Tutsis seem to be depicted by Westerners as inherently, unfathomably "foreign"; even when national policies and players are invested, as was the case in the 1994 Rwanda genocide where French weapons contractors fueled the conflict, UN peacekeepers failed to protect victims, and Clinton administration officials blocked the UN from effective intervention to block the genocide. For an analysis of the genocide in which 70 percent of the Tutsis and 20 percent of moderate Hutus, who opposed the slaughter and mass rape, were killed, see Philip Gourevitch's *We Wish to Inform You That Tomorrow We Will Be Killed with Our Families: Stories from Rwanda* (New York: Farrar, Straus, and Giroux, 1998).

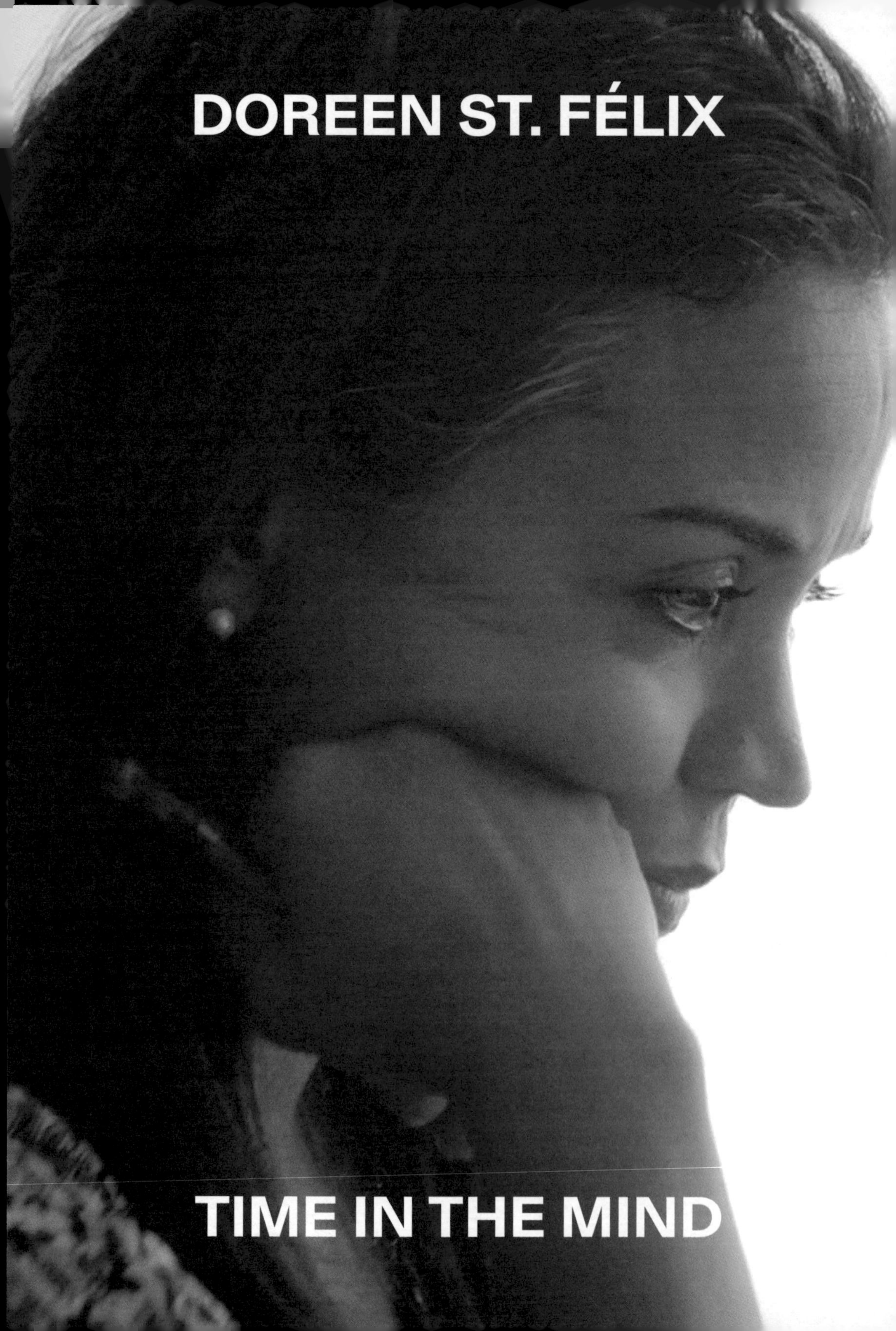

DOREEN ST. FÉLIX

TIME IN THE MIND

Garrett Bradley warped the clock. In her masterwork *Time* (2020), the present is the past is the future—which is to say, the lie of linearity gets emptied. Virginia Woolf comes up, when I think of artists who have comparably seized on the "extraordinary discrepancy between time on the clock and time in the mind"—to quote the novelist, peering as she did over the ledge of modernity come to her imperial country. For Bradley—reporting from her own nation, the carceral nation of the United States—focusing on and possibly reproducing, in the cinema, the fractured flow of "time in the mind" from the vantage of Black women is a decolonizing move. And so *Time,* Bradley's second feature-length film and first feature-length documentary, is a womanist biography of an American family, led by the singular being we call Fox Rich, made and unmade by the prison experience, spanning, if you'll allow the insufficient temporal term, nearly two decades. The country pretends to turn on the axis of innocence and guilt. The shifting lens of subjectivity is the real source of order.

Bradley's body of work—which encompasses fiction and nonfiction filmmaking, episodic television, and gallery installation—is unbound by genre. How *Time* assumed its final, layered form is a testament to its director's liberated process. The thirty-five-year-old artist is a personal filmmaker; many of her works are spawned from the intimate relationships of her life and within her extended community in New Orleans and its environs. Going down South, her reverse migration, gave the native New Yorker a new view of the invention of Blackness in the country. In 2017, Bradley made what she calls the sister film to *Time,* the twelve-minute short *Alone,* a portrait of her friend Aloné Watts, in collaboration with the *Op-Docs* desk at the *New York Times.* The contours of the cultural crisis of mass incarceration are there in the works. But Bradley is constitutionally an image maker, not a documentarian per se. The mandates of the nonfiction filmmaking mode, its predilection for the fantasy of critical distance, cannot leak into Bradley's portrait of Aloné, because Bradley trusts Aloné to be the authority on her own experience.

It is Aloné, in voice-over, who gives us the situation: Desmond Watson, her incarcerated lover, would like to marry. "What would it look like to marry Desmond in prison?" Aloné thinks in bed, her hair preserved in a bonnet. The subjunctive—*what would it look like*—is the grammatical mood in Bradley's examinations of unfulfilled desire, her studies of women forced by institutions and by society to find succor in the perpetual promise of a hypothetical better life. Trying on a bridal gown she may or may not get to wear, Aloné says, "I am beautiful in this dress." So plunged are we into the interiority of Aloné that when the aperture of the film widens, five minutes in, the moment, one of intergenerational confrontation, shocks. The confrontation is conveyed through crashing, heaving sound. Bradley's camera sits yards away from the door of the home inside which Aloné informs her family of her intentions to marry, as if the camera, too, is being rebuked. And it is. Out of a desire to steer their child away from the carceral destiny, the film's mother figures—Bradley is drawn to ruptures and continuities in the Black matriarchal line—scream at and admonish and lacerate Aloné for deigning to waste her one and precious life. On what? On *love*? *What would it look like?* That closed door, that emblem of no exit from the pull of family and the burden of history and the intoxicant of respectability, is the portal to understanding why this is a scene that cannot be overtly "seen"—the withholding embedded in the view of the film paradoxically dramatizes the custom of kitchen secrecy, of not running your mouth and letting your business out. Of having the temerity to control the record. And records—who in society is given license to create them—occupy Bradley. Aloné too. Mired in doubt, the young woman encounters a maternal figure, Rich, whom Bradley, with mythos on the mind, films at a canted angle. Rich identifies the problem. The system, she speechifies, "is designed, just like slavery, to tear you apart. And instead of using the whip, they use Mother Time." The tilt, and the intercutting of what looks like a religious crowd absorbing the good word, turns Rich and her preaching into the prophet figure and prophecies augured by her government name, Sibil.

That's who opens *Time*: Sibil Fox Richardson, before she was Fox Rich, the orator and prison abolitionist and matriarch. Before a twenty-year fight to gain clemency for her incarcerated husband, Rob, who was sentenced to prison for sixty years without the possibility of probation or parole; before the three youngest of her six sons were born; before the fight returned its reward. A young mother in profile, cheeks round, torso round with life, fussing with a camcorder in Shreveport, Louisiana, in the late nineties. The frame is everything to Fox, because the video she records is meant to substitute memory for Rob, if not *become* memory. Fox, and as he grew older, Remington, her eldest son, recorded the mundane and the monumental—the amusement-park rides; the birth of the twins, Justus and Freedom, named after the elusive ideals; the car rides; the offhand reprimands—to replace the human experience Rob could not have. The moving image as surrogate life, then. The very texture of Fox's digital footage seems alive because it is deteriorating, like bodies do, showing the effects of age. It's not difficult to understand why Bradley, when assembling this opening montage, a kind of shadow film, was attracted to the archive, its totemic meaning, for it contains not just the vital stuff of family maintenance but the awareness of history being made. Notice the instances of talk Bradley makes sure to include in her selections. Fox talking to Rob, showing the smile she will give him when he comes home. Remington, in the car, discovering the bounds of his identity through the technology of the lens. "So, Pops, this is me. This is myself. Back to you," says the child. Black elders love to hyperbolize that they blink and a child is full-grown; Bradley's edit of Remington's life, from grade-schooler to graduate of dental school, punctuated by a coda shot of the man ascending in a transparent elevator, is a miniature film in and of itself, implicitly told, I think, from the imagined perspective of Rob, whom for most of the film we see only in a snapshot of a kiss between the lovers, and hear only on the other end of inhumanely truncated prison phone calls.

The subject-director binary is a Western one that Bradley wants to trouble. She has called Fox her codirector. Originally, Bradley and her team of cinematographers—Nisa East, Zac Manuel, Bron Moyi, and Justin Zweifach—had observed Fox and her family in the present tense. The treatment would have been another short, like *Alone,* called *Flat Rob,* after the cardboard effigy Fox made to stand in in her husband's absence. When Fox handed over to Bradley a bag full of MiniDV tapes, one hundred hours of footage captured over the years, Bradley knew the project had to change. The use of this borrowed footage, her interest in antinarrative, puts Bradley in connection with speculators such as the artist and filmmaker John Akomfrah, the scholar Saidiya Hartman, the late filmmaker William Greaves, and Bradley's closest contemporary of the group, RaMell Ross, creator of the poetic 2018 documentary *Hale County This Morning, This Evening.*

Bradley is in attunement with the voices of her subjects too. The Black subject, in too much Black art, is flattened to the easily recognized facts of her existential emergency. Of primary importance to Bradley, a cineaste, is the transformation of real life into art. The techniques of fiction filmmaking are available to her. A signature of her films is the voice-over; in *Time,* Fox and Remington and Freedom speak as if angels of history. It is through Fox's narration that the viewer receives the précis of the situation. Back in the nineties, Fox and Rob opened a streetwear business in Shreveport. After a loan fell through, they decided to rob a local credit union, with the

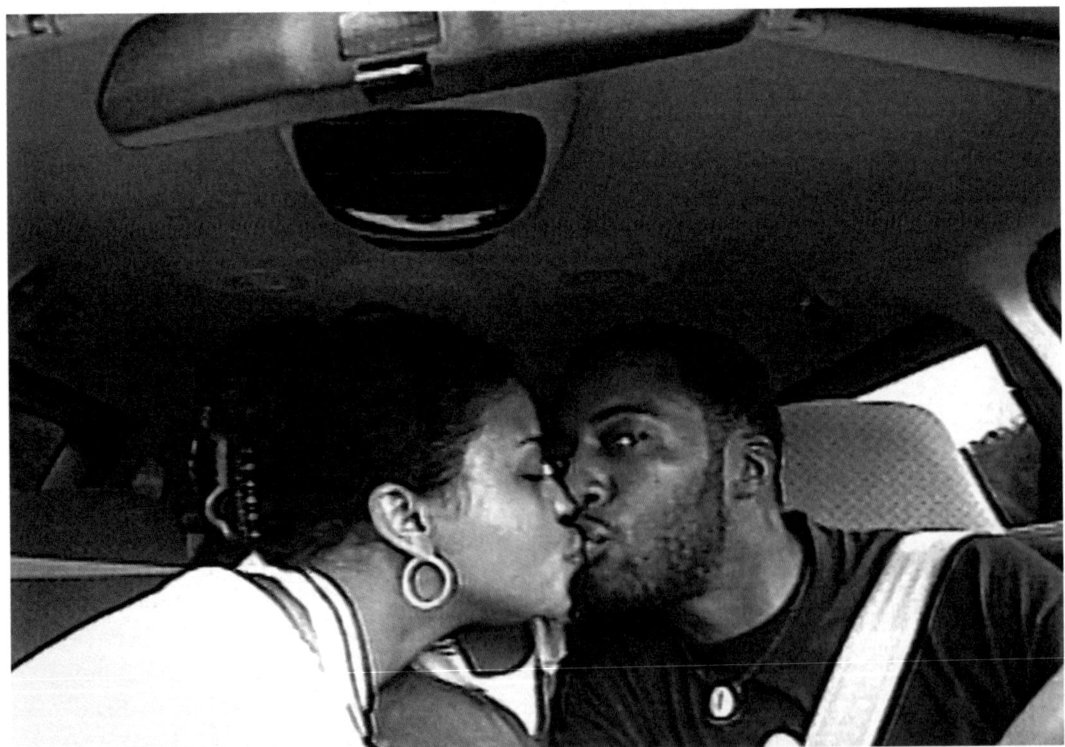

Garrett Bradley, *Time,* 2020

assistance of Rob's nephew. The robbery failed, and the couple were incarcerated; with Rob receiving his abominably long sentence and Fox one for thirty-six months, of which she served a shortened term. The texture of *Time* usually vacillates between the refinement of Bradley's footage and the pixelated surface of the family footage. But to visualize the Louisiana State Penitentiary, Bradley consults the tropes of the southern gothic. Thick fog envelops the campus. The drone shot of Angola, as the facility is more commonly known, makes the institution a terrible cosmos. We do not need to enter the prison to know the awful work it wreaks on America. The prison is in the expression of Freedom, feigning poise, as an instructor begins a lesson on criminal justice. The prison is in the expression of Rich—somewhere between Sibil and Fox—as she asks her church for forgiveness. Exposition and exposure, this film implicitly argues, is not the singular way to shift consciousness. Bradley reaches for the evocative, rather than the denotative, in *Time;* she wants the Black lives in this film, and Black life in general, which the public loves to pin down and diagnose, to retain an aura of unknowability.

This is not to say that Bradley—her gaze, her presence—is wholly deferential to the perspective of the family, or self-annihilating. She is no annotator. Bradley has her own agenda, political and aesthetic. There is the imposition of her signature palette, the color-sapping gray scale, on the sequences, both archival and contemporaneously composed. There is the piano score, taken from the oeuvre of Emahoy Tsegué-Maryam Guèbrou, an Ethiopian nun, which gives the portrait a diaspora-minded sound, epic in its scope of late-century styles. There is the repeated canted angle of Fox, this time primarily reserved for her delivery of an abolitionist address at Tulane University. And, of course, there are the indirect associative connections made by Bradley and Gabriel Rhodes, the editor of the film, in their merging of the material. Bradley *lives* in the cut. *Time* is very much the director's vision of the Richardson family odyssey, a slant that is fascinating, and slightly dissonant with the material, if you look closely. The subjects are keen self-stylers and practiced lay documentarians. The most indelible scene in a film dense with indelible scenes is our first contemporary view of Fox. Now the owner of a successful car dealership in New Orleans, she is in her office being filmed for a commercial. Her voice is deeper, her enunciation clearer by orders of magnitude than what we have seen in the home footage. She is a commanding presence. She directs the director of the commercial with a certitude of purpose that is disproportionate to the project. "No," Bradley's zoom seems to nearly vocalize, "Fox Rich, who has had life taken away from her and her family, completes all activities with conviction." Bradley's camera pushes in on grooming scenes throughout—hair being pin-curled, lashes being lacquered, slacks being pressed, beards being stroked—and these slight montages wordlessly convey the Black Christian correlation: physical hygiene as moral hygiene. Status, how one looks to society, is important to the Richardson family.

It was not until my third viewing of *Time* that I noticed how infrequently Bradley films the family together, so powerful is the love and loyalty that otherwise courses between them. Even when they are in the same building—say, at Remington's graduation—the director separates the members, so the unit stays visually elusive. The splintering evokes for the viewer the radiating traumas of incarceration, its creation of attendant loneliness: every experience of the nearly two and a half million people who are in prison in the US, and their families, is different. Time passes at undecipherable rates. Progress is inertia. Time whizzes by; it freezes. For Fox, the system is a predatory bureaucratic hell. She is often observed alone in her office, on the phone, pressing an administrator for an update on a judge's parole decision. The phone calls are rendered in suspenseful real time; we as viewers share, for merely a matter of minutes, an infinitesimal sample of what life has been for Fox for years. For Freedom, a political science student, the absence of his father stoked in him a desire to continue the work of his abolitionist mother. And for Fox's mother, Ms. Peggy—the most stirring camera presence in the film besides her daughter—the system is something to be avoided. "Right don't come to you doing wrong," says Ms. Peggy. Ms. Peggy, and her bitter remembrance of time lost, or wasted, brings an ambivalence, so clearly softened by the years, that recalls that of Aloné's mother figures. The forgiveness weighted by the not-forgetting—this is a history brought to the fore too.

Time won the US Documentary Directing Award at the Sundance Film Festival, making Bradley the first Black woman to win the prize, and afterward, she was nominated for the Academy Award for Best Documentary. Bradley may have made the most discussed documentary of 2020. The film is often talked about in terms of omission. It does not resemble any other prison documentary. It does not contain identifying time stamps. It does not deploy experts. It does not polemicize. Presidencies passed, and storms raged, and wars were launched and lost, and no part of the torrent explicitly comes into frame. All that talk of subtraction, however, obscures the creative powers of the artist, who has, ultimately, made for the Richardson family a love story for their spiritual consumption. It is almost a miracle, the way the film ends. The momentum, the drive to the final act, puts us in mind of fiction. Rob is released into the arms of Fox. We are stupefied by the simple fact of his physicality, and we the viewers have gone without seeing him in the flesh for only seventy or so minutes. What of a lifetime? The two pile into a car, and the camera lingers on the activity of connection, the most human work; Rob lying down, Fox's shoulders heaving. All of a sudden this film, built on abstraction and impression and absence, sees love made incarnate. From this point, Bradley's final montage, a rewinding of her film, which is to say, the *undoing* of her film, is counterintuitively a picture of life reinstated.

Sixty years. Sixty years. Sixty years. Sixty years. It is as if, at the Tulane talk, Fox is attempting to will the absurd length of her husband's sentence into corporeal shape. No container can hold the raw mass of sixty years, Bradley knows, but that of a life, and every day gained is paradoxically one lost. What is created is destroyed. To describe one of Bradley's final, ritualistic images: the effigy is burned to ash, and the man lives in its stead.

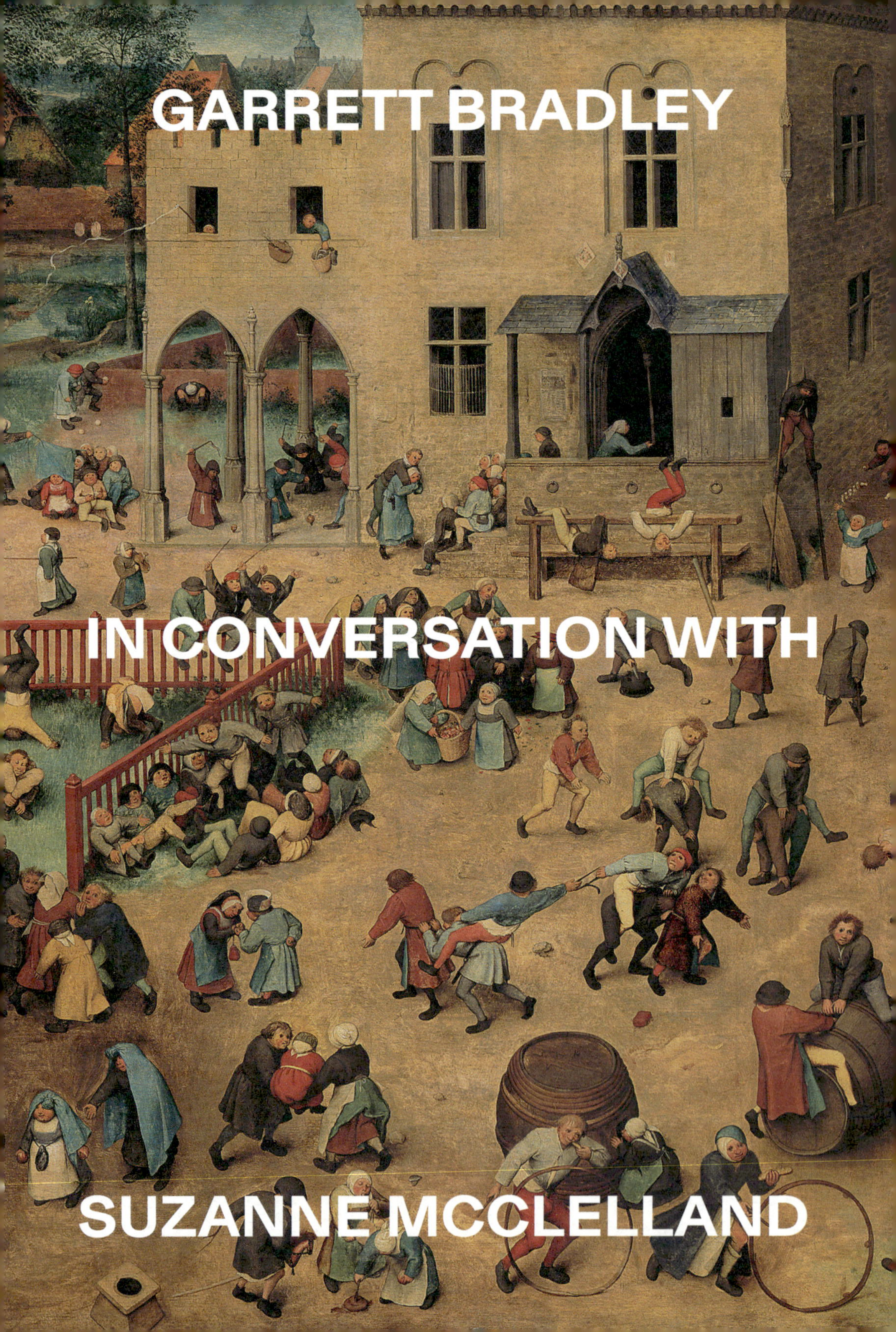
GARRETT BRADLEY
IN CONVERSATION WITH
SUZANNE MCCLELLAND

Suzanne McClelland: Robert Altman's *Nashville* [1975]—let's talk about it ... I love how it winds around itself. Loosely, Altman weaves together individual story lines, then he sort of tightens up the weave near the end of the film and yet nothing is packaged or resolved.

Garrett Bradley: I would say the Coen Brothers have that same tendency, but yes, *Nashville*. Or maybe we start earlier, with Bruegel and work our way up? I love the idea of thinking about him relative to Altman.

SM: Which paintings? He always offered viewers multiple scenes all at once. *The Tower of Babel* [1563] by Pieter Bruegel [the Elder] was a painting I encountered in the summer of 1980, traveling through Vienna to Greece and spending hours in the Kunsthistorisches Museum. I have kept a postcard of it up in every studio since then. In middle school, when you were studying the development of written language—cuneiform, Babylonia, Sumerian clay tablets—you talked about it a lot and were deep into the mythology and history. We talked about the origins of written language and divisions of languages around the globe and how writing is drawing and the physical trace of speech At that time, I was listening to speech and drawing from it in the city, in playgrounds, courtrooms and the streets but your study took me to the origins—the history of this subject. You got deep into it probably around eleven years old. I think it's fascinating that you recall that painting now. I'm wondering why?

GB: One of the earliest paintings I remember talking about was *The Tower of Babel* and feeling like the concept of the ziggurat was really interesting, this idea of things being piled on top of each other. The mythology and stories around *The Tower of Babel* stayed with me in ways that I didn't expect. It looks like a narrative. It's from Genesis [11:1]: "Now the whole earth had one language and the same words. And as they migrated from the east, they came up upon a plain in the land of Shinar and settled there and they said to one another, 'Come, let us make bricks, and burn them thoroughly.' And they had brick for stone, and bitumen for mortar."

A lot of the older paintings made me think about primary text as potent sources for visual material, for narrative.

SM: I understand why so many artists addressed this subject and it's especially relevant in this day of conflicting facts and confusion. Babel is all about misunderstanding. Bruegel did three versions and while his characters and interactions are often extravagantly bizarre, they are mixed up with mundane tasks like baking and laying bricks. The overview is always there but one's mind can only engage with parts of the landscape. It's easy to get lost in the various time zones in his paintings.

You were always interested in belief itself. That's an area where I think you and I cross over, as artists, this interest not so much in religion or its structure, but in why and when human beings believe in the things they believe in—where truths lie and how we behave in relationship to beliefs. You have faith. Maybe it's optimism, but I think it's deeper than positivity. I guess you connected with your Old Testament studies in college. You got deep into the stories in a way that I resisted, maybe because my own mother studied religion and also participated in the institutions built out of them. I abhor those patriarchal structures that exist in every religion.

GB: Do you not have faith, Mom?

SM: I have faith in human beings and the power of language and I believe in the destructive and constructive forces of us and I believe in the powers of the natural world, both what we can see and what is hidden. I believe that science has the capacity to heal and reveal.

GB: I like the idea of different time zones or the impossibility of experiencing his work in its entirety. It does bring up time in an interesting way. Like, in what tense does awareness live in? We may be looking at the laying of bricks in one area of the painting, yet to know there is a lot going on elsewhere. There's something you're getting at that creates an interesting parallel for our capacity to receive and engage with parallel realities. Where is your interest in it?

SM: Mistakes, misunderstandings and translation glitches. The Bruegel painting was made around the time of the Reformation, a Protestant and Catholic divide. Christians sat through their services in Latin. They were sending their money to Rome. Lots of reasons for separation. The Polyglot Bible was printed right around the time that this painting came out and I think the Antwerp version was printed in six languages around 1566. As far as I know, the sixteenth century was one of the first times that the Bible was made accessible in such a wide range of languages. Building the Tower of Babel is all about the impossibility of a single language and then I guess it's God punishing this king who wanted to build this vertical tower—these guys were always in a state of conflict in their absurd scramble to climb.

Garrett, back to Altman's film *Nashville*. He clearly identifies fierce divisions in American culture. The Vietnam War was ending and the protests were everywhere in the musical landscape of the country. A peace agreement was signed in January 1973 but the war didn't end until April of 1975. I recall as a teenager that the world seemed divided between pro-war and anti-war citizens and it was especially complex because the American and European expansions were so violent, both covert and overt. When artists dig deep into a subject it reflects things that are going on in their immediate world, it has to in some way. Misunderstandings come from a lack of listening and lack of observation.

GB: *Nashville* was made during a time when zoom lenses were a kind of dominating aesthetic, at least in the US. What I love about watching his films and films of this period, were those multiple focal lengths within a single frame. And, you know, how he used sound to connect different story lines. You might have five people in a room, and every person has a mic, it's a very precise way of creating chaos, and also mimicking reality—connecting multitudes and simultaneity into a single frame. I can't think of any other mainstream theatrical film space where that had really been done previously. Normally, a sense of connection is created through physical cuts between people or spaces. So, it was unusual and I think totally new, to create the same effect in two very different ways.

SM: Yes he shows those divisions and the synchronism—just as Bruegel illustrates. What do you think about the humor in Altman? Is it to address division or perhaps simultaneity? He's showing people's isolation from one another and then, the unexpected connections.

GB: The film riffs on its own playfulness and construction. It is interesting to think about another Bruegel painting in this context, *Children's Games* [1560]: Is this chaos or coexistence? I feel like the humor you're tapping into is like, it's remarkable that anything gets done in the world, that we don't bump into each other more often. Maybe coexistence is chaos [laughing].

SM: There might be harmony in what appears to be chaos—a beautiful dissonance? Certain things work when they overlap. Beliefs, or maybe intentions, become shared on some level. Bruegel's *Children's Games* tells us so much about shared desires and a need for human exchange, play, fantasy, joy, physical intimacy and the thrill of spinning and hanging upside down. I'm going back to the *Tower* because it remained in your memory banks for so long—since your childhood. Why did it stick for you? There's this ambition to conclude or create a unified thing in *The Tower of Babel* painting. Do you relate to that?

GB: Yes. And not to be too literal, but making a film can be exactly like these two paintings. Reaching for a collective goal, working toward a unified thing—having to learn multiple languages that span, mood, culture, money, time. The chaos of these paintings has deep emotional resonance for me because they feel real and they move away from the romanticism of "order," of fascistic notions of efficiency or perfection in order to get something done. I do believe hierarchy is necessary in achieving a goal, but it can be done so horizontally. Intention for instance, could be a 'north star' which, as long as it's maintained, can be achieved in a variety of different ways and which from a distance, could look exactly like this – chaos.

SM: There are multiple intentions at play in *Nashville*, just as there are in *Children's Games*. And all of those individual, isolated scenarios in *Nashville* reflect major differences in American cultures. Altman builds structure from the beginning within the recording studio scenes—each studio isolates a genre but also a political ideology, as well as various types of faith and collectivity. Each genre has its own sense of timekeeping, its own rhythm, with gospel singers all in the same room but the country dude in his isolation booth yelling at the "long hair" piano player. Musicians play, but artists work?

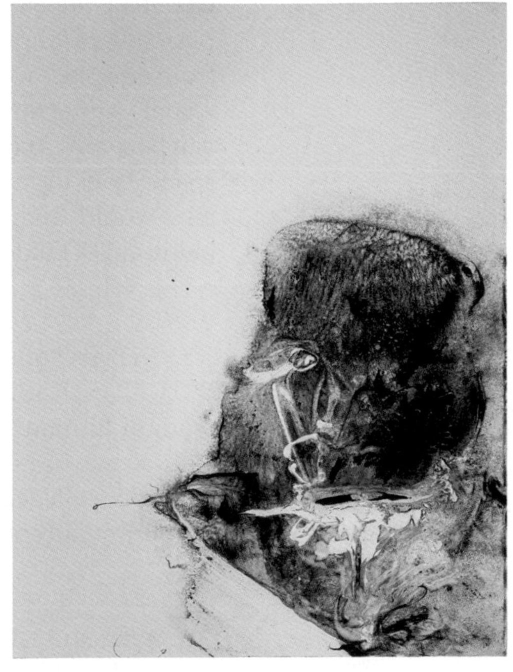

Also the overall connective tissue is the roving, wandering political van with its body-less voice. It is a thread running throughout the whole film, even during the car crash—the pileup—one of the most deeply absurd scenes I've seen in any film. The van keeps talking unaware of its surroundings because it's on monologue. Another thread throughout the film is the British reporter, loony, insensitive, projecting her assumptions upon reality. Mesmerizingly hungry—for what? A singular "story"?

GB: Geraldine Chaplin.

SM: She exhibits all of the misunderstandings between two English-speaking countries, assuming similarities when there

Suzanne McClelland, *MUTE Y- an Alphabet*, one of 26 panels, 2019 is so much difference. Every scene she barges into, she enters with her mouth open and eyes and ears shut, never reading the room. "Opal from the BBC". (She loves saying "BBC" as she inserts herself into the bubbles of life). She has no sense of space or observational capacities, therefore no respect for the worlds she invades. No neutrality, and her curiosity wanes as reality presents itself.

GB: Yeah, her character was disturbing and also strategically placed. As a "reporter" she allowed "us" and Altman to jump from one place to the next. She was, in addition to sound, our visual connector between spaces, in the same way that the van becomes a chariot for the audience, a way to get through space. Looking at *The Tower of Babel*, or at *Children's Games* who would Chaplin be in this? Does that translate over to painting? A guide?

SM: Bruegel displays an overview of social behaviors—the way we move around and with each other. He allows the viewer to absorb a large swath of humanity from an impossibly powerful position up high, so maybe his point of view is as the guide. The only character who really seems to have the benefit of an overview is us, but perpetually outside of the frame.

GB: What is outside of the frame is complicated with moving images, because the amount of time you can film something is finite. The film will run out. I assume that's in part why we edit. The implementation of editing might be one reason that a guide feels necessary, because films work off the premise that you can't stay in one place forever—change is inevitable.

Switching subjects a little, I was excited to talk with you about duration and thinking about painting as durational. You mentioned that you make a distinction between external and internal duration. What does that mean, exactly?

SM: With film, television, theater, literature, life itself, there's a linearity that runs through time—it's actually a physical matter and one must roll with it or jump ship. I consider this an external duration. Most poetry is considered in a spatial way I think, so I separate this practice from literature. I think that with painting we experience form spatially.

A scene takes time to absorb—at different speeds, of course—then we are left with memories. There is the use of memory in both internal and external duration, but they sit in my body differently. I experience painting as internal duration, because the object itself is sitting still, but you're having an experience, looking at it, reading it closely and from various distances, and feeling it in a sensory way, all simultaneously, and then you leave the painting, and you still have those memories in your body and come back to them and nothing is ever the same as the first impression. We may all have really precise memories of the same object but different points of view. I am curious about the difference between memory of an object and the perception standing in front of it. I don't think that any two people ever have had the same exact experience with a work of art and yet we try to connect through the experience.

How do you feel about duration in sculpture or something physical that you walk through or around three-dimensionally —urban plans, design, architecture, landscape? Anything that forces you to move.

GB: I love the idea of thinking about sculpture as this thing that exists between film and painting.

SM: In the case of *America* [2019] the circularity makes it sculptural or architectural, really. By passing each screen or moving around it like a carousel it ends up functioning both as a still object and a moving picture. It's as though we are passing through the forms—with them—in time. And then maybe transparency allows for stillness? It depends on how you use your camera, if you let your camera function in a passive way, and there's no action in the scene it does give you the option of experiencing it like a still object—as in *Alone* [2017].

GB: I was interested in a physical metaphor for how history, memory and insight develop. *America* is both a circle and an

X, a place of intersection, a time capsule. The transparency of the flags offered a space for viewers to make their own connections by way of their own curiosity, height, or movement through the room and would inform how they were going to see things that were just for them, that were totally unique to their own time and their choices in the space.

To be able to sit and look at a painting and allow things to unfold and reveal themselves and change with a timeframe dictated by the viewer. I envy that there is no pressure or fear that something is going to change before you're ready for it to. When we think about duration in painting, things are going to unfold at a natural pace, you know, and that is not the case with films. Filmmaking is so human, but so unnatural in a way.

SM: I see. What's natural, though? Let's stay with your word "unfold", that's a really beautiful movement. It's true that film moves of its own volition and that a painting allows the viewer to control the changes, so then the anxiety comes with not knowing when those things will change?

GB: I think I'm building off something mentioned earlier, around the finite nature of filmmaking and the impossibility of filming forever. That it does stop and so in anticipation of that end, a certain kind of method is developed to maybe deal with that anxiety. I'm interpreting it as anxiety. Anxiety that in and of itself gave birth to an entirely new artform which is editing. Films are about movement and light, even if they are "still." Maybe it's something different that I'm responding to, something that has more to do with the era we live in. An anxiety around the role that screens play in our lives and the effect this has on the work. So I'm saying two things, really.

SM: Every day there is something that demands your evaluation or wants to convince you of something, or pushes you into action or maybe subdues you if you are too present, too loud. That creates anxiety. It challenges our internal belief systems. Then there's friction between what we want, what we believe, and what the external world is telling us we need. We have pressure to participate politically in order to have agency in our lives and improve the social landscape. Then there is pressure to believe in singular leaders rather than collaborative entities, which is problematic. Political social movements like the women who started Black Lives Matter did it successfully. They succeeded in dismantling the charismatic singular star "leader." BLM is more of a network of mini-systems. Bruegel shows us a map of social interdependence and bubbles of isolation on the same field. He allows us to view intimate human activities without obscuring or erasing anything—no cluster interrupts another. Erasure and blocking can cause anxiety.

GB: Maybe that's also part of this screen problem, or today problem, feeling as though we have fewer options for ways to observe and experience. Questioning if the ideas we have are really our own or just echoes of things that follow us? Going outside, getting away from the screen is radical. But what if the screens follow us? On the street, in the train. How do we go sit in a movie theater or a space and watch something after all that? A new kind of anxiety. Painting and writing feel exceptionally comforting in their ability to ground us in a certain kind of way, this unfolding can be grounding.

SM: A painting has a frame—you are either in or out. Painting takes time to absorb, but it's the viewer's time. You can pick up and leave at any point. You talk about a desire for a kind of groundedness, but the ground is always shifting in life. Experiencing film is like swimming in a river, you enter it and you can either let yourself go with it, or stiffen and resist the current. But getting out of moving water is harder to do than walking away from a still frame. There are choices in both experiences.

Are viewers looking for a comfort zone—searching for a reflection of themselves, whether idealized or reduced—or to be faced with the unfamiliar? Maybe what you're saying also is that we're constantly being challenged, because we're constantly being preached at and convinced and controlled by rapid image production and this has been a problem since television took over. When viewing or making a painting I always ask: What is legible? Do we demand a nameable subject? Where's the energy? Where's the air? What's the gravity? Where is the light emanating from? What's the point of view?

GB: Yeah, there's a sort of intolerance for a lack of legibility. Fundamentally, what we're up against, in every faction of society, is the premium that's put on something that is explicit, something that is black or white, good or bad. The actual duration is quite illusionary in filmmaking and I'm wondering for you, when you watch—rather, when you look at a painting ...

SM: Oh, I like that, "watch" a painting.

GB: Are paintings in real time? How are you thinking about that for your own work or for Bruegel? Like, is this real time?

SM: Looking takes time and a painting hangs back, demands nothing, whereas a film expects you to stay with it. I'm still stuck on this idea of watching a painting. Or "looking" at a film. When watching, the still object opens out, it unfolds, to use your word. Sometimes form becomes nameable or spatially positioned, creating stability. Sometimes I make a predefined scheme and then execute the recipe. It gets interesting as I dismantle any stability, like taking blocks out of a mound to test its sturdiness, the reverse of the *Tower of Babel*. I think about finding a point of precise satisfaction, a precarious balance, mainly because I'm interested in how doubt looks.

GB: Right.

SM: Water and air move in a way that film can capture or *be with*. Painting can only display or depict, or provide an impression of one frame that lingers after a visit.

The *Yes*, *No*, and *Maybe* paintings I've been making over the past year have a lot to do with the process of making a picture that is constantly remaking and interrupting itself. They point to anxiety in the air where nobody gets to finish their thoughts or speak a complete sentence anymore without interruption.

Recently I revisited Audre Lorde's essay "Uses of the Erotic: The Erotic as Power" [1978]. I am still compelled by her notion of maintaining connections to the "yes" within us. Sometimes when we focus on resisting larger moving forces, we neglect internal desires that are *still*. I liken it to standing up and resisting the currents in that river and not sinking into the muddy bottom. Also I am reminded of the eel, Anguilla, in Rachel Carson's "Journey to the Sea" [1941]. She travels from salt to fresh water, returning to the sea to spawn and die; an end that is predetermined by 'nature'. Duration suggests an end at some point, walking away from the relentlessness of a frame or abandoning the plan, or is it interrupting it?

GB: Wow, yeah I interpret water and air as elements that are powerful and even domineering yet also totally malleable, adapting the shape of whatever it fills. And so in that way, it seems to me that duration is less linear than it is dependent on the medium it's working in. Also, I love the idea of a painting that interrupts itself. It feels connected in some way to the challenges that archive presents—this idea of something that is both fixed and fluid all at once. Duration suggests an end point, but maybe the question is: Who ends it?

SM: Maybe you do and that's a good ending in and of itself!

LEGACY RUSSELL

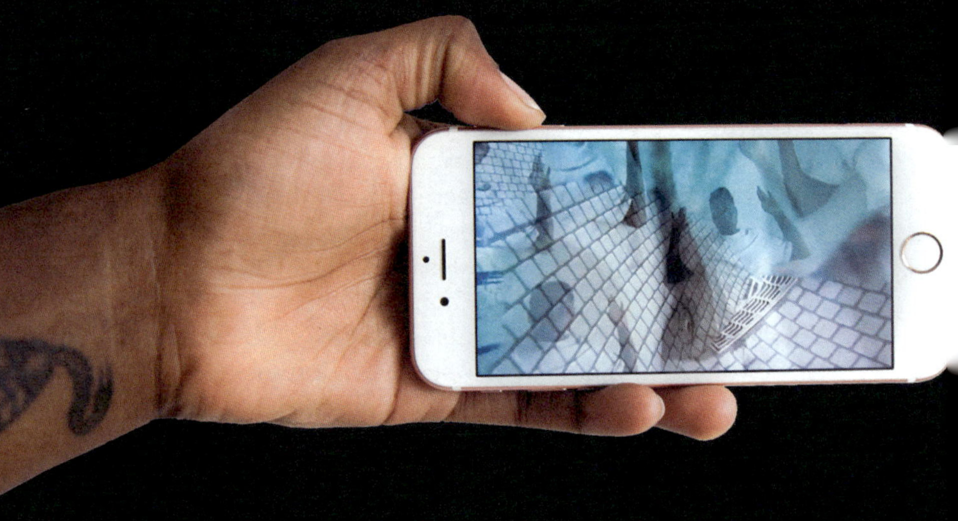

GLITCH GHOSTS

Imagine being useless.
—Richard Siken, "Seaside Improvisation"

By definition, "to ghost" is to end a relationship by ending all communication, and subsequently disappearing.

As glitch feminists, we want to ghost the binary body.

Gender is a scaled economy: it is a mode of regulation, management, and control. It allows for the reification of process, the division of labor, and the exchange of value under the umbrella of capitalism. In order to ghost on the binary body, to abandon it as a failed idea, we must step back and look at the world as a body, an assemblage that has been constructed. The body, like the world, is a tool in and of itself.

Ghosting on the binary body is a threefold process: First, it requires us to realize that the relationship between the *idea of the body* and *gender as a construct* is a damaging one that we need to exit.

Second, it requires us to identify that we have agency either to consent or refuse our current "relationship status." Too often we forget that *we have the right to leave if we want to*. We have the right to deny our use, and, through this, close the wounds created by a world fed on the binary rhetoric.

Third, it requires us to claim our continuous range of multitudinous selves. As we fail to assimilate into a binary culture, we do so by asserting all components of ourselves—the masculine, the feminine, and everything in-between—as being part of a continuous narrative, rather than existing as polar points.

The scaling of the economy of gender features most prominently across discussions surrounding "big data." For example, every forty-eight hours online we as a global community generate as much information as was generated in written history from the beginning of civilization until 2003.[1] This data we generate triggers monumental questions about mass surveillance and how the information tied to our digital selves can be used to track our every movements. Our Internet search histories, social media habits, and modes of online communication—what sociologist David Lyon calls "factual fragments" —expose our innermost thoughts, anxieties, plans, desires, and goals.[2] Gender binary is a part of this engine: a body read online as male/female, masculine/feminine fulfills a target demographic for advertising and marketing. Google Ads explains gleefully to its users, "With demographic targeting in Google Ads, you can reach a specific set of potential customers who are likely to be within a particular age range, gender, parental status, or household income. For instance, if you run a fitness studio exclusively for women, demographic targeting could help you avoid showing your ads to men."[3]

Lyon identifies "disappearing bodies" as a "basic problem of modernity," citing that the increase of surveillance correlates directly with the "growing difficulties of embodied surveillance that watches visible bodies." This is not always restricted to the easy monitoring of a physical self but also comes from the tracking of "personal traces"[4] such as when we use our bank cards, the scraping of our travel data, our mobile phone signals. Lyons's concept of disappearing bodies speaks to the reality of an increasingly networked world, where online exchange and interaction is now just as, if not more, common than physical AFK interaction. On the Internet we go to the bank, we pay our student loans, we speak to our friends, we read news and learn about the world.

With these various modes of online engagement, we leave traces of ourselves scattered across the digital landscape, vulnerable to be tracked and traded for profit. This presents a darkly modern paradox: as bodies disappear within the everyday interactions of the Internet, that which we might have assumed as inherently private—our physical bodies—remain at risk of becoming increasingly public, the abstracted fragments of our online selves making moves independent of those chosen of our own volition.

How can ghosting on the binary body help us keep safe our factual fragments as we fight to maintain our abstract bodies, our cosmic selves?

There is a long legacy to the attempts to split the body into autonomous parts. However, glitch feminism demands that we look at it another way, through the vision of another ghost—the ghost in the machine. The continuity between online and AFK selfdom problematizes the proposition of digital dualism. With this in mind, we can deepen our understanding of digital dualism further by reaching back to the idea of "the ghost in the machine," a term coined in 1949 by the philosopher Gilbert Ryle.

The *ghost in the machine* presupposed that the mind and body were somehow separate entities, operating autonomously. Those critical of this position pointed out that the "ghost" of our minds ought not to be made distinct from the "machine" of our physical selves, as the loop between the two is a crucial component of what makes us human—it is what gives us life. Artist Cécile B. Evans "argues that in today's society, where drones are used for warfare and romantic relationships begin online, we can no longer distinguish between the so-called real and the virtual."[5]

As the body in its contemporary context and the machines it engages become increasingly difficult to splice, this offers an opportunity to see that the machine is a material through which we process our bodily experience. And, as such, bodies navigating digital space are as much computational as they are flesh. Still, the movement of our data within a gendered economy is not self-determined. In the world we live in today, a body that refuses binary is one that is regularly reminded that, standing in-between, it is at threat of ceasing to exist in its failure to be recognized and categorized by the normative hegemony of the mainstream.

What is a body, therefore? Artist and writer Rindon Johnson ponders this in his 2019 essay "What's the Point of Having a Body?" asking: "What's the point of having a body if I theoretically could make or step into so many?"[6] Johnson reflects on the "malleable" self as a form of language that can teach, learn, signify, code. Johnson, a poet himself, creates a link between poetry and virtual reality as virtual reality maps to the body's experiential immersion within it: "The more you are inside of [virtual reality], the more you read it, the easier it is to quickly disappear within it."[7]

Perhaps, then, as we work toward ghosting the binary body, we also work toward dissolving ourselves, making the boundaries that delineate where we begin and end, and the points where we touch and come into contact with the world, disappear completely. In this, perhaps our factual fragments can be scrambled, rendered unreadable. If existence within a hegemonic culture today requires the gender binary to delineate the self and even to be recognized as human, then is ceasing to exist within a gendered framework the most skillful of disappearing acts? In rejecting binary gender, can we challenge how our data is harvested, and, in turn, how our data moves? *Can we become useless, too?*

The question of "What is a body?" as it intersects with our musing on how we might ghost on the binary body, presents itself as a *question of becoming*. In becoming, we shape-shift, deepen, evolve, as we leave the edifice of a gendered architecture. Thus, our movement—our ability to ghost on the idea of the body, moving away from it—is a key component of becoming. The movement of ghosting creates a generative void that makes space for new alternatives. *Becoming* prompts questions of who we are, who we would like to be, and triggers a spatial interrogation of boundaries and how we might break through them. It brings us as well to explore the experience of touch in ways that might transform us. Black feminist theorist and critic Hortense Spillers notes, "The question of touch—to be at hand without mediation or interference—might be considered the gateway to the most intimate experience and exchange of mutuality between subjects ... [it is] the absence of self-ownership."[8]

This "absence of self-ownership" *is* the consent to not be a single being, an embrace of a cosmic corporeality. The digital experience is defined by a touch that breaks limits; it "is not a non-existent reality, because we live it, feel it, can be changed by it."[9] As we engage with the digital, it encourages us to challenge the world around us, and, through this constant redressing and challenging, change the world as we know it, prompting the creation of entirely new worlds altogether.

When we reject the binary, we reject the economy that goes

along with it. When we reject the binary, we challenge how we are valued in a capitalist society that yokes our gender to the labor we enact. When we reject the binary, we claim uselessness as a strategic tool. Useless, we disappear, ghosting on the binary body.

NOTES

1. M.G. Siegler, "Eric Schmidt: Every Two Days We Create as Much Information as We Did Up to 2003," *TechCrunch*, August 5, 2010.

2. David Lyon, *Surveillance Society: Monitoring Everyday Life* (Buckingham: Open University Press, 2012), 2.

3. "About Demographic Targeting," Google Ads Help, support. google.com/google-ads/answer/2580383.

4. Lyon, *Surveillance Society*, 15.

5. "Cécile B. Evans: The Virtual Is Real," *HuffPost*, August 4, 2017.

6. Rindon Johnson, "What's the Point of Having a Body?," *DazedDigital*, March 6, 2019.

7. Ibid.

8. Hortense Spillers, "To the Bone: Some Speculations on Touch," talk given at "Hold Me Now—Feel and Touch in an Unreal World" conference organized by the Gerrit Rietveld Academie at the Stedelijk Museum, Amsterdam, March 23, 2018.

9. Johnson, "What's the Point of Having a Body?"

GARRETT BRADLEY

IN CONVERSATION WITH

LINDA GOODE BRYANT, ARTHUR JAFA

A 2023 discussion between Linda Goode Bryant, founder of the gallery Just Above Midtown (JAM) and two artists she commissioned to produce a work influenced by its collaborative spirit: Garrett Bradley and Arthur Jafa, whose a Negro, a Lim-o *(2022) consists of two films projected simultaneously in dialogue with one another. It was first exhibited at 'Just Above Midtown: Changing Spaces,' which was curated by T Lax at The Museum of Modern Art, New York, from October 9, 2022 – February 18, 2023*

Garrett Bradley: Before jumping into this, I haven't centred myself in our work together since we made it a year ago now?

Arthur Jafa: I come across it just because it's on my Vimeo link. But it is very different seeing it on a monitor than in the space.

GB: Right. I am in Joshua Tree right now and I realized that I'm in the same house we were in, in our early conversations between the three of us, with T Lax. Which feels like two years ago now maybe? And that was when we were just like, yeah, trying to figure it out. So, I wonder if it makes sense for us to go backwards a little bit?

Linda Goode Bryant: I mean, the initial concept was, or it was more of a feeling, but you know, so JAM always put together artists who hadn't worked together in collaboration before. And, working on the show, I just got an itch. I wanted to see what happens when AJ and Garrett come together, like what is the energy? And how does that manifest into something that's made? If there was a new collaboration that I wanted to do for the show, I knew it was the two of you. So there's that.

And then, when we first started talking, we were leaving it open about how you might want to work together is how I'm recalling the sequence of events. You all landed on an idea of working together where you had conversations with one another, but not necessarily about the piece – only that you would create work that was inspired by JAM, your relationship to it or how you perceive JAM. That fuelled what was created. And I have to say, it's so funny when you try to explain work and I can't do it very well, but this is an important piece. I wish

I could articulate it. But I know for a fact this is a significant piece. And I'm glad it was made.

GB: I remember a big part of the conversations being this question around 'what black art is or isn't' and both of us, as you said, coming to our memories of JAM. I had this experience in Atlanta two days ago for a convention, and there was this really interesting conversation between between civil rights leader and former Mayor, Andrew Young, and Pastor Jamal Harrison Bryant. Bryant was saying that there is a pervasive sense of hopelessness in the world right now and that a good deal of his work within the church was focused on addressing that. And Young responded by sort of refusing to believe that hopelessness was a premise from which a congregation could be lead in this day and age, because of its sharp contrast to what his generation had experienced. His feeling was that society doesn't get to where it is through hopelessness. The debate was really this JAM moment, where there was space for deep love and debate and disagreement to co-exist. It was also a passionate intergenerational dialogue that didn't tip toe around itself. In a way, the opportunity or framework that you offered us, Linda, or the essence of JAM really as I see it, was to facilitate this very thing among artists—unapologetically.

AJ: Just to go back for a second to Linda and the intuition thing. Talking is a big part of my sound, so highfalutin'; it's a practice, but it's a big part of what I do. I even sort of increasingly make the joke that, my art is hit or miss, but my rap is elite. My only eternal metric is like, how do I close the gap between my rap and what I actually do? Because people think of me as verbose—that would be a nice way to put it—but I don't really talk about core stuff, like the meaning of specific works. It's very rare. I've never said to anybody that *Love is the Message, the Message is Death* [2016] is about X, Y and Z. I'm really proficient at talking about process and aesthetics and things like that, but not how I arrived at making the work.

I personally hate going into art spaces with museum curators in general. I've had terrible, exasperating experiences, where every time you walk in front of something, they start explaining it, like the worst man, the worst. It's like if you listen to some music, and a person was whispering in your ear: *B flat, A sharp*, as you listen to it... 'Wow, can we just experience the thing, you know?' And so, I think sometimes when people have really tried to press me to say something declarative about what the thing is supposed to be, I always come to thinking, 'I just want to be dope'. People think you're being evasive when you say that. But dope is a good word, because it's so abstract and so indeterminate. Just like you want to make something that does something.

In the spirit of JAM, I didn't really have any preconceptions about what this work was going to be beyond it was gonna be video, you know? You talk, just talk, talk, talk and then you do something. I kept waiting, I was like, I know, Garrett's gonna do something. And when she does something, I'm gonna respond to that—if you move left, my tendency is to move right, just to make space.

GB: Ha, yeah, I mean I guess I was waiting for you too—we were waiting for each other. Although, I have to admit, I did kind of have an agenda from jump, which was to avoid anything figurative. It felt like a challenge for me personally in how I was going to work with the camera.

AJ: The whole thing of black people being in the art world is so much about us negotiating the complex space that we occupy as we make things like, saying 'this is my position'—there is no contemporary art without black aesthetics. Contemporary art doesn't look like anything, there is no way it looks like how it looks without the impact of African artifacts.

It's this complicated dance when you enter this space, because it looks like as a black artist, you're doing what your culture expects you to do and that you're second rate or you come in later... And they have cubism, which is just like them calling black music rock and roll or something. It's just a rebranding, you know. Romare Bearden was always really important to me in this line of thought, because you see cubism, those formal tactics, which are interesting, and artistically legitimate, as well as Picasso and Matisse. But when you see Bearden's use of it in his photo collages, you can see that that formal tactic is tied to a philosophy of how you understand the universe, because you recognize black urban life doesn't literally look like that, but that is exactly what it feels like. And that's interesting, completely legitimate as an artistic thing.

LB: I gotta jump in here. Someone told me, I can't remember who, but that Bearden was represented by Cordier & Ekstrom, so he became one of the few artists who had a gallery when he was working. Anyway, Bearden was really working in the abstract and it was the gallery that asked him to do figurative work. And that was his response to it, which is what he's known for, right? That is, they were saying you need to make a figurative step, so I find that interesting in the context of what you're saying. And when he was working, like Norman Lewis, they were really working in the abstract.

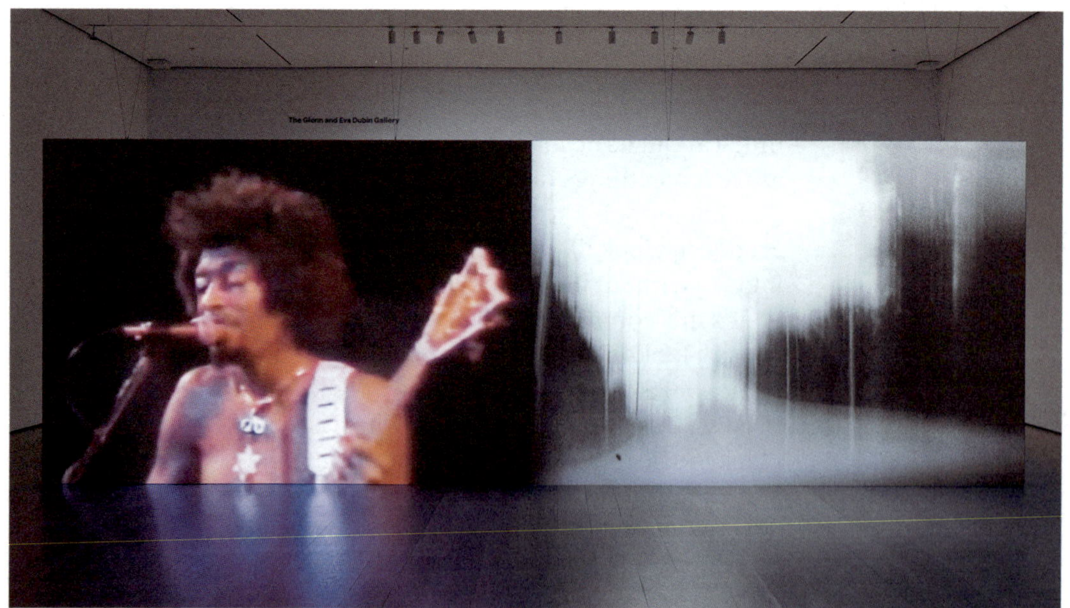

Garrett Bradley and Arthur Jafa, *a Negro, a Lim-o*, 2022

AJ: Right. And this is why I thought of it in the first place, because of the question of collaboration. My understanding of how Bearden arrived at the photo collages was that he was in a group called Spiral, this kind of jazz collaborative way to make visual art. But he said nobody else took it up. He tried, but nobody else really wanted to do it, so he just kept doing it himself. Now, I don't doubt for a second that the gallery saw it and said, "Oh, this is gonna be easier to sell then that abstract thing you're doing"... but I always thought those paintings were very, very interesting. Pollock doesn't exist without jazz, there's just no way you get to Pollock without jazz. Lee Krasner said he would listen to the same jazz record 100 times in a row.

GB: I think about that a lot—when the source of something is hidden but is simultaneously serving as inspiration, the pockets wherein that source are allowed to be seen, will inevitably appear secondary and in fact as by-products of the very thing it helped create. That's why the question of what 'Black art is' feels like a trick question.

AJ: One of the reasons that I'm reticent to talk about the meaning of things is I don't want to overdetermine... because people place extra emphasis on the 'art' or the 'author', as if what you say is supposed to be some kind of final word.

Obviously, I have a privileged relationship to the work, because I'm making it or channelling it or ushering it into existence. But, what the fuck do I know? My shit is just as much of a guess as anybody else's at a certain point—when the thing gets out, it's its own thing.

One of the things that was really exciting to me, when I saw this work both figuratively and literally come together, was that it is definitely rendering a space that we're in now, one that's hard to name.

Like, we have a name for post-segregation, post-reconstruction, abolitionism, integration and anti-slavery, but I feel to a certain degree, over the past 40 years, black political thinkers have not been able to name the thing or call it—we just out here reacting to the situation. I mean, the closest thing to it is Black Lives Matter—but saying 'our lives matter', is that the best we can do? I'm not trying to critique it, because people are doing something. They came up with a hashtag and they mobilized under it, it's all right, but it just seems so fucking ass-backwards. I just read this thing yesterday, not to defend Kanye, but I read this startling account of his 'white lives matter' t-shirt. He said, "When I see white folks walking around with these Black Lives Matter t-shirts, I'm like, 'no fucking kidding', so I just decided I was gonna say y'all lives matter too!" Although I and most people took it as some kind of super retrograde move, in a way he was just showing the absurdity of it and I kind of more agree with that than I don't, you know what I mean?

GB: Kanye was stating the obvious and I'm not mad at him trying to get philosophical in the mainstream, but he carelessly or conveniently forgot how mainstream works in that moment. And I agree on the BLM phrasing—I think about what it means for young minds to affirm defence. I wonder if 'Black is Beautiful' operates differently in our own bodies? To self-identify with something not in relationship to another? I'm not downing BLM but I wonder if it was more of a mantra for non-Black people to know and remember, not so much for us. And maybe that's part of what made it so powerful in 2020, is that it did seem to have an unprecedentedly interracial effect.

AJ: But see, that's the thing. And this is the main problem I always had with being an artist in the art world. I used to feel like Black artists get penalized for subtlety. Like, do you remember *Tree* [video, 2001]. Well, I don't know if my career would have ever gotten any traction with *Tree* at all. It was closer to what you did Bradley, in our collaboration, those blurred things that you were doing. *Tree* is like an extended pushing in that space. But it's kind of like Bearden's abstraction—it's like, we can't see the niggers' bodies in it. So how, how are we supposed to have some relationship to it... how are people gonna know I'm hanging a negro's product on my wall if you don't see a black person's body? I have a lot of internal ambivalence about this because like, honestly, frankly, most of the times when I hear 'black figurative art', I'm just like, that shit is jive. I'm sorry. It's retro and it's jive... Now at the same time, I love Kerry's work. Kerry [James Marshall] is preoccupied with a single thing at the core: How come, if it's a white body it can be universal, but if it's a black body it *can't* be universal? There's so many people coming out of art schools generating a whole lot of figurative art, but I'm really shocked at how much of it is bad. The majority of it, I would even say, I'm sounding very elitist now, but is just like illustration. You know?

LB: Let's be clear about that. They're driving a market for white folks that want that imagery. I think of that in terms of our creativity, we are not dictated to by the marketplace.

GB: I mean that feels like what's in the market. Not necessarily what exists. Once we get into the future and we look back this will be one moment that was like. You know, just like what Dawoud [Bey] says, there's multiple art worlds, not just one.

AJ: We know that better than anyone.

GB: Can I ask then, with respect to the market, do you feel we love each other the same way? Is it bringing us together or pulling us further apart?

AJ: For sure. it's the Negro League Baseball versus the major leagues, and now they have to put asterisks next to people's names, because this person was hitting more home runs in the Major League, but they didn't hit more than Josh Gibson. And they weren't going up against the best pitcher in the world, which was Satchel Paige. The white baseball stars would go down to Cuba and play against him just to test themselves. And nobody could hit him. He was Rookie of the Year, 42 years old, when he finally came to the major leagues. That's the vision of black people in the art world that I don't think younger black artists even have a handle on. We were totally segregated from it. We were outside of it. And we had our own sort of pantheon, let's say, but, it's a complicated trajectory, which I traced to a few people. I mean, oh, man, we could go in so many directions in this conversation.

GB: Those are two different things, are we more connected? And are we more in love? How do you love someone you're not connected to?

AJ: On a slave ship?

GB: But you're still connected...

AJ: I mean, in other words, a lot of our sense of continuity is from shared oppression and misery... Linda is frowning at that.

LB: No, there are a couple of things. I would say we are not family the way we used to be.

AJ: And you don't love everybody in your family. Or you don't like everybody in your family. You love them but you don't like them.

LB: That's right, we're not that now. And I think that is critical to being able to be as creatively expressive as possible. Much of the work that's being presented to the public, there are not the relationships between artists there were probably 10 or 15 years ago.

You know going to dinner parties that I was invited to with artists, I was really offended that you could spend two, three hours in a house with artists and maybe one or two collectors and all they could talk about was who sold what at auction. I would usually get pissed off and finally say, you know, are you making products now? I mean, what the fuck are you talking about?

And when we are family, you know, going back to what you were referring to AJ, in terms of Spiral, we were family, being creative together. I'm a mentor to Columbia MFA students for the last two years. And I can assure you that for the black and other artists of color, they are torn by the fact that they're being indoctrinated into making product, into being IKEA makers, and fearful of not having a chance to be in that market. It goes back to who you're making it for, we make something because we want something to do something. It's less and less about that. We are not family.

AJ: I agree with everything you just said, of course. But it's like, even when we say family for us, you know, I have conversations with people at different levels. I don't mean levels, like better, but just different realms. But what I am digging into when we say family, you know, that's just a problematic thing for black Americans, that most times we don't unpack.

We have our families who we grew up with, but when we talk about the larger sense of family, much of what we call family is not in our native context in Africa, where you're talking about a family's continuity, where you can trace it back to more generations than you can count.

But for us, family wasn't that, because we were put in circumstances where we create family in situations where we had no control of who we are or we were having intercourse with —that's at the deep core of our family structures. And so our family thing is, I don't say it's abnormal, but it's not natural. Maybe no family's natural, but I know that's both the superpower of it, because it's a vision of kinship, that goes beyond blood that's what's futuristic about it. People say to me, 'Hey, what do you want to say?' I just laugh. 'Oh, I say a lot in my work, but I'm not trying to say anything, I'm doing something', you know what I mean? Declaring something is not the only way to make meaning in the world, and mostly what I end up trying to do, and I increasingly I'm looking for situations that allow me to do that, is I just want to make something that's as complicated and fucked up and beautiful as I am and the people I know. But it's not like an idealized portrait as much as my work always has an aspect of leaning into, let's say, black pride or something like that. But like, even with *love is the message*,

I never understood that it was an uplift moment. I was like, I don't do the lifting, it's not my it's not my natural move to do uplift. And I even have jokingly said, I'm an undertaker, I'm not an uplifter. I'm really attracted to the underside of shit.

LB: I'm not going to be able to articulate it in this moment, but it's tying back to what Garrett was saying about this desire to do something with image and I feel that that desire might be driven by more than the figure. Let me see if I can express it in a different way? Increasingly, people who make things aren't necessarily clear about who they're making it for. You need to know your audience, but that isn't a demographic. Who is the family you're creating for? And I say family in the context of JAM, because it was a family. There were people who didn't like each other in that family. But we loved each other because we shared an energy, a spirit, a need, that we supported each other in pursuing. Each of us needed to be around people who were experiencing the world around them and within them and articulating it in their unique way. We needed and wanted that family and we still do.

AJ: It's like being on a team together. Like [Michael] Jordan, most of them hated him, but they were on the same team, they had a shared mission. I mean, of all the things that Greg [Tate] ever said to me in our long runnings together, was: 'So you think everybody in Duke Ellington's band liked each other?' He was like: 'Drop the dumb shit. Just get on with the work. Sometimes you like people sometimes you don't'.

GB: Right. I don't know why this is bringing up *Gemini Man* for me. Ang Lee's film with Will Smith? The premise is deeper now, since 'The Slap,' but it's like young Will fighting current (adult) Will. And you have The Man in between the two of them. It's not a good movie, but it could be... the very idea of it is enough for me. Anyway, maybe part of what we need—and what JAM did for us—was a reminder that there is more than one market. And also that the more time we create to be with one another allows for a healthy dialogue that doesn't need to be polite. The open disagreement might be an antidote to alienation, to isolation, to what ultimately separates us. In discussing our lack of familyhood that we have right now, what is it going to take for us to come back to that?

I should watch *Gemini Man* again because I can't remember how it ended. I'm assuming it ended well you know because they killed the market, right? They killed the man in between...

AJ: That's such a generous reading of that film.

GB: Thank you (laughing).

LB: One last thing. Garrett, when you said: 'How do I create figures or non-figures in this medium that I'm using?' I just flashed in my mind on themes in your work and I realized just how kindred you both are as as creators. Very different as people but very kindred. Because, AJ, guess what popped in my mind? Your Spike Lee film, *Crooklyn* when you stretched the image and the digital work you've been doing. I didn't want this conversation to end without someone saying out loud that you both have very similar drives, you really do.

AJ: I don't want to be dissing the figurative. My impulse has always been more of a vibration thing, I will say that's the continuity between everything. I'm only interested in the figure to the degree that you can see vibration on the surface of it, whether it's motion or a body or whatever...

LB: I would invoke vibration in a way that includes motion and emotion, because your work is emotion and Garrett's work is emotion. I think the piece that you created together—and not together —is a very significant piece, if for no other reason that your two energies are very kindred. So, thank you so much. I love you both.

JEFFREY SKOLLER

KILLER OF SHEEP

The need to confront those specters of a past that, though unseen, still powerfully impacts the present becomes even more necessary as the events themselves recede into a distant past. The catastrophe of African American slavery lasted for hundreds of years and visibly ended generations ago. How to understand the ways in which events long past continue to inhere in the present becomes even more difficult to pinpoint and harder to represent visually. It has been the challenge for some artists to find different ways to speak about the spectral nature of such events in an attempt to produce more complex and deeply felt representations of people as beings who are affected and transformed by the movement of time.

The film *Killer of Sheep* (1977) by Charles Burnett reveals the ways in which legacies of events from the past actually inhere in the present, invisibly inflecting daily life with a force that is powerfully tangible. This film can be seen as an attempt to understand how elements of a past come to bear on the present in ways that are not always identifiable. These are the "hauntings" of the present, which, although invisible in positivist social science notions of historicism, when given close attention, begin to reveal just how dynamic the relationships are between past and present. As Avery F. Gordon suggests, "'Invisible things are not necessarily not-there' [and] encourage the complementary gesture of investigating how that which appears absent can indeed be a seething presence."[1] This suggests a need to refocus attention away from what is simply visible toward the temporal as the meanings of an event, its legacies and effects, transform in time. For a medium like film, in which its indexical literalness is the basis for its historiographic authority, conventions of historical narrative are harnessed to that of the seeable. The larger problem of narrating the history of African American slavery is compounded not only by the formal problems of how to show it but also by American society's reluctance to integrate its history of slavery into narratives of the present. This is why these histories tend to produce such powerful boundaries that close off the past. The insistence on closure limits the complex ways that different moments of time commingle, inscribe, and inflect each other. This often forecloses possibilities of understanding the continuing effects of such a past as they impact the present. To take up daily life in the present in relation to the specters of the past is to counter the notion that African slavery is a closed chapter in American history, and to show that its haunting legacy continues to be a powerful part of the present—a force that continues to brutalize Black America and unsettle the entire nation. The vision of a life and a community haunted by the cultural inheritance of the catastrophe of slavery and hundreds of years of racist brutalization permeates the images in *Killer of Sheep*. While it is one of the only films I have taken up that is an entirely dramatic film, and does not appear to fit into many of my criteria for materialist avant-garde film practices, I find that the film's formal and aesthetic style not only is cinematically innovative and perhaps unique but also reflects an aesthetic designed to evoke the haunting legacy of American slavery. Burnett uses cinematic duration, especially the continuous take and long shot, as the central formal element of the film's visual style, allowing viewers to engage their own thoughts in relation to what is seen and heard. *Killer of Sheep* pro-

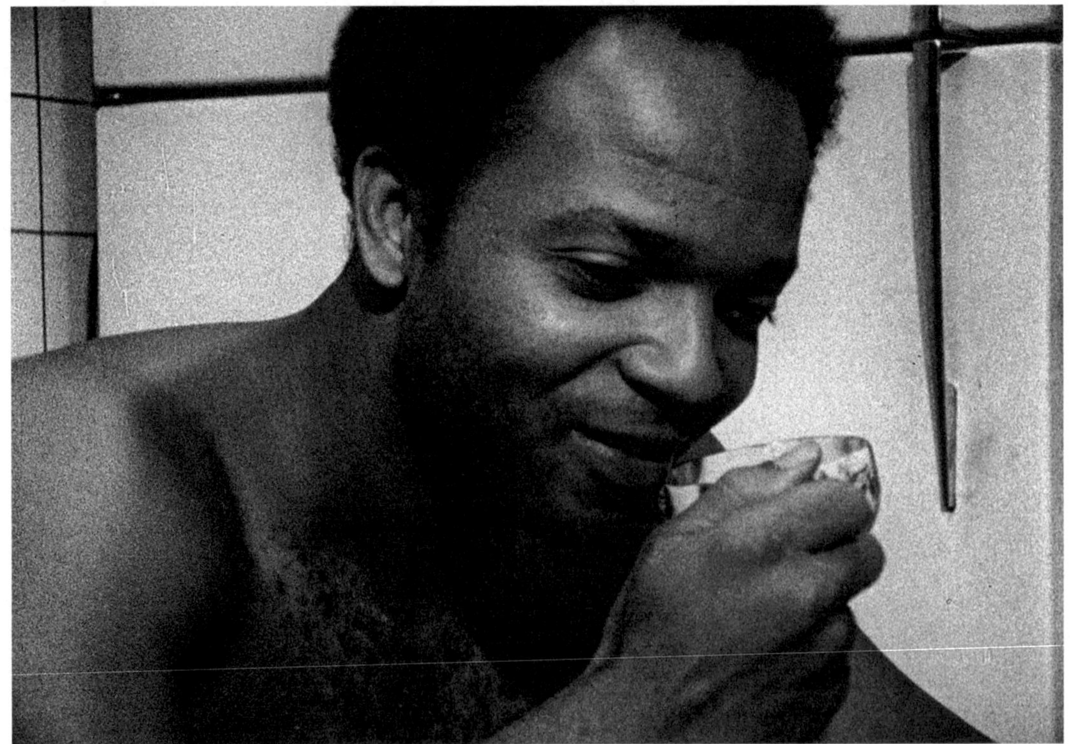

Charles Burnett, *Killer of Sheep*, 1977

duces both a representation of a state of being in the film's fictional characters and a concrete real-time experience for the viewer. The film evokes, rather than represents, the daily rhythms and psychological conditions of the film's central character and community. A good deal has been written about the emerging Pan-African cinema of the last thirty years. Much of this writing has focused on the social and political contexts of these films, either as artifacts of marginalized cinematic practices or as communities within a larger context, as does Thomas Cripps, for example, when he writes about African American cinema as a genre within the larger context of American film:

> We shall seek to define black genre film through social and anthropological rather than aesthetic factors. In this light, films are different from those fine arts in which the artist and his audience share a fund of common knowledge and experience. Rather, films bridge the gap between producer and mass audience, not through shared arcane tastes, but because a team of filmmakers shares a knowledge of genre formulas, more than an artistic tradition with its audience.[2]

Here Cripps implies that because African American cinema is specifically a minority cinema, the films should largely be understood in sociological terms or as artifacts because marginalized Black sensibilities and "tastes" are inaccessible to wider audiences outside Black culture, or worse, that the only ground Black filmmakers and their audiences share is the knowledge of cinematic genre formulas. The danger with Cripps's contention is that it implies that Black cinema is simply a subgenre working off the dominant ones, rather than a dynamic and innovative cinema capable of creating complex and nuanced expressions of an individual filmmaker and his or her community in the context of other advanced work in contemporary world cinema.

In *Killer of Sheep*, Burnett innovatively uses the cinematic element of duration instead of literary elements of emplotment to show the intimate details of the daily lives encountered in the film's characters. He has also pared down plot elements to the barest minimum in order to reveal other elements within the film as complex components in the production of the film's meanings. In *Killer of Sheep* the depiction of place as opposed to events is foregrounded. The characters' interaction with the environment in which they live reveals their psychological or emotional condition rather than the forward movement of melodramatic conflict-resolution forms so common to conventional dramatic films. The film places the main characters' psychological states in the context of larger social conditions, suggesting that it is social contexts that have produced the characters' personal condition. *Killer of Sheep*, however, is not a sociological study. Rather, the attempt is to produce the experience of the characters' conditions as cinematic experience for the viewer. To do this, the film departs radically from the cinematic conventions of film melodrama, such as the continuity constructions of the classical Hollywood form with its seamless flow of time moving from one scene to the next according to the dictates of plot requirements. The film has reduced to a minimum spoken dialogue between the characters as a way of propelling the narrative forward. Rather, the film shows the characters in detailed visualizations of their daily activities and their physical relationships to the people around them.

The narrative form of the film's story is more typically modernist than classical. The story in *Killer of Sheep* is episodic and fragmentary, constructed through a series of loosely knit sequences depicting the daily life of this working-class African American family, each separate scene a self-contained narrative with its own formal logic. While the accumulation of these sequences produces specific meaning as a whole, each shot has its own integrity temporally and compositionally. Narrative time is constantly being constructed within each shot and then broken by colliding with another. The narrational intensity comes from the accumulation of discrete shots, each successive one deframing the next. This is a quintessentially anti-illusionist gesture that fractures narrative continuity and repeatedly throws the viewer back into the context of his or her own present by constantly having to work to reconnect one sequence to another.

In *Killer of Sheep*, the formal style is constructed around two major kinds of shots: the long shot, in which the entire object shown is contained in the frame; and the long take, in which the duration of the shot is continuous. These shots emphasize complete actions and images of whole objects. These types of shots emphasize the real-time continuity of an action rather than the expansion or elision that results from putting together individual shots to make up a whole action. These two shots are deviated from in the occasional use of the close-up or moving camera. The long shot and the continuous take, however, create the rhythms of the film, which are languid and produce a contemplative relation to the events in the story.

Killer of Sheep produces interesting tensions between traditional modes of storytelling and more purely visual and experiential modes of filmmaking. It shows, through a loosely connected string of sequences, elements of daily

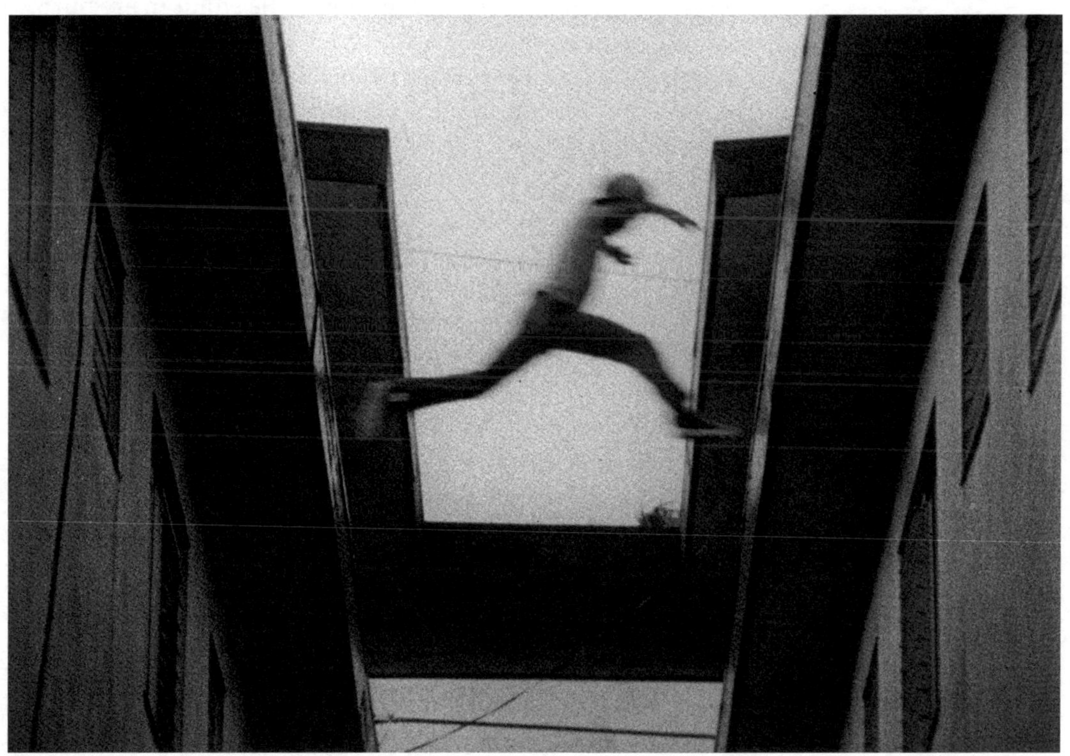

life in a working-class Black community. The story is structured in alternating sequences between the activities and interactions of the adults in the family and neighborhood and the play of the children in its streets and buildings.

The film centers on Stan, who has a wife and two kids and works in a slaughterhouse. We see him interact with family members and friends. We see him involved in different activities that show the uneventful, prosaic quality of his life. He is repairing the kitchen sink, cashing a check, disciplining his son, going through the routinized activities at work. The adults talk to each other about their lives either in stammering, soul-searching discussions or by arguing. In both cases they seem to be trying to articulate their emotional condition, but with little success. Through objective positioning of the film's mostly static camera and long takes, the viewer is given the time to see the characters' eyes, expressions, and bodies. We see what cannot be expressed verbally. In contrast to the adults, we see the children of the neighborhood playing in the streets, in vacant lots, and in buildings. The children are pure motion, like kinetic apparitions who are defined by movement. There is little for them to do or play with, so they play with each other, inventing games, running and biking around the neighborhood. Their youthful energy and constant invention of activities keep them in motion and occupied. No one, adult or child, is doing anything out of the ordinary, and nothing particularly dramatic happens, again emphasizing the prosaic nature of life in this neighborhood. Intermittently we see Stan at work, herding the sheep to slaughter. These moments at the slaughterhouse that show the sheep unknowingly being led to slaughter are placed in relief against the activities of the adults and children. The metaphor of the archetypal image of the innocent lamb being led to slaughter is the only specific comment the director makes about the condition of his characters. Otherwise the activities of the people are recorded objectively with a static camera shot largely in a series of long shots with the occasional cut to a close-up of a face. Burnett rarely leads the viewer to specific conclusions through conventional master-shot/close-up combinations but rather lets his or her eye wander through the details of a shot's richly composed framing.

Killer of Sheep creates rhythms rather than stories. It is in the contrast between the alternating rhythms created by the kinetic energy of the children at play and the slow movements of the quietly serious adults placed in the unremarkable, crumbling environment of South Central Los Angeles that the condition of many African Americans in the late twentieth-century United States is most profoundly articulated. These rhythms emerge as the central element of the film, giving *Killer of Sheep* a strange, otherworldly quality. While the film is located specifically in South Central Los Angeles, in the present day, the highly formalized rhythms render the place and time slightly unfamiliar and ephemeral. Rather than being realistic, the film produces a spectral-like aura around the characters that makes them appear to be slightly out of time.

In his essay "New US Black Cinema," Clyde Taylor, who has emphasized the realism and documentary quality that characterizes the visual style of *Killer of Sheep*, writes:

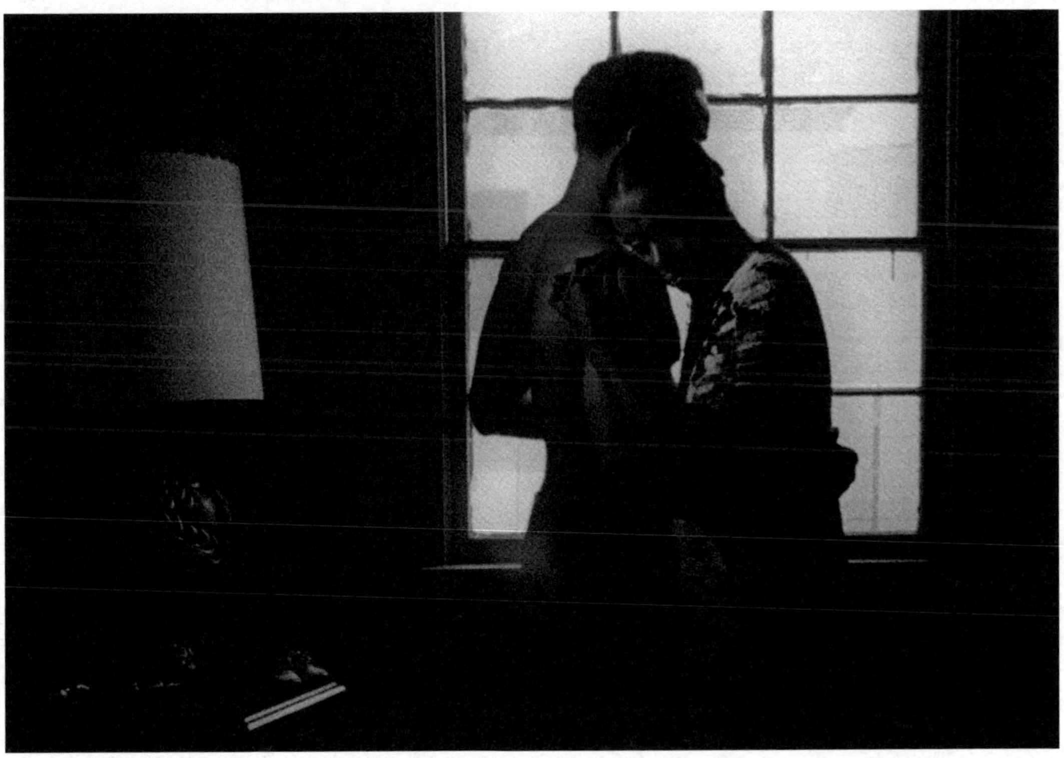

> The basic palette of the indigenous Afro screen is closer to that of Italian neorealism and Third World cinema than to Southern California. Charles Burnett, in *Killer of Sheep,* for instance, makes effective use of the open frame, in which characters walk in and out of the frame from the top, bottom and sides—a forbidden practice in the classical code of Hollywood.[3]

The realism of the film's mise-en-scène, with its unadorned locations and real interiors instead of sets, is unmistakable. The film, however, is also a tightly controlled and formally rigorous construction, which defies the documentary-like quality associated with early neorealist cinema such as *The Bicycle Thief* (1948) by Vittorio De Sica or *Rome, Open City* (1945) by Roberto Rossellini. Rather, *Killer of Sheep* can be seen more productively in relation to later highly formal and stylized modernist films that grew out of neorealism such as *L'eclisse* (*The Eclipse*) (1962) by Michaelangelo Antonioni. *L'eclisse,* while

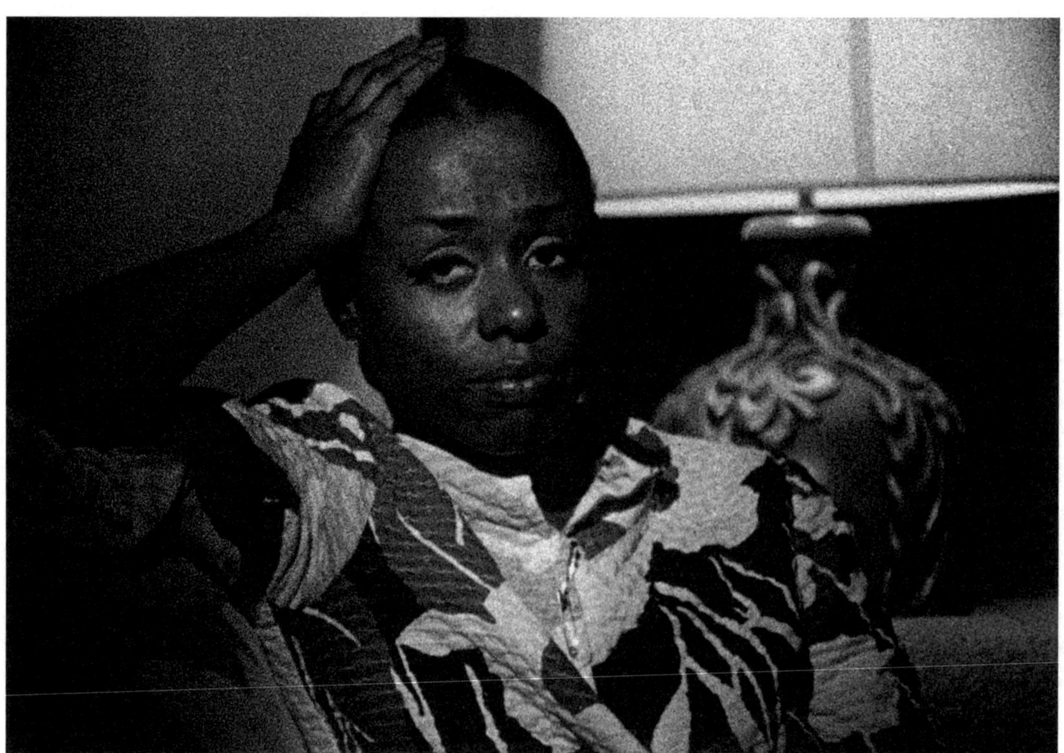

using real locations, also expresses the traumatized, out-of-time quality of its characters, who in the wake of World War II are no longer able to express a sense of personal agency. As with Stan in *Killer of Sheep*, they seem to be disconnected from the lives they lead and are seen in rigorously composed shots existing in depersonalized urban landscapes.

Unlike the more spontaneous style of neorealism, in *Killer of Sheep* every shot is formally composed using the graphic elements of the frame to compositionally foreground the interplay between characters and the constricting reality of inner-city life with its buildings, narrow stairways, sidewalks blocked with other children, dogs running uncontrolled, and boulevards filled with cars. In these tightly composed framings—rather than documentary spontaneity—we see the thwarted desire for the freedom of open spaces that characterizes inner-city life. This becomes a graphic cinematic metaphor for the African American lives that are filled with compromise, the negotiation with a hostile environment, and the ultimate inability to live the way one wants.

The high-contrast black and white used in the film emphasizes the graphic compositional elements of the shots as opposed to the use of black and white to heighten a sense of realism, another element often ascribed to early neorealism. From the beginning of the film, the black and white is used to create contrasts, producing otherworldly spaces and separations between people and cultures. From the opening, the images of a father chastising his son are shot in low-key expressionist lighting in which space is deterritorialized, as in a dream. The next sequence begins with the screen literally divided between black and white. It is a rock fight in a sandlot, and a boy is using a sheet of plywood as a shield. By framing the plywood to completely cover half the frame, Burnett uses the flatness of the screen to create divisions between dark and light. Throughout the film, the high contrasts of the black and white make palpable the sense of claustrophobia and frustration of daily life in this ghetto. In this sense, the black and white of the film creates a much more abstract and metaphorical world than a realistic one. There is no clearer instance of this than the graphic quality of the white sheep disappearing into the black space of the chute in the slaughterhouse. The contrast between black and white is made even more potent when the image of the white sheep going to slaughter is reversed in the viewer's mind—through the film's central metaphor—into the black skins of the film's subjects.

The metaphor of innocence then continues as the sheep silently go off to slaughter, intercut with images of the also innocent Stan, helplessly watching the neighborhood children. Stan, as the killer of sheep, is at once murderer and victim as he bears witness to the trauma of the African American experience. Stan's silence comes from the slow and steady diminution of a sense of self through the lack of control over his life. As the killer of sheep, he kills, as he himself is being killed by the lack of possibilities and his lost dreams. In *Killer of Sheep*, this can be seen as his trauma—and also the collective one—embodied by his silence and listless gaze.

In his essay "Notes on Trauma and Community," Kai Erikson describes traumatized subjects as those who "look out at the world through a different lens. And in this sense they can be said to have experienced not only a changed sense of self and a changed way of relating to others but a changed *worldview*."[4] Looking out at the world through a different lens is an apt way to describe a film like *Killer of Sheep*. It is one that presents a completely different image of the Black experience in America, by looking closely, carefully, and intimately at the rhythms of daily life in an African American community. In the film, Stan's silent gaze can be seen as that of the traumatized subject, through whom the viewer bears witness both to the spirit of endurance and to the abjection in African American life. Through Stan's silence, the film privileges the visual over the written, opening the film and its viewers to insights and modes of expression perhaps not possible by literary means. Because of the film's prosaic and quiet qualities, we are able to see the world around him. Nothing much happens to Stan, and he does little besides his job. This invites us to move beyond the actions of the protagonist and to look at the world around him.

In one of the most moving scenes in the film, Stan tries to speak in a way that reveals his deep sensitivity, however dotted and sedimented under his silence it may be. Late one night, he is sitting at the kitchen table playing dominoes with a friend; they are drinking tea out of china cups. Stan has the friend put the hot teacup against his cheek and asks what it reminds him of. The friend says he has no idea. Stan ventures that it feels like a woman's forehead while making love. The friend bursts out laughing incredulously. We see in the background his longing wife in the darkness of the hallway, silently observing this exchange. The camera holds on Stan as he rubs the cup against his cheek; we see him struggle with his emotions as if he is using the hot cup to evoke the memory of another world now inaccessible to him. Throughout the film, despite the advances of his wife and other women, he shows little interest in sex, or sensual experience of any kind. So the realization of the warm cup as something connected to pleasure takes on much larger

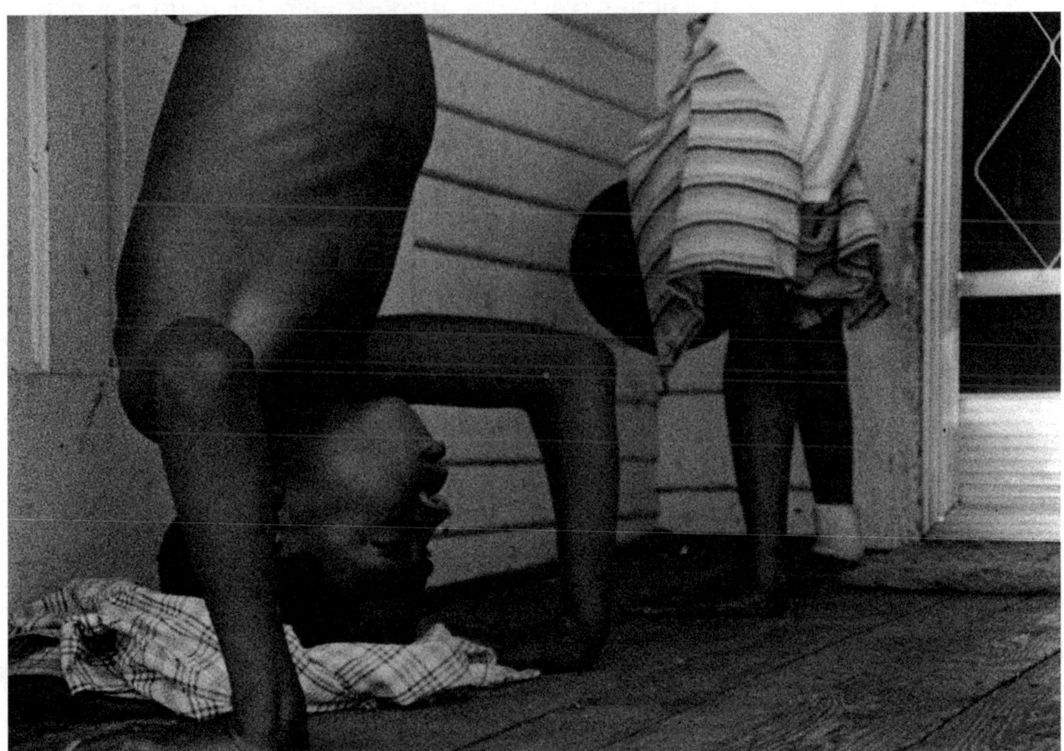

symbolic proportions than a sexual fantasy. In the disparities between his quietly reflective attempt to describe an ephemeral sensation, the boisterous ridicule of the uncomprehending friend's laughter, and his wife's silent presence, the viewer can see evidence of Erikson's notion of a worldview changed by trauma. All bear witness to Stan but are unable to perceive as he does the memory evoked by the heat of the teacup, thus separating Stan from his wife, his friend, and the viewer, isolated as he is in his own world.

The relationship between a traumatized subject of catastrophe and the act of witnessing is central to understanding this reading of the film's form. The fixed camera quietly records these poignant moments in Stan's domestic life in which his wife and children try to find ways of crossing into the isolated world that surrounds Stan. In a single fixed-camera shot, Stan and his wife are seen alone in their darkened living room. She is trying to get him to dance with her. They are in silhouette, framed by a window in which nothing can be seen in the window but the bright white light of the overexposed outside world. In this heartbreaking scene, he spurns her attempts at lovemaking and walks away. Like a moth to the light, she rushes to the window, throwing her body against it as if she might crash through. Such otherworldly images graphically open the film beyond the present. In Burnett's formal style of real time observed through the continuous take, we are able to sense the specters of past trauma that creates such affect in the present.

The African American community is haunted by the specter of the trauma of slavery. As Avery Gordon writes:

> Slavery has ended, but something of it continues to live on, in the social geography of where peoples reside, in the authority of collective wisdom and shared benightedness, in the veins of the contradictory formation we call New World modernity, propelling, as it always has, a something to be done. Such endings that are not over is what haunting is about.[5]

The profound accomplishment of *Killer of Sheep* is its quiet construction of the rhythms of the quotidian. It creates the sense of the wavering present by asking the viewer to think beyond what is represented and perhaps opens up a space where one can experience the ways in which ephemeral and ungraspable elements of the past are always present and inflect daily life. Through the long and lingering shots of his camera pointed at his own community, Burnett creates a conjuring tool with which to witness a present that evokes a past far from over.

Killer of Sheep reflects a vastly different culture and social reality than other avant-garde films; their connection, however, lies in the way they all use time as the central formal element to move viewers away from the specificity of stories told, toward the experience of the temporal rhythms of daily life lived. Burnett is committed to an image of time as a way of exploring a prosaics of the quotidian that might sensitize the viewer to the complexity and richness of African American cultures past, present, and future. Certainly *Killer of Sheep* is a politically situated expression of the African American reality in the late twentieth century—coming at the end of the civil rights and Black Power movements of the sixties. The film can even be seen as social realist in the ways some critics have cited. As I have argued, however, the film's power lies in what remains unseeable, but felt, through Burnett's use of the formal elements of duration, composition, and the contrasts of black, whites, and grays that evoke in the present the specters of the catastrophic past of slavery that continues to haunt America.

NOTES

1. Avery Gordon, *Ghostly Matters: Haunting and the Sociological Imagination* (Minneapolis: University of Minnesota Press, 1997), 17.

2. Thomas Cripps, *Black Film as Genre* (Bloomington: Indiana University Press, 1979), 9.

3. Clyde Taylor, "New US Black Cinema," *Jump Cut: A Review of Contemporary Media* 28 (April 1983): 47.

4. Kai Erikson, "Notes on Trauma and Community," in *Trauma: Explorations in Memory*, ed. Cathy Caruth (Baltimore: Johns Hopkins University Press, 1995), 194.

5. Gordon, *Ghostly Matters*, 139.

KEVIN QUASHIE

THE CAPACITIES OF WAITING

If we go back to the image of Tommie Smith and John Carlos on the podium in 1968, it is evident that quiet is a call to rethink expressiveness. That is, rather than imagine expressiveness as public and dramatic, the argument for quiet asks about expressiveness that is shaped by the vagaries of the inner life. Such expressiveness is not necessarily articulate—it isn't always publicly legible, and can be random and multiple in ways that makes it hard to codify singularly. And yet reconsidering expressiveness is important, given the high premium that publicness carries in Black culture. So, what can a notion of quiet do for how we understand expressiveness? Specifically, what are the qualities that characterize quiet expressiveness?

These questions are related to larger discussions about the nature of language. Modern linguists have argued varyingly about how language works, but it is the study of poetry that most exposes the tension between the literal and figurative aspects of language. The concept of figurative language "has always involved a contrast with the 'proper' meaning of a word, its supposed rightful meaning, the idea which comes directly to mind when the word is used," literary theorist Thomas McLaughlin asserts ("Figurative Language," 81). What McLaughlin is trying to make clear is the balance between the expectation of language as a vehicle for expressing shared notions and the almost inherent multiplicity in the meaning of words. Figurative language is language as an inexact medium, abundant at the same time that it approximates precision; it is language that resembles the wild copiousness of the interior.[1]

These ideas about language are relevant to thinking about expressiveness and Black culture. For one, McLaughlin's distinction between proper and figurative meaning makes reference to the fact that communication presupposes a listener, invoking the issue of audience negotiation that is readily apparent in Black expressiveness. Furthermore, the acknowledgment of language's figurative capacities is heightened by the particular role that language has played as a tool of Black oppression and liberation. As Keith Byerman notes, "language ... has always been a source of power in black life, and its ramifications continue to be explored in black literature. A recurrent theme is the conflict between those who use words to constrict, objectify, and dehumanize, and those who insist on the ambiguous, ironic, liberating aspects of language"

(*Fingering the Jagged Grain*, 6). This historical reality inflects any discussion of what Black expressiveness can mean.[2]

It is poetry as a genre that best exploits these conundrums of expressiveness, the gaps and insinuation and juxtaposition that make meaning tenuous and rich. As Aimé Césaire argues, poetic language respects the "knowledge born in the great silence of scientific knowledge" ("Poetry and Knowledge," 134). Césaire is distinguishing between the exactness of scientific thinking, and the truths that poetry can reveal about human life. For him, what is transcendent about poetry is its reliance on a kind of inexpressible expressiveness, its pursuit and celebration of that which cannot fully be revealed (146). Césaire is not alone in this line of argument; the poet Carl Phillips notes that poetry speaks not as "documentation – which is part of the business of prose—but as confirmation — echo—of something essential to being human, flawed, mortal" (*Coin of the Realm*, p.161). Phillips is referring to the way that poetry often abandons the sequential logic of prose and surrenders to what is random and excellent. In fact, because poetry does not depend on characters to tell its story, it does not have a reliance on identity as fiction does; poetry can be about a sensation, a moment, a something that is impressive and coherent—or not. In this regard, the aesthetic of poetry is almost intrinsically quiet.

The point here is not to privilege poetry as a genre, but instead to use what we know about the capacities of poetic language as a frame for rethinking expressiveness. One could argue that all language use is figurative in the ways described above, functioning on gaps, elision, accidents, coincidence; the truth of its expression is always partial, though no less significant for its partiality. There is a humanness to the partiality, in fact, a sense that what is true is beyond the limits of our social rules, so the best we can have is a glimpse. This is a notion of language as the domain not of meaning but the stuff of dreams, abundance, and inexactness.[3]

Essential to poetry's expressiveness is form, the particular shape of a poem. Indeed, it is the form of a poem that contributes mightily to its figurative qualities: whereas content can be easy to comprehend—what happens, where it happens and to whom, what is being described—form is often more implicit, and its contributions to meaning are not always clear or definitive. One can see this in thinking about how a line break or an example of alliteration inflects what is being said, or how the overall shape of the poem (is it in predictable stanzas?) influences what we read. Even aspects of form that are explicit, for example particular genres such as a sestina or a sonnet, do not contribute to meaning in conclusive or predictable ways. It might seem counterintuitive to suggest that form creates spaciousness since, on the surface, form implies structure; after all, a sonnet is fourteen lines and a sestina ends each line with one of six repeated words. But in reading a poem, structure itself becomes another variable of the process of deciphering.

In Black cultural studies, considerations of form are often secondary to those of content. That is, the critical emphasis tends to be on what a work says or means, more than on the impact of its structure or genre or literary features. This prevalence of content is not exclusive to Black culture; instead it is a common disposition of everyday readers that results from the fact that asking and understanding "what" is easier than thinking about "how" (the latter requires technical knowledge and language). And still the emphasis on content in Black culture is particular to the issue of publicness: Racist discourses expect Black art to tell the true story of Black life unvarnished by craft, which is also an expectation of nationalism. This reinforces the social imperative of Black art and it encourages us to read Black cultural works as social documents or as texts of resistance. What is lost here is not only an appreciation of artistic value but also a sense of how form can disturb the assumed precision of content and support a reconsideration of expressiveness.[4]

The impact of form is hard to talk about in the abstract, so let's look at Natasha Trethewey's "Incident", a poem from her Pulitzer Prize-winning collection *Native Guard*. "Incident" is a pantoum and therefore it is composed of quatrains that rely on overlapping repetition: the second and fourth lines of a stanza become the first and third of the next, and the final line of the poem repeats the very first. Trethewey's poem reads:

We tell the story every year—
how we peered from the windows, shades drawn—
though nothing really happened,
the charred grass now green again.

We peered from the windows, shades drawn,
at the cross trussed like a Christmas tree,
the charred grass still green. Then
we darkened our rooms, lit the hurricane lamps,

At the cross trussed like a Christmas tree,
a few men gathered, white as angels in their gowns.
We darkened our rooms and lit hurricane lamps,
the wicks trembling in their fonts of oil.

It seemed the angels had gathered, white men in their gowns.
When they were done, they left quietly. No one came.
The wicks trembled all night in their fonts of oil;
by morning the flames had all dimmed.

When they were done, the men left quietly. No one came.
Nothing really happened.
By morning all the flames had dimmed.
We tell the story every year.

The content of the poem is easy to summarize—it is about the violence of a cross burning by Klansmen in a family's front yard in the American South—but what is the impact of Trethewey's rendering of this iconic narrative in such a tight form? For one, the story seems to unfurl and has more dimensions and points of understanding than an anecdote about a cross burning might otherwise have. For example, the meaning of the repeated phrase "nothing really happened" is broadened to suggest at least four things: nothing but the cross burning happened, though the family was bracing for much more; or no one—no neighbors or law officials—intervened, that night or in the days after; or, the men were disappointed that family did not agitate in a way that would authorize violence greater than the burning; or that the term "nothing" is an understated assessment made in the safety of being at some relative distance from this moment. It is the repetition and juxtaposition inherent to the pantoum that amplifies the simple idiom "nothing really happened," and which helps to give roundedness to a story that could be told with less dimension. Another example of the poem's expansiveness is how the men become white via repetition—at first, whiteness is not clearly identified as their racial identity ("a few men gathered, white as angels in their gowns") but instead is part of the narrator's reading of the symbols of the incident. It is only in the next iteration that the harshness of that name—"white men"—is so much more threatening and definitive than the earlier line. Again, repetition provides greater texture.[5]

Like many poetic forms that rely on strict rules of repetition, the pantoum is highly structured, even awkwardly so; still the form is key to the multiplicity and ambivalence of the story that the poem tells. This is quite an achievement, since cross burnings are so quintessentially fraught with meaning that they can efficiently sum up whole chapters of the public discourse of race in the US. And yet Trethewey's poem offers a nuanced portrait that has varying levels of horror and concern, as well as a sense of everydayness (it is casually titled "incident"). There is more than one story here, even as the narrator says that "we tell the story every year," and as the poem unfolds, one can imagine the competing stories in the annual telling—some filled with fear and resentment, some with humor, some with bravado and invented bravery, and so on. The humanness of the people who experienced this incident and the fact that it must have involved a range of emotions, not only in the moment it was happening but especially in the recollection from year to year—this humanness is sustained via the form of the poem, the way none of the emotions is expressed definitively or singularly. The poem and the story it tells are haunted, packed full of what is unsettled and unresolved, complicated and multiple. Violence happened for sure, but amid that violence were the ones who experienced it; their experience was and is still, in each telling, magnificent, and it cannot be narrated completely, and hence the poem repeats lines of the story as if to create a narrative that respects the flexibility of expression. This is the achievement of the poem—to use form to tell a story quietly, which is to tell it with the expressive complexity of the inner life.[6]

The language of Trethewey's poem is spare and simple, even as the anecdote extends beyond the boundaries of realism. This is a crucial point, since realism is the de facto aesthetic expectation of Black art. Whether from within or outside of Black culture, realism is attractive because it emphasizes the real and promises to represent an object or experience in a straightforward and concrete manner. This promise is compatible with the political dimensions of Blackness, especially the argument that art has the obligation to challenge racist characterizations. Because of its easy fit with nationalism, realism has accrued a kind of authority in Black culture. And though one is hard pressed to argue against the important role that realist depictions have played in documenting Black humanity and experience—and the benefit of those depictions to civil rights achievements—the prevalence of realism also reinforces the troubling idea that Blackness is singular. Besides, rather than reinforce facile notions of Blackness, realism, as an aesthetic concept, should remind us of the constructedness of the real, the fact that a thing is being represented.[7] The limitations of realism might explain the popularity of surrealism amongst some Black artists: Surrealism moves away from a commitment to realistic representation and focuses instead on the unconscious, the marvelous, and the fantastic. The surrealist aesthetic is interested in the magic of unexpected intersections—not a characterization of the social notion of time, for example, but time as it is felt in lived experience, morphing and irregular and sometimes mundane. Surrealism is a language of possibility, a dream language that honors the inexpressible. This language is poetic in its approximation of abundance, feeling, excellence, intensity.[8]

Such an expressiveness is legible in the work of Lorna Simpson. One of the most celebrated contemporary visual artists, Simpson first gained wide attention for her black-and-white photographic series in the late 1980s and early 1990s. These pieces mostly feature Black female subjects whose bodies are cropped and whose faces are hidden from the viewer; they highlight repetition as each piece showcases two or more figures in similar postures, dressed in stark, simple clothing (suits or white shifts). Simpson's striking visuals are sometimes accompanied by phrases or sentences, and their overall composition have a documentary quality, as if each subject is being catalogued for study, as if her hair and body and temperament are being diagnosed. In this way, the work evokes a sense of realism and speaks to the larger social narratives about Black women (facelessness as marginalization, for example). Yet this realism is complemented, even disturbed, by the surreal ghostliness of the repetition: Each duplicated figure exhibits subtle differences in posture or the fall of her dress, as if the careful viewer is seeing shades of one person's complexity. The subject becomes a body of multiplicity, a being of nuance whose humanity is illegible if one only reads through a social lens. These are magical women who seem timeless and mysterious. Simpson's work doesn't offer an objective truth about Black women but instead indulges in whimsy. Indeed, in her odd and beautiful juxtapositions Simpson offers a visual language that unravels our racialized and gendered expectations. As Holland Cotter writes in a 2011 *New York Times* review of Simpson's work, "Most of the figures in her pictures ... [are] ... generic presences, adaptable to any narrative. The implication is that there are many narratives of race available, all of them conditional and subjective, created by the pressures of personal experience, interpretation and memory." There is no single integrity here—not of body or politic or agency; just the vagary that is more reflective of the wildness of life as it is lived.[9]

One of Simpson's achievements as an artist is the ability of her work to take on matters of gender, race, and violence without disavowing complexity in her visual language. This is evident in looking closely at one of her more iconic works, *Waterbearer*. The composition here is consonant with Simpson's aesthetic—a Black woman figure, dressed simply in a shift, whose face is out of view and who is framed by a text that is foreboding and vague—though the piece is different from the others because of its single subject. The expansive capacity of Simpson's language is noticeable in the dissonance between the text and the image, for while the figure evokes strength and vulnerability and dancerly grace, the caption seems to deny this very humanity. Here we have a Black woman, holding two water vessels (one plastic, one pewter). Her water-pouring could be an act of labor and subjection, something spiritual and cleansing, something more mundane. Her pose is rife with motion, not just in the tilt of her head or the creases in her dress or the cascade of the water, but also in the engagedness of her action, as if we are watching her move. The posture also calls to mind Themis, the Greek titan of justice, or even the emblem of crucifixion. And yet, in all this, this Black woman is mysterious to us. We have to ponder who she is, what she is doing and thinking; we are struck by the competing litheness and firmness of her bearing of water, and she seems to float in a timeless nowhere. All of this ambiguity is in contrast to the caption [She saw him disappear by the river, They asked her to tell what happened, Only to discount her memory], which speaks to racial and gendered violence in an iconic way: a man missing, a "they" who are questioning, a woman who bears witness and who is discounted. The astute viewer knows this narrative and might be inclined to use it to frame the figure. But even the caption itself is ambivalent, not in terms of the threats it describes, but in the exactness of what it says—Is the man who disappeared Black? Is he killed or on the run? What is his relationship to the woman, and who are the inquisitors? Is the woman in the image the same as the woman announced in the text?

There are more questions in the caption than there is clarity, and the questions multiply when you consider the accompanying image; as a result, the overall expressiveness of Simpson's piece work is figurative: It doesn't say any one thing, though it is powerful and articulate. Moreover, it pulls the viewer into imagining the inner life of the subject, for though we are called to notice the racialized and gendered body in a political context, we are also compelled to pay attention to the very human simplicity of the body posed as elegantly as it is. We don't, in fact, know very much about this woman who is turned from us and engaged in pouring water; it is as if Simpson is showcasing her inner world by reminding us of our lack of access to that world. This is an important achievement in the piece because some of its compositional aspects are so dramatic that it could easily be more shrill or categorical. And in this regard, Simpson's *Waterbearer* seems to marvel in an expressiveness that is quiet.[10]

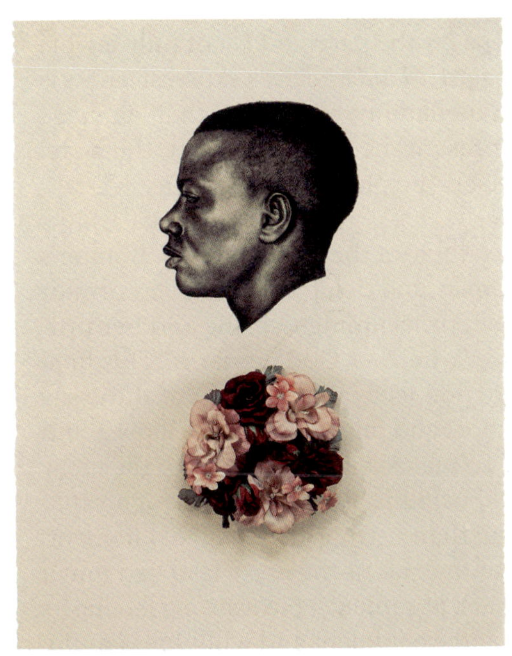

Simpson's use of juxtaposition and sparseness to explode expressiveness is reminiscent of the qualities of Whitfield Lovell's *KIN VII (Scent of Magnolia)*, depicted here. Lovell's piece seems to invite the viewer to imagine a broad inner life for his figure. What sustains this invitation is the spare quality of the composition, and the relationship of the image to the artifact—each placed just so, just next to each other without excessiveness. Lovell's work is pure visual poetry, his drawing enjambed and aligned above the wreath, and meaning left open: Who is that man? What was he thinking then, and what was the taste he liked the most? Was he a poet, a lover of words, or did he prefer the lilt of a soft piano? What to make of these flowers that are part of his profile? These questions are only askable if we forgo a lens of public expressiveness, and instead allow the possibility that he has an interior life that is largely inaccessible to us. Commentators have noted a certain haunting quality in both Simpson's *Waterbearer* and Lovell's work overall, an assessment that makes sense given how their subjects seem so exposed and vulnerable, not just to violence but to life itself. In this regard, they are ghostly in the way that Avery Gordon uses the term—that ghosts are bodies of wild agency that are not fully comprehensible to our social and political language.

The expressiveness of poetic language works on a level beyond what is social or political. One might even say that it is a language that tries to approximate sensation rather than ideology. It can be definitive or dramatic, this language, but it is reflective of the interior and so its sureness is fleeting or at least multiple. This point is hard to describe clearly, though there is an example in Gwendolyn Brooks's *Maud Martha*: part of it is the way the novel approximates a short story whose economy requires that most of the action is left unarticulated. The chapters are anecdote-sized and are catalogues of sensation rather than the full-fledged declaration of belief. The breadth of *Maud Mar-*

Whitfield Lovell, *Kin VII (Scent of Magnolia)*, 2011

tha's interiority happens off the page and is not fully legible to the reader. In this regard, *Maud Martha*'s expressiveness is respectful of a certain ineffability, of the idea that language cannot sufficiently represent the interior; in fact, the novel seems to be built on that principle.

There is yet another example at the end of Marita Bonner's "On Being Young, a Woman, and Colored," where the narrator launches into a flourish, proclaiming that she and her protagonist are "ready to go wherever God motions." This final section is written more poetically than the rest of the essay —sentences that are short and full of allusions, ellipses, and incomplete thoughts. To make sense of the end of the essay is to engage these juxtapositions, the pieces of thoughts that form a composite rather than a strong declarative statement. Indeed, what is clear at the end of the essay is not so much the specificity of Bonner's arguments, but a strong feeling— the wealth of anxiety and excitement and willfulness of the narrator's ambition. This palpable feeling is a proxy for what is not fully said or fully sayable in words; it is the sublime of quiet, an awesome quality of experience that is hard to express clearly. As the narrator gives up clarity and instead surrenders to these wild feelings, it is the surrender that is expressive.[11]

Another idiom for thinking about quiet expressiveness is prayer. Conceptually, prayer is an expression of one's contemplation and dreaming. And yet this expressiveness cannot be articulated completely or precisely; it is figurative and poetic. In this sense, prayer is a type of exceptional communication that is "much richer than speech alone. It is a particular kind of speech that acts, and a peculiar kind of action that speaks to the depths and heights of being" (Zaleski and Zaleski, *Prayer*, 5). The language of prayer is fashioned from a deep level of human understanding that exists beneath or beyond what is conscious. And the very magic of prayer, its will and ability to make something happen, is consonant with ineffability.[12]

Inherent in prayer is the idea of self as audience; that is, the praying subject speaks to a listener who is manifest in his or her imagination. Even in many orthodox or evangelical contexts, the closeness one has to God in a moment of prayer is related to the strength of one's faith. The emphasis in prayer is not so much on the deity who is listening as it is on the subject who is praying and his or her capacity and faithfulness. In this way, prayer reflects the most perfect communication—to speak to one who is and is not one's self. This excellent conversation exposes the praying self as both needy and capable.[13]

An essential aspect to the idiom of prayer is waiting: the praying subject waits with agency, where waiting is not the result of having been acted upon (as in being made to wait), but is itself action. In waiting, there is no clear language or determined outcome; there is simply the practice of contemplation and discernment. This is a challenge to the way we commonly think of waiting, which is passive; it is also a disruption of the calculus of cause and effect which shapes so much of how we understand the social world. Conceptually, prayer makes space, and in this space the praying subject explores the inner life, encounters and tries to give name to desires and vulnerabilities. One waits, waits to see one's own self revealed, to feel the range of sentiments that manifest when one sits and ... waits. This waiting is tingly and it can momentarily liberate the self from the strictures of its social identity. "Waiting is something full-bodied" and voluptuous, and it is in waiting that the self becomes more capable of its own human bigness.[14]

Waiting has no audience or cause. We often think of waiting as a term in need of a preposition—waiting *for* someone or something, waiting *to* embark or retreat. There are many examples of this in classical literature where seafaring or war-making men, or even just men of adventure, head off and leave behind women, children, and the old to wait for their return. But waiting is not the opposite of adventure and discovery, as Zora Neale Hurston shows in various moments in her novel *Their Eyes Were Watching God*. In a scene discussed earlier, after Jody slaps her for burning dinner, Janie, the novel's protagonist, "stood where he left her for unmeasured time and thought. She stood there until something fell off the shelf inside her. Then she went inside there to see what it was" (67). This is a terrific characterization of waiting as a place of stillness that is also filled with change. In her waiting, Janie finds "that she has a host of thoughts she had never expressed to him, and numerous emotions she had never let Jody know about" (68). Waiting here is active, even renegade; it is surrender. It can be wild and energetic, but it is not urgent; waiting is its own thing, self-indulgent, like falling into water. As it is for Marita Bonner's narrator ("So being a woman you can wait"), there is no waiting "for," no result expected; the act itself is the result, the encounter with one's interior is the achievement.[15]

There is a sublime agency to be found in waiting, a point that is demonstrated in Dionne Brand's poem, "Blues Spiritual for Mammy Prater". Brand's poem is the standout from her 1990 collection *No Language Is Neutral*, which was shortlisted for Canada's Governor General Award, and which explores the politics of language through the experiences of various Caribbean women subjects. "Blues Spiritual" is a fifty-one-line description of its title subject, a woman who was born into slavery. No specific date or place is given though we are told, in an epigraph, that Prater was 115 years old when she sat for a photograph. It is this image and gesture that serves as inspiration for Brand's narrator.

Like Trethewey's "Incident", Brand's "Blues Spiritual" relies on repetition; it consists of three stanzas of almost equal length, each describing the same few details in unadorned language with minimal punctuation and no capitalization. The story the poem tells is not of Prater, but of her waiting to take the photograph. The narrator describes, over and again, Prater's waiting—waiting until technology was capable, waiting through a century of labor and struggle, waiting with what looks like silent patience but which is really something more difficult to pin down precisely. This reiteration of Prater's capacity to wait is complemented by the few details the poem offers about her age, her pose, her marked legs, her black dress, her expressive eyes. Because the details are so few, much of the poem studies her waiting and theorizes what it means.

Brand's piece is a straightforward narrative poem and it reads without effort, but if you could see it, you might notice the way its simplicity belies the dynamism of the narrator—that it is the narrator's meditation on the photograph that is being described in the poem, more than it is anything essential about

Mammy Prater. The narrator is determined to read Prater's life and agency through the image, and to find the story that she, the narrator, needs to hear. To the narrator, the photograph is evidence of Mammy Prater's agency; Prater's waiting is an act of willfulness and defiance. The narrator is looking for a forebear, for inspiration, and Prater's waiting is the perfect legacy to claim. In this way, the photograph is a story of triumph in the narrator's rendering.

And yet, the poem, in its repetitive stanzas, seems incapable of telling us much about Mammy Prater other than the few stark details. Indeed, Prater's life seems to evade capture and what we get is a glimpse of her—a snapshot—while the fullness of her humanity is left inexpressible. This is the genius of Brand's poem—that the narrator gets to use Mammy Prater for her self-indulgent needs, even as the poem itself avoids caricaturing its title subject. The poem cannot tell us what Mammy Prater was thinking on the day of the photograph. Did the act of sitting remind her of anything? Was she tired? Was she hearing her heartbeat? Were there birds overhead, or was the day cloudy—and how did this affect her mood? As the narrator repeatedly engages the few details in the photograph, and muses on the meaning of Prater's waiting, she also confirms what we ought to know already: that it is not possible to sum up 115 years of living—of any kind of living, never mind the kind that Prater was sure to have had—in a poem or novel or in any language. And even when we need definitive stories to inspire us, that need should not override the reality that human life is beyond neat description. What is most important about Mammy Prater cannot be known, and the poem respects the sovereignty of the inner life. In its wishfulness the poem is the narrator's prayer, full of her desire and vulnerability, her expression of faith and neediness; it is an expression of the narrator's longing.

Brand's poem illustrates at least two different examples of waiting: the first is what the narrator imagines for Prater, that she waited for the right moment to take this photograph. In the narrator's mind, this waiting is robust—it has anger and impatience, is intentional and not, is a mark of strength and despair. But there is a second quality of waiting exhibited by the form of the poem—the way that the repetition of the few details of the poem slowly produces a distinct but incomplete image of Mammy Prater. That is, in reading and rereading the three stanzas and noticing how they revisit the same scant details, the image of Prater unfolds in slow motion, arriving in pieces and never in full clarity. The poem sets us up to wait for Mammy Prater, to wait for her to reveal herself (or to be revealed). And the waiting is rewarded, though not with a picture of a representative Black woman, but instead with the realization that the incompleteness is as it should be; the reward is noticing how beautiful Mammy Prater is because she is left unknowable. There is a respect for what cannot be expressed, even in a poem of such capable expressiveness.

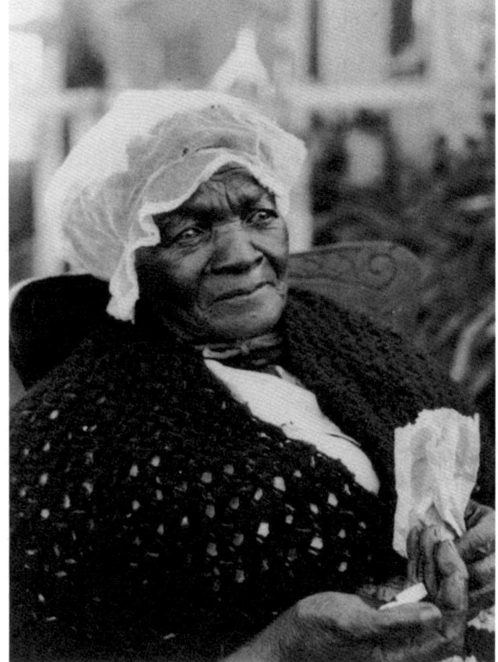

Prayer is dreaming and self-assessment, wild motion rapt with possibility and ache, a self-conversation that is driven by the abundance of imagination. And yet this self-indulgence does not correlate with solitude. In fact, the connective intimacy of prayer is evident in the narrator's effort to study Mammy Prater: "Who were you," she seems to ask, "and how did you live? What can I learn from your living?" And though her questions go unanswered in one sense, the connection she has with Mammy Prater is vibrant, an exchange between the praying subject and her imagined, perfect listener.[16]

This idea that prayer can articulate beyond its own self-indulgence is important to thinking about the bowed heads of Tommie Smith and John Carlos; that is, to read their protest as quiet expressiveness does not disavow their capacity to inspire. In fact, nothing speaks more to their humanity—and against the violence of racism—than the glimpse of their inner lives. The challenge, though, is to understand how their quiet works as a public gesture, without disavowing its interiority. This is always a conundrum because of the ease with which the terms of publicness overdetermine how we read human

Anon., *Age has not dimmed Mammy Prater's love for sweets*, 1920 behavior, though the novelist Colm Tóibín provides an instructive example in an essay, "A Gesture Life," on Pope John Paul II. Remembering his experience of a papal mass, Toibin writes:

> The ceremony lasted for hours. He did not once lose the full rapt attention of the crowd. He did nothing dramatic, said nothing new. Before he spoke—and every word he said was translated into many languages on our radios—he remained still. There must have been music. But it was the lights that I remember and the sense that he had no script for this, that it was natural and improvised and also highly theatrical and professional. More than anything, it was unpredictable.
>
> And in that first hour, or maybe half-hour, he did something genuinely astonishing. With a million of us watching, he lifted his hands and cupped them over his face. It was nothing like a gesture of despair; he did not put his head in his hands out of unhappiness. He held his head high and proud so that it could be seen, and he left his hands in place covering it. The crowd watched him, presuming this would last a few moments as he sought some undistracted purity for his prayer or his contemplation. We waited for him to lower his hands, but he did not. He stayed still, the world gazing up at him. What he did ceased to be a public gesture, but became instead intensely private. It was like watching somebody sleeping. I do not know how long it lasted. Maybe twenty minutes; maybe half an hour. He was offering the young who had come here in the infant years of Eastern European democracy not a lesson in doctrine or faith or morals but some mysterious example of what a spiritual life might look like. Somehow he managed to put a sort of majesty into it. Even those among us, like myself, who had no faith anymore and a serious argument with the church had to watch him in awe. He was showing us his own inner life as beautifully simple as well as strange and complex.

Tóibín captures what is sublime in the pope's display, how this gesture that is done in public also retains all of the vulnerability and unpredictability of the interior. There is inspiration in this gesture which serves both the pope (his moment of contemplation, as if seeking a clear inner space from which to pray) and those in attendance, especially Tóibín. This is prayer as self-indulgence and connection, and it is also true of Smith and Carlos's expression of protest—not so much the fists and the gloves, but the bowing of the heads. However planned that bowing was, it is also such a human act that it manifests as a sign of their inner lives; it makes the whole thing transcendent in a way that is beyond words. And their capacity to speak to collectivity is not hindered by the interiority of their gesture; in fact, the inspiration of their public display is in seeing its deep human privacy.

This is the expressiveness of quiet.

NOTES

1. The nature of language is studied in various scholarly traditions, though the comments here are informed by Ferdinand de Saussure's work in linguistics and Jacques Lacan's in psychoanalysis. Also see José Medina's book *Language: Key Concepts in Philosophy*. McLaughlin's essay "Figurative Language" is useful because it is related to literature and also because he suggests that language is, in part, interior.

2. It is in this regard that language and literacy are part of the celebrated nature of Black expressiveness; see, for example, Henry Louis Gates Jr.'s *Figures in Black*. Many writers have engaged the idea of language as ambivalence; see my discussion in chapters 6 and 7 of *(Un)Becoming the Subject*.

3. Many poets have written about the nature of poetic language; see, for example, Mary Oliver's excellent *A Poetry Handbook*. In her poem "Morgan Harris," Cheryl Clarke notices the interior of poetic language: "To her, poetry is the smallest thing, / her greater depth" (*Experimental Love: Poems*, 14). This sense of what is small, what is tender and fragile, is the aim of poetry; as Rita Dove notes, poetry is a form that "connects you to yourself, to the self that doesn't know how to talk or negotiate. We have emotions that we can't really talk about, and they're very strong" (quoted in Clarence Major's *The Garden Thrives*, xxvi). Dove goes on to suggest that "I really don't think of poetry as being an intellectual activity. I think of it as a very visceral activity." The claim that is being made about the language of poetry is also relevant to the short story, which works with limited space and therefore relies on brevity and symbolism, at least as much as the novel (see note 11 below). This is even truer of music, where pieces are made up of gaps and silence as much as they are of notes played, a point that is especially legible in listening to jazz. I am grateful to L.H. Stallings for the reference to Clarke's poem.

4. For a consideration of the tension between form and content in Black literature, see Gates's *Figures in Black* (especially "Introduction" and "Literary Theory and the Black Tradition"), "Criticism in the Jungle," and his introduction to *The Signifying Monkey*; also see Madelyn Jablon (*Black Metafiction*) and Keith E. Byerman (*Fingering the Jagged Grain*). Additionally, see William Andrews's formulation of "posing as artless" (*To Tell a Free Story*), John Michael Vlach's *By the Work of Their Hands* (especially the introduction and chapter 1), and Robin Kelley's *Yo Mama's Disfunktional* (especially chapter 1). An anxiety about form fuels many of the aesthetic debates of the Harlem Renaissance (including varying essays by Romare Bearden ["The Negro Artist and Modern Art"], W.E.B. Du Bois ["Criteria of Negro Art"], Langston Hughes ["The Negro Artist and the Racial Mountain"], Zora Neale Hurston ["What White Publishers Won't Print"], Alain Locke ["The Negro Takes His Place in American Art"], and George Schuyler ["The Negro-Art Hokum"]), and of the Black Arts Movement in the 1960s (for example, Amiri Baraka's "Black Art," Addison Gayle's "The Black Aesthetic," and Hoyt Fuller's "Towards a Black Aesthetic"). For a more general consideration of form, see Hayden White's *The Content of the Form*, and Michael Boccia's *Form as Content and Rhetoric in the Modern Novel*.

5. Of repetition, James Snead writes, "whenever we encounter repetition in cultural forms, we are indeed not viewing 'the same thing' but its transformation." Snead's comment is from his truly excellent essay "Repetition as a Figure of Black Culture," 59.

6. In keeping with the aesthetic of the entire collection, Trethewey uses the intimacy of family (mother/daughter relationship; biracial child's relationship to the South; interracial family; Black men's relationship to the national family) to explore big narratives of race, loyalty, war.

7. In this regard, realism is authority, as Wahneema Lubiano has phrased it in "'But Compared to What?' Reading Realism, Representation, and Essentialism," and as has often been advocated, implicitly or explicitly, by cultural leaders. The intent of authoritative realism is to document, a goal that means being attuned to a public audience as well as committed to a notion of truth that necessarily compromises the representation of complexity. The best overall work on realism and Black culture is Gene Andrew Jarrett's *Deans and Truants*. Some key examples of the advocacy of realism by cultural leaders include Alain Locke's "The Saving Grace of Realism," Richard Wright's "Blueprint for Negro Writing," Amiri Baraka's poem "Black Art," and Addison Gayle's "The Black Aesthetic." Also see Gates's discussion of the politics of realism in his introduction to *Figures in Black*, especially pages xxvi–xxvii. For other discussions of the presence and limits of "racial realism," see Dubey's *Signs and Cities*, Tate's *Psychoanalysis* (especially the introduction), Jablon's *Black Metafiction*, and Eversley's *The Real Negro*; as well as the general discussions of realism by Michael Elliott (*The Culture Concept*, especially chapters 2 and 3), Kenneth Warren (*Black and White Strangers*), Amy Kaplan (*The Social Construction of American Realism*), and Michael Bell (*The Problem of American Realism*).

8. Part of the consideration of surrealism must include its political inclinations—that many proponents of the aesthetic saw it as a way to advocate progressive, even revolutionary, ideas. This merger of the political and the imaginative made surrealism attractive to the Negritude poets and other Black writers; see Jean-Claude Michel's *The Black Surrealists* and Robin Kelley's *Freedom Dreams*, especially the chapter "Keepin' It (Sur)real: Dreams of the Marvelous." Some scholars suggest that surrealism, conceptually, is natural to black experience, as Kelley does in discussing Richard Wright: "For Wright, black people did not have to go out and find surrealism, for their lives were already surreal" (183). One challenge in thinking about surrealism is its use of primitivism, which seems similar to racist notions about Black identity; as T. Denean Sharpley-Whiting notes: "Reason, Absolute Truth, Logic—ideals held as unique to the European Enlightenment—are denounced by Césaire in favor of the madness, the illogical, uncivilized, cannibalistic tendencies ascribed to blacks by Europeans" (*Negritude Women*, 9). Sharpley-Whiting goes on to argue that the primitivism of surrealism was not exclusive to Black people, though there was general acceptance of the idea that "people of color ... were more in touch with the id" (85). The overall ideas about surrealism as an alternative to realism might apply to other ideologies of fantastical expression, for example magical realism.

   Another example in thinking about the quality of language described here is Mark Rothko's late works, those brilliant paintings of two or three blocks of colors. These pieces evoke terrific fluidity and intensity, a sense of being overwhelmed by the ocean of feeling. That such simple and abstract blocks of color could produce such abundance and intimacy arises from the poetic capacity of Rothko's language. His aesthetic is not minimalist or even economical, and is not merely beyond what is real (or hyper-real); instead, it is accessible and supple, expressive as well as ambiguous, a bigness of feeling. See Jeffrey Weiss, who quotes Rothko's claim that his work is about intimacy (*Mark Rothko*, 262). Rothko's work has been described as abstract expressionism, though he never embraced the term. He has also been described as minimalist, though minimalism—which is sometimes based on objectivity—is different from the capacity being described here. On minimalism, see Kirk Curnutt's *Wise Economies* (especially pages 205–16) and Cynthia Whitney Hallett's *Minimalism and the Short Story*.

9. Here I am referring largely to pieces like *Same*, *Time Pieces*, *Easy for Who to Say*, *Guarded Conditions*, and *Dividing Lines*. These pieces and further discussion of Simpson's work can be found in Beryl Wright and Saidiya Hartman's *Lorna Simpson: For the Sake of the Viewer*, Deborah Willis's *Lorna Simpson*, and Coco Fusco's *English Is Broken Here* and "Uncanny Dissonance"; also see my discussion of Simpson in chapter 1 of *Black Women, Identity, and Cultural Theory*.

10. André Bazin claims that "The photographic image is the object itself, the object freed from the conditions of time and space that govern it" ("The Ontology of the Photographic Image," 8). This claim might be too bold to be entirely true (for example, Smith and Carlos's image is informed by time and space), but it does speak to the way that Simpson plays with timelessness.

11. There is a predicament of expression with the sublime that makes it an interesting framework for thinking about quiet. Historically, as a part of the discourse of aesthetics, the term "sublime" has been used to describe an excellent and awesome quality of experience, a sense of transcendence. The sublime is a revelation of what is beyond our social understanding of humanness, an awe that is divine; in its capacity to take us beyond what is human, the sublime is a disturbance or even loss of identity. The sublime has been used interchangeably with the beautiful, though beginning in the Enlightenment, the sublime was theorized as superior to the beautiful. The distinction between the two lies in the argument that the sublime is beyond nature, while the beautiful is limited to and by nature; the sublime is "the inhuman, the realm of things beyond ourselves, the dimension of otherness we can never know" (Mary Arensberg, *The American Sublime*, 1). This is all part of the long intellectual history of aesthetics, a discourse that has shaped thinking from ancient Greece to the Enlightenment to postmodernism and has been central to philosophy, religion, art, psychology, and sociology. Most interesting to thinking about quiet is the notion of beauty as a human capacity to perceive, experience, judge—beauty as a quality of being or measure of being human. Some useful general resources here include Jeremy Gilbert-Rolfe's *Beauty and the Contemporary Sublime* (especially pages 1–10, where he argues that the expressiveness of the sublime is freedom), Umberto Eco and Alastair McEwen's *History of Beauty*, and Jerome Stolnitz's essay "'Beauty': Some Stages in the History of an Idea." Also see Stolnitz's and Stephen Ross's encyclopedia entries on "beauty." Of course, the concept of beauty also has historical relevance to racist ideas about Black inferiority, especially physically; see Maxine Craig's *Ain't I a Beauty Queen?* and Noliwe Rooks's *Hair Raising*. In terms of thinking about the sublime as a loss of identity, see Donald Pease's "Sublime Politics," Helen Regueiro's "Dickinson and the Haunting of the Self," and Frances Ferguson's *Solitude and the Sublime* (which argues that the beautiful is social and the sublime is isolation); also see Barbara Freeman's construction of the "feminine sublime" as an engagement of otherness. For other discussions of the sublime and beauty, see Marc Conner (*The Aesthetics of Toni Morrison*, especially pages 49–76), Dolan Hubbard's "W.E.B. Du Bois and the Invention of the Sublime in *The Souls of Black Folk*," and Gilbert-Rolfe's discussion of Schiller in *Beauty and the Contemporary Sublime*.

   Another way of describing this kind of language is to notice its gaps and hesitations, as if it were working "by some more intuitive method of communication, by rhythm, or as the structuralists would say, by a deep structure that lies beneath the conscious level of concept" (Charles May, *The New Short Story Theories*), a level of human capacity and understanding that exists beneath what is conscious. This is Charles May's way of thinking about the language of short story, and it seems to be consonant with the idea of interiority. Discussions of the aesthetic of the short story as a genre have informed the consideration of language in this chapter; see, for example, May's and Julio Cortazar's essays in *The New Short Story Theories*, Michael Wood's *Children of Silence*, Curnutt's *Wise Economies*, Raymond Carver's "On Writing," Valerie Shaw's *The Short Story, a Critical Introduction*, and Susan Lohafer and Jo Ellyn Clarey's *Short Story Theory at a Crossroads* (especially Lohafer's excellent introduction to part one and Austin Wright's essay). Also see Suzanne Ferguson's argument about interior action ("Defining the Short Story").

12. Prayer is a vast concept, hardly representing a defined set of notions. Philip and Carol Zaleski, in their highly readable and comprehensive book *Prayer: A History*, note that prayer merges "the absurd and the sublime ... the fantastic and the banal," action and contemplation, the material and the imaginative, being and becoming (3–6). Furthermore, it may be interior, even a sense of stillness, but it is concerned with the world of things and is also motion (as in the African proverb "when you pray, you move your feet"). For further references on prayer, see Patricia Carrington's *Freedom in Meditation*, George Maloney's *Inward Stillness*, and D.Z. Phillips's *The Concept of Prayer*.

13. Within various religious traditions, the discussion of audience and even double consciousness would be different from that above. The discussion here is predicated on the concept of prayer drawn from its general practice. No distinction is being made here between ritual and personal prayer, for example, or the ways that religious communities can serve as an external audience; instead, prayer is being spoken of in its most essential and idealized sense.

14. The quotation is from Natalie Goldberg's distinction between procrastination and waiting (*Wild Mind*, 211).

15. Hurston herself notices the gendered difference between men and women's concept of adventure in the opening paragraphs of the novel, which starts "Ships at a distance carry every man's wish on board." In contemporary literature, works like Sena Naslund's *Ahab's Wife* challenge the construct of women who wait for men's return from epic adventure. And of course Mary Helen Washington famously critiqued the characterization of Black men's adventures as being more meaningful than Black women's stories of interior journeys (see the introduction of *Invented Lives*).

16. This is part of the magic that Brand's narrator is able to manifest. Magic is a part of the Zaleskis' history of prayer: "prayer partakes of magic and sacrifice yet reserves to itself something altogether more mysterious, more difficult to define" (90); see especially chapters 2 and 3. Also, in thinking about prayer as a means to connection, see D. Z. Phillips, who makes a convincing argument about the tenuousness of such connection (*The Concept of Prayer*, especially chapters 1 and 4).

BIBLIOGRAPHY

Byerman, Keith. *Fingering the Jagged Grain: Tradition and Form in Recent Black Fiction*. Athens: University of Georgia Press, 1985.

Césaire, Aimé. "Poetry and Knowledge." In *Refusal of the Shadow: Surrealism and the Caribbean*. Edited by Michael Richardson. Translated by Michael Richardson and Krzysztof Fijalkowski, 134–46. London: Verso, 1996.

Cotter, Holland. "Lorna Simpson, Gathered." *New York Times*, July 2, 2011.

McLaughlin, Thomas. "Figurative Language." In *Critical Terms for Literary Study*. Edited by Frank Lentricchia and Thomas McLaughlin, 80–90. Chicago: University of Chicago Press, 1995.

Phillips, Carl. *Coin of the Realm: Essays on the Life and Art of Poetry*. St. Paul, MN: Graywolf, 2004.

Zaleski, Philip, and Carol Zaleski. *Prayer: A History*. Boston: Houghton Mifflin, 2005.

GARRETT BRADLEY

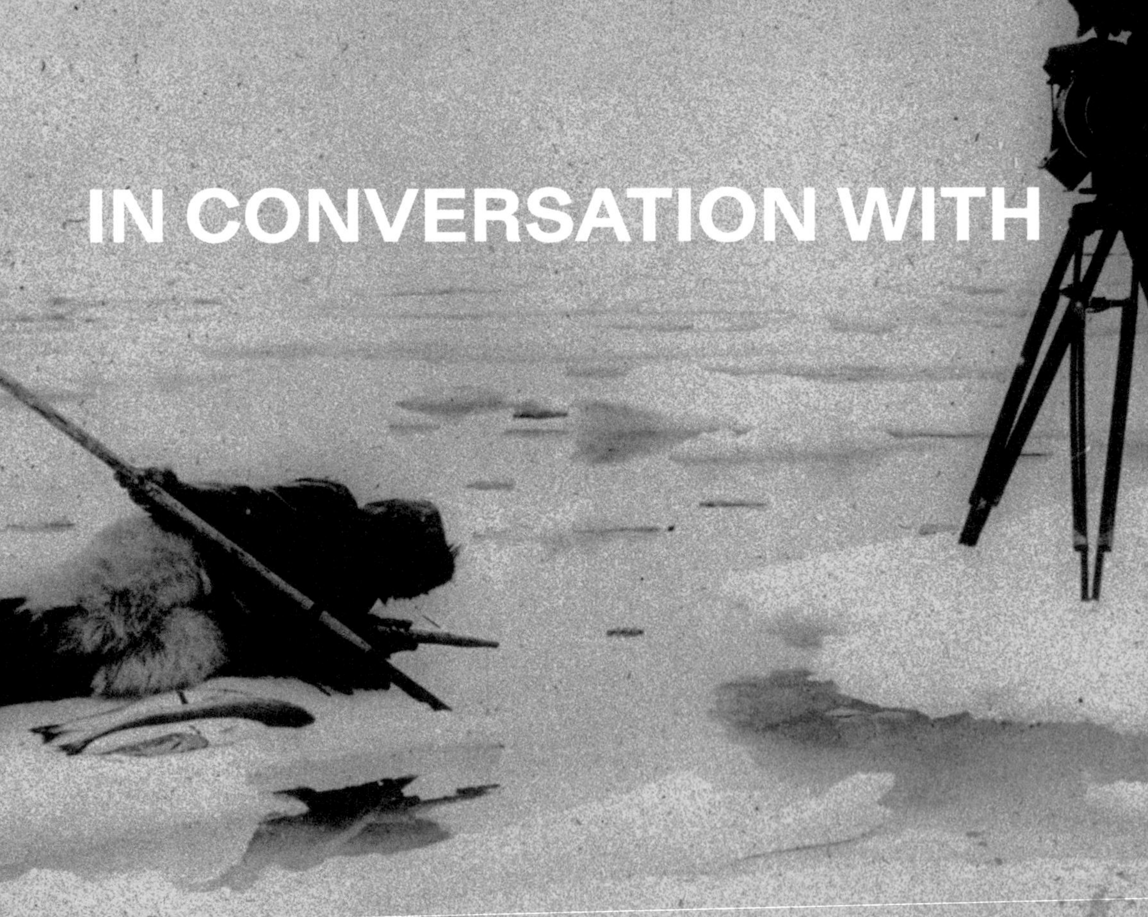

IN CONVERSATION WITH

ALEXANDRA BELL

Alexandra Bell: I often think about the overlap between journalism and documentary. I know in a sense they are the same thing, but documentary has a type of freedom to it that I'm not sure journalism has. Documentary is a more robust subjective space than journalism. Anyway, there is something you said at BAM [Brooklyn Academy of Music], when you were in conversation with Julie Dash [as part of *Garrett Bradley's* America*: A Journey Through Race and Time* October 11–17, 2019]. And you said in journalism and in documentary, I think, there are questions about the role of beauty... and whether beauty can incite action in the same way that trauma can. And I'm very much in the camp of yes, beauty can do that. So, I think I enter my work and my process from that point of view. Can you say more about this?

Garrett Bradley: Sure, although quickly on documentary and journalism: John Grierson was a Scottish filmmaker credited with coining the term "documentary," in reference to Robert J. Flaherty's 1922 film, *Nanook of the North.* From what I understand Flaherty went to the Arctic to film the Inuk people from this "ethnographic perspective," then somehow lost all of his film. So, he went *back* to the same place and had members of the Inuk community reenact their own lives and practices. And that film was then coined "a documentary," by Grierson in a review—which cemented the notion of a new genre. In Grierson's essay, "First Principles of Documentary" (1932) he makes the case that "acting" and scripted films are not only bourgeois but have less potential to reflect "the spirit" of the real world.

Today, Wikipedia defines a documentary as "a non-fictional motion picture (intended) to document reality, primarily for the purpose of instruction, education or maintaining a historical record." The documentary works I've made have often started with a conversation that centers itself on if and how larger societal issues affect us on a personal level. And from there—really just facilitating a visual articulation of how those questions are answered. And that does go into aesthetics, into your question on the role of beauty versus trauma, or pain?

I should be clear that I'm not qualifying those two things. I don't mean to imply that it's a matter of choosing between violence and trauma, but rather of incorporating them both as modes of expression that can create the opposite effect, that create the peace, the beauty. Both likely need a platform because both are true. I think what I was getting at is the complication that occurs in parallel, when something becomes public, it can also become definitive. And there is a tendency, that I'm personally invested in counteracting, in which we are defined by the problem, by the pain, by the trauma. Black people—Black Americans in particular—have shaped and defined global culture through music, clothing, language, art, through forms of beauty. And that place, the outcome of a grim reality, is where I've personally been most interested, most focused.

AB: In journalism, I think violence is central to the way the field operates. Journalism trains you for trauma being the point of arousal—it's supposed to galvanize people. In fact, a lot of people enter journalism school dreaming of uncovering some human rights abuse or some high-level corruption. It isn't as common for beauty to be the catalyst in news. I think solutions journalism tries to get at this by asking a very central question, What is actually working? And from there those stories often contain great examples of communal love, perseverance and problem-solving, but this isn't the norm. Most news is doom and gloom. You know, if it bleeds it leads.

GB: I want to talk a bit about form because I think our processes work to similar ends in very different ways. When I'm cutting something, I find myself aspiring toward a seamless or invisible change. I don't want anyone to feel the construction. And it's interesting because I realized that makes the work opaque again in some way.

I want to read a very brief description of your process by Doreen St. Félix for the *New Yorker*. It's brilliant in its brevity, because your work is doing so many things, so it's a good place to start. She writes, "[Bell] uses redaction, omission, annotation and text editing to alter articles. She then prints out large versions of her deconstructions and plasters them onto walls around the city."

Can you talk a little about your process—particularly the role of visibility? Being able to see what you've changed with your red marker, the error and correction in one space. The construction is made visible. Are you interested in being able to see a multifaceted truth? Or is it a new truth?

AB: It's an old truth, right? I'm most often trying to narrow it down to something really singular and specific. When it comes to reporting on violence against Black people, there's a certain level of nuance allowed. So, a part of me is trying to remove all doubt. I'm trying to erase all the gray areas, many of which are hidden in the framework or structure of the article.

I once returned a used book because it had too many margin notes. I remember it felt impossible to read and form my own view with all the side-talking going on. I think about *Counternarratives* in this way. The goal is to be disruptive and to distract, so that people can see your construction. The edit needs to be intrusive and domineering. It needs to be visible. Also, visible edits on top of an already published *New York Times* article is a power move. It's my way of saying, "Not so fast, we are not done yet."

I feel like I noticed some of your edit in *Alone* (2017) or is it technique? There's a parallel between your distance from the subjects and their distance from one another. It happens in the conversation with the lawyer and when she's waving to him as he's been transferred. Also, you use montage in *America* (2019) and isn't that sort of bossy?

GB: Both of those instances in *Alone* are in-camera. The distance—the placement of the lens in relation to what's happening—is a type of editing in that it's a choice but it takes on a different process once I start cutting. There are hard cuts or dissolves, essentially lots of different ways to "cut" or transition from one thing to the next. All of which reflect, from a formal standpoint, what the message is. *America* was a series of 12 vignettes. It's funny because I never thought about it as a montage but I like that: twelve years in montage. And montage is bossy, but in my mind, the whole process is a layering of points of view, connected to a certain end, a certain goal.

AB: Ah yes. Well for me, construction and edits sometimes feel like the same thing, but I get there is a clear difference. I'm perhaps overreading, because I'm in the early stages of film and video in my art practice. I've been thinking through broadcast news segments and montages so I'm hyper-attuned to every little thing these days.

This new thing I'm working through emerged out of my stay in LA, where I spent a great deal of time with Kahlil Joseph and folks at BLKNWS. I got to sit in on editing and make suggestions and also share my own thoughts about news and media. When it came time for me to prepare a segment, I felt a number of limits: first my own editing abilities and that I really wanted to put a lot of text on screen.

I remember feeling a bit frustrated, but it became an opening for me. I really wanted to embrace the idea of the news segment and consider what it might mean to pull video from two screens and put it into another form, one that felt more in line with the way I read. Does this make sense?

Montage feels so abstract to me and I feel so painfully literal at times. One place that always feels radical for me when it comes to my practice is that I use old news. I don't think drawing from the archive is this mind-blowing thing, but in journalism and news media *when* something occurs is very important, reaching back to something that is considered "old" is disruptive.

In this sense, time becomes part of my technique. Can we talk about the use of time in your work? Obviously, you have the film *Time* (2020), but you also have *America* which moves across time. There's something thematically happening for me. For you?

GB: All three of those films were made around the same time, very much overlapping with each other. *America* took almost six years to make and I was really invested in the idea of trying to formally challenge myself to create something within the technical limitations of the turn of the century. That's why it's on 35mm film, even though it's expensive as fuck, and I knew color wasn't an option at that point [in the early twentieth century]. I'm mentioning that because that's also why *Alone* is in black and white, I was having a hard time seeing in color and I didn't feel it would add another layer to Aloné's or her family's experience, or that it was even appropriate. It was actually one of her sons, Jay, who said, "It's so cool that it's in black and white, because it's like nothing's changed in time." I wish I had thought of that. *Time* and *Alone*, in my mind, are always sister films, because I met Fox in the process of making *Alone* and the methodology that I established remained exactly the same. But getting to your larger question around conceptual ideas of time, my feeling is that there's just one tense, so when we remember things from the past, they become present inside of us. In the same sort of corny New Age way that you talk to your future self and it becomes your present. And that's how you manifest, right?

AB: Yeah. Alright. I was thinking about that. It's the thing that stands out to me. When I get asked about time my feeling is just that nothing is ever really old.

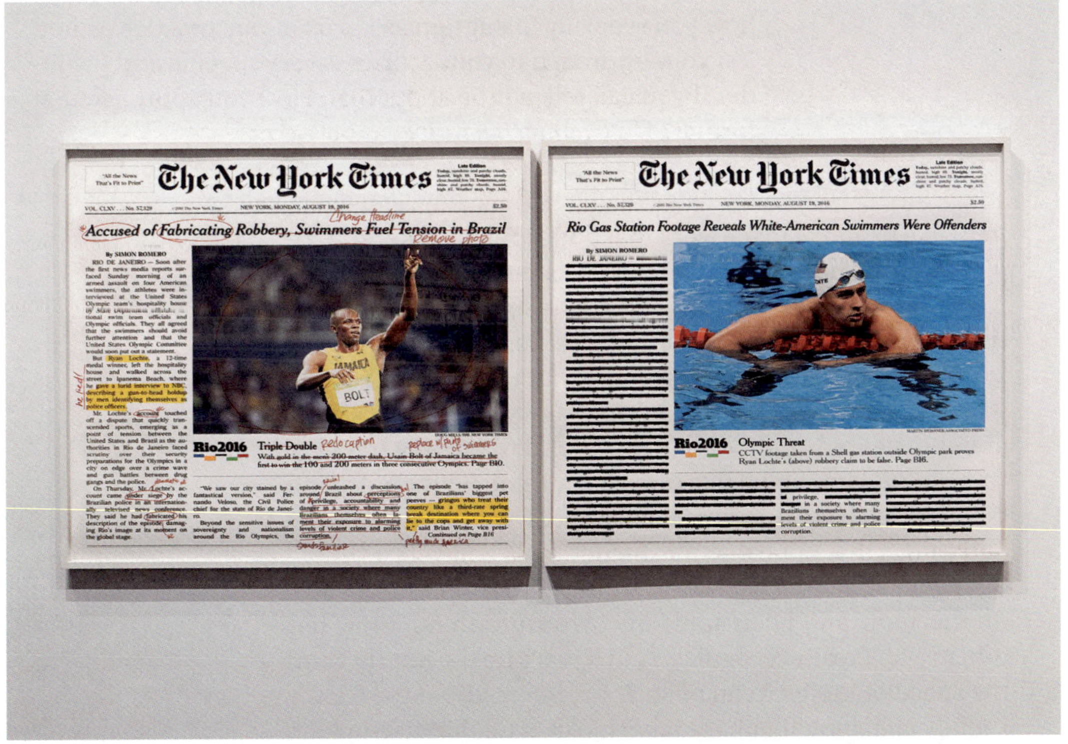

Alexandra Bell, *Olympic Threat*, 2020

GB: Right, exactly, and those three films in particular were really operating under that belief system that the past and the present were one in the same. With *Time* it was interesting, because I didn't know Fox had this whole archive of films and it forced me to reconsider how to edit the piece. And the film became about how they stayed connected over the course of Robert's incarceration, and how love, ritual and routine operated for them in their life, and how they were able to hold on to themselves as individuals, to resist the ways in which the prison industrial complex aims to remove one's identity and sense of self. The juxtaposition from past to present allowed for them to always be in the same tense of time, even if it was twenty years prior. But I wouldn't have been able to do that had I not tried to do something similar with *America*, namely how to force flexibility out of material I myself did not shoot, how to evoke or pull out something I discern, through movement, timing and juxtaposition. Through its editorial construction. That challenge is what I think, really defined the next film, thereafter. And *Osaka* actually.

But so, while we're talking about construction, I don't know how you see your Instagram as a part of our practice or not, but your approach to your Stories is very specific and I wonder if you can talk a little about that. How you approach that format? Do *Counternarratives* apply here?

AB: I like to think I make work that both appreciates and complements my neurosis and also breaks me out of it. I can be painfully literal and ordered and as a result linear in the way that I don't always love. I'm always looking for the moment a system or setup or gadget breaks me out of this sort of 1, 2, 3, 4 feeling I constantly have. And you know, there's something about Instagram and how it's structured that really frees me from, or perhaps highlights the way my mind bounces around before I even have a chance to intervene. That said, it has limits and things that appeal to me. Structure is good. Ten slides? I got you. I can make effective, funny, incisive commentary on this topic and I can apply my own rules that I know but others won't really recognize. And it plays on the internet and the speed of things. I can make a statement about the CDC's rapidly changing incubation period and tie that to Amazon working conditions in ten slides using a meme featuring a Tyler Perry character. It's so fucking funny to me and I really love the way this site holds my humor and idiosyncrasies in this way. And I guess another thing that is important—it doesn't feel forced or contrived.

I try to respect my limits but it's never the end of things for me. I'm always trying to figure out how to say something and when I feel stuck or that I don't fully have the skills to pull something off, I seek other ways while also reaching back to build up those other muscles. Instagram puts me in the video conversation. I'm inching my way there. It's me inching my way toward collage. It's me inching my way toward assemblage. I've been really devouring the work of Raymond Saunders, Hervé Télémaque, as well as returning to Lorna Simpson, Mickalene Thomas, and Arthur Jafa. There's a certain readability for me now that I'm trying to tackle a different set of challenges.

This is an opening for me, you know? And I've been trying to figure out how to take this skill that exists in the very specific arena that is Instagram and figure out how to make a physical work or installation. How does one give form to or say concretize these seemingly ephemeral moments that are so rich and so informative? They all represent the power of the internet and I guess inherently the danger of it too, depending on where you stand in the world. Also, without getting too conspiracy theory on you, one day they are gonna up and unplug the whole thing without notice. Watch. I think it is really necessary to find these moments of meaning and house them somewhere.

GB: The anxiety that you're talking about around being unplugged is really interesting—it makes me think, in much the same way of needing to house and archive likely off the internet, that part of the revolution in this moment is that it is, unplugging. And unplugging is deceivingly simple because we know how difficult and complicated that actually is when our emotional, economic, even increasingly our human connections are through devices. But if that dependence is what colonization looks like today, are we not in a profound moment wherein it's easier than ever to revolt? I don't know how I feel about what I'm saying. It's truly a question I'm agnostic about at the moment. I am curious how you might think about that proposal. If it is a matter of just turning the phone off—not buying appliances with cameras and microphones—focusing on the physical world, are we potentially in the least violent and most powerful position historically to resist?

AB: Ehhh. I'm not sure if it is anxiety so much as it feels like an inevitability. I imagine it is not even possible for people to decide to unplug and I think people who are able to achieve a certain level of analog-only life are financially secure and have the option to carve out a niche way of living.

GB: I'm saying the technological age that we are entering, tells us that our own bodies and the physical world are more and more obsolete. And I'm wondering what past revolutionaries whose bodies were so integral to the resistance, what they would say to us in this moment? The violence in other words, maybe, is staying plugged in.

AB: I'm reading David Walker's *Appeal* from 1829. It's this small pamphlet he wrote in Boston calling out slavery, calling out white folks, with a call for Black unity to fight back against oppression. He was smuggling it down to North Carolina on ships by sewing it into sailors' clothing. Its presence in the South resulted in one of the first quarantines. They were really trying to make sure the book didn't get around. Anyway, I mention this because one of the remarkable things about the pamphlet and about Black newspapers is that they represented mobility. Especially so at a time when Black people couldn't move because of slavery and Northern terrorism, the mobility of paper was revolutionary.

I think about the internet in this light. Obviously, it's supervised and there is probably zero likelihood of privacy, but it's a form of distribution. Cheap distribution. The internet is a place to get information out and to connect with other people. To mobilize if one desires, or at least get the ball rolling toward this kind of place. I think that's important and again, I think people have to do the work of traversing the digital and the in-person.

If I have any anxiety, it's that there is limited infrastructure in place for when—not if—the internet goes away. Goes offline. Maybe this is a question for Nam June Paik. You know he basically used his work to predict the internet and that we would be uploading ourselves. I think both are likely, but I lean more toward there being some grand and extreme blackout and a great unplugging. If the powers that be don't make it happen, climate change will get us there soon enough.

GB: I would agree that we have innovated every situation we've found ourselves in—and yet in almost every instance, it's revealed, identified and co-opted. And so again, we are forced to find another mode of mobilization, maybe hence the internet. But I wonder if we've reached that point now where it's been revealed. They know what Black Twitter is. And so I'm sort of forced to wonder if it's a matter at this point of getting back to another, physical in-this-world method.

AB: Well I hope while people are logged in, they are gathering up all the connections and all the tools we will need for whatever is coming. Speaking of, I know you are working on an Octavia Butler project. I read *Parable of the Sower* (1993) in LA at the height of the pandemic, when people were running out of oxygen, that was intense. It's a book that considers how we might get on the other side of something. I'm wondering, what's it like to make a film like *Parable* now?

GB: It doesn't feel like a jump. I've, from the beginning, talked about it as a documentary because there is nothing about it that isn't real. Not even, [the main character] Lauren's hyper-empathy. One of humanity's great downfalls is our own amnesia, our tendency to forget. And I think that's where both the problem and the solution lie in this present moment. Lauren as a central character—and as us—is very much sifting through all of that.

AB: I think sometimes the alternative or the seemingly fictional setup is sometimes the best way to smuggle in these new ideas. I have an in-progress work, *The Freedom Papers*. I'm going to do predictive reporting but with a touch of fantasy to consider solutions to things that, in the moment, feel insurmountable. It's also a way I'm trying to break out of my own gaze. You know, the work that I've done, in many ways, centers Black trauma and doesn't always upend it or turn us toward solution. I left 2020 and perhaps the early part of the pandemic thinking about how to challenge myself: How do I make something that is of my own mind? Something that doesn't use as its source a particular, perhaps painful news story as a jumping point.

And I leaned into that question in a very literal way. What would it look like if I made something in my own words? My neon series, *Disputations on the Power and Efficacy of the Fourth Estate*, emerged from that thinking. I have a lot of insecurities about the work, but it also feels like an important moment. I'm giving myself freedom to use each work, each series, as a springboard to something else. And it feels good that it came out of a challenge I gave myself.

GB: I love the idea of thinking about neon writing as a way to take a break from your own aesthetic. Especially when you think about neon as an announcement. How do I break my own tendencies? That's a good question. I think that's a challenging thing when you're working with film, because of its elusiveness to a certain extent. The closest relationship I have to touching my films is in the edit and then they become things I can't touch again. It's like making a memory seven times—in ideation, in production, in post, in sound, in color, in typeface and in its release. I like thinking more and more about physical space as a final space to experience the work and maybe shifting away from linearity.

AB: Ah yes, the challenge of linearity. I guess that's where we end?

GB: Good idea.

Re:

FILMOGRAPHY CAPTIONS

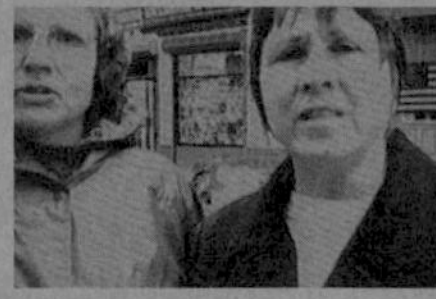

Autumn, 2001
Single-channel film, video (color, black and white, stereo sound)
9 minutes, 41 seconds

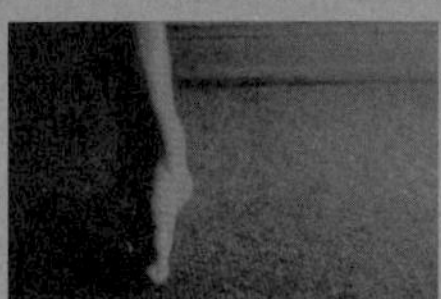

Practice, 2004
16mm film, transferred to video (black and white, stereo sound)
49 seconds

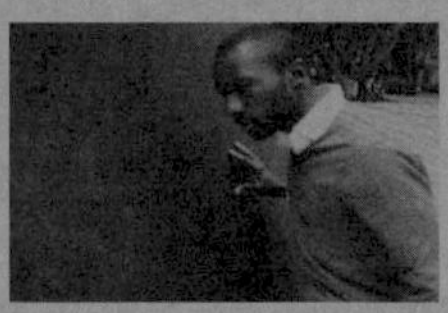

Sardines (Torqued Ellipse by Richard Serra), 2008
Single-channel film, 16mm transfer (black and white, stereo sound)
3 minutes

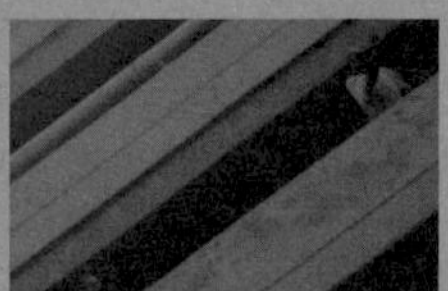

Dante 9–5, 2013
Single-channel film, HD video (color, stereo sound)
23 minutes, 16 seconds

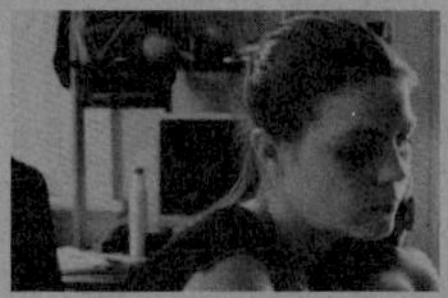

Below Dreams, 2014
Single-channel film, HD video (color, stereo sound)
74 minutes

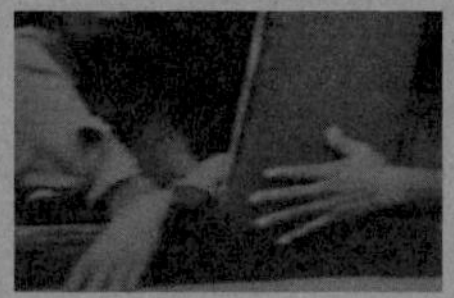

Like, 2016
Single-channel film, HD video (color, stereo sound)
9 minutes, 47 seconds

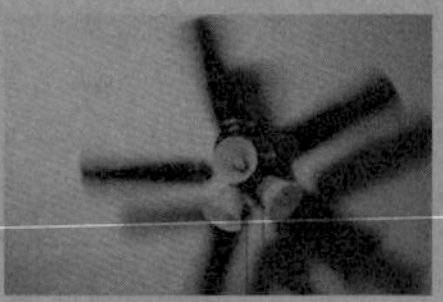

Alone, 2017
Single-channel film, HD video (black and white, stereo sound)
13 minutes

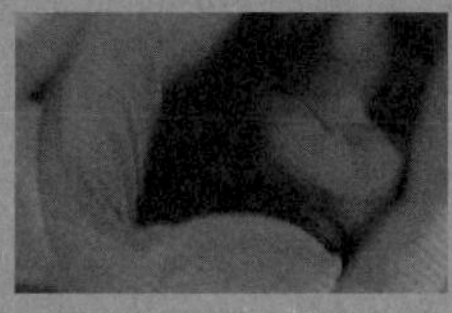

The Earth is Humming, 2018
Single-channel film, HD video (color, stereo sound)
13 minutes, 28 seconds

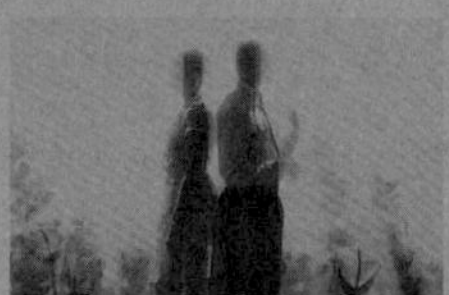

America, 2019
Multi-channel video installation, 35mm film transferred to HD video (black and white, 5.1 sound), continuous

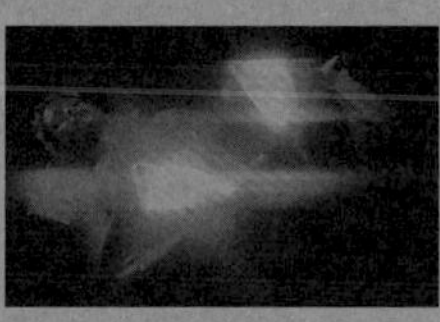

AKA, 2019
Single-channel video, HD video (color, stereo sound)
8 minutes, 17 seconds

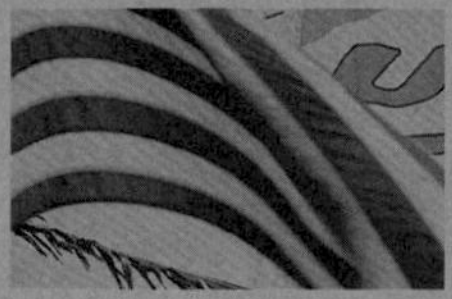

Time, 2020
Single-channel video, (black and white, stereo sound)
81 minutes

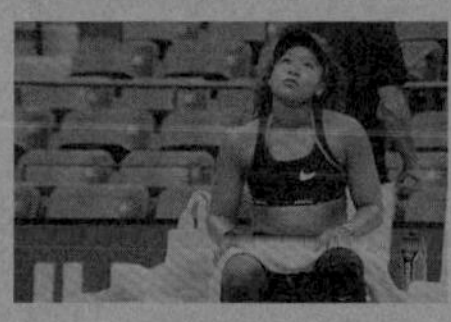

Naomi Osaka, 2021
Netflix, limited mini-series (3 episodes)

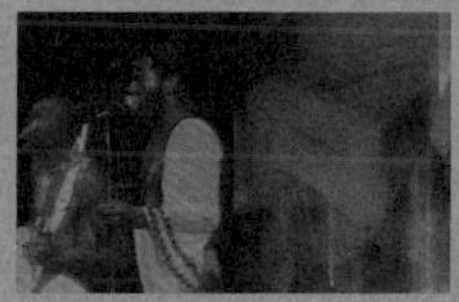

Garrett Bradley and Arthur Jafa
a Negro, a Lim-o, 2022
Two-channel video, HD video (color, black and white, surround sound), continuous

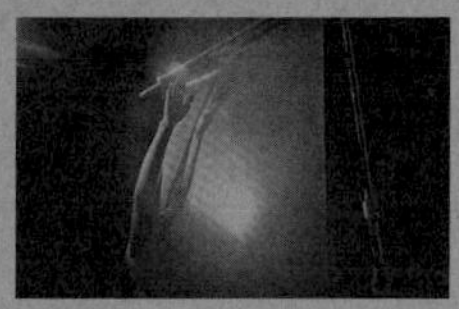

Safe, 2022
Three-channel video, HD video (color, black and white, surround sound), continuous

IMAGE CREDITS

Pages 128–132	Stills from T. Hayes Hunter, Edwin Middleton, *Lime Kiln Club Field Day*, 1914/2014. Courtesy of The Museum of Modern Art, New York.
Page 135	Garrett Bradley, *America*, 2019, multi-channel video installation, 35mm film transferred to HD video (black and white, 5.1 sound), continuous (detail). Installed at the Museum of Modern Art, New York, 2020. © Garrett Bradley; Digital Image © 2023 The Museum of Modern Art, New York. Photo by Robert Gerhardt.
Pages 138–156	Stills from William Greaves, *Symbiopsychotaxiplasm: Take One*, 1968. © William Greaves.
Page 162	Image of Orson Welles as Harry Lime from Carol Reed, *The Third Man*, 1947 Photo by Ernst Haas/Getty Images.
Page 188	Jayson Musson (as Hennessy Youngman), *ART THOUGHTZ: How to Be a Successful Black Artist*, 2010 (detail). © Jayson Musson; Courtesy of the artist.
Page 196	Garrett Bradley, *America*, 2019, multi-channel video installation, 35mm film transferred to HD video (black and white, 5.1 sound), continuous (detail). Installed at Contemporary Arts Museum Houston, Texas, 2019. © Garrett Bradley, Contemporary Arts Museum Houston. Photography by Will Michels.
Pages 202	Garrett Bradley, *AKA*, 2019, single-channel video, HD video (color, sound), 8 minutes 17 seconds. Installed at COMA in Sydney, Australia, 2023. © Garrett Bradley. Courtesy COMA.
Page 207	Garrett Bradley, *AKA*, 2019, single-channel video, HD video (color, sound), 8 minutes 17 seconds. Installed at Whitney Biennial, May 17–September 22, 2019. © Garrett Bradley. Courtesy Whitney Museum of American Art, New York. Photography by Ron Amstutz.
Page 210	Zora Neale Hurston photographed at a football game at Carolina College for Negroes in 1939. Photo by Alexander Rivera/North Carolina Central University via Getty Images.
Pages 228–239	*Fire!! A Magazine of the Younger Negro Artist*, November 1926. Cover design by Aaron Douglas. Courtesy of HathiTrust.
Page 244	Sleeping Position of Africans on Slave Ship, 1957, the *Illustrated London News*, June 20, 1857.
Page 250	Girl (Simone Leigh and Chitra Ganesh), *my dreams, my works must wait till after hell*, 2011, single-channel video, color, sound; 7 minutes, 14 seconds. © Girl. Courtesy Matthew Marks Gallery and Gallery Wendi Norris.
Page 254	Jennifer Packer, *Blessed Are Those Who Mourn (Breonna! Breonna!)*, 2020, oil on canvas. © Jennifer Packer. Courtesy of the artist; Corvi-Mora, London; Sikkema Jenkins & Co., New York.
Page 260	Garrett Bradley, still from *Below Dreams* 2014, single-channel film, HD video (color, stereo sound), 74 minutes (detail). © Garrett Bradley. Courtesy of the artist.
Page 268	Tyler Mitchell, *Tenderly*, 2022, archival pigment print 20 x 16 in / 50.8 x 40.6 cm. © Tyler Mitchell. Courtesy of the artist.
Page 270	Assata Shakur (JoAnne Chesimard), being taken from Riker's Island to Middlesex County jail to await trial, January 29 1976. Photo by Frank Hurley/NY Daily News Archive via Getty Images.
Pages 280–284	Stills from Garrett Bradley, *Time*, 2020, single-channel video (black and white, stereo sound) 81 minutes. © Garrett Bradley. Courtesy Lisson Gallery.
Page 288	Pieter Bruegel the Elder, *Children's Games*, 1560, oil on panel (detail); 46 x 63 in / 118 x 161 cm. Kunsthistorisches Museum Wien, Gemäldegalerie. Image © KHM-Museumsverband.
Page 293	Suzanne McClelland, *MUTE Y- an Alphabet*, 2019, mixed media on canvas (one of 26 panels), 40 x 30 in / 102 x 76 cm © Suzanne McClelland. Courtesy of the artist.
Page 300	Rindon Johnston, *My Daughter, Aaliyah (Norf, Norf)*, 2016 (detail). © Rindon Johnston; courtesy of the artist.

Pages 306–310	Garrett Bradley and Arthur Jafa, *a Negro, a Lim-o*, 2022 (detail), two-channel video, HD (color, black and white, surround sound), continuous. Soundscape combines score, atmosphere and excerpted audio from JAM archive which includes dialogue from: Steve Cannon, John Farris, Peter Bradley, Martha Wilson, Jack Tilton and Linda Bryant, 27 mins. Installation view of the exhibition *Just Above Midtown: Changing Spaces*, The Museum of Modern Art, New York, October 9, 2022–February 18, 2023. Presented by Project EATS. © Garrett Bradley and Arthur Jafa; Digital Image © 2022 MoMA, N.Y. Courtesy The Museum of Modern Art, New York. Photo by Emile Askey.
Pages 318–329	Stills from Charles Burnett, *Killer of Sheep*, 1977. © Charles Burnett.
Page 332	Tommie Smith and John Carlos raise their gloved fists in the Black Power salute, during the US national anthem, at the Mexico Olympic Games, October 16, 1968. Photo by Bettmann/Getty Images.
Page 341	Whitfield Lovell, *Kin VII (Scent of Magnolia)*, 2011 © Whitfield Lovell; Courtesy DC Moore Gallery, New York.
Page 346	Anon., *Age has not dimmed Mammy Prater's love for sweets*, ca. 1920.
Page 352	Allakariallak performing as Nanook for Robert Flaherty's documentary, *Nanook of the North*, 1922. Revillon Frères Fonds / Library and Archives Canada / Copy no. 315 and 316 (figure)
Page 357	Alexandra Bell, *Olympic Threat*, 2020, screenprint and archival pigment print on paper 48 x 52 x 2" each; (Diptych). © Alexandra Bell. Courtesy of the Artist.

TEXT CREDITS

Ashley Clark: First published online as "Back to black: the 101-year making of the oldest black American-starring feature" by the British Film Institute, May 26, 2015.

Charles P. Linscott: First published as part of Close-Up: Black Film and Black Visual Culture in *Black Camera* 8, no. 1 (Fall 2016): 169–90.

Hilton Als with Joan Didion: First published in the *Paris Review*, no. 176, Spring 2006. Copyright © Hilton Als, used by permission of The Wylie Agency LLC.

Claudia Rankine: First published as Part II in *Citizen: An American Lyric* (Minneapolis: Graywolf Press, 2014), 23–36. Copyright © 2014 by Claudia Rankine. Reprinted with the permission of The Permissions Company, LLC on behalf of Graywolf Press, graywolfpress.org.

Garrett Bradley with Huey Copeland: First published in *Garrett Bradley: American Rhapsody*, exh. cat. (Houston: Contemporary Arts Museum Houston, 2020). Courtesy the Contemporary Arts Museum Houston.

Valerie Boyd: Excerpted from *Wrapped in Rainbows: The Life of Zora Neale Hurston* (New York: Scribner, 2003), 184–97. © Simon & Schuster.

Zora Neale Hurston: First published in *Fire!!*, November 1926, 7–14.

Josie Roland Hodson: Excerpted from the essay first published in *October*, no. 176 (Spring 2021): 7–24. Reprinted courtesy of the MIT Press.

Joy James: Excerpted from the essay "The Womb of Western Theory: Trauma, Time Theft, and the Captive Maternal" first published in *Carceral Notebooks* 12 (2016): 253–96. The essay is part of a larger project entitled "Fulcrum: Captive Maternals, Leverage, and a Theory of Democracy."

Doreen St. Félix: First published online by the Criterion Collection, January 18, 2022.

Legacy Russell: First published in *Glitch Feminism: A Manifesto* (New York: Verso Books, 2020).

Jeffrey Skoller: Excerpted from the chapter "Specters: The Limits of Representing History" in *Shadows, Specters, Shards: Making History in Avant-Garde Film* (Minneapolis: University of Minnesota Press, 2005). Courtesy University of Minnesota Press.

Kevin Quashie: First published in *The Sovereignty of Quiet: Beyond Resistance in Black Culture* (New Brunswick, NJ: Rutgers University Press, 2012).

All other conversations are courtesy the contributors, 2023.

CONTRIBUTOR BIOGRAPHIES

Hilton Als is a writer at the *New Yorker* and was previously a staff writer for the *Village Voice* and an editor-at-large at *Vibe*. Als edited the catalogue for the 1994–95 Whitney Museum of American Art exhibition *Black Male: Representations of Masculinity in Contemporary American Art*. His first book, *The Women*, was published in 1996. Other books include: *White Girls* (2013), a finalist for the National Book Critics Circle Award in 2014. He won the Pulitzer Prize for Criticism in 2017. In 1997, the New York Association of Black Journalists awarded Als first prize in both Magazine Critique/Review and Magazine Arts and Entertainment. He was awarded a Guggenheim for creative writing in 2000 and the George Jean Nathan Award for Dramatic Criticism for 2002–3. Als is an associate professor of writing at Columbia University's School of the Arts and has taught at Yale University, Wesleyan, and Smith College.

Alexandra Bell is an interdisciplinary artist who investigates the complexities of narrative production, consumption, and perception. Utilizing various media, she deconstructs language and imagery to explore the tension between subaltern experiences and dominant histories. Through investigative research, she considers the ways media frameworks control how narratives involving marginalized communities are depicted and in turn disseminated under the aegis of journalistic "objectivity." She is the recipient of numerous awards and fellowships including the International Center of Photography's Infinity Award, CatchLight Fellowship, Soros Equality Fellowship, Sarah Arison Artadia Award, and the Radcliffe Fellowship at Harvard University. Her work is in the collections of the Whitney Museum of American Art, Harvard Art Museums, and the Museum of Fine Arts Boston among others. She received her B.A. in humanities from the University of Chicago and an M.S. from Columbia University's School of Journalism.

Valerie Boyd (1963–2022) was the author of the critically acclaimed biography *Wrapped in Rainbows: The Life of Zora Neale Hurston*, winner of the Southern Book Prize and the American Library Association's Notable Book Award. She also edited *Gathering Blossoms Under Fire: The Journals of Alice Walker 1965–2000*, and was at work on an anthology titled *Bigger Than Bravery: Black Resilience and Reclamation in a Time of Pandemic*, which was released in 2022 by Lookout Books at the University of North Carolina, Wilmington. She was the founder and director of the MFA program in narrative nonfiction and the Charlayne Hunter-Gault Professor of Journalism at the University of Georgia. She was editor-at-large at the University of Georgia Press and senior consulting editor for the *Bitter Southerner*. She also taught creative nonfiction in the graduate writing program at Antioch University in Los Angeles and was a consultant to the Zora Neale Hurston Trust.

Garrett Bradley is an American artist, educator and filmmaker. She received a BA in religion from Smith College (2003) and an MFA in film production from UCLA (2012). Bradley works across narrative, documentary and experimental modes of filmmaking to address themes such as race, class, familial relationships, social justice and socio-political histories within the US. Her collaborative and research-based approach is often inspired by the real-life stories of her protagonists, exploring the space between fact and fiction and blurring the boundaries between notions of narrative and documentary cinema. Bradley's rigorous explorations of the social, economic, and racial politics of everyday life—its joys, pleasures, and pains—are lyrically and intimately rendered on screen. In 2020, Bradley's debut feature documentary, *Time* was nominated for 57 awards and won 20 times, including an Oscar Nomination, a Peabody Award and Best Director, Documentary at Sundance, making her the first Black woman to win this award. Bradley was a 2015 resident at Skowhegan School and is a recipient of the Prix de Rome (2019), the Art Award from the American Academy of Arts and Letters (2022) and the 2023 Eye Filmmuseum's Eye Art & Film Prize (2023). In 2017, Bradley co-founded Creative Council, an artist-led after-school program aimed at developing college portfolios and applications for public high schools, supported by New Orleans Video Access Center (NOVAC). Recent presentations include *Just Above Midtown: Changing Spaces*, Museum of Modern Art, New York (2022); *Grief and Grievance: Art and Mourning in America*, New Museum, New York (2021); *Projects: Garrett Bradley*, Museum of Modern Art, New York (2020); and *Garrett Bradley: American Rhapsody*, Contemporary Arts Museum Houston (2019), which toured to The Momentary, Crystal Bridges, Arkansas (2021); August Wilson African American Cultural Center, Pittsburgh (2022); and Museum of Contemporary Art, Los Angeles (2022). Bradley lives and works in New Orleans, Louisiana.

Linda Goode Bryant's decades of art-based activism began with her founding of Just Above Midtown (JAM) gallery in 1974, a self-described laboratory that foregrounded the work of African American artists, including David Hammons, Maren Hassinger, Lawrence D. "Butch" Morris, Senga Nengudi, Lorraine O'Grady, Howardena Pindell, and many others. JAM's explicit purpose was to be "in, but not of, the art world," offering early and often unique opportunities to artists to experiment and create freely, away from art market pressures. After closing JAM in 1986, Goode Bryant dedicated herself to filmmaking, directing the Peabody Award–winning documentary *Flag Wars* (2003), an intimate portrait of a community in flux that explores the tensions between preservation and gentrification. Over her nearly fifty-year career, Goode Bryant has and continues to advocate for a connection to "our innate ability to use what we have to create what we need." Most recently, Goode Bryant founded Project EATS, a "living installation" of neighborhood-based, small-plot, high-yield farms that use art, urban agriculture, partnerships, and social enterprise to sustainably grow and equitably distribute fresh, local, organically grown food in communities across New York City.

Ashley Clark is the curatorial director at the Criterion Collection. Previously, he worked as director of film programming at the Brooklyn Academy of Music, and he has curated film series at BFI Southbank, the Museum of Modern Art, TIFF Bell Lightbox, and the Smithsonian National Museum of African American

History and Culture, among other venues. His writing has appeared in the *New York Times*, *Vulture*, *Sight & Sound*, *4Columns*, and *Reverse Shot*. He is the author of the book *Facing Blackness: Media and Minstrelsy in Spike Lee's* Bamboozled (2015).

Huey Copeland is BFC Presidential Associate Professor of History of Art and Africana Studies at the University of Pennsylvania. A contributing editor of *Artforum*, Copeland is the author of *Bound to Appear: Art, Slavery, and the Site of Blackness in Multicultural America* (University of Chicago Press, 2013), in addition to more than sixty articles and interviews, including forthcoming essays on Marcel Duchamp (Museum für Moderne Kunst, Frankfurt am Main) and the writing of Afrotropic art histories (Duke University Press). Along with Steven Nelson, Copeland edited *Black Modernisms in the Transatlantic World* (Yale University Press, 2023), a Seminar Papers volume that at once aims to undo hegemonic modernist narratives in the West and to move toward the discipline's intersectional futures. The same ambition characterizes Copeland's book of collected writings forthcoming from the University of Chicago Press, *Touched by the Mother: Black Men, American Art, Feminist Horizons.*

Joan Didion (1934–2021) was a world-renowned journalist, novelist, memoirist, essayist, and screenwriter. She published her first novel, *Run River*, in 1963. Didion's other novels include *Play It as It Lays* (1970), *A Book of Common Prayer* (1977), *Democracy* (1984), and *The Last Thing He Wanted* (1996). Didion's first volume of essays, *Slouching Towards Bethlehem*, was published in 1968, and her second, *The White Album*, in 1979. Her nonfiction works include *Salvador* (1983), *Miami* (1987), *After Henry* (1992), *Political Fictions* (2001), *Where I Was From* (2003), *We Tell Ourselves Stories in Order to Live* (2006), *Blue Nights* (2011), *South and West* (2017), and *Let Me Tell You What I Mean* (2021). Her memoir *The Year of Magical Thinking* won the National Book Award for Nonfiction in 2005. In 2005, Didion was awarded the American Academy of Arts and Letters Gold Medal in Belles Lettres and Criticism. In 2007, she was awarded the National Book Foundation's Medal for Distinguished Contribution to American Letters. In 2013, she was awarded a National Humanities Medal by President Barack Obama and the PEN Center USA's Lifetime Achievement Award.

Josie Roland Hodson is a writer and art historian based in Brooklyn, New York. She is currently a PhD candidate in African American studies and history of art at Yale University. Her scholarly writing and criticism have appeared in *October*, *Art in America*, *Grove Dictionary of Art*, and *Texte zur Kunst*.

Zora Neale Hurston (1891–1960) was an American folklorist and writer associated with the Harlem Renaissance who celebrated African American culture of the rural South. She attended Howard University from 1921 to 1924 and in 1925 won a scholarship to Barnard College, where she studied anthropology under Franz Boas. She graduated from Barnard in 1928 and for two years pursued graduate studies in anthropology at Columbia University. She also conducted field studies in folklore among African Americans in the South. Her trips were funded by folklorist Charlotte Mason, who was a patron to both Hurston and Langston Hughes. For a short time Hurston was an amanuensis to novelist Fannie Hurst. In 1930 Hurston collaborated with Hughes on a play (never finished) titled *Mule Bone: A Comedy of Negro Life in Three Acts* (published posthumously 1991). In 1934 she published her first novel, *Jonah's Gourd Vine*, which was well received by critics for its portrayal of African American life uncluttered by stock figures or sentimentality. *Mules and Men*, a study of folkways among the African American population of Florida, followed in 1935. *Their Eyes Were Watching God* (1937), a novel, *Tell My Horse* (1938), a blend of travel writing and anthropology based on her investigations into voodoo (Vodou) in Haiti, and *Moses, Man of the Mountain* (1939), a novel, firmly established her as a major international author. For a number of years Hurston was on the faculty of North Carolina College for Negroes (now North Carolina Central University) in Durham. She also was on the staff of the Library of Congress. *Dust Tracks on a Road* (1942), an autobiography, is highly regarded. Her last book, *Seraph on the Suwanee*, a novel, appeared in 1948.

Arthur Jafa is an artist, filmmaker, and cinematographer. Across three decades, Jafa has developed a dynamic practice comprising films, artifacts and happenings that reference and question the universal and specific articulations of Black being. Underscoring the many facets of Jafa's practice is a recurring question: How can visual media, such as objects, static and moving images, transmit the equivalent power, beauty and alienation embedded within forms of Black music in US culture? The receipent of Best Cinematographer at Sundance Film Festival in 1992 and the Golden Lion at the Venice Biennale in 2019, Jafa's films have garnered acclaim at the Los Angeles, New York, and BlackStar Film Festivals and his artwork is represented in celebrated collections worldwide including at the Metropolitan Museum of Art, Museum of Modern Art, Tate Modern, San Francisco Museum of Modern Art, the Studio Museum in Harlem, High Museum of Art, Dallas Museum of Art, MCA Chicago, the Stedelijk Museum Amsterdam, LUMA Foundation, Pérez Art Museum Miami, Museum of Contemporary Art, Los Angeles, Hirshhorn Museum and Sculpture Garden, and the Smithsonian American Art Museum, among others.

Joy James is Ebenezer Fitch Professor of Humanities at Williams College. She is the author of *Resisting State Violence*, *Shadowboxing: Representations of Black Feminist Politics*, *Transcending the Talented Tenth*, and *Seeking the Beloved Community*. James has published numerous articles on: political theory, police, prison and slavery abolition; radicalizing feminisms; diasporic anti-Black racism; and US politics; and writes on the Captive Maternal through the lens of "The Womb of Western Theory." Creator of the digital Harriet Tubman Literary Circle at UT Austin, James is editor of *The New Abolitionists: (Neo)Slave Narratives and Contemporary Prison Writings*, *Imprisoned Intellectuals*, *Warfare in the American Homeland*, *The Angela Y. Davis Reader*, and co-editor of the *Black Feminist Reader*. James's most recent books include *In Pursuit of Revolutionary Love* and *New Bones Abolition: Captive Maternal Agency and the Afterlife of Erica Garner*.

Charles P. Linscott is assistant professor of instruction and associate director of undergraduate studies at the J. Warren McClure School of Emerging Communication Technologies, Ohio University.There he teaches a series of classes on virtual reality theory, history, criticism, and production. Linscott has been exploring audio production and experimental sound in various capacities since the late 1980s. He is the head of audio at the GRID Lab, where he oversees audio production and leads student employees. His writing deals principally with the implications of sound, image, technology, and mediation for Blackness (and vice versa). His book project, *Sonic Overlook: Blackness between Sound and Image*, examines the ways in which sonicity intervenes in Black visuality. Linscott's writing has appeared in *Black Camera*, *In Media Res*, *liquid blackness*, *ASAP/J*, *Journal of Cinema and Media Studies*, and the anthology *At the Crossroads*. Linscott recently published a lengthy chapter on XR in the textbook *Now Media* (Routledge, 2021). He is on the editorial board of *liquid blackness* journal, which is due to be archived by the Library of Congress because of its historical significance.

Suzanne McClelland's practice includes large-scale paintings, works on paper, and books. These often extract fragments of speech or text from various political or cultural sources, explore the social, symbolic, and material possibilities that reside within language, and celebrate the physicality of speech and sound. McClelland has participated in the 1993 and 2014 Whitney Biennials and has been the subject of solo presentations at the Aldrich Contemporary Art Museum, curated by Amy Smith-Stewart; the University of Virginia Museum of Art, curated by Jennifer Farrell; and the Whitney Museum of American Art, Philip Morris branch, curated by Thelma Golden. Her paintings are held in numerous public collections, including the Museum of Modern Art, the Metropolitan Museum of Art, the Brooklyn Museum, the Yale University Art Gallery, the Albright-Knox Gallery, and the Walker Art Center. Her awards include a Guggenheim Fellowship, Nancy Graves Foundation Grant, American Academy of Arts and Letters, and Anonymous Was a Woman Award. Her residencies include PS1/Clocktower, Berg Contemporary, Skowhegan School of Painting and Sculpture, Lab Grant with Dieu Donné papermill, Urban Glass, and Trodeson Villa. Recent publications include the monograph *Suzanne McClelland: 36-24-36* with an essay contribution by Thierry de Duve, published by team (gallery, inc.) in 2016 and distributed by D.A.P.

Tyler Mitchell is an American artist, photographer, and filmmaker living and working in Brooklyn, New York. He received his B.F.A. in film and television from NYU Tisch School of the Arts. His work introduces new narratives about Black beauty and desire, embracing themes of the past and creating fictionalized moments of the imagined future. Mitchell's work is characterized by a visual representation of Black life that emphasizes empowerment, play, and self-determination. He is often inspired by pastoral and domestic scenes from his upbringing in suburban Georgia. In 2018, he made history as the first Black photographer to shoot a cover of American *Vogue* for Beyoncé's appearance in the September issue. The following year, a portrait from this series was acquired by the Smithsonian National Portrait Gallery for its permanent collection. Other collections that hold Mitchell's work include the Los Angeles County Museum of Art, Brooklyn Museum, High Museum of Art, Museum of Fine Arts Boston, FOAM Fotografiemuseum, Hessel Museum of Art, Columbus Museum of Art, and the National Gallery of Victoria. Mitchell has been the subject of solo and two-person exhibitions at numerous institutions including FOAM Amsterdam, the International Center of Photography, Cleveland Museum of Art, the Gordon Parks Foundation, CONTACT Photography Festival, Toronto and SCAD Museum of Art. Mitchell has been a visiting artist and lecturer at a number of institutions including Yale University, Harvard University, NYU, and Paris Photo.

Kevin Quashie teaches Black cultural and literary studies and is a professor in the Department of English at Brown University. Primarily, he focuses on Black feminism, queer studies, and aesthetics, especially poetics. He is the author or editor of many books, including *Black Aliveness, or A Poetics of Being* (2021), *The Sovereignty of Quiet: Beyond Resistance in Black Culture* (2012), and *Black Women, Identity, and Cultural Theory: (Un)Becoming the Subject* (2004). Among his honors are a fellowship from the National Endowment for the Humanities (2015) and a grant from the Andrew W. Mellon Foundation (2004), as well as citations for teaching excellence from Brown University and Smith College. *Black Aliveness* has been awarded two prizes: the James Russell Lowell Prize from the Modern Language Association (2022) and the Pegasus Award for Poetry Criticism from the Poetry Foundation (2022). Currently, he is thinking about literary criticism as a form of estrangement and consolation or, said another way, he is thinking about the workings and potency of Black sentences.

Claudia Rankine is the author of five books of poetry, including *Citizen: An American Lyric* and *Don't Let Me Be Lonely: An American Lyric*; three plays including *HELP*, which premiered in March 2020 (The Shed, NYC), and *The White Card*, which premiered in February 2018 (ArtsEmerson/American Repertory Theater) and was published by Graywolf Press in 2019; as well as numerous video collaborations. Her recent collection of essays, *Just Us: An American Conversation*, was published by Graywolf Press in 2020. She is also the co-editor of several anthologies including *The Racial Imaginary: Writers on Race in the Life of the Mind*. In 2016, Rankine co-founded the Racial Imaginary Institute. Among her numerous awards and honors, Rankine is the recipient of the Bobbitt National Prize for Poetry, the Poets & Writers' Jackson Poetry Prize, and fellowships from the Guggenheim Foundation, Lannan Foundation, MacArthur Foundation, United States Artists, and the National Endowment for the Arts. A former chancellor of the Academy of American Poets, Rankine joined the NYU Creative Writing Program in fall 2021.

Legacy Russell is a curator and writer. Born and raised in New York City, she is the executive director & chief curator of the experimental new media, art, and performance institution The Kitchen. Recent exhibitions include *The Condition of Being Addressable*, Institute of Contemporary Art, Los Angeles (2022); *The New Bend*, Hauser & Wirth, New York (2022); *Sadie Barnette: The New Eagle Creek Saloon*, The Kitchen, New York (2022);

Projects: Kahlil Robert Irving (2021), *Projects: Garrett Bradley* (2020), and *Projects: Michael Armitage* (2019), all with the Studio Museum in Harlem in partnership with the Museum of Modern Art, New York; *(Never) As I Was* (2021), *This Longing Vessel* (2020), and *MOOD* (2019), all with the Studio Museum in Harlem in partnership with MoMA PS1; *Thomas J Price: Witness* (2021), *Dozie Kanu: Function* (2019), *Chloë Bass: Wayfinding* (2019), and *Radical Reading Room* (2019), all at the Studio Museum in Harlem; and *LEAN* with Performa's Radical Broadcast (online, 2020) and at Kunsthall Stavanger, Norway (on-site, 2021). She is the recipient of the 2019 Thoma Foundation Arts Writing Award in Digital Art, 2020 Rauschenberg Residency Fellowship, 2021 Creative Capital Award, 2022 Pompeii Commitment Digital Fellowship, and the 2023 Center for Curatorial Leadership Fellowship. Her first book is *Glitch Feminism: A Manifesto* (2020). Her second book, *BLACK MEME*, is forthcoming from Verso Books.

Jeffrey Skoller is a filmmaker, writer, and professor emeritus of film and media at University of California Berkeley. He teaches film/video production and courses on the histories and theories of experimental/avant-garde film and video art, documentary/nonfiction film, Third Cinema, activist and other counter-media practices. As a filmmaker, Skoller has made over a dozen films that have been exhibited at international venues including the Pacific Film Archive, Berkeley; Museum of the Moving Image, New York; Getty Museum, Los Angeles; Whitney Museum, New York; P.S. 1, New York; Flaherty Film Seminar, New York; Arsenal Kino, Berlin; Mannheim Film Festival, Germany; The Latin American Film Festival, Havana; and the National Film Theatre, London. As a writer he has published numerous essays and articles on nonfiction and experimental film and video in anthologies, artist catalogues, and media journals. He is the author of two books, *Shadows, Specters, Shards: Making History in Avant-Garde Film* (2005) and *POSTWAR: The Films of Daniel Eisenberg* (2010). Skoller was a founding faculty member of the School of the Art Institute of Chicago's Film/Video/New Media/Animation Department.

Doreen St. Félix is a staff writer at the *New Yorker*. She was previously a staff writer at MTV News, and an editor-at-large at Lenny Letter. She was a 2017 finalist for the The American Society of Magazine Editors' National Magazine Award in Columns and Commentary and won that same category in 2019. In 2016, she was named as one of *Forbes* magazine's "30 Under 30.". Her writing has appeared in the *Times Magazine*, *New York* magazine, *Vogue*, *The Fader*, and *Pitchfork*, among others.

Ossian Ward is content director at Lisson Gallery and a writer on contemporary art. As well as leading the gallery's communications and publishing teams, he was co-curator of the major off-site exhibition, *Everything at Once* and editor of the gallery's fiftieth anniversary book, *ARTIST / WORK / LISSON* (both 2017). He was the chief art critic and visual arts editor at *Time Out London* for over six years and has contributed to magazines such as *Art in America*, *Art + Auction*, *World of Interiors*, *Esquire*, *News Statesman* and *Wallpaper**, as well as newspapers including the *Evening Standard*, the *The Guardian*, *The Observer*, *The Times*, and the *Independent on Sunday*. Formerly editor of *ArtReview* and the *V&A Magazine*, he has also worked at the *Art Newspaper* and edited a biennial publication, *The Artists' Yearbook*, for Thames & Hudson from 2005 to 2010. His book, *Ways of Looking: How to Experience Contemporary Art* was published by Laurence King in 2014. A sequel, *Look Again: How to Experience the Old Masters*, was published by Thames & Hudson in 2019.

Re:

Lisson Gallery and the MIT Press present a new series of books entitled *Re:*, beginning with Garrett Bradley and continuing in 2025 with Rodney Graham

READER
RENDER
REMARK
RESOLVE
REDEEM
REVISIT
REMAINDER
REPETITION
REASON
REVISE
RESOW
REMAIN
REEL

LISSON GALLERY 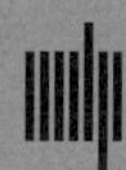

Co-published by Lisson Gallery and the MIT Press

ISBN 978-0-262-04879-8
Library of Congress Control Number: 2023932923

Distributed by the MIT Press

Edited by: Ossian Ward
Design and Production: Zoë Anspach
Printed by: VeronaLibri, Italy

British Library Cataloguing-in-Publication Data
A catalogue record for this book is available from the British Library.